This edition published by Parragon, 13 Whiteladies Road, Clifton, Bristol BS8 1PB, United Kingdom
ISBN 0-75252-386-4
Printed in France

FORMULA 1 YEARBOOK

1997-98

Pictures
Steve Domenjoz
Thierry Gromik
Masakazu Miyata

Conception and texts
Luc Domenjoz

Translated by
Eric Silbermann

Page layout, statistics and results
Ruth Domenjoz-Leibold

Drawings and circuit maps
Pierre Ménard

PHOTOGRAPHIC CREDIT

Steve Domenjoz: 88/89, 138/139, 186/187, 210/211. *Thierry Gromik / SIPA Press*: 92/93, 96/97, 100/101, 106/107, 110/111, 114/115, 120/121, 124/125, 130/131, 134/135, 146/147, 150/151, 154/155, 158/159, 170/171, 174/175, 178/179, 182/183, 194/195, 202/203, 206/207. *Vincent Kalut*: 80/81, 82/83, 162/163. *Masakazu Miyata*: 16/17, 42/43, 54/55, 142/143, 198/199. *Jean-Paul Thomas / SIPA Press: 166/167. Manfred Giet: 190/191.*

Contents

Foreword

"I am very happy to be putting my name to the preface of "The Formula 1 Yearbook" for the first time. I have been reading it for years now and I hope you will enjoy reading it and admiring the superb photos as much as I will.

Each one of its chapters brings back memories of different stages of the season, about which I have mixed emotions. On the one hand it was a year of revival, with Alain Prost taking control of the team. I have never driven a single seater as competitive as the JS45, which was not far off the pace of the Williams and Ferraris. On the other hand, I will always think of 1997 as the year of my accident. As far as I am concerned, it was just part of the job. When you are a racing driver, this type of misfortune is simply one of the risks you run and must accept.

However, I now want to forget about 1997 and concentrate on 1998. With the Peugeot engine and a new car designed under the guidance of Alain Prost, we will be mounting a terrific challenge next season.

I think I will have a car with which I can win a few grands prix and I am more than a touch impatient to be back on the grid in Melbourne in March 1998. In the meantime, to make the time pass more quickly, I am going back to the pages of "The Formula 1 Yearbook." Good reading..."

Olivier Panis

One turn of the wheel too far, one wheel bearing too soon

Rarely had we known such tension before the start of a grand prix. Side by side on the grid at Jerez for the final showdown of the season, Jacques Villeneuve and Michael Schumacher both knew that an entire season's work was going to be decided in the course of the next two hours. Formula 1 had not seen such a finale in a long time.
That sort of pressure is bound to end in tears and so it did on lap 48, after the two men had slugged it out, tooth and nail.
In second place, Jacques Villeneuve could not allow himself to stay behind the Ferrari. To take the world title, he had to win or at least finish ahead of his rival. On lap 48, shortly after his pit-stop, he knew the time had come, so that he could make the most of his new tyres to scale the barricade.
It was now or never. Out in front, Schumacher was playing a different game, with the plan of trying to save his tyres.
In a desperately daring move, Villeneuve slid his car inside the Ferrari at Dry Sack corner. It all happened in a fraction of a second. The Canadian was travelling so quickly, he was likely to end up in the gravel. But, at that moment, Schumacher, in a fit of road rage steered into the Williams. It kept the Williams on course and sent the Ferrari into the gravel on the outside of the corner, its wheels spinning helplessly.
The next miracle for Villeneuve, was that his car was not too badly damaged and he was able to keep going. If the Ferrari had hit one of his wheels, rather than the side of the car, his race might have been over. But the blow to the side pod proved how strong a car is the Williams. While the knock upset the handling, it was still able to finish the race.
The world championship had yet again been decided by a coming together of the two protagonists: a stroke of luck for Villeneuve and a huge mistake from Schumacher.
The incident was a fair reflection of what we had seen before during this season. It was not the first time Villeneuve had benefited from a stroke of luck to win, as happened at Silverstone, Budapest and Nurburgring.
Luck had not always gone Schumacher's way. At Silverstone, he was let down by his Ferrari when he was about to dominate the race. A victory there would have changed the course of the season, but it was not to be, after he was sidelined with a seized wheel bearing - a very rare failure.

Williams - a catalogue of errors.

A bit of luck has always come in handy in winning a world title, but Jacques Villeneuve's crown was certainly not tarnished in any way by circumstances.
Indeed the Canadian richly deserved the title. On that epic and decisive Sunday in Jerez, he put on a masterful display of outright speed and control. In the course of an amazing race, he swept away all the criticism that had been laid at his feet and wiped out the memory of all the mistakes attributed to him during the course of the season.
Errors there were aplenty. With the equipment at his disposal, the Canadian admitted he should have wrapped up the championship well before the final race, if it had not been for errors on his part and that of the Williams team, which allowed Schumacher to be a threat right to the end. The most flagrant examples occurred at Monaco and Spa. On both occasions, Williams made a complete hash of their tyre choice in the wet conditions.
Before the European Grand Prix, it seemed that Michael Schumacher deserved to pick up his third world championship. He had driven some incredible races in the wet, conditions which were literally heaven sent for Ferrari and his talent marked him down as favourite.
At Jerez, this judgement was turned on its head on lap 48. With a vulgar attempt to push Jacques Villeneuve off the track, the German's cavalier conduct not only allowed his rival to take the world championship, but also made the achievement seem even more worthy.
In his role of victim who still managed to secure the title, Villeneuve became the hero of what was an unforgettable season.

1997 WORLD CHAMPIONSHIP

Drivers:

	Driver	Points
1.	Jacques VILLENEUVE	81
2.	Michael SCHUMACHER	78
3.	Heinz-Harald FRENTZEN	42
4.	David COULTHARD	36
	Jean ALESI	36
6.	Gerhard BERGER	27
	Mika HAKKINEN	27
8.	Eddie IRVINE	24
9.	Giancarlo FISICHELLA	20
10.	Olivier PANIS	16
11.	Johnny HERBERT	15
12.	Ralf SCHUMACHER	13
13.	Damon HILL	7
14.	Rubens BARRICHELLO	6
15.	Alexander WURZ	4
16.	Jarno TRULLI	3
17.	Mika SALO	2
	Pedro DINIZ	2
	Shinji NAKANO	2
20.	Nicola LARINI	1

Constructors :

	Constructor	Points
1.	Williams / Renault	123
2.	Ferrari	102
3.	Benetton / Renault	67
4.	McLaren / Mercedes	63
5.	Jordan / Peugeot	33
6.	Prost / Mugen Honda	21
7.	Sauber / Petronas	16
8.	Arrows / Yamaha	9
9.	Stewart / Ford	6
10.	Tyrrell / Ford	2

This year, Frank Williams entered the pages of motor racing history. His team won its ninth Constructors' Championship, an outright record in F1, However, it must be remembered that the Constructors' title only came into being in 1958 and so some great performances from Ferrari do not feature in this list. ▽▷

△
Scuderia Ferrari celebrated its fiftieth anniversary with a dazzling return to form. 1997 confirmed that the Scuderia is well and truly back at the top of the pile. It has even been predicted that we are witnessing the dawning of an all-red future over the next few seasons.
◁ ▽

A magnificent season

Formula 1 today is becoming less and less of a sport. It is a global show which mixes political intrigue and lavish financial contracts with high technology and purely sporting contests. This strange mix is becoming more and more popular.
Formula 1 attracts increasing interest all over the world, especially from Asia, which is just discovering the sport. As Max Mosley explained in Jerez, in 1997, 70% of the television audience is in the Far East, Malaysia and Korea. With no historical F1 baggage, these new enthusiasts take the sport as they find it with all the complications and intrigue of a soap opera and they like what they see.

Even if a few clouds appeared on the horizon in the latter part of the 1997 season - some suspected Ferrari of cheating, others felt Jacques Villeneuve's disqualification in Japan was unjust - 1997 was a vintage year, full of suspense.
This was due in part to the return to form of Ferrari, the mythical team of the sport, which meant that observing the duel between Villeneuve and Schumacher, Williams and Ferrari, was far more exciting than watching the championship disputed between two Williams drivers, as happened in 1996.
In a nutshell it was a fantastic season and one can only hope it continues this way in the future.

Youth policy

Over the past few years, the leading lights of Formula 1 tended to put down roots in the sport. For young drivers, it was very difficult to get a seat and then it tended to be restricted to the second division teams.
All that changed in 1997 and now the young drivers seem to come into the sport through the role of team test driver. They gain experience and do not hang about once they get themselves onto a grid.
Thanks to this policy, no less than seven rookies, or at least near-rookies, raced in grands prix this year, with top teams like Jordan and Benetton: Ralf Schumacher, Giancarlo Fisichella, Shinji Nakano, Norberto Fontana, Alexander Wurz, Tarso Marques and Jan Magnussen.
From this list of young guns, two names stood out: Giancarlo Fisichella and Alexander Wurz and it is no fluke that both of them will drive for Benetton in 1998. It now seems that some teams are ready to take a gamble on youth, which is a good thing for the future of the sport.

◁
Do not get the wrong impression from this photo: Giancarlo Fisichella did not make many mistakes this season. On the contrary, he proved to be remarkably consistent at the same time as being very quick. Just ask Ralf Schumacher for his opinion on the subject.

Many are called, but only one is chosen

Yet another lacklustre season for Jean Alesi. Apart from his superb pole position at Monza, the Frenchman will not have many pleasant memories of 1997.

At the end of the season, it is always an amusing exercise to compare the declared hopes and aspirations of the different competitors as expressed at the start of the season, with their actual results at the end. One can see that optimism is rife at the start, but often takes a cold bath when reality bites. By the end, the protagonists either offer excuses or keep silent.

However, at Benetton, no explanation was given, but action was taken. Confronted with another shambles which was 1997, Alessandro Benetton decided on sweeping changes in the team's structure, pushing David Richards into the driving seat of Benetton Formula.

Will it be enough? There is reason for doubt, but new blood in the form of Giancarlo Fisichella and Alexander Wurz, should at least change things on the surface for next season, so Benetton's results might improve.

Another notable disappointment was Damon Hill's season. Over the winter, the Englishman declared he hoped to win at least one race in 1997. While he got very close in Hungary, it seems likely this owed more to exceptional circumstances and the superiority of his Bridgestone tyres, rather than to the quality of his car.

Also on the debit list: the sad performances of Heinz-Harald Frentzen who only managed to win one race, while his team-mate racked up seven.

Sauber also had a nondescript season. While the Swiss team modestly refrained from making any pre-season predictions, one could have expected more from a car equipped with the 1996 Ferrari engine.

Damon Hill was not very convincing this season.

Against a backdrop of political turmoil

While the 1997 season was one of the most hotly contested on the tracks under the Sunday afternoon sun, it was no less heated in the shadier climes of the motorhome awnings.

A constant thread throughout the year was the discord surrounding the 1997 Concorde Agreement: an agreement in existence since 1981, which ties all the F1 teams together. It defines everyone's role, even and especially, detailing the division of shares of the revenue generated by the television rights and the on-track advertising.

These revenues increased considerably in recent months, thanks to contracts signed by Bernie Ecclestone with the new digital television channels. For a team like Minardi, its share represented almost half its running costs budget, or a bonus of 25 million dollars.

In August 1996, when the new agreement was drawn up, Williams, McLaren and Tyrrell refused to sign the document.

Throughout the season, Bernie Ecclestone tried to convince them to sign, as their procrastination prevented him from floating Formula 1 on the stock exchange, as the financiers insisted that F1 put its house in order before any deal could be struck.

By the end of the season, nothing had changed. An agreement seemed "close," but Ron Dennis had been saying this for over a year.

On the up and up at McLaren and Ferrari

While most teams had cause to be disappointed with their season, this was not the case throughout the pit-lane. The nice surprises came from McLaren-Mercedes and their three wins; the Anglo-German team having waited since 1995 to toast their partnership with winner's champagne.
However, to listen to Ron Dennis was to discover this was not enough. When this year's car was launched at a cost and level of excess never before seen in Formula 1, he had predicted a brilliant season for his team. The three wins in 1997 did not match this level of expectation, especially as the Australian and European wins owed something to luck.
In fact, the McLaren team was only truly dominant at Monza, where David Coulthard owed his win to a better race strategy, decided on by his engineers and the speed with which his mechanics sent him on his way after the pit-stop.
There were several ominous clouds still hanging over McLaren's resurgence and the silver arrows retired on several occasions when victory was in their grasp, most notably at Silverstone and especially at the Nurburgring, when both cars led the field.
Mario Ilien, the designer of the Mercedes engine, will have his work cut out this winter to get to the bottom of the problems.
The other pleasant surprise this season was naturally Ferrari. They were the only team to do better than their stated objectives at the beginning of the season, with the exception of Williams of course, who never deign to make predictions.
Jean Todt had said he wanted four wins in 1997 and his team actually went on to win five, but more importantly the team was in contention for the title until the very last race. The season served to show that, with Ross Brawn as technical director, Rory Byrne in charge of designing the car, and with Jean Todt running the team, the Scuderia looks set to get back on the road to victory. They are all foreigners of course, but luckily the Italians are not chauvinistic.

△ *The key moment of David Coulthard's win at Monza: The Scotsman, who had been stuck behind Jean Alesi for several laps, made his pit-stop at the same time as the Frenchman. He got out again just fractions of a second earlier (photo.) Victory was in the bag.*

Going out in a blaze of glory

In June 1996, people could not believe their ears when Renault announced it was pulling out of Formula 1, as the French constructor had every reason to be proud of its achievements in the blue riband of motor racing.
It had won everything and its successes had conferred a young and dynamic image on the marque.
But all good things must come to an end and so, on Sunday evening after the race in Jerez, in an atmosphere of euphoria created by Jacques Villeneuve's world title, the eleventh for the company, Renault was able to leave the stage, its head held high.
Its record is so exceptional that it merits a few moments close scrutiny:
Renault in Formula 1 is:
• 6 Constructors' World Championships and 5 Drivers's World Championships.
•95 wins
•135 pole positions (23 courtesy of Alain Prost)
•105 lap records
• 250 podiums
• 2016 points
• 76 all-Renault front rows
• 2 top four finishes (France 1996 and Luxembourg 1997)
• 10 top three finishes
• 34 top two finishes
• 34 drivers
Figures which are unlikely to be beaten for many a year

◁ *The Sauber-Petronas were not the quickest of cars, but they were among the most aesthetically pleasing with a hint of purple running through their colour scheme.*

Tyre wars

The common consensus is that winning in F1 is dependent more on the car than on the driver, who is credited with making a contribution of between 5 and 20% to the overall performance of the car.
Even though the fans might be more interested in the private lives of the drivers, technology is still of great import in F1 and the arrival of a new idea, a new team or a new constructor is worthy of as much interest as a new driver.
In this context, the Formula 1 debut of the Bridgestone tyre company caused a minor revolution in the paddock. Until then, the American company Goodyear enjoyed a monopoly and had a quiet life.
With the arrival of the Japanese company, all that changed and the Goodyear engineers went back to work with a vengeance.
The result was that lap times dropped by as much as two seconds compared with the previous year. The changes to the regulations for 1998 (see page 216) destined to slow the cars down, will only just compensate for this huge step forward.

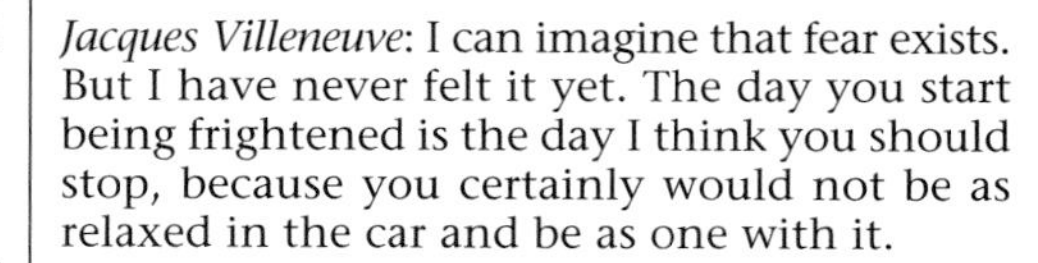

Jacques Villeneuve, the casual champion

At the end of a ceaseless struggle with Michael Schumacher, Jacques Villeneuve won his first Formula 1 world championship title at the wheel of his Williams-Renault this year. However, he still has his feet firmly on the ground.

Often unshaven, with his denim shirt hanging out over his trousers, the laid-back Jacques Villeneuve stands out from the crowd of Formula 1 drivers, most of whom prefer clothes by Cerruti and briefcases bearing the Louis Vuitton label. The Canadian maintains he has not deliberately cultivated this image, it is simply the way he is and F1 will not make him change his ways.

Jacques Villeneuve knows nothing of political correctness. He always says what he thinks, even if this has caused him all sorts of problems, as when in June, he was hauled over the coals by the FIA for his comments on the new regulations for Formula 1.

While he is now a millionaire, Villeneuve has no desire to join in the race to have the best private jet, as do some of his fellow drivers. He is more than happy tinkering around with his 1951 Chevy pick-up.

You do not seem to have expensive tastes. Is that true?

Jacques Villeneuve: That's right, I do not. I have no private plane as I don't see the point. But if it is easier to get somewhere in a private plane, then I hire one. More basic things make me happy. My luxuries are my old pick-up, which has been completely restored. I also like buying CDs or new bits for my computer. But I am not into big watches with diamonds, or fancy cars or ten room apartments when I only need two.

Do you think you know the value of things?

Jacques Villeneuve: I think I do. On the other hand, if I go down to the supermarket, I don't seek out the cheapest brand. I just buy what I like. I do not know how much I spend or even how much money I have in the bank. But I know I have got enough and I do not throw my money out of the window.

What is the difference between the Jacques Villeneuve the public sees at the race track and the private man?

Jacques Villeneuve: When I am at home, I can act more my age and relax. I don't know really, it is hard for me to judge. In public I am a bit more introverted. I hate being in the middle of a crowd of people all shouting my name.

Do you not like the life of a personality?

Jacques Villeneuve: I hate being the centre of attention, for example when an entire restaurant turns to stare at me. In Monaco, in the summer, with all the tourists, it becomes a bit difficult.

So I tend to stay shut away in my apartment. However, at the race track I accept being surrounded by people. They have come to see me and it is my job. But if I go to watch a tennis tournament and people start asking for my autograph, then that bothers me. In Montreal once, at a hockey game, the crowd gave me a bigger round of applause than the players. It was embarrassing.

In general, are you self-confident?

Jacques Villeneuve: Yes I think so. It has nothing to do with motor racing, but I believe that to do anything well, you must have self belief.

What is fear for a driver?

Jacques Villeneuve: I can imagine that fear exists. But I have never felt it yet. The day you start being frightened is the day I think you should stop, because you certainly would not be as relaxed in the car and be as one with it.

Are you a happy man?

Jacques Villeneuve: Yes, very happy. There are things that upset me, just as there are for anyone, but I have never been unhappy for a long period. I am quite positive by nature and my career is going rather well, which helps. (Laughs)

It is said you are a perfectionist, to the point of getting angry abut things.

Jacques Villeneuve: It depends. I am with the people who work with me. If Craig (Pollock, his manager) fixes up ten interviews for me and I have to interrupt a briefing with my engineer, then I get mad. It is true that even when everything is going well there is room for improvement.

What does this first world championship mean to you?

Jacques Villeneuve: I am completely happy in my life, so that winning the championship changed nothing in this respect. However, from a professional point of view it means everything to me. I would have taken it very badly if I had not won.

Do you already think about life after Formula 1?

Jacques Villeneuve: You always have to look far into the future. But in fact you never know which way to go. After Formula 1, it would surprise me if I stayed in motor sport. Once you have given twenty years of your life to something, it is time to turn the page. There are so many interesting things to do. I don't know, computers, music....lots of things. A human being can discover so many things, it would be a shame to do the same all one's life.

Is there any other activity you apply yourself to?

Jacques Villeneuve: I play the piano a bit in my spare time. Sometimes I can sit at the piano for four hours at a time. I like to get stuck into something when I get into it.

Into the history books

By winning this year's Formula 1 title, Jacques Villeneuve has put his name in the pages of history. Along with the American, Mario Andretti, they are the only two men to have won the Indy 500, the Indycar championship and the F 1 World Championship.

Jacques Villeneuve was born on 9th April 1971 at St. Jean sur le Richelieu in Quebec. As the son of Gilles Villeneuve, his entire childhood was spent in a racing environment and he took up karting when he was 15 years old. He then did three years of Italian Formula 3, from 1989 to 1991, one year of Formula 3 in Japan in 1992, before switching to Formula Atlantic and Indycar in 1994.

The following year he won the Indycar title and the Indy 500. In 1996, he made his F1 debut with Williams-Renault and finished second in the championship. A perfect trajectory that finally reached its ultimate goal the F1 title, this year in Jerez.

Jacques Villeneuve gives the appearance of cruising through the world of Formula 1 with an air of detached determination. It is hard to understand the character that lurks behind the mischievous smile.

An image that is upmarket "grunge"

Jacques Villeneuve, son of Gilles has no intention of living off his surname. He has already scored more victories than his father, not to mention his world champion's crown. *«It took us a year for people to stop thinking about Gilles whenever they mentioned Jacques,»* explained his manager, Craig Pollock. *«We had to deal with the same thing in Formula 3, in Japan, then in Formula Atlantic and Indycar.»*
Craig Pollock with dual Swiss and British nationality, was Jacques Villeneuve's sports teacher for five years, when the driver attended a private school at Villars sur Ollon in Switzerland. Their friendship, which endures to this day, was born on the ski slopes.
Wherever you see the Williams driver, you can be sure Pollock is not far behind. *«My job is to look after all Jacques' activities outside the cockpit,»* he continued. *«He must be able to come to the track and get in his car, without having to think about anything other than his set-up.»*
Pollock is even responsible for his clothing. *«Jacques prefers the natural look. He dresses the way he does, because that is his taste. The role of a manager is to study what is available and get the best out of it. When he was in Indycar, his clothes had a definite North American flavour and now we have modified them to give him a European touch. He dresses like a young guy, but I give him a few hints. We have made a deliberate choice to dress him this way as part of keeping up a certain image.»*

Craig Pollock with Frank Williams. 41 years old, Villeneuve's manager is always one of the most elegantly turned out people in the paddock. With perfect creases in his shirts and trousers, he watches over his charge to allow him to concentrate on driving.
▽

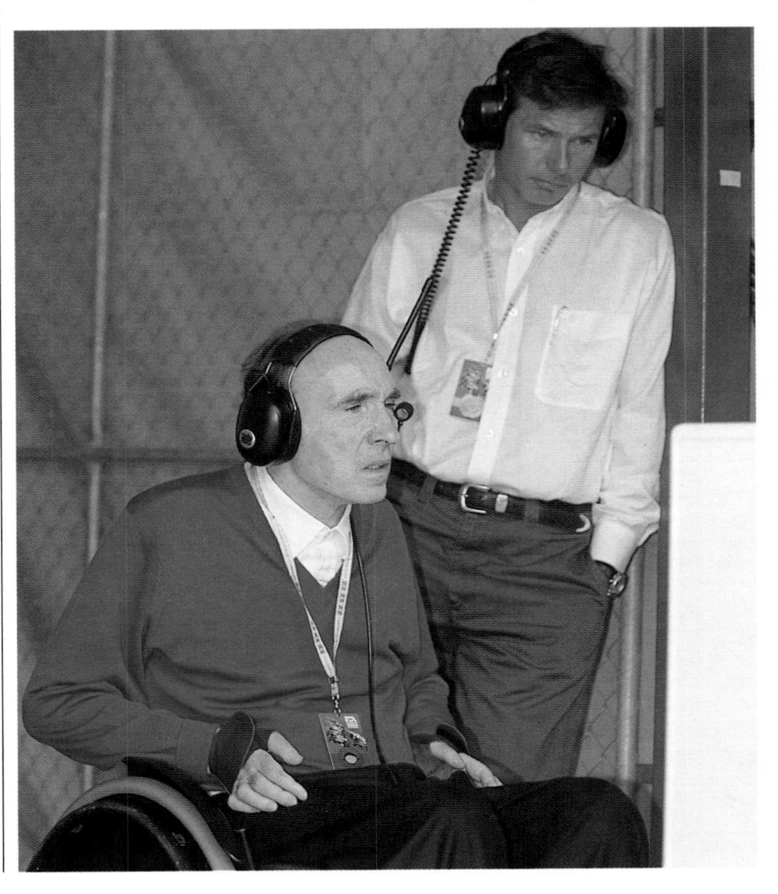

Pleasure comes first

In his heart Jacques Villeneuve is an epicurean. Above all he likes to have fun and can spend hours playing Dungeons and Dragons on his computer.
For him, the pleasure of driving comes before everything else. He openly admits that winning a race easily gives him less satisfaction than having a good fight for a place. This season, the Canadian certainly got his money's worth.
Brought up in the American way of racing, his style is most definitely non-conformist, which has led to some of the most memorable overtaking moves, like his overtaking of Schumacher at Estoril in 1996. This sometimes brings him into conflict with Williams Technical Director Patrick Head, who occasionally does not approve of his driver's strange settings on the car.
To be honest, Villeneuve does not exactly have a laugh with the Williams-Renault team, noted for its austerity.
But at least it gave him the FW19 with which to win the championship. Sometimes you have to make concessions in the pursuit of happiness.

Set course for a second title

With the Indy 500, the Indycar title and now the F1 crown in his pocket, Villeneuve has achieved all his ambitions.
What could be his next target. *«Why a second world championship of course!»* he replied without hesitation on Sunday night after the European Grand Prix. *«This year we should have led easily for the whole season, but that was definitely not the case. I had to fight all the way and I hope 1998 will be a bit easier.»*
Having won the title, Villeneuve could have invoked a clause in his contract, allowing him to leave the Williams team if he was champion.
The rumours of a transfer to the Prost team made a lot of waves at the time of the Luxembourg Grand Prix. However, the season over, it seems we can forget that idea. Jacques Villeneuve will stay put with the championship winning team in 1998, to fight for his crown once more.

The actors

The Formula 1 circus has a lot of acts. There are the stars of course, who occupy centre stage on Sunday afternoon. But there are also the backroom boys and girls, the team owners and engineers. Before the curtain goes up, it is time to meet the cast.

Arrows-Yamaha

1. Damon HILL

DRIVER PROFILE

- Name : *HILL*
- First names : *Damon Mark*
- Nationality : *British*
- Date of birth : *September 17, 1960*
- Place of birth : *London (GB)*
- Lives in : *Dublin (IRL)*
- Marital status : *married to Georgie*
- Kids : *3 kids (Oliver, Joshua, Tabatha)*
- Hobbies : *golf, music, motorbike, tennis*
- Favourite music : *Elvis Presley, Otis Redding*
- Favourite meal : *traditional english cuisine*
- Favourite drinks : *milk, wine, beer, champagne*
- Height : *182 cm*
- Weight : *70 kg*

STATISTICS

- Nber of Grand Prix : *84*
- Victories : *21*
- Pole-positions : *20*
- Best laps : *19*
- Accident/off : *12*
- Not qualified : *6*
- Laps in the lead : *1325*
- Km in the lead : *6062*
- Points scored : *333*

PRIOR TO F1

1983 : *Motorcycle 500cc*
1984 : *F. Ford 1600 (10th)*
1985 : *F. Ford 1600 (3rd)*
1986 : *F. 3 GB (9th)*
1987 : *F. 3 GB (5th)*
1988 : *F. 3 GB (3rd)*
1989 : *F. 3000 (11th)*
1990 : *F. 3000 (13th)*
1991 : *F. 3000 (7th)*

F1 CAREER

1992 : *Brabham / Judd. 0 point.*
1993 : *Williams / Renault. 69 points. 3rd of champ.*
1994 : *Williams / Renault. 91 points. 2nd of champ.*
1995 : *Williams / Renault. 69 points. 2nd of champ.*
1996 : *Williams / Renault. 97 pts.* ***World Champion.***
1997 : *Arrows / Yamaha. 7 points. 13th of championship.*

2. Pedro DINIZ

DRIVER PROFILE

- Name : *DINIZ*
- First names : *Pedro Paulo*
- Nationality : *Brazilian*
- Date of birth : *May 22, 1970*
- Place of birth : *São Paulo*
- Lives in : *Monte Carlo, São Paulo*
- Marital status : *single*
- Kids : *-*
- Hobbies : *traveling, reading, tennis*
- Favourite music : *soft rock, Sade*
- Favourite meal : *spaghetti alla crudaiola*
- Favourite drink : *mineral water*
- Height : *174 cm*
- Weight : *69 kg*

STATISTICS

- Nber of Grand Prix : *50*
- Victories : *0*
- Pole-positions : *0*
- Best laps : *0*
- Accident/off : *8*
- Not qualified : *0*
- Laps in the lead : *0*
- Km in the lead : *0*
- Points scored : *4*

PRIOR TO F1

1987-88 : *Karting*
1989 : *F. Ford Brazil*
1990 : *F. 3 South America*
1991 : *F. 3 GB*
1992 : *F. 3 GB*
1993-94 : *F. 3000*

F1 CAREER

1995 : *Forti / Ford. 0 point.*
1996 : *Ligier / Mugen. 2 points. 15th of championship.*
1997 : *Arrows / Yamaha. 2 points. 18th of championship.*

Shown the door by Williams too late in the '96 season to pick up a good drive, Damon Hill had to fall back on Arrows, knowing his new mount would not put him in a position to defend his title. All the same, Damon hoped to win at least one race and nearly managed it in Hungary. The rest of his season was very disappointing as he retired five times in the first six grands prix. Relations between the driver and team soon took a downward turn. His boss Tom Walkinshaw accused him of not giving value for money for the 4.5 million pounds salary he was on.
In the end, Damon stayed on to the end of the season, through thick and thin, but he is looking forward to Jordan next year!

Well, it seems one cannot judge the talent of Pedro Diniz by the thickness of his wallet alone. In 1997, the Brazilian was sometimes quicker than his team-mate, although he was no doubt helped by the Englishman's lack of motivation. All the same, he managed to pick up two points at the Nurburgring, which given the performance of his chassis, was quite an achievement.
However, he was still capable of getting it wrong. Although his tally of spins does not put him on a par with Katayama or Ralf Schumacher, it was not far off.

ARROWS-HART A18 – DAMON HILL
HUNGARIAN GRAND PRIX

Arrows-Yamaha A18

SPECIFICATION

• Chassis :	*Arrows A18*
• Engine :	*Yamaha OX11A*
• Tyres :	*Bridgestone*
• Wheels :	*BBS*
• Fuel / oil :	*Elf*
• Brakes (discs) :	*Carbone Industrie*
• Brakes (calipers) :	*AP Racing*
• Transmission :	*Arrows 6 gears*
• Radiators :	*Secan*
• Plugs :	*NGK / FIAMM*
• Electronic mgt :	*Zytek*
• Shock absorbers :	*Dynamic*
• Suspensions :	*push rods (ft/bk)*
• Dry weight :	*600 kg, driver included*
• Wheelbase :	*3000 mm*
• Front track :	*1650 mm*
• Rear track :	*1600 mm*
• Total length :	*4700 mm*

TEAM PROFILE

• Address :	*Arrows Grand Prix Int. Ltd.* *Leafield Technical Centre* *Leafield* *NR Witney* *Oxon OX8 5PF* *United Kingdom*
• Telephone :	*(44) 1993 87 10 00*
• Fax :	*(44) 1993 87 14 00*
• Established in :	*1977*
• First Grand Prix :	*Brazil 1978*
• General director :	*Tom Walkinshaw*
• Technical director :	*John Barnard*
• Team-manager :	*John Walton*
• Chief mechanic :	*Lee Jones*
• Nber of employees :	*170*
• Sponsor :	*Danka*

STATISTICS

• Number of Grand Prix :	*305*
• Number of victories :	*0*
• Number of pole-positions :	*1*
• Number of best laps during the race :	*0*
• Number of drivers' world titles :	*0*
• Number of constructors' titles :	*0*
• Total number of points scored :	*150*

POSITION IN WORLD CHAMPIONSHIP

1978 : *9th – 11 points*	1988 : *4th – 23 points*
1979 : *9th – 5 points*	1989 : *7th – 13 points*
1980 : *7th – 11 points*	1990 : *9th – 2 points*
1981 : *8th – 10 points*	1991 : *not classified*
1982 : *10th – 5 points*	1992 : *7th – 6 points*
1983 : *10th – 4 points*	1993 : *9th – 4 points*
1984 : *9th – 6 points*	1994 : *9th – 9 points*
1985 : *8th – 14 points*	1995 : *8th – 5 points*
1986 : *10th – 1 points*	1996 : *9th – 1 point*
1987 : *6th – 11 points*	1997 : *8th – 9 points*

Tom Walkinshaw spent a lot of money to buy the services of Damon Hill, to no great effect.
▽

A sledgehammer to crack a nut

Damon Hill said he had been impressed by the facilities at Leafield, Tom Walkinshaw's operations centre where he based the Arrows team. The Scotsman did not stint in speculating to accumulate in order to reach his goal of the world championship. Unfortunately for him, he is not the only one with this goal, nor the only one with an ultra-modern factory. When the time came to look at the score sheet, one wonders if the resources Arrows used were not a sledgehammer to crack a nut. Nine points were the only consolation for a disappointing season. The only ray of sunshine that pierced the gloom was the Hungarian Grand Prix and one still wonders how this ever happened. The atmosphere in the team deteriorated rapidly and the arrival of John Barnard in May, did little to change the situation.

TEST DRIVERS 1997

Jörg MÜLLER (D), Martin BRUNDLE (GBR)

SUCCESSION OF DRIVERS 1997

• Damon HILL :	*all Grand Prix*
• Pedro DINIZ :	*all Grand Prix*

◁
"Just seven more grands prix and it's time for a change of scenery." At the Hungarian Grand Prix, Hill was already looking to his future, which would certainly not involve Arrows-Yamaha.

Williams-Renault

3. Jacques VILLENEUVE

DRIVER PROFILE

• Name :	*VILLENEUVE*
• First name :	*Jacques*
• Nationality :	*Canadian*
• Date of birth :	*April 9, 1971*
• Place of birth :	*St-Jean-sur-Richelieu, Quebec, CAN*
• Lives in :	*Monaco*
• Marital status :	*single*
• Kids :	-
• Hobbies :	*music, computer, movie theatre*
• Favourite music :	*rock and pop*
• Favourite meal :	*pasta*
• Favourite drink :	*milk*
• Height :	*171 cm*
• Weight :	66,5 kg

STATISTICS

• Nber of Grand Prix :	*33*
• Victories :	*11*
• Pole-positions :	*13*
• Best laps :	*9*
• Accident/off :	*5*
• Not qualified :	*0*
• Laps in the lead :	*634*
• Km in the lead :	*2972*
• Points scored :	*159*

PRIOR TO F1

1986 : Jim Russel School
1987 : Driving school Spenard-David
1988: Ital. Champ. Alfa
1989-91 : F3 (-, 14th, 6th)
1992 : F3 Japan (2nd)
1993 : F. Atlantic (3rd)
1994 : IndyCar (6th)
1995 : IndyCar (Champion)

F1 CAREER

1996 : *Williams / Renault. 78 points. 2nd of championship.*
1997 : *Williams / Renault. 81 pts.* **World Champion.**

World Champion! With seven wins from 17 races, the Canadian's first world title was richly deserved. This year, Jacques proved he is one of those drivers who can dig deep within himself when the pressure is on. His race in Jerez was a masterpiece of aggression, speed and control. If some of his successes - Silverstone, Budapest and Nurburgring - were gifted him, Villeneuve did not always get the full support he would have wished of his team. It makes his crown all the more deserved.

4. Heinz-Harald FRENTZEN

DRIVER PROFILE

• Name :	*FRENTZEN*
• First name :	*Heinz-Harald*
• Nationality :	*German*
• Date of birth :	*May 18, 1967*
• Place of birth :	*Mönchengladbach (D)*
• Lives in :	*Monaco*
• Marital status :	*single*
• Kids :	-
• Hobbies :	*running, mountain-bike, eating*
• Favourite music :	*funk, soul, rap*
• Favourite meal :	*fish, paella*
• Favourite drink :	*apple juice*
• Height :	*178 cm*
• Weight :	*64,5 kg*

STATISTICS

• Nber of Grand Prix :	*64*
• Victories :	*1*
• Pole-positions :	*1*
• Best laps :	*6*
• Accident/off :	*14*
• Not qualified :	*0*
• Laps in the lead :	*76*
• Km in the lead :	*379*
• Points scored :	*71*

PRIOR TO F1

1980-84 : *Karting*
1981 : *German Jr Karting Champion*
1885-87 : *F. Ford 2000 of Germany*
1988 : *F. Opel Lotus Champion*
1989 : *F. 3 of Germany*
1990-91 : *F. 3000*
1992-93 : *F. 3000 Japan*

F1 CAREER

1994 : *Sauber / Mercedes. 7 points. 13th of championship.*
1995 : *Sauber / Ford. 15 points. 9th of championship.*
1996 : *Sauber / Ford. 7 points. 12th of championship.*
1997 : *Williams / Renault. 42 pts. 3rd of championship.*

If one was handing out medals for bad luck this season, Heinz-Harald Frentzen would qualify for it. Because, while the German found it very difficult adapting to the Williams team and if he made some spectacular errors, above all he was the victim of spectacular misfortune. The most glaring example was Budapest, when a win looked on the cards, till the fuel filler on his car fell off. "This apart, "Heinzi's" season was very disappointing. Quite frankly, one expected more from a driver, whom Michael Schumacher has always described as his closest rival in terms of pure speed.

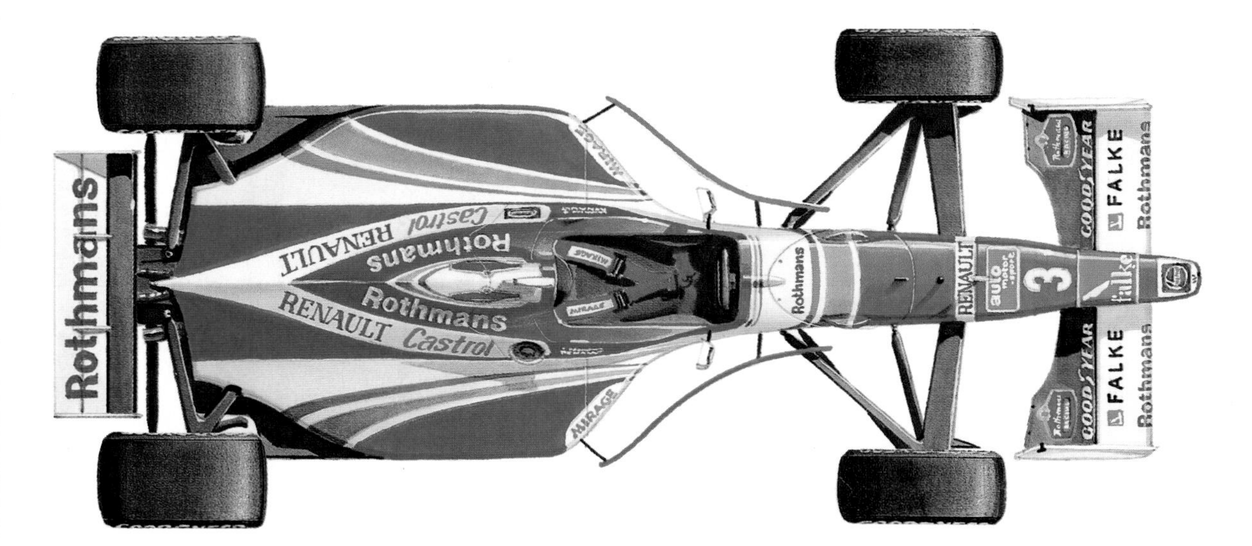

WILLIAMS-RENAULT FW19 – JACQUES VILLENEUVE ARGENTINIAN GRAND PRIX

Williams-Renault FW19

SPECIFICATION

- Chassis : *Williams FW19*
- Engine : *Renault RS9 V10*
- Tyres : *Goodyear*
- Wheels : *OZ*
- Fuel / oil : *Elf*
- Brakes (discs) : *Carbone Industrie*
- Brakes (calipers) : *AP Racing*
- Transmission : *Williams 6 gears*
- Radiators : *Secan (water) / IMI (oil)*
- Plugs : *Champion*
- Electronic mgt : *Magneti Marelli*
- Shock absorbers : *Williams / Penske*
- Suspensions : *Williams (push rods)*
- Dry weight : *600 kg, driver included*
- Wheelbase : *2890 mm*
- Front track : *1670 mm*
- Rear track : *1600 mm*
- Total length : *4150 mm*

TEAM PROFILE

- Address : *Williams Grand Prix Engineering, Grove, Wantage, Oxfordshire OX12 0DQ, United Kingdom*
- Telephone : *(44) 1235 77 77 00*
- Fax : *(44) 1235 76 47 05*
- Established in : *1969*
- First Grand Prix : *Argentina 1975*
- General director : *Frank Williams*
- Technical director : *Patrick Head*
- Team-manager : *Dickie Stanford*
- Chief mechanic : *Carl Gaden*
- Nber of employees : *220*
- Sponsor : *Rothmans*

STATISTICS

Number of Grand Prix :	*379*
Number of victories :	*103*
Number of pole-positions :	*107*
Number of best laps during the race :	*109*
Number of drivers' world titles :	*7*
Number of constructors' titles :	*9*
Total number of points scored :	*1909.5*

POSITION IN WORLD CHAMPIONSHIP

1975 :	*9th – 6 points*	1987 :	***1st – 137 points***
1976 :	*not classified*	1988 :	*7th – 20 points*
1977 :	*not classified*	1989 :	*2nd – 77 points*
1978 :	*9th – 11 points*	1990 :	*4th – 57 points*
1979 :	*2nd – 75 points*	1991 :	*2nd – 125 points*
1980 :	***1st – 120 points***	1992 :	***1st – 164 points***
1981 :	***1st – 95 points***	1993 :	***1st – 168 points***
1982 :	*4th – 58 points*	1994 :	***1st – 118 points***
1983 :	*4th – 38 points*	1995 :	*2nd – 112 points*
1984 :	*6th – 25.5 points*	1996 :	***1st – 175 points***
1985 :	*3rd – 71 points*	1997 :	***1st – 123 points***
1986 :	***1st – 141 points***		

A pensive Patrick Head. By his own admission, the Williams technical director lived through a difficult season. But once again, victory awaited him at the end of the road. ▽

Simply the best

Year after year, the Williams team rack up the successes with a consistency which must irritate the opposition. This season however, the FW19 was nothing more than an evolution of the 1996 FW18 and was not the perfect winning machine.

As far as reliability is concerned there is nothing to say: the FW19 only let its drivers down 3 times from 34 starts (Villeneuve in Imola; Frentzen in Argentina and Hungary.) From a chassis point of view, the team noticed at the mid-season in Hockenheim that the car had a problem with its aerodynamic balance. Heinz-Harald had complained about it since the start of the season, but he was not listened to as he had just joined the team and Jacques was not complaining.

The problem solved, the FW19 was once again on top form throughout the summer grands prix. The Constructors' Championship was richly deserved, all the more so as Renault had made a big effort with the RS9, which never once failed in a race.

TEST DRIVER 1997

Jean-Christophe BOULLION (F)

SUCCESSION OF DRIVERS 1997

- Jacques VILLENEUVE : *all Grand Prix*
- Heinz-H. FRENTZEN : *all Grand Prix*

Ferrari

5. Michael SCHUMACHER

DRIVER PROFILE

- Name : *SCHUMACHER*
- First name : *Michael*
- Nationality : *German*
- Date of birth : *January 3, 1969*
- Place of birth : *Hürth-Hermühlheim (GER)*
- Lives in : *Vufflens-le-Château (CH)*
- Marital status : *married to Corinna*
- Kids : *one daughter (Gina Maria)*
- Hobbies : *karting, mountain-bike, biking*
- Favourite music : *Phil Collins, M. Jackson, T. Turner*
- Favourite meal : *Italian cuisine*
- Favourite drink : *apple juice with mineral water*
- Height : *174 cm*
- Weight : *74,5 kg*

STATISTICS

- Nber of Grand Prix : *102*
- Victories : *27*
- Pole-positions : *17*
- Best laps : *28*
- Accident/off : *18*
- Not qualified : *0*
- Laps in the lead : *1568*
- Km in the lead : *7211*
- Points scored : *440*

PRIOR TO F1

1984 : *German junior karting Champion*
1987 : *European karting Champion*
1988 : *German Champion of F. Ford*
1990-91 : *Sportscar championship with Mercedes*

F1 CAREER

1991 : *Jordan / Ford & Benetton. 4 points. 12th du champ.*
1992 : *Benetton / Ford. 53 points. 3rd of championship.*
1993 : *Benetton / Ford. 52 points. 4th of championship.*
1994 : *Benetton / Ford. 92 points.* ***World Champion.***
1995 : *Benetton/Renault. 102 pts.* ***World Champion.***
1996 : *Ferrari. 49 points. 3rd of championship.*
1997 : *Ferrari. 78 points. 2nd of championship.*

6. Eddie IRVINE

DRIVER PROFILE

- Name : *IRVINE*
- First name : *Edmund*
- Nationality : *British*
- Date of birth : *November 10, 1965*
- Place of birth : *Newtownards (IRE)*
- Lives in : *Dublin, Oxford (GB) & Conlig (IRE)*
- Marital status : *single*
- Kids : -
- Hobbies : *golf, swimming, fishing*
- Favourite music : *rock, Van Morrison*
- Favourite meal : *Chinese*
- Favourite drink : -
- Height : *178 cm*
- Weight : *75 kg*

STATISTICS

- Nber of Grand Prix : *65*
- Victories : *0*
- Pole-positions : *0*
- Best laps : *0*
- Accident/off : *23*
- Not qualified : *0*
- Laps in the lead : *23*
- Km in the lead : *125*
- Points scored : *52*

PRIOR TO F1

1983-87 : *F. Ford 1600*
1988 : *F. 3 GB*
1989 : *F. 3000*
1990 : *F. 3000 (3rd)*
1991 : *F. 3000 Japon (7th)*
1992 : *F. 3000 Japon (8th)*
1993 : *F. 3000 Japon (2nd)*

F1 CAREER

1993 : *Jordan / Hart. 0 point.*
1994 : *Jordan / Hart. 6 points. 14th of championship.*
1995 : *Jordan / Peugeot. 10 points. 12th of championship.*
1996 : *Ferrari. 11 points. 10th of championship.*
1997 : *Ferrari. 24 points. 8th of championship.*

We all knew Michael Schumacher was the best of the current crop. This year, he simply confirmed that fact with some of the most memorable performances of his career. At Monaco, he was regal in the rain and in Belgium he was the king of the damp conditions.
His technical genius also allowed Ferrari to have an above average season, even though the F 310 B chassis was described by Schumacher as "catastrophic" the first time he tried it in January. Unfortunately, this idyllic tableau was somewhat spoilt by the incident in Jerez. Even though Michael refuses to admit it, it seemed like a deliberate attempt to push Jacques Villeneuve off the track. It was an inelegant move which has seriously damaged the Ferrari driver's reputation. The public will not forget it until the next time he produces a brilliant performance.

In his role as Schumacher's lieutenant, Eddie Irvine did an even better job this year than last. Quick and effective, he is just the man for the job. Indeed, the German described him as the quickest team-mate he has ever had.
Unfortunately, Eddie knows he will never become world champion as Schumacher's Number Two. He has already had to sacrifice his first potential win at Suzuka, on the altar of his loyalty to his team. Irvine knows it and is patient. As he has said on many occasions, he is learning a lot from Michael Schumacher.

FERRARI F310B – MICHAEL SCHUMACHER
BELGIAN GRAND PRIX

Ferrari F310B

SPECIFICATION

- Chassis : *Ferrari F310B*
- Engine : *Ferrari 046/2 V10*
- Tyres : *Goodyear*
- Fuel / oil : *Shell*
- Brakes (discs) : *Carbone Industrie*
- Brakes (calipers) : *Brembo*
- Transmission : *Ferrari 7 gears*
- Radiators : *not revealed*
- Plugs : *NGK*
- Electronic mgt : *Magneti Marelli*
- Shock absorbers : *not revealed*
- Wheels : *BBS*
- Suspensions : *push rods (ft/bk)*
- Dry weight : *600 kg, including driver*
- Wheelbase : *2935 mm*
- Total length : *4358 mm*
- Total height : *968 mm*
- Front track : *1690 mm*
- Rear track : *1605 mm*

TEAM PROFILE

- Address : *Ferrari SpR, Via Ascari 55, 41053 Maranello (MO), Italy*
- Telephone : *(39) 536 94 91 11*
- Fax : *(39) 536 94 64 88*
- Established in : *1929*
- First Grand Prix : *Monaco 1950*
- General director : *Luca Di Montezemolo*
- Technical director : *Ross Brawn, Paolo Martinelli (engines)*
- Concepteur chassis : *Rory Byrne*
- Recherche : *Gustav Brunner*
- Team-manager : *Jean Todt*
- Chief mechanic: *Nigel Stepney*
- Nber of employees : *330*
- Sponsors : *Marlboro, Fiat, Shell, Asprey*

STATISTICS

- Number of Grand Prix : *586*
- Number of victories : *113*
- Number of pole-positions : *121*
- Number of best laps during the race : *126*
- Number of drivers' world titles : *9*
- Number of constructors' titles : *8*
- Total number of points scored : *2082.5*

POSITION IN WORLD CHAMPIONSHIP

1958 : *2nd – 40 points*
1959 : *2nd – 32 points*
1960 : *3rd – 24 points*
1961 : ***1st – 40 points***
1962 : *5th – 18 points*
1963 : *4th – 26 points*
1964 : ***1st – 45 points***
1965 : *4th – 26 points*
1966 : *2nd – 31 points*
1967 : *4th – 20 points*
1968 : *4th – 32 points*
1969 : *5th – 7 points*
1970 : *2nd – 55 points*
1971 : *4th – 33 points*
1972 : *4th – 33 points*
1973 : *6th – 12 points*
1974 : *2nd – 65 points*
1975 : ***1st – 72,5 points***
1976 : ***1st – 83 points***
1977 : ***1st – 95 points***
1978 : *2nd – 58 points*
1979 : ***1st – 113 points***
1980 : *10th – 8 points*
1981 : *5th – 34 points*
1982 : ***1st – 74 points***
1983 : ***1st – 89 points***
1984 : *2nd – 57,5 points*
1985 : *2nd – 82 points*
1986 : *4th – 37 points*
1987 : *4th – 53 points*
1988 : *2nd – 65 points*
1989 : *3rd – 59 points*
1990 : *2nd – 110 points*
1991 : *3rd – 55,5 points*
1992 : *4th – 21 points*
1993 : *4th – 23 points*
1994 : *3rd – 71 points*
1995 : *3rd – 73 points*
1996 : *2nd – 70 points*
1997 : *2nd – 102 points*

Almost there

This time, it seems that Ferrari is on the right road. In January 1997, when the new F 310 B was unveiled, Jean Todt's avowed objective was to win more races than in 1996. With Schumacher winning five races that objective has been reached.
Naturally, as the season evolved, the target shifted to the world championship as the German driver headed the table from the Monaco GP onwards.
Finally they missed out. But it was close. All the same, Ferrari has enjoyed its best season since 1983 - the last time the Scuderia won the Constructors' title. By the end of the year, the F 310 B seemed a match for the Williams. Therefore, it looks as though everything is in place for 1998 to be the year that all of Italy can celebrate.

TEST DRIVER 1997

Gianni MORBIDELLI (I)

SUCCESSION OF DRIVERS 1997

- Mich. SCHUMACHER : *all Grand Prix*
- Eddie IRVINE : *all Grand Prix*

◁ *Accomplices at all times: Michael Schumacher and Jean Todt, the team's sporting director.*

Benetton-Renault

7. Jean ALESI

DRIVER PROFILE

- Name : *ALESI*
- First name : *Jean*
- Nationality : *French*
- Date of birth : *June 11, 1964*
- Place of birth : *Avignon (F)*
- Lives in : *Nyon (CH)*
- Marital status : *divorced, fiancée Kumiko*
- Kids : *two daughters*
- Hobbies : *skiing, tennis, golf, water skiing*
- Favourite music : -
- Favourite meal : *pasta*
- Favourite drink : *Vichy Menthe*
- Height : *170 cm*
- Weight : *75 kg*

STATISTICS

- Nber of Grand Prix : *135*
- Victories : *1*
- Pole-positions : *2*
- Best laps : *4*
- Accident/off : *23*
- Not qualified : *0*
- Laps in the lead : *239*
- Km in the lead : *1113*
- Points scored : *225*

PRIOR TO F1

1981-82 : *Karting*
1983-84 : *Renault 5 Turbo*
1985 : *F. Renault of France (5th)*
1986 : *F. 3 of France (2nd)*
1987 : *French Champion of F. 3*
1988 : *F. 3000 (10th)*
1989 : *Champion F. 3000*

F1 CAREER

1989 : *Tyrrell / Ford. 8 points. 9th of championship.*
1990 : *Tyrrell / Ford. 13 points. 9th of championship.*
1991 : *Ferrari. 21 points. 7th of championship.*
1992 : *Ferrari. 18 points. 7th of championship.*
1993 : *Ferrari. 16 points. 6th of championship.*
1994 : *Ferrari. 24 points. 5th of championship.*
1995 : *Ferrari. 42 points. 5th of championship.*
1996 : *Benetton / Renault. 47 points. 4th of champ.*
1997 : *Benetton / Renault. 36 points. 5th of champ.*

8. Gerhard BERGER

DRIVER PROFILE

- Name : *BERGER*
- First name : *Gerhard*
- Nationality : *Austrian*
- Date of birth : *August 27, 1959*
- Place of birth : *Wörgl (A)*
- Lives in : *Monte Carlo, Kundl (A)*
- Marital status : *married to Ana*
- Kids : *two daughters (Christina, Sarah M.)*
- Hobbies : *skiing, motorcycle, sleeping*
- Favourite music : *Beatles*
- Favourite meal : *Italian cuisine*
- Favourite drink : *water*
- Height : *184 cm*
- Weight : *74 kg*

STATISTICS

- Nber of Grand Prix : *210*
- Victories : *10*
- Pole-positions : *12*
- Best laps : *21*
- Accident/off : *26*
- Not qualified : *0*
- Laps in the lead : *654*
- Km in the lead : *3184*
- Points scored : *382*

PRIOR TO F1

1981 : *European Cup Alfa Sprint (7th)*
1982 : *F. 3 of Germany (3rd)*
1983-84 : *European F. 3 (8th and 3rd)*

F1 CAREER

1984 : *ATS / BMW. 0 point.*
1985 : *Arrows / BMW. 3 points. 17th of championship.*
1986 : *Benetton / BMW. 17 points. 7th of championship.*
1987 : *Ferrari. 36 points. 5th of championship.*
1988 : *Ferrari. 41 points. 3rd of championship.*
1989 : *Ferrari. 21 points. 7th of championship.*
1990 : *McLaren / Honda. 43 points. 3rd of championship.*
1991 : *McLaren / Honda. 43 points. 4th of championship.*
1992 : *McLaren / Honda. 49 points. 5th of championship.*
1993 : *Ferrari. 12 points. 8th of championship.*
1994 : *Ferrari. 41 points. 3rd of championship.*
1995 : *Ferrari. 31 points. 6th of championship.*
1996 : *Benetton / Renault. 21 points. 6th of championship.*
1997 : *Benetton / Renault. 27 points. 6th of champ.*

Yet another season with not a single win for Jean of Avignon. It was not for lack of trying and once again he put up some exceptional performances this season.
But his B197 was too much of a lunatic piece of equipment to give him any real hope. Once again, Jean was often forced to fight for minor placings, unworthy of his talent. Jerez was a case in point - he finished 13th! His only high moment was pole position in Monza.
Apart from that, Jean racked up another four second places. Always the best man but never the bridegroom.

Gerhard Berger had a strange season, a mixture of great performances and all-time lows. Gerhard blamed his sinus problem which started at the Argentinian Grand Prix. The infection bothered him in San Marino, Monaco and Spain, before his doctors forbade him from driving in the Canadian Grand Prix.
When he made his comeback, he stopped the clocks. A man possessed, he took both pole position and victory in Hockenheim, before returning to anonymity, once again bothered by his sinusitis. Finally, after much thought, Gerhard decided to retire at the end of the season, although he says it could be "temporary." Formula One's grand old man has finally reached for the pipe and slippers.

BENETTON-RENAULT B197 –
GERHARD BERGER
GERMAN GRAND PRIX

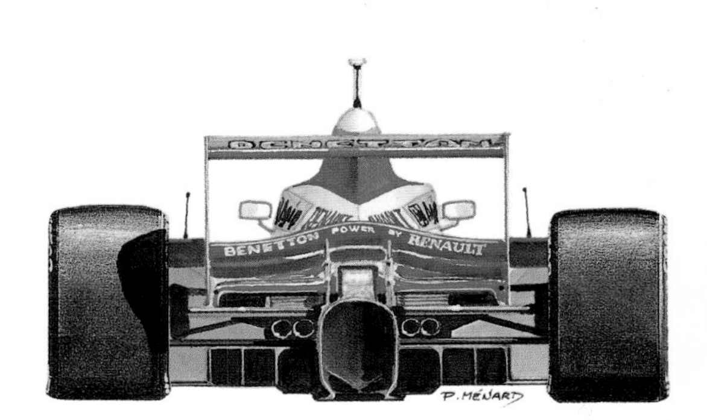

Benetton-Renault B197

SPECIFICATION

• Chassis :	*Benetton B197*
• Engine :	*Renault RS9 V10*
• Tyres :	*Goodyear*
• Wheels :	*BBS*
• Fuel / oil :	*Agip*
• Brakes (discs) :	*Carbone Industrie*
• Brakes (calipers) :	*Brembo*
• Transmission :	*Benetton 6 gears*
• Radiators :	*Benetton*
• Plugs :	*Champion*
• Electronic mgt :	*Magneti Marelli*
• Shock absorbers :	*Bilstein*
• Suspensions :	*push rods (ft/bk)*
• Dry weight :	*550 kg (without driver)*
• Wheelbase :	*2880 mm*
• Front track :	*1700 mm*
• Rear track :	*1600 mm*

TEAM PROFILE

• Address :	*Benetton Formula Ltd. Whiteways Technical Centre Enstone, Chipping Norton Oxon OX7 4EE United Kingdom*
• Telephone :	*(44) 1608 67 80 00*
• Fax :	*(44) 1608 67 86 09*
• Established in :	*1970 (under the name Toleman)*
• First Grand Prix :	*Italy 1981*
• General director :	*Flavio Briatore / David Richards*
• Technical director :	*Pat Symonds*
• Team-manager :	*Joan Villadelprat*
• Chief mechanic :	*Mike Ainsley-Cowlishaw*
• Nber of employees :	*175*
• Sponsors :	*Mild Seven, United Colors of Benetton*

STATISTICS

• Number of Grand Prix :	*251*
• Number of victories :	*26*
• Number of pole-positions :	*15*
• Number of best laps during the race :	*36*
• Number of drivers' world titles :	*2*
• Number of constructors' titles :	*1*
• Total number of points scored :	*797.5*

POSITION IN WORLD CHAMPIONSHIP

1981 : *not classified*
1982 : *not classified*
1983 : *9th – 10 points*
1984 : *7th – 16 points*
1985 : *not classified*
1986 : *6th – 19 points*
1987 : *5th – 28 points*
1988 : *3rd – 39 points*
1989 : *4th – 39 points*
1990 : *3rd – 71 points*
1991 : *4th – 38,5 points*
1992 : *3rd – 91 points*
1993 : *3rd – 72 points*
1994 : *2nd – 103 points*
1995 : ***1st – 137 points***
1996 : *3rd – 68 points*
1997 : *3rd – 67 points*

Alexander Wurz only drove in three grands prix as Berger's replacement, but he made a big impression, finishing on the podium at Silverstone.
▽

Another disappointment!

In this chapter of the 1996 version of "Formula One Yearbook," it explained that Benetton's 1997 season could hardly be worse than 1996. But it was! This year, the multi-coloured team scored one less point than last year.
However, it at least salvaged its honour with one win, thanks to a surge of energy from Gerhard Berger, when he returned to the wheel at the German Grand Prix.

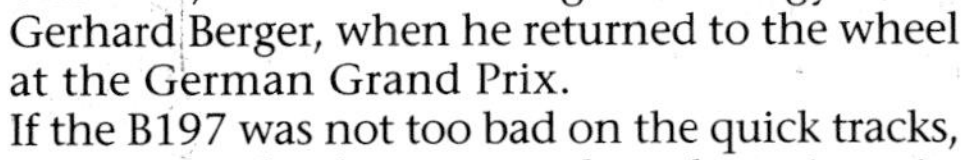

If the B197 was not too bad on the quick tracks, it was completely out-paced on the twisty circuits, as when Berger qualified a humiliating 18th in his home grand prix in Austria.
There were many reasons for the problem and they were all the harder to solve as the creators of the car, Ross Brawn and Rory Byrne had defected to Ferrari. They were replaced with a team of young engineers who evidently could not pull their weight.

Flavio Briatore did not have a brilliant season. Shown the door by Alessandro Benetton, he was replaced by David Richards after the Luxembourg Grand Prix.
▽

TEST DRIVER 1997

Alexander WURZ (AUT)

SUCCESSION OF DRIVERS 1997

• Jean ALESI :	*all Grand Prix*
• Gerhard BERGER :	*AUS-BRE-ARG-RSM-MON-ESP-D-HON-BEL-ITA-AUT-LUX-JAP-EUR*
• Jarno TRULLI :	*CAN-FRA-GB*

McLaren-Mercedes

9. Mika HAKKINEN

DRIVER PROFILE

- Name : *HAKKINEN*
- First names : *Mika Pauli*
- Nationality : *Finnish*
- Date of birth : *September 28, 1968*
- Place of birth : *Helsinki (SF)*
- Lives in : *Monte Carlo*
- Marital status : *single*
- Kids : -
- Hobbies : *skiing, swimming, golf, tennis*
- Favourite music : *Michael Jackson, Phil Collins*
- Favourite meal : -
- Favourite drinks : *water, milk*
- Height : *179 cm*
- Weight : *70 kg*

STATISTICS

- Nber of Grand Prix : *96*
- Victories : *1*
- Pole-positions : *1*
- Best laps : *1*
- Accident/off : *14*
- Not qualified : *2*
- Laps in the lead : *66*
- Km in the lead : *319*
- Points scored : *118*

PRIOR TO F1

1974-86 : *Karting (5 times Champion of Finland)*
1987 : *Champion F. Ford*
1988 : *Opel Lotus Euroseries*
1989 : *F. 3 (GB, 7th)*
1990 : *F. 3 / Champion West Surrey*

F1 CAREER

1991 : *Lotus / Judd. 2 points. 15th of championship.*
1992 : *Lotus / Ford. 11 points. 8th of championship.*
1993 : *McLaren / Ford. 4 points. 15th of championship.*
1994 : *McLaren / Peugeot. 26 points. 4th of champ.*
1995 : *McLaren / Mercedes. 17 points. 7th of champ.*
1996 : *McLaren / Mercedes. 31 points. 5th of champ.*
1997 : *McLaren / Mercedes. 27 points. 7th of champ.*

10. David COULTHARD

DRIVER PROFILE

- Name : *COULTHARD*
- First name : *David*
- Nationality : *British*
- Date of birth : *March 27, 1971*
- Place of birth : *Twynholm (Scotland)*
- Lives in : *Monaco*
- Marital status : *single*
- Kids : -
- Hobbies : *motorsport, golf, swimming*
- Favourite music : *Queen, Phil Collins*
- Favourite meal : *pasta*
- Favourite drink : *tea*
- Height : *182 cm*
- Weight : *75 kg*

STATISTICS

- Nber of Grand Prix : *58*
- Victories : *3*
- Pole-positions : *5*
- Best laps : *5*
- Accident/off : *10*
- Not qualified : *0*
- Laps in the lead : *330*
- Km in the lead : *1596*
- Points scored : *117*

PRIOR TO F1

1983-88 : *Karting*
1989 : *Junior F. Ford 1600 Champion*
1990 : *F. Opel Lotus*
1991 : *F. 3 GB (2nd)*
1992 : *F. 3000 (9th)*
1993 : *F. 3000 (3rd)*

F1 CAREER

1994 : *Williams / Renault. 14 points. 8th of champ.*
1995 : *Williams / Renault. 49 points. 3rd of champ.*
1996 : *McLaren / Mercedes. 18 points. 7th of champ.*
1997 : *McLaren / Mercedes. 36 pts. 4th of champ.*

The undisputed talent of the super-fast Mika Hakkinen was rewarded with a victory in the dying seconds of the season at Jerez where he won on the very last lap of the final grand prix. Until then, the Finn had suffered from his usual appalling bad luck. At Silverstone he was seven laps from victory when his engine let go. In Spielberg it was the same story, albeit on the first lap and then at the Nurburgring it happened again. Not to mention that he was stripped of his hard fought third place in Belgium.
The Jerez win was some compensation for all these efforts. It would certainly serve to buck up the morale of a driver who has always seemed down in the dumps this season. At the beginning of the season, he seemed to struggle, but towards the end he always beat his team-mate in qualifying.

It was a good season for David Coulthard. In 1997, the Scotsman managed to better his team-mate in six of the qualifying sessions. But it was at the start and towards the end, Hakkinen was definitely quicker.
David made up for it with some demon starts, which could not be entirely explained away by McLaren's form of traction control. He was always very aggressive in the races and nearly always impossible to overtake.
After giving the matter deep thought, the McLaren team decided to retain his services for a further season. He certainly would not have deserved to get the push.

McLAREN-MERCEDES MP4/12 – DAVID COULTHARD AUSTRALIAN GRAND PRIX

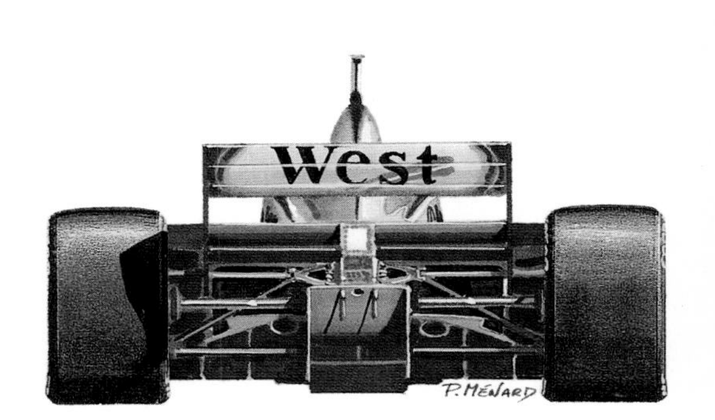

McLaren-Mercedes MP4/12

SPECIFICATION

- Chassis : *McLaren MP 4/12*
- Engine : *Mercedes-Benz FO 112 V10*
- Tyres : *Goodyear*
- Wheels : *Enkei*
- Fuel / oil : *Mobil*
- Brakes (discs) : *Hitco*
- Brakes (calipers) : *AP Racing*
- Transmission : *McLaren 6 gears, semi-autom.*
- Radiators : *McLaren / Calsonic*
- Plugs : *NGK / GS Battery*
- Electronic mgt : *TAG Electronic System*
- Shock absorbers : *Penske*
- Suspensions : *push rods*
- Dry weight : *600 kg, driver included*
- Wheelbase : *not revealed*
- Front track : *not revealed*
- Rear track : *not revealed*

TEAM PROFILE

- Address : *McLaren International Ltd. Woking Business Park Albert Drive Woking, Surrey GU21 5JY United Kingdom*
- Telephone : *(44) 1483 728 211*
- Fax : *(44) 1483 720 157*
- Established in : *1963*
- First Grand Prix : *Monaco 1966*
- General director : *Ron Dennis*
- Technical director : *Adrian Newey*
- Team-manager : *Jo Ramirez*
- Chief mechanic : *Paul Simpson*
- Nber of employees : *210*
- Sponsors : *Reemtsma, Hugo Boss, Tag-Heuer*

STATISTICS

- Number of Grand Prix : *460*
- Number of victories : *107*
- Number of pole-positions : *80*
- Number of best laps during the race : *71*
- Number of drivers' world titles : *9*
- Number of constructors' titles : *7*
- Total number of points scored : *2049.5*

POSITION IN WORLD CHAMPIONSHIP

1966 : *7th – 3 points*
1967 : *8th – 1 points*
1968 : *2nd – 51 points*
1969 : *4th – 40 points*
1970 : *4th – 35 points*
1971 : *6th – 10 points*
1972 : *3rd – 47 points*
1973 : *3rd – 58 points*
1974 : *1st – 73 points*
1975 : *3rd – 53 points*
1976 : *2nd – 74 points*
1977 : *3rd – 60 points*
1978 : *7th – 15 points*
1979 : *7th – 15 points*
1980 : *7th – 11 points*
1981 : *6th– 28 points*
1982 : *2nd – 69 points*
1983 : *5th – 34 points*
1984 : ***1st – 143.5 points***
1985 : ***1st – 90 points***
1986 : *2nd – 96 points*
1987 : *2nd – 76 points*
1988 : ***1st – 199 points***
1989 : ***1st – 141 points***
1990 : ***1st – 121 points***
1991 : ***1st – 139 points***
1992 : *2nd – 99 points*
1993 : *2nd – 84 points*
1994 : *4th – 42 points*
1995 : *4th – 30 points*
1996 : *4th – 49 points*
1997 : *4th – 63 points*

Ron Dennis in happy mood. His team found the road to success once more this season.
▽

A building year

The McLaren-Mercedes team had changed colour over the winter, from Marlboro red to West grey. It allowed the team to adopt the "Silver Arrows" look and their cars were by far the prettiest on the grid this year.
But underneath the paint job, progress had also been made. After several barren years, the McLaren-Mercedes duo saw its partnership crowned with success for the first time in Melbourne. It was something of a lucky win, but it was reinforced by the subsequent win in Monza. A final win in Jerez, a one-two finish at that, had the bosses dancing in the aisles, but there were still too many mechanical failures, mainly on the engine side and this robbed them of several good results.
It was McLaren's best season for a long time and 1998 promises to be even better with a car designed by Adrian Newey, poached from Williams.

Who dares say they are not a bright bunch at McLaren? At least their luminous clothing lights up as soon as the flash guns go off.
▽

TEST DRIVER 1997

-

SUCCESSION OF DRIVERS 1997

- Mika HAKKINEN : *all Grand Prix*
- David COULTHARD : *all Grand Prix*

Jordan-Peugeot

11. Ralf SCHUMACHER

DRIVER PROFILE

- Name : *SCHUMACHER*
- First name : *Ralf*
- Nationality : *German*
- Date of birth : *June 30, 1975*
- Place of birth : *Hürth (D)*
- Lives in : *Monte Carlo*
- Marital status : *single*
- Kids : -
- Hobbies : *karting, tennis*
- Favourite music : *soft rock*
- Favourite meal : *pasta*
- Favourite drink : *apple juice with mineral water*
- Height : *178 cm*
- Weight : *73 kg*

STATISTICS

- Nber of Grand Prix : *17*
- Victories : *0*
- Pole-positions : *0*
- Best laps : *0*
- Accident/off : *5*
- Not qualified : *0*
- Laps in the lead : *0*
- Km in the lead : *0*
- Points scored : *13*

PRIOR TO F1

1978-92 : *Karting*
1993 : *Jr. Champ. ADAC*
1994 : *Champ. F. 3 (D, 3rd)*
1995 : *Champ. F. 3 (D, 2nd), winner world final F.3 in Macao*
1996 : *F. 3000 Champion (Japan)*

F1 CAREER

1997 : *Jordan / Peugeot. 13 points. 12th of championship.*

12. Giancarlo FISICHELLA

DRIVER PROFILE

- Name : *FISICHELLA*
- First name : *Giancarlo*
- Nationality : *Italian*
- Date of birth : *January 14, 1973*
- Place of birth : *Roma (I)*
- Lives in : *Monte Carlo*
- Marital status : *single*
- Kids : -
- Hobbies : *skiing, fishing, football, tennis*
- Favourite music : *disco music, Zucchero*
- Favourite meal : *pasta, pizza, steaks and fish*
- Favourite drink : *orange juice*
- Height : *172 cm*
- Weight : *69,5 kg*

STATISTICS

- Nber of Grand Prix : *25*
- Victories : *0*
- Pole-positions : *0*
- Best laps : *0*
- Accident/off : *6*
- Not qualified : *0*
- Laps in the lead : *7*
- Km in the lead : *48*
- Points scored : *0*

PRIOR TO F1

1984-88 : *Karting*
1989 : *World Championship Karting (4th)*
1991 : *F. Alfa Boxer; karting (EUR) (2nd)*
1992-94 : *F 3 (ITA), champion in1994*
1995 : *DTM/ITC Alfa Romeo*

F1 CAREER

1996 : *Minardi / Ford. 0 point.*
1996 : *Minardi / Ford. 0 point.*
1997 : *Jordan / Peugeot. 20 points. 9th of championship.*

Clearly it cannot be easy coming into Formula 1 as Michael Schumacher's brother.
This apart, Ralf Schumacher might have hoped for a better debut season in F1. Pretentious, arrogant and dangerous on the track (Giancarlo Fisichella in Argentina and Johnny Herbert in Italy know all about it.) Ralf was quickly nicknamed "Rex" in the paddock. There was no doubt he was fast, but that was all. Throughout the second half of the season, he was always out-qualified by his team-mate. In fact, Ralf will be best remembered for the incredible number of times he flew off the track, especially in qualifying. To sum up, it was a very poor year. Ralf will have a lot to do to rebuild his image for next season.

The ladies think he is cute and the team owners think he is very quick. Giancarlo Fisichella was certainly the revelation of the season.
This was only his first full season in F1, but "Fisico" performed beyond his level of experience. On top of that, he is a nice guy. It is hardly surprising that Jordan and Benetton fought over his services for 1998.

JORDAN-PEUGEOT 197 –
GIANCARLO FISICHELLA
BELGIAN GRAND PRIX

Jordan-Peugeot 197

SPECIFICATION

• Chassis :	*Jordan 197*
• Engine :	*Peugeot A14 V10*
• Tyres :	*Goodyear*
• Wheels :	*OZ*
• Fuel / oil :	*Total*
• Brakes (discs) :	*Carbone Industrie*
• Brakes (calipers) :	*Brembo*
• Transmission :	*Jordan 6 gears*
• Radiators :	*Secan / Jordan*
• Plugs :	*FIAMM / FIAMM*
• Electronic mgt :	*TAG Electronics*
• Shock absorbers :	*Jordan*
• Suspensions :	*push rods (ft/bk)*
• Dry weight :	*600 kg, driver included*
• Wheelbase :	*2950 mm*
• Front track :	*1700 mm*
• Rear track :	*1618 mm*

TEAM PROFILE

• Address :	*Jordan Grand Prix Ltd. Buckingham Road, Silverstone, Northants NN12 8TJ United Kingdom*
• Telephone :	*(44) 1327 857 153*
• Fax :	*(44) 1327 858 120*
• Established in :	*1981*
• First Grand Prix :	*USA 1991*
• General director :	*Eddie Jordan*
• Technical director :	*Gary Anderson*
• Team-manager :	*Trevor Foster*
• Chief mechanic :	*Tim Edwards*
• Nber of employees :	*80*
• Sponsors :	*Benson&Hedges, Total*

STATISTICS

• Number of Grand Prix :	*114*
• Number of victories :	*0*
• Number of pole-positions:	*1*
• Number of best laps during the race :	*2*
• Number of drivers' world titles :	*0*
• Number of constructors' titles :	*0*
• Total number of points scored :	*118*

POSITION IN WORLD CHAMPIONSHIP

1991 : *5th – 13 points*
1992 : *11th – 1 point*
1993 : *10th – 3 points*
1994 : *5th – 28 points*
1995 : *6th – 21 points*
1996 : *5th – 22 points*
1997 : *5th – 33 points*

"Bye Giancarlo. Wait and see, you will miss us next year."

Fifth yet again

Once again, the Jordan team finished fifth in the championship, which means that compared to the previous season, progress has not exactly been spectacular!
As far as results go, the high point of the season was without a doubt Giancarlo Fisichella's second place in Belgium. However, the bare results do not tell the whole story as, on the track, the Jordans occasionally looked like they were about to take the top slot. Fisichella could have won in Hockenheim for example, but for some bad luck. The Jordans unfortunately suffered from recurring reliability problems. What is more, entrusting the development of the car to two novice drivers was not the best solution. The situation was aggravated as the two young lions were already at one another's throats after the third race. Finally, Eddie Jordan lost Peugeot for 1998. He landed on his feet with Mugen, but at what cost in terms of performance.

TEST DRIVER 1997

–

SUCCESSION OF DRIVERS 1997

• Ralf SCHUMACHER : *all Grand Prix*
• Giancarlo FISICHELLA: *all Grand Prix*

Prost-Mugen

14. Olivier PANIS

DRIVER PROFILE

• Name :	*PANIS*
• First names :	*Olivier Denis*
• Nationality :	*French*
• Date of birth :	*September 2, 1966*
• Place of birth :	*Lyon (F)*
• Lives in :	*Grenoble (F)*
• Marital status :	*married to Anne*
• Kids :	*one son (Aurélien)*
• Hobbies :	*skiing, bike, karting, weight-lifting*
• Favourite music :	*Stevie Wonder*
• Favourite meal :	*pasta*
• Favourite drink :	*Coca Cola*
• Height :	*173 cm*
• Weight :	*76,1 kg*

STATISTICS

• Nber of Grand Prix :	59
• Victories :	1
• Pole-positions :	0
• Best laps :	0
• Accident/off :	10
• Not qualified :	0
• Laps in the lead :	0
• Km in the lead :	0
• Points scored :	70

PRIOR TO F1

1981-87 : *Karting*
1988 : *Champion Steering Wheel Elf Paul Ricard*
1989 : *Champion F. Renault of France*
1990 : *F. 3 of France (4th)*
1991 : *F. 3 of France (4th)*
1992 : *F. 3000*
1993 : *Champion F. 3000*

F1 CAREER

1994 : *Ligier / Renault. 9 points. 11th of championship.*
1995 : *Ligier / Mugen. 16 points. 8th of championship.*
1996 : *Ligier / Mugen. 13 points. 9th of championship.*
1997 : *Prost / Mugen Honda. 16 points. 10th of champ.*

15. Shinji NAKANO

DRIVER PROFILE

• Name :	*NAKANO*
• First name :	*Shinji*
• Nationality :	*Japanese*
• Date of birth :	*April 1, 1971*
• Place of birth :	*Osaka (JAP)*
• Lives in :	*Marseilles*
• Marital status :	*single*
• Kids :	-
• Hobbies :	*tennis, squash, skiing, biking*
• Favourite music :	*no special taste*
• Favourite meal :	*Japanese cuisine*
• Favourite drink :	*water*
• Height :	*174 cm*
• Weight :	*63 kg*

STATISTICS

• Nber of Grand Prix :	17
• Victories :	0
• Pole-positions :	0
• Best laps :	0
• Accident/off :	3
• Not qualified :	0
• Laps in the lead :	0
• Km in the lead :	0
• Points scored :	2

PRIOR TO F1

1987 : *Karting (JAP, 2nd)*
1988 : *Champion Super Kart (JAP)*
1989 : *Ch. F3 JAP (7th)*
1990-91 : *F. Opel-Lotus*
1992 : *Champ. F3 and F3000 (JAP)*
1993-94 : *Champ. F3 (JAP)*
1995-96 : *Champ. F3000*

F1 CAREER

1997 : *Ligier / Mugen Honda. 2 points. 19th of champ.*

If anyone still had any doubts, 1997 confirmed that Olivier Panis is an exceptional talent. At the wheel of his JS45, the Frenchman was the author of some great performances which were all the more astounding as he was the only driver to contribute to the development of the car.
Of course, his season was completely ruined by his accident in the Canadian Grand Prix, a race which he looked like winning as he rocketed towards the head of the field on his Bridgestone tyres. He would doubtless have gone well at Magny-Cours as well. When he returned to an F1 cockpit for the first time in September, he set a time which would have given him pole position in the French Grand Prix.
When he made his comeback at the Nurburgring, he proved he had not lost his touch. 1997 is now forgotten and Panis is anxiously awaiting 1998 and the Peugeot engine.

It cannot be easy fitting into a French team when you are Japanese and Nakano had great difficulty coping with the season. This situation was exacerbated by the fact that his boss, Alain Prost obviously wanted to get rid of him as soon as possible. Thanks to support from Mr. Honda, Nakano hung on until the end of the season. To be fair, he must be credited with some good performances - his point in Hungary for example. However, it is not enough to get him a drive for 1998. Even Honda did not try and foist him on Jordan.

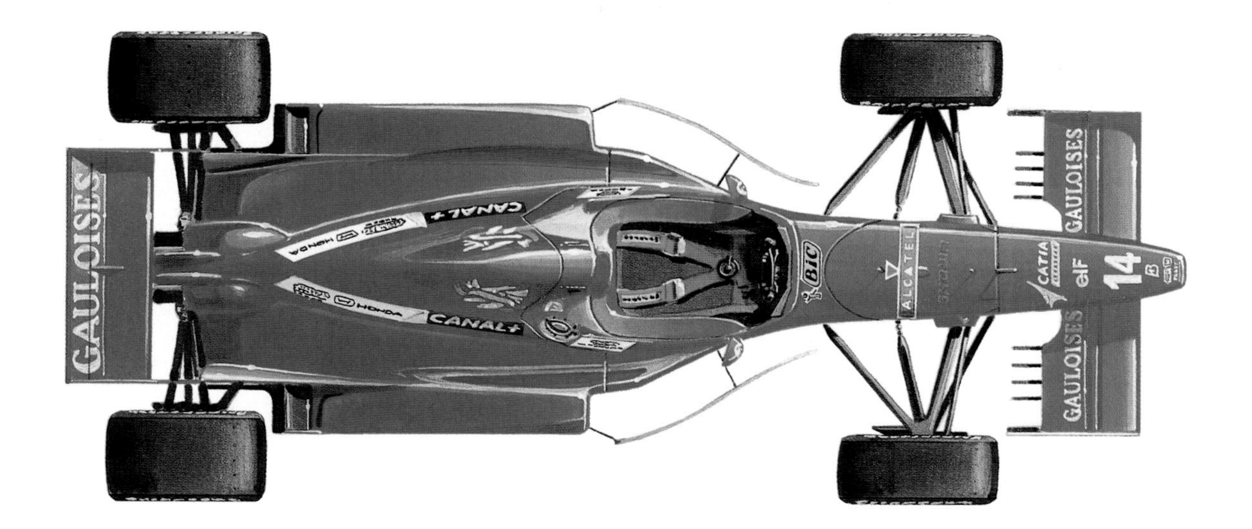

PROST-MUGEN HONDA JS45 –
OLIVIER PANIS
SPANISH GRAND PRIX

Prost-Mugen JS45

SPECIFICATION

• Chassis :	*Prost JS45*
• Engine :	*Mugen-Honda MF-301HB-V10*
• Tyres :	*Bridgestone*
• Fuel / oil :	*Elf*
• Brakes (discs) :	*Carbone Industrie*
• Brakes (calipers) :	*Brembo*
• Transmission :	*Ligier 6 gears*
• Plugs :	*NGK / FIAMM*
• Shock absorbers :	*Showa*
• Suspensions :	*push rods (ft/bk)*
• Dry weight :	*600 kg, driver included*
• Wheelbase :	*2995 mm*
• Front track :	*1693 mm*
• Rear track :	*1608 mm*
• Total length :	*4335 mm*
• Total height :	*950 mm*

TEAM PROFILE

• Address :	*Prost Grand Prix* *Technopole du Circuit* *58470 Magny-Cours* *France*
• Telephone :	*(33) 4 86 60 62 00*
• Fax :	*(33) 4 86 21 22 97*
• Established in :	*1969*
• First Grand Prix :	*Brazil 1976*
• General director :	*Alain Prost*
• Technical director :	*Loïc Bigois*
• Team-manager :	*Cesare Fiorio*
• Chief mechanic :	*Robert Dassaud*
• Nber of employees :	*80*
• Sponsors :	*Gauloises Blondes, Alcatel,BIC*

STATISTICS

• Number of Grand Prix :	*343*
• Number of victories :	*9*
• Number of pole-positions :	*9*
• Number of best laps during the race :	*11*
• Number of drivers' world titles :	*0*
• Number of constructors' titles :	*0*
• Total number of points scored :	*408*

POSITION IN WORLD CHAMPIONSHIP

1976 : *5th – 20 points*	1987 : *11th – 1 point*
1977 : *8th – 18 points*	1988 : *not classified*
1978 : *6th – 19 points*	1989 : *13th – 3 points*
1979 : *3rd – 61 points*	1990 : *not classified*
1980 : *2nd – 66 points*	1991 : *not classified*
1981 : *4th – 44 points*	1992 : *7th – 6 points*
1982 : *8th – 20 points*	1993 : *5th – 22 points*
1983 : *not classified*	1994 : *6th – 13 points*
1984 : *10th – 3 points*	1995 : *5th – 24 points*
1985 : *6th – 23 points*	1996 : *6th - 15 points*
1986 : *5th – 29 points*	1997 : *6th - 21 points*

A concerned Alain Prost. As he admitted this season, the role of team owner is far more stressful than that of a driver.
▽

On the way up

14th February 1997. In Peugeot's head office at Avenue de la Grande Armee in Paris, Alain Prost announced his takeover of the Ligier team. The team would now be known as "Prost Grand Prix." A new name for new ambitions. Just a few weeks had gone by before the whole world had forgotten the Prost team had ever had a past. The four times world champion had blown in with a wind of change and the results were not long in coming: third place in Brazil, second in Spain.
The road to success lay before them and new sponsors were queuing up. Nothing it seemed could resist the Prost team. Jacques Villeneuve even said that the French team would be capable of winning the world championship that very year.
Olivier Panis' accident put a spoke in their wheels. But it is only temporary. Next year, Prost Grand Prix should be one of the leading players.

TEST DRIVER 1997

–

SUCCESSION OF DRIVERS 1997

• Olivier PANIS :	*AUS-BRE-ARG-RSM-MON-ESP-CAN-LUX-JAP-EUR*
• Jarno TRULLI :	*FRA-GB-D-HON-BEL-ITA-AUT*
• Shinji NAKANO :	*all Grand Prix*

Jarno Trulli was called up to replace Olivier Panis. The young Italian was not unworthy, as he led for 160 kms in Austria and scored 3 points in Germany.
▽

Sauber-Petronas

16. Johnny HERBERT

DRIVER PROFILE

- Name : *HERBERT*
- First name : *Johnny*
- Nationality : *British*
- Date of birth : *June 27, 1964*
- Place of birth : *Romford (GB)*
- Lives in : *Monaco*
- Marital status : *married to Rebecca*
- Kids : *two daughters (Amy, Chloe)*
- Hobbies : *golf, squash, fishing*
- Favourite music : *rock, pop*
- Favourite drink : *apple juice*
- Height : *167 cm*
- Weight : *65 kg*

STATISTICS

- Nber of Grand Prix : *112*
- Victories : *2*
- Pole-positions : *0*
- Best laps : *0*
- Accident/off : *17*
- Not qualified : *3*
- Laps in the lead : *27*
- Km in the lead : *149*
- Points scored : *82*

PRIOR TO F1

1984-85 : *F. Ford 1600*
1986 : *F. Ford 2000*
1987 : *GB F. 3 Champion*
1988 : *F. 3000*

F1 CAREER

1989 : *Benetton / Ford & Tyrrell / Ford. 0 point.*
1990 : *Lotus / Lamborghini. 0 point (only 2 GP).*
1991 : *Lotus / Judd. 0 point.*
1992 : *Lotus / Ford. 2 points. 14th of championship.*
1993 : *Lotus / Ford. 11 points. 8th of championship.*
1994 : *Lotus / Honda. 0 point.*
1995 : *Benetton / Renault. 45 points. 4th of champ.*
1996 : *Sauber / Ford. 4 points. 14th of championship.*
1997 : *Sauber / Petronas. 15 points. 11th of champ.*

17. Gianni MORBIDELLI

DRIVER PROFILE

- Name : *MORBIDELLI*
- First name : *Gianni*
- Nationality : *Italian*
- Date of birth : *January 13, 1968*
- Place of birth : *Pesaro (ITA)*
- Lives in : *Monte-Carlo*
- Marital status : *single*
- Kids : -
- Hobbies : *music, gym*
- Favourite music : *disco*
- Favourite drink : *water, Coca Cola Light*
- Height : *167 cm*
- Weight : *59 kg*

STATISTICS

- Nber of Grand Prix : *68*
- Victories : *0*
- Pole-positions : *0*
- Best laps : *0*
- Accident/off : *11*
- Not qualified : *2*
- Laps in the lead : *0*
- Km in the lead : *0*
- Points scored : *8.5*

PRIOR TO F1

1980-85 : *Karting*
1987 : *Italian F. 3 Champ. (6th)*
1988 : *Italian F. 3 Champ. (5th)*
1989 : *Italian F. 3 Champion*

F1 CAREER

1990 : *Dallara / Ford & Minardi / Ford. 0 point. (3 GPs)*
1991 : *Minardi / Ferrari & Ferrari (1 GP). 0.5 point. 24th*
1992 : *Minardi / Lamborghini. 0 point.*
1994 : *Arrows / Ford. 3 points. 22nd of championship.*
1995 : *Arrows / Hart. 5 points. 14th of championship.*
1997 : *Sauber / Petronas. 0 point. (8 GPs)*

Johnny Herbert is one of the nicest drivers in the paddock and when the mood takes him he can pull something out of the bag; witness his performance when, to everyone's surprise, he topped the time sheets in Thursday's practice at Monaco.
He drove an honourable season without ever throwing in the towel. With Jean Alesi by his side next season, he will finally have some help in developing the car. Things can only get better in 1998.

Gianni Morbidelli is not a Sauber driver. He was simply loaned to the Swiss team by Ferrari, as a replacement for the Italian Nicola Larini, who turned out to be a lightweight.
Morbidelli took his job seriously, but he was never capable of beating Johnny Herbert.
He then broke his arm in private testing at Magny-Cours, which forced Peter Sauber to find a replacement for the French Grand Prix. Gianni was back in business in Budapest, but hurt his wrist again in Suzuka. Once again it was Norberto Fontana who took over the second Sauber. Hardly ideal conditions to develop the car.

Originally, Nicola Larini was supposed to drive for the whole of the 1997 season for Sauber. But his results were so poor that the Swiss team replaced him from the Spanish Grand Prix onwards. It did not change much. ▽

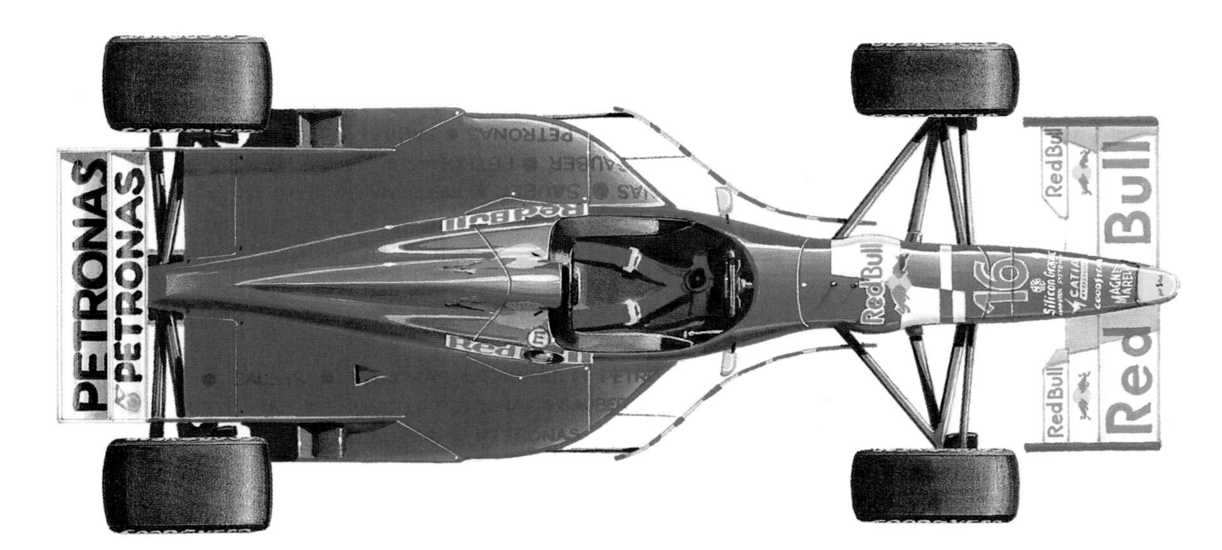

SAUBER-PETRONAS C16 –
JOHNNY HERBERT
HUNGARIAN GRAND PRIX

Sauber-Petronas C16

SPECIFICATION

- Chassis : *Sauber C16*
- Engine : *Petronas SP01*
- Tyres : *Goodyear*
- Fuel / oil : *Shell*
- Brakes (discs) : *Carbone Industrie*
- Brakes (calipers) : *Brembo*
- Transmission : *Sauber 6 gears*
- Radiators : *Behr/Secan*
- Plugs : *NGK*
- Electronic mgt : *Magneti Marelli*
- Shock absorbers : *Sachs*
- Suspensions : *push rods (ft/bk)*
- Dry weight : *600 kg, driver included*
- Wheelbase : *2940 mm*
- Front track : *1660 mm*
- Rear track : *1610 mm*

TEAM PROFILE

- Address : *Red Bull Sauber AG, Wildbachstrasse 9, 8340 Hinwil, Switzerland*
- Telephone : *(41) 1 938 14 00*
- Fax : *(41) 1 938 16 70*
- Established in : *1972*
- First Grand Prix : *South Africa 1993*
- General director : *Peter Sauber*
- Technical director : *Leo Ress*
- Team-manager : *Max Welti*
- Chief mechanic : *Beat Zehnder*
- Nber of employees : *80*
- Sponsors : *Red Bull, Petronas*

STATISTICS

- Number of Grand Prix : *81*
- Number of victories : *0*
- Number of pole-positions : *0*
- Number of best laps during the race : *0*
- Number of drivers' world titles : *0*
- Number of constructors' titles : *0*
- Total number of points scored : *68*

POSITION IN WORLD CHAMPIONSHIP

1993 : *6th – 12 points*
1994 : *8th – 12 points*
1995 : *7th – 18 points*
1996 : *7th – 11 points*
1997 : *7th – 16 points*

Very average

The 1997 season was not one to remember for the Sauber team. With an engine which was supposed to be first class, the Petronas power unit was none other than the 1996 Ferrari V10, the season looked set fair. The only glitch was the total lack of pre-season testing as the car was not ready until the very last minute. Apart from a podium finish in Hungary, the team did not set the world alight this year. The chassis had inherent and severe understeer and was difficult to set-up. At every track, both drivers had to work hard to solve these faults. Unfortunately, Johnny Herbert was the only driver to score any points. Three drivers passed through the second car without ever making any sort of impression.

TEST DRIVER 1997

Norberto FONTANA (ARG)

SUCCESSION OF DRIVERS 1997

- Johnny HERBERT : *all Grand Prix*
- Nicola LARINI : *AUS-BRE-ARG-RSM-MON*
- Gianni MORBIDELLI : *ESP-CAN-HON-BEL-ITA-AUT-LUX-JAP*
- Norberto FONTANA : *FRA-GB-D-EUR*

Johnny Herbert's most frightening moment of the season: he went off the track at Monza, doing over 300 km/h. Caught unawares, we will forgive the photographer for the less than perfect photograph of the incident.
▽

Tyrrell-Ford

18. Jos VERSTAPPEN

DRIVER PROFILE

• Name :	*VERSTAPPEN*
• First names :	*Johannes Franciscus*
• Nationality :	*Dutch*
• Date of birth :	*March 4, 1972*
• Place of birth :	*Montfort (HOL)*
• Lives in :	*Monte-Carlo*
• Marital status :	*married to Sophie (pregnant)*
• Kids :	-
• Hobbies :	*squash, jogging, mountain-bike*
• Favourite music :	*pop, UB40, Phil Collins*
• Favourite meal :	*pasta*
• Favourite drink :	*Coca-Cola*
• Height :	*175 cm*
• Weight :	*73 kg*

STATISTICS

• Nber of Grand Prix :	48
• Victories :	0
• Pole-positions :	0
• Best laps :	0
• Accident/off :	12
• Not qualified :	0
• Laps in the lead :	0
• Km in the lead :	0
• Points scored :	11

PRIOR TO F1

1980-91 : karting
1983+84 : HOL Champion
1986 : Benelux Champion
1989 : European Champion
1991 : BEL Champion
1992 : F. Opel Lotus (Benelux Champion)
1993 : Champion F3 D; F. Atlantic

F1 CAREER

1994 : *Benetton / Ford. 10 points. 10th of championship.*
1995 : *Simtek / Ford. Forfeit after 5 races.*
1996 : *Arrows / Hart. 1 point. 16th of championship.*
1997 : *Tyrrell / Ford. 0 point.*

19. Mika SALO

DRIVER PROFILE

• Name :	*SALO*
• First names :	*Mika Noriko Endo*
• Nationality :	*Finnish*
• Date of birth :	*November 30, 1966*
• Place of birth :	*Helsinki (SF)*
• Lives in :	*London*
• Marital status :	*single, fiancée Noriko*
• Kids :	-
• Hobbies :	*ski-doo, squash, mountain-bike*
• Favourite music :	*rock*
• Favourite meal :	*meat balls, pasta*
• Favourite drink :	*milk*
• Height :	*175 cm*
• Weight :	*66 kg*

STATISTICS

• Nber of Grand Prix :	52
• Victories :	0
• Pole-positions :	0
• Best laps :	0
• Accident/off :	4
• Not qualified :	0
• Laps in the lead :	0
• Km in the lead :	0
• Points scored :	12

PRIOR TO F1

1989 : *British F. 3*
1990 : *F. 3 GB (2nd)*
1991-94 : *F. 3000 Japan*

F1 CAREER

1994 : *Lotus / Mugen. 0 point. (only 2 GP)*
1995 : *Tyrrell / Yamaha. 5 points. 14th of championship.*
1996 : *Tyrrell / Yamaha. 5 points. 13th of championship.*
1997 : *Tyrrell / Ford. 2 points. 17th of championship.*

The confrontation between "The Boss" and Mika Salo promised much, with both men confident of their own ability. It was going to be interesting to see which one destroyed the other. Whichever one was beaten could probably kiss his career goodbye.
In the end, it was pretty much a draw between the two Tyrrell drivers in qualifying, with Mika Salo enjoying a slight advantage. Jos "The Boss" defended his corner, but always for the lesser placings on the grid.
This did not stop the Dutch fans from turning up in their thousands to cheer on their hero. With 10,000 members, Verstappen has the next biggest fan club after Michael Schumacher. Strange these Dutch folk.

Yet another far from convincing season for Mika Salo. The man who claims to be quicker than Michael Schumacher was beaten on six occasions by his team-mate. It is difficult to pillory him however. His Tyrrell was powered by the feeble Ford V8 and no one could have got more out of it. The Finn still managed to score two points, thanks to the chaos that was the Monaco Grand Prix and the rain that hid his car's weak points. Next year, he drives for Arrows instead of Damon Hill. He will renew his acquaintance with the Yamaha engine which brought him so much suffering in 1996 with Tyrrell.

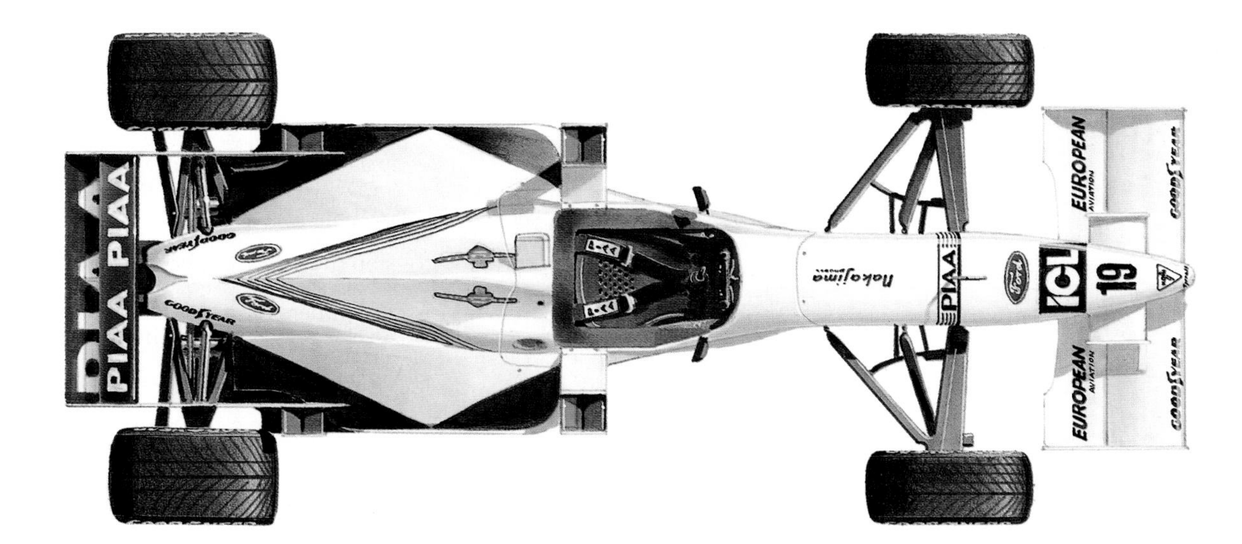

TYRRELL-FORD 025 – MIKA SALO
MONACO GRAND PRIX

Tyrrell-Ford 025

SPECIFICATION

• Chassis :	*Tyrrell 025*
• Engine :	*Ford Cosworth ED4*
• Tyres :	*Goodyear*
• Fuel / oil :	*Elf*
• Brakes (discs) :	*Hitco*
• Brakes (calipers) :	*AP Racing*
• Transmission :	*Tyrrell 6 gears*
• Radiators :	*Secan*
• Plugs :	*NGK*
• Electronic mgt :	*Ford*
• Shock absorbers :	*Koni*
• Suspensions :	*push rods (ft/bk)*
• Dry weight :	*600 kg*
• Wheelbase :	*2990 mm*
• Front track :	*1700 mm*
• Rear track :	*1610 mm*
• Total length :	*4430 mm*
• Total height :	*950 mm*

Courage and perseverence

Ken Tyrrell's story is more and more incredible. In 1996 his car barely had a sponsor on it, apart from the Mild Seven logos which accompanied Ukyo Katayama. But when the Japanese driver went to Minardi, poor old Uncle Ken had even less in the piggy bank. His situation was all the more critical as he had not signed the Concorde Agreement and therefore did not receive any of the television rights money. To add to his misfortune he was no longer in partnership with Yamaha and had to pay through the nose for the down on power Ford engines that no one else wanted. Despite these financial worries, the team kept on track and morale was good (see page 79.) Harvey Postlethwaite, the team's technical director even came up with a few unique innovations like the cockpit mounted wings for use on slow tracks. It did not however, make up for the missing 100 horsepower.

TEST DRIVER 1997

Toranosuke TAKAGI (JAP)

SUCCESSION OF DRIVERS 1997

• Jos VERSTAPPEN :	*all Grand Prix*
• Mika SALO :	*all Grand Prix*

TEAM PROFILE

• Address :	*Tyrrell Racing Organisation Ltd.* *Long-Reach, Ockham* *Woking, Surrey GU23 6PE*
• Telephone :	*(44) 1483 284 955*
• Fax :	*(44) 1483 284 892*
• Established in :	*1960*
• First Grand Prix :	*Canada 1970*
• General director :	*Ken Tyrrell*
• Technical director :	*Harvey Postlethwaite*
• Sports director :	*Satoru Nakanjima*
• Team-manager :	*Steve Nielsen*
• Chief mechanic :	*Nigel Steer*
• Nber of employees :	*75*
• Sponsor :	*PIAA*

STATISTICS

• Number of Grand Prix :	*402*
• Number of victories :	*23*
• Number of pole-positions :	*14*
• Number of best laps during the race :	*20*
• Number of drivers' world titles :	*2*
• Number of constructors' titles :	*1*
• Total number of points scored :	*617*

POSITION IN WORLD CHAMPIONSHIP

1971 :	***1st – 73 points***	1985 :	*9th – 7 points*
1972 :	*2nd – 51 points*	1986 :	*7th – 11 points*
1973 :	*2nd – 82 points*	1987 :	*6th – 11 points*
1974 :	*3rd – 52 points*	1988 :	*8th – 5 points*
1975 :	*5th – 25 points*	1989 :	*5th – 16 points*
1976 :	*3rd – 71 points*	1990 :	*5th – 16 points*
1977 :	*5th – 28 points*	1991 :	*6th – 12 points*
1978 :	*4th – 38 points*	1992 :	*6th – 8 points*
1979 :	*5th – 28 points*	1993 :	*not classified*
1980 :	*6th – 12 points*	1994 :	*6th – 13 points*
1981 :	*8th – 10 points*	1995 :	*8th – 5 points*
1982 :	*7th – 25 points*	1996 :	*8th – 5 points*
1983 :	*7th – 12 points*	1997 :	*10th – 2 points*
1984 :	*not classified*		

Jos Verstappen and Mika Salo enjoyed a good relationship this season, even if they should have made for an explosive cocktail.

Minardi-Hart

20. Ukyo KATAYAMA

DRIVER PROFILE

- Name : *KATAYAMA*
- First name : *Ukyo*
- Nationality : *Japanese*
- Date of birth : *May 29, 1963*
- Place of birth : *Tokyo (J)*
- Lives in : *Monte Carlo and Tokyo*
- Marital status : *married to Rumiko*
- Kids : *one son (Ryui), one daughter (Risa)*
- Hobbies : *golf, reading, fitness*
- Favourite music : *all kinds of music*
- Favourite meal : *Japanese and Italian cuisine*
- Favourite drink : -
- Height : *165 cm*
- Weight : *60 kg*

STATISTICS

• Nber of Grand Prix :	95
• Victories :	0
• Pole-positions :	0
• Best laps :	0
• Accident/off :	30
• Not qualified :	1
• Laps in the lead :	0
• Km in the lead :	0
• Points scored :	5

PRIOR TO F1

- 1983 : *Japan champion of F. Ford 1600 B*
- 1984 : *Japan champion of F. Ford 1600 A*
- 1985 : *F. 3 Japan (6th)*
- 1986-87 : *F. 3 France*
- 1988-90 : *F. 3000 Japan*
- 1991 : *Champion F. 3000 Japan*

F1 CAREER

1992 : *Venturi / Lamborghini. 0 point.*
1993 : *Tyrrell / Yamaha. 0 point.*
1994 : *Tyrrell / Yamaha. 5 points. 17th of championship.*
1995 : *Tyrrell / Yamaha. 0 point.*
1996 : *Tyrrell / Yamaha. 0 point.*
1997 : *Minardi / Hart. 0 point.*

21. Tarso MARQUES

DRIVER PROFILE

- Name : *MARQUES*
- First name : *Tarso*
- Nationality : *Brazilian*
- Date of birth : *January 9, 1976*
- Place of birth : *Curitiba (BRA)*
- Lives in : *Curitiba (BRA)*
- Marital status : *single*
- Kids : -
- Hobbies : *water-skiing*
- Favourite music : *rock*
- Favourite meal : *pasta*
- Favourite drink : *orange juice*
- Height : *175 cm*
- Weight : *64 kg*

STATISTICS

• Nber of Grand Prix :	9
• Victories :	0
• Pole-positions :	0
• Best laps :	0
• Accident/off :	1
• Not qualified :	0
• Laps in the lead :	0
• Km in the lead :	0
• Points scored :	0

PRIOR TO F1

- 1988-91 : *Karting*
- 1992 : *Formula Opel (BRA)*
- 1993 : *Champ F. 3 BRA and South America*
- 1994 : *Int. champ. F 3000*
- 1995 : *Int. champ. F 3000 (2nd)*

F1 CAREER

1996 : *Minardi / Ford. 0 point. (2 GPs)*
1997 : *Minardi / Hart. 0 point.*

Ukyo Katayama lived up to his reputation this season: several off-track excursions, a lot of spins and several small problems. The Japanese driver's best results were two tenth places. Nothing to celebrate and not the way to bring his F1 career to an end in style.
Katayama announced his retirement in Suzuka. He will not be missed as a driver, although he will be regretted as a really nice guy with a sense of humour. At the end of the day, he got his seat year after year, thanks to the millions he brought with him from Mild Seven.

Reckoned to be very talented by those who knew him when he raced at home in Brazil, Tarso Marques did not make a strong impression at Minardi this year. He was test driver until he was called up to replace Jarno Trulli, who moved to Prost.
It is difficult to see how he could shine. A Minardi-Hart is hardly a state of the art race car as it is the only car which did not score a single point this season. For the pleasant Brazilian, the season boiled down to several battles with the Tyrrells.

MINARDI-HART M197 – UKYO KATAYAMA
SAN MARINO GRAND PRIX

Minardi-Hart M197

SPECIFICATION

• Chassis :	*Minardi M197*
• Engine :	*Hart 830 AV 7*
• Tyres :	*Bridgestone*
• Fuel / oil :	*Agip / Motul*
• Brakes (discs) :	*Carbone Industrie*
• Brakes (calipers) :	*Brembo*
• Transmission :	*Minardi/ XTrac 6-speed*
• Radiators :	*Minardi*
• Plugs :	*Champion / FIAMM*
• Electronic mgt :	*Magneti Marelli*
• Shock absorbers :	*Penske*
• Suspensions :	*pushrod*
• Dry weight :	*600 kg, driver included*
• Wheelbase :	*2900 mm*
• Front track :	*1680 mm*
• Rear track :	*1620 mm*

TEAM PROFILE

• Address :	*Minardi Team SpA Via Spallanzani 21 (Z.I.) 48018 Faenza Italy*
• Telephone :	*(39) 546 620 480*
• Fax :	*(39) 546 620 998*
• Established in :	*1974*
• First Grand Prix :	*Brazil 1985*
• General director:	*Gian Carlo Minardi*
• Technical director :	*Gabriele Tredozi*
• Team-manager :	*Frédéric Dhainaut*
• Chief mechanic :	*Gabriele Pagliarini*
• Nber of employees :	*80*
• Sponsors :	*Mild Seven, Fondmetal, Bossini*

STATISTICS

• Number of Grand Prix :	*205*
• Number of victories :	*0*
• Number of pole-positions :	*0*
• Number of best laps during the race :	*0*
• Number of drivers' world titles :	*0*
• Number of constructors' titles :	*0*
• Total number of points scored :	*27*

POSITION IN WORLD CHAMPIONSHIP

1985 : *not classified*	1992 : *11th – 1 point*
1986 : *not classified*	1993 : *8th – 7 points*
1987 : *not classified*	1994 : *10th – 5 points*
1988 : *10th – 1 point*	1995 : *10th – 1 point*
1989 : *10th – 6 points*	1996 : *not classified*
1990 : *not classified*	1997 : *not classified*
1991 : *7th – 6 points*	

No progress in sight

Naturally, no one expected miracles from the Minardis this season, even though Giancarlo Minardi had managed to trade in his 1996 "customer" Fords for a supply of Brian Hart engines. Nevertheless, Minardi could count on help from several Italian racing personalities, from Flavio Briatore to Alessandro Nannini. They could also count on the excellent Jarno Trulli and had the luxury of a test driver in the shape of Tarso Marques. Unfortunately this positive perspective never materialised, added to which, Trulli, who had been developing the car, was snatched from Minardi at the French Grand Prix. Today, even Giancarlo Minardi himself admits it is unlikely his team will ever win a race.

A Minardi on the limit with its brakes glowing red. All this effort and no reward this year.
▽

TEST DRIVER 1997

–

SUCCESSION OF DRIVERS 1997

• Ukyo KATAYAMA :	*all Grand Prix*
• Jarno TRULLI :	*AUS-BRE-ARG-RSM-MON-ESP-CAN*
• Tarso MARQUES :	*FRA-GB-D-HON-BEL-ITA-AUT-LUX-JAP-EUR*

Stewart-Ford

22. Rubens BARRICHELLO

DRIVER PROFILE

- Name : *BARRICHELLO*
- First names : *Rubens Gonçalves*
- Nationality : *Brazilian*
- Date of birth : *May 3, 1972*
- Place of birth : *São Paulo (BRA)*
- Lives in : *Monaco*
- Marital status : *married to Silvana*
- Kids : -
- Hobbies : *running, jet-ski*
- Favourite music : *pop, rock*
- Favourite dish : *pasta*
- Favourite drink : *Diet Pepsi, Pepsi Max*
- Height : *172 cm*
- Weight : *71 kg*

STATISTICS

- Nber of Grand Prix : *81*
- Victories : *0*
- Pole-positions : *1*
- Best laps : *0*
- Accident/off : *12*
- Not qualified : *0*
- Laps in the lead : *8*
- Km in the lead : *47*
- Points scored : *46*

PRIOR TO F1

1981-88 : *Karting (5 times Brazilian Champion)*
1989 : *F. Ford 1600 (3rd)*
1990 : *Champion Opel Lotus Euroseries*
1991 : *Champion F. 3 (GB)*
1992 : *F. 3000*

F1 CAREER

1993 : *Jordan / Hart. 2 points. 17th of championship.*
1994 : *Jordan / Hart. 19 points. 6th of championship.*
1995 : *Jordan / Peugeot. 11 points. 11th of championship.*
1996 : *Jordan / Peugeot. 14 points. 8th of championship.*
1997 : *Stewart / Ford. 6 points. 14th of championship.*

23. Jan MAGNUSSEN

DRIVER PROFILE

- Name : *MAGNUSSEN*
- First name : *Jan*
- Nationality : *Danish*
- Date of birth : *July 4, 1973*
- Place of birth : *Roskilde (DK)*
- Lives in : *Silverstone*
- Marital status : *single*
- Kids : *1 son (Kevin)*
- Hobbies : *Art, gliding*
- Favourite music : *dance, pop*
- Plat favori : *McDomald's*
- Favourite drink : *Coca-Cola*
- Height : *170 cm*
- Weight : *58 kg*

STATISTICS

- Nber of Grand Prix : *17*
- Victories : *0*
- Pole-positions : *0*
- Best laps : *0*
- Accident/off : *3*
- Non-qualifications : *0*
- Laps in the lead : *0*
- Km in the lead : *0*
- Points scored : *0*

PRIOR TO F1

1987-89 : *Karting (Junior world champion)*
1990 : *Karting World Champion*
1991-92 : *Formula Ford*
1993 : *Vauxhall Lotus + F3*
1994 : *Champion F3 (GB)*
1995 : *DTM (Mercedes), 8th*
1996 : *ITC and Indycar*

F1 CAREER

1995 : *McLaren / Mercedes. 0 point (1 GP)*
1997 : *Stewart / Ford. 0 point.*

After spending his entire four year F1 career at Jordan, Rubens Barrichello was in for a minor revolution this season. Not only was he changing teams, but he was also having to contribute to its development from Day One.
Now comes the difficult task of assessing his performance, because he only finished two grands prix this season. On one of these occasions, at Monaco, "Rubinho" made it to the second step of the podium which goes a long way to redressing the balance of this difficult year.

When the team was launched in a London hotel in December 1996, the Stewart family described Jan Magnussen as the most talented young driver it had ever come across. Jackie Stewart even went so far as to compare him to a new Ayrton Senna.
These words of praise meant the young Dane was the centre of much attention for the start of his first season. The pressure evidently got to him, as he made several errors at the start. During the year he only twice managed to outqualify Barrichello. Having hesitated for a long time about keeping him on for another season, Stewart finally decided to show confidence in him. It is a second chance which he should not waste.

STEWART-FORD SF01
– RUBENS BARRICHELLO
MONACO GRAND PRIX

Stewart-Ford SF01

SPECIFICATION

• Chassis :	*Stewart Ford SF-1*
• Engine :	*Ford Zetec R V10*
• Tyres :	*Bridgestone*
• Fuel / oil :	*Texaco*
• Brakes (discs) :	*Carbone Industrie*
• Etriers :	*AP Racing*
• Transmission :	*Stewart / XTrac*
• Radiators :	*Secan*
• Plugs :	*Champion / FIAMM*
• Electronic mgt :	*Ford*
• Shock absorbers :	*Stewart / Penske*
• Suspensions :	*push rods (ft/bk)*
• Dry weight :	*600 kg, driver included*
• Wheelbase :	*2950 mm*
• Front track :	*1690 mm*
• Rear track :	*1585 mm*

TEAM PROFILE

• Address :	*Stewart Grand Prix* *16 Tanners Drive, Blakelands* *Milton Keynes, MK14 5BW* *United Kingdom*
• Telephone :	*(44) 1908 216122*
• Fax :	*(44) 1908 216133*
• Established in :	*1996*
• First Grand Prix :	*Australia 1997*
• General director :	*Paul Stewart*
• Technical director :	*Alan Jenkins*
• Team-manager :	*David Stubbs*
• Chief mechanic :	*Dave Redding*
• Nber of employees :	*75*
• Sponsors :	*HSBC, Visit Malysia, Havoline, Sanyo*

STATISTICS

• Number of Grand Prix :	*17*
• Number of victories :	*0*
• Number of pole-positions :	*0*
• Number of best laps during the race :	*0*
• Number of drivers' world titles :	*0*
• Number of constructors' titles :	*0*
• Total number of points scored :	*6*

POSITION IN WORLD CHAMPIONSHIP

1997 : *9th – 6 points*

Not very convincing

Naturally the project had been meticulously put together. Jackie Stewart was personally launching his own team, which made it seem like a very serious project. It was certainly enough to convince Ford to jettison the Sauber team, with which the American company had collaborated since 1995.
The 1997 results sheet is hardly positive. Out of 34 starts, the team only saw its cars cross the finish line on six occasions. A broken engine was the cause of 10 retirements, the Ford V10 proving unfortunately as unreliable as it was low powered.
No doubt Jackie Stewart's admirers had expected too much from this first season. These things take time and it will only be in 1998, when the lessons of this first season have been learned, that we will be able to judge the team. Whatever happens, next year cannot be worse than 1997 for the Scottish team.

TEST DRIVER 1997

–

SUCCESSION OF DRIVERS 1997

• Rubens BARRICHELLO: *all Grand Prix*
• Jan MAGNUSSEN: *all Grand Prix*

◁
The Stewart clan, father and son. With this new challenge, Jackie was once again confronted with a worthwhile task, all the more so as he continued to be an adviser to Ford.
Signed Stewart: although totally new, the team had left nothing to chance. The tartan pattern that adorned everything from trousers to caps, had been registered as an intellectual property.

The engines

FERRARI 046/2

SPECIFICATIONS
- Output : *760 hp at 14 800 rpm*
- Maximum speed : *15 300 rpm*
- Weight : *140 kilos*
- Capacity : *2998.1 cc*
- Configuration : *75 degrees V10*
- Material : *iron block*
- Valves : *4 per cylinder*

RACE PROFILE
- First Grand Prix : *Monaco 1950*
- Team 1997 : *Ferrari*
- Nber of victories 1997 : *3*
- Nber of pole-positions 1997 : *5*

STATISTICS
- Number of Grand Prix : *587*
- Number of constructors' titles : *8*
- Number of pole-positions : *121*
- Number of victories : *113*

FORD ZETEC-R V10

SPECIFICATIONS
- Output : *720 hp at 15 100 rpm*
- Maximum speed : *16 000 rpm*
- Weight : *120 kilos*
- Capacity : *2998 cc*
- Configuration : *72 degrees V10*
- Material : *iron, aluminium and titanium block*
- Valves : *4 per cylinder*

RACE PROFILE
- First Grand Prix : *Brazil 1994*
- Team 1997 : *Stewart*
- Nber of victories 1997 : *0*
- Nber of pole-positions 1997 : *0*

STATISTICS
- Number of Grand Prix : *66*
- Number of constructors' titles : *0*
- Number of pole-positions : *6*
- Number of victories : *8*

FORD COSWORTH ED4

SPECIFICATIONS
- Output : *665 hp at 13 700 rpm*
- Maximum speed : *14 200 rpm*
- Weight : *130 kilos*
- Capacity : *2998 cc*
- Configuration : *75 degrees V8*
- Material : *aluminium block*
- Valves : *4 per cylinder*

RACE PROFILE
- First Grand Prix : *USA 1963*
- Teams 1997 : *Tyrrell*
  Lola
- Nber of victories 1997 : *0*
- Nber of pole-positions 1997 : *0*

STATISTICS
- Number of Grand Prix : *451*
- Number of constructors' titles : *12*
- Number of pole-positions : *131*
- Number of victories : *165*

HART TYPE 830 AV7

SPECIFICATIONS
- Output : *680 hp at 13 100 rpm*
- Maximum speed : *13 600 rpm*
- Weight : *115 kilos*
- Capacity : *2996 cc*
- Configuration : *78 degrees V8*
- Material : *aluminium block*
- Valves : *4 per cylinder*

RACE PROFILE
- First Grand Prix : *Italy 1981*
- Team 1997 : *Minardi*
- Nber of victories 1997 : *0*
- Nber of pole-positions 1997 : *0*

STATISTICS
- Number of Grand Prix : *135*
- Number of constructors' titles : *0*
- Number of pole-positions : *1*
- Number of victories : *0*

MERCEDES-BENZ FO 112

SPECIFICATIONS
- Output : *760 hp at 15 800 rpm*
- Maximum speed : *16 600 rpm*
- Weight : *not revealed*
- Capacity : *3000 cc*
- Configuration : *75 degrees V10*
- Material : *aluminium block*
- Valves : *4 per cylinder*

RACE PROFILE
- First Grand Prix : *France 1954*
- Team 1997 : *McLaren*
- Nber of victories 1997 : *0*
- Nber of pole-positions 1997 : *0*

STATISTICS
- Number of Grand Prix : *77*
- Number of constructors' titles : *0*
- Number of pole-positions : *13*
- Number of victories : *12*

The engines

MF-301HB MUGEN-HONDA

SPECIFICATIONS

- Output : *710 hp at 13 900 rpm*
- Maximum speed : *14 500 rpm*
- Weight : *140 kilos*
- Capacity : *3000 cc*
- Configuration : *72 degrees V10*
- Material : *iron block*
- Valves : *4 per cylinder*

RACE PROFILE

- First Grand Prix : *South Africa 1992*
- Team 1997 : *Prost*
- Nber of victories 1997 : *0*
- Nber of pole-positions 1997 : *0*

STATISTICS

- Number of Grand Prix : *98*
- Number of constructors' titles : *0*
- Number of pole-positions : *0*
- Number of victories : *1*

SP01 PETRONAS

SPECIFICATIONS

- Output : *760 hp at 14 500 rpm*
- Maximum speed : *15 200 rpm*
- Weight : *140 kilos*
- Capacity : *2998.1 cc*
- Configuration : *75 degrees V10*
- Material : *iron block*
- Valves : *4 per cylinder*

RACE PROFILE

- First Grand Prix : *Australia 1997*
- Team 1997 : *Sauber*
- Nber of victories 1997 : *0*
- Nber of pole-positions 1997 : *0*

STATISTICS

- Number of Grand Prix : *17*
- Number of constructors' titles : *0*
- Number of pole-positions : *0*
- Number of victories : *0*

A14 PEUGEOT

SPECIFICATIONS

- Output : *740 hp at 13 900 rpm*
- Maximum speed : *14 400 rpm*
- Weight : *133 kilos*
- Capacity : *2998 cc*
- Configuration : *72 degrees V10*
- Material : *iron block*
- Valves : *4 per cylinder*

RACE PROFILE

- First Grand Prix : *Brazil 1994*
- Team 1997 : *Jordan*
- Nber of victories 1997 : *0*
- Nber of pole-positions 1997 : *0*

STATISTICS

- Number of Grand Prix : *66*
- Number of constructors' titles : *0*
- Number of pole-positions : *0*
- Number of victories : *0*

RS 9 / 9B RENAULT

SPECIFICATIONS

- Output : *755 hp at 14 600 rpm*
- Maximum speed : *15 300 rpm*
- Weight : *132 kilos*
- Capacity : *3000 cc*
- Configuration : *71 degrees V10*
- Material : *aluminium block*
- Valves : *4 per cylinder*

RACE PROFILE

- First Grand Prix : *United Kingdom 1977*
- Teams 1997 : *Williams*, *Benetton*
- Nber of victories 1997 : *9*
- Nber of pole-positions 1997 : *13*

STATISTICS

- Number of Grand Prix : *286*
- Number of constructors' titles : *6*
- Number of pole-positions : *135*
- Number of victories : *95*

OX 11 A YAMAHA

SPECIFICATIONS

- Output : *700 hp at 14 000 rpm*
- Maximum speed : *14 400 rpm*
- Weight : *105 kilos*
- Capacity : *2996 cc*
- Configuration : *72 degrees V10*
- Material : *aluminium block*
- Valves : *4 per cylinder*

RACE PROFILE

- First Grand Prix : *USA 1991*
- Team 1997 : *Arrows*
- Nber of victories 1997 : *0*
- Nber of pole-positions 1997 : *0*

STATISTICS

- Number of Grand Prix : *116*
- Number of constructors' titles : *0*
- Number of pole-positions : *0*
- Number of victories : *0*

Atmosphere

«A picture is worth a thousand words,» so the saying goes. That is why "The Formula One Yearbook," has traditionally opened its account with a veritable explosion of photographs, to help you get into the mood of the season.

Tough competition among the girls

While the drivers fight it out on the tracks, the young ladies in the paddock try and out-do one another in the beauty stakes. It is still not clear which is the most hotly contested of these two forms of competition.

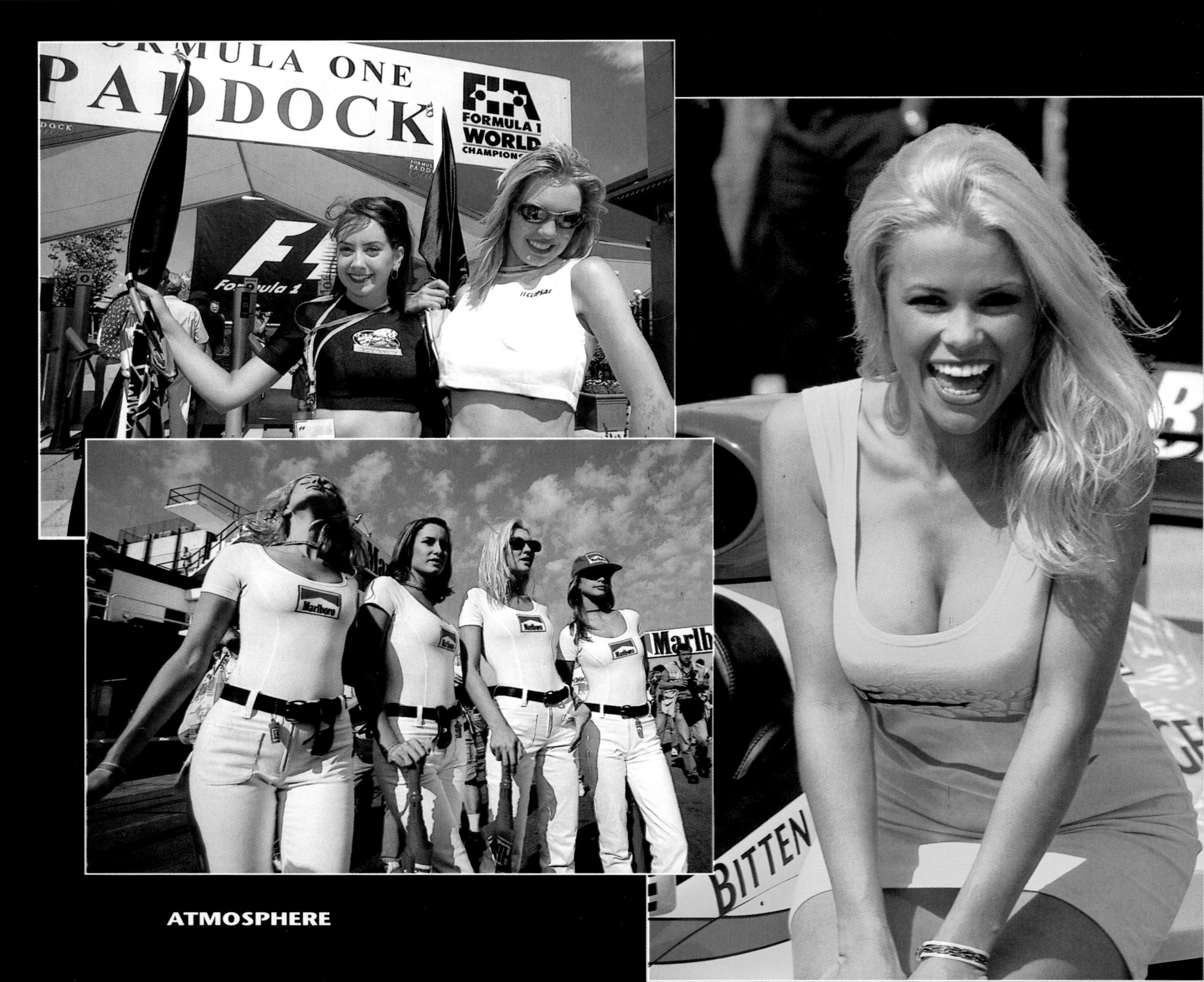

ATMOSPHERE

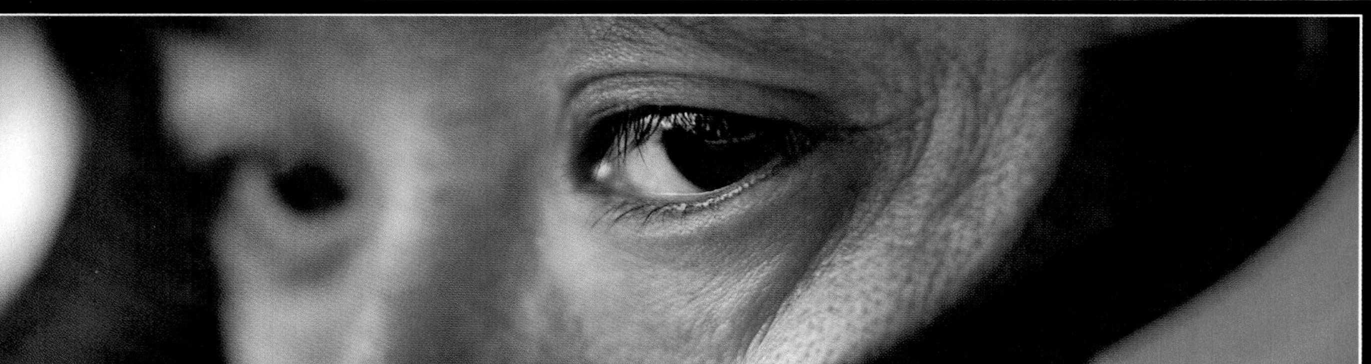
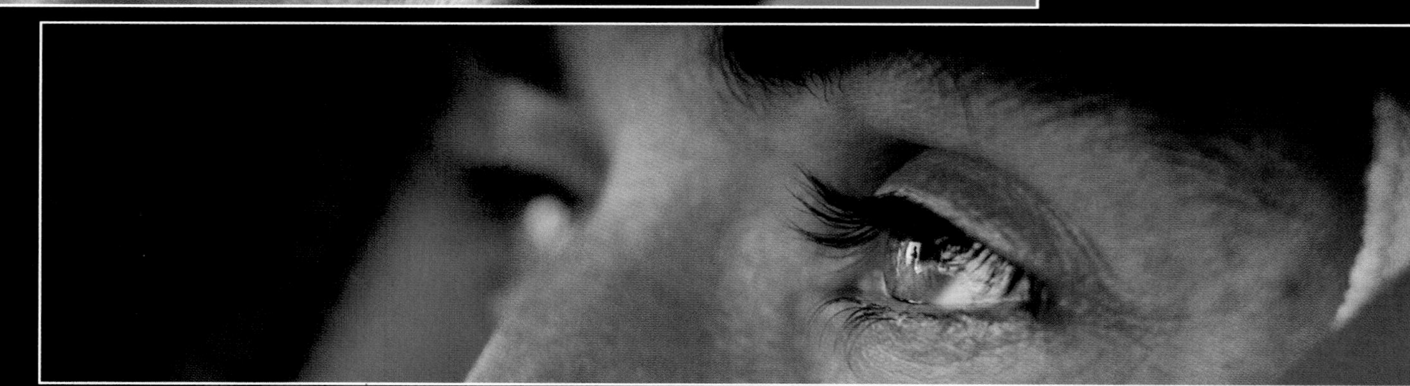
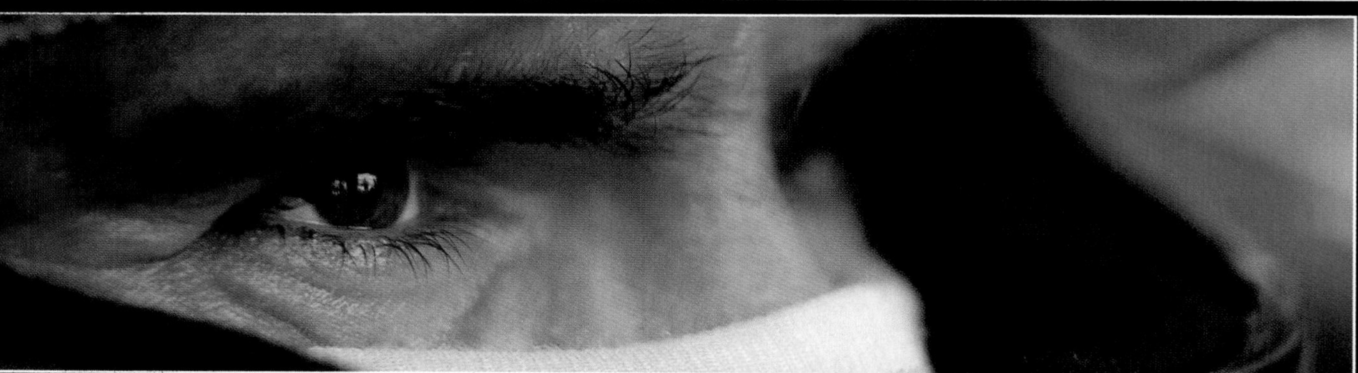
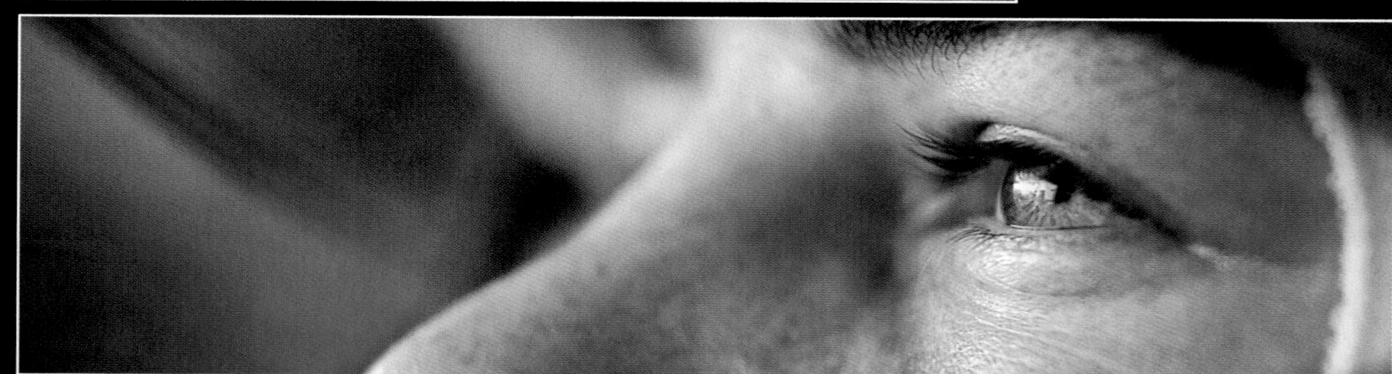

The eyes have it

The drivers all have such individual features that they serve as signatures. Can you spot them?

(in order: Mika Salo, Ukyo Katayama, Jean Alesi, Damon Hill, Jacques Villeneuve and Jos Verstappen)

The Bold and the Beautiful

There is not enough room in «The Formula One Yearbook» to describe Ralf Schumacher's dozens of off-track excursions this season, either in practice or the race. All of them have brought a smile to the lips of Giancarlo Fisichella, whom the girls tell us is the cutest driver in the paddock.

BiC
ALCATEL
POTENZA
BRIDGESTONE
BBS
CANAL+
PlayStation
HONDA
LVS
15

ATMOSPHERE

he perfect career change

ince he quit driving at the end of 993, Alain Prost seemed lost. After uying the Ligier team, "The rofessor" found a suitable outlet for is talents.

Ie did not have long to wait for the esults to come in this season. Alain rost is going for the record of five orld championships. He will not be t the wheel for the fifth one, but it ill probably be his toughest hallenge.

POWER BY
YAMAHA

Better late than never: The McLaren-Mercedes made significant progress this season. But David Coulthard's two wins were not enough to slake the silver team's thirst for victory.

Mobil 1

Spotlight

Destined to provide a better understanding of this sport, these «spotlights» give five of the world's most eminent Formula 1 journalists, carte-blanche to address their chosen topic and unveil some of the secrets of the sport of Grand Prix.

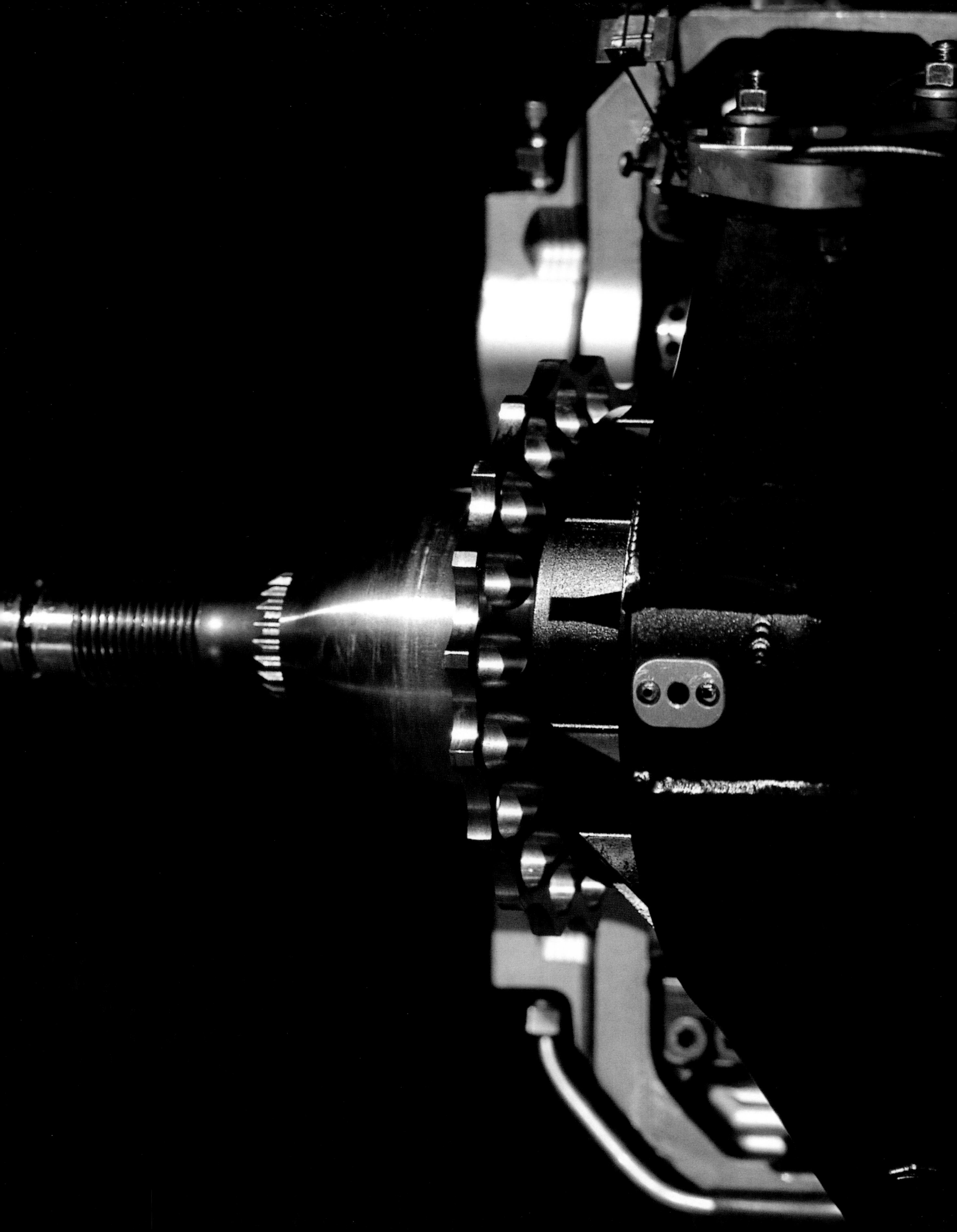

1997 : a British point of view

How to mess up an F1 season in 17 easy lessons...

by Nigel Roebuck
«Autosport»

«*Do I feel like favourite for the world championship?*» said iacques villeneuve, in response to a question at the launch of the Willians-Renault FWI9 in January. *«Well, it'd be great to feel like that, but it would be dangerous, too, because you never know what's going to happen.*

«My main opposition? Well, my team mate (Heinz-Harald Frentzen), *definitely, because he's got the same equipment. Apart from him, you have to mention Michael* (Schumacher) - *if Ferrari manage to make it work.*

«You have to consider, too, that Willians had the best car in 1996, so it will be more difficult to improve our car significantly than for the teams that had a worse car last year.»

Cautious, we thought at the time. Very cautious. In 1996, after all, Williams had won a dozen of the 16 grands prix, with Damon Hill taking eight en route to the world championship.

As the year had progressed, Villeneuve got more and more on terms with Hill, and now, for 1997, he was team leader, with Damon unaccountably replaced bv Frentzen. Given that FW19 was not a wholly new car, but rather a refinement of the one dominant in 1996, in only his second season Jacques was looking at perhaps the best chance of the world championship he would ever have.

Not all was good, however. First, Adrian Newey was gone, and although Patrick Head, the engineering chief at Williams, of course remained, the significance of Newey's departure could not be underestimated, least of all by Head: *«Adrian's leaving means change, and it would be foolish to suggest that it has had no ripple effect. I'd give him a very considerable amount of credit for our success over the last few years. For some time now, he has been responsible for the general layout of the car, with particular emphasis on aerodynamics. It'll be interesting to see how we get on without him, but the effects of his departure probably won't be as apparent this year as next.»*

That much was sure. By the time he precipitately left, in mid-November of 1996, Newey had done most of the design work for the new FW19, for one thing; for another, he was leaving williams for McLaren. *«Losing someone as good as Adrian is only half the story,»* Frank Williams said. *«The other half is that in future he will be working against you... »*

Working against Williams, too, would be Hill, although not in any significant sense, for by the time he bad been informed that his services would not be required for 1997, it was too late for him to find any sort of vaguely comparable drive. Eventually he signed for Arrows, where the prospects were not spectacular, but at least the pay cheques were cheering.

The Williams decision to replace Hill with Frentzen seemed eccentric, to say the least, and stemmed from the proprietors fears that Ferrari would ultimately provide Schumacher with a truly competitive car. *«If you really want to know why we're replacing Hill,»* another team member tersely said at the time, *«It's because he can't bloody pass people.»*

That seemed a touch harsh, for overtaking in the contemporary era is near impossible at the best of times, but it was indisputable that getting through backmarkers quickly – a Schumacher speciality – was not Hill's strongest suit. Williams suspected that, in Frentzen, he would have not only an ultra-quick driver, but also a harder racer than Hill.

There is, however, rather more to being a successful driver than that. Gerhard Berger was astonished by Williams's decision: *«First, Frentzen is not exactly proven. Second, while Damon way not be the most naturally-talented driver, he knows how to win races - and that's something you can't teach. You have it, or you don't.»*

Williams had something else going with Hill, too. There is probably no better test driver than Damon, and those skills would be missed. Broadly, his tastes in set-up followed conventional Formula 1 practice, whereas Villeneuve, schooled in Indycar racing, had more radical ideas, which sometimes worked, sometimes didn't.

Hill, in other words, provided a baseline, which in his absence would be less clearly drawn. At the start of the season, though, Williams-Renault gave every sign of continuing where they had left off in 1996.

In Melbourne qualifying, Villeneuve was stupefying, taking pole position by a scarcely believable 1.8 seconds, and none was more demoralised than his new team mate Frentzen, who scrabbled on to the front row only in the dying seconds of the session.

If Villeneuve was thus an overwhelming favourite that day in Australia, his race was over in seconds.

After an indifferent start, he was bundled off the road by Eddle Irvine, and although Heinz-Harald Frentzen led for a while, he fell back on the pit stops, and was running second when a front brake disc exploded towards the end.

Williams therefore returned from the Antipodes without a point, but in Brazil and Argentina, Villeneuve restored normality, winning both races, albeit not by accustomed Williams margins. A worry, though, was that Frentzen was nowhere near his team mate, in Brazil qualifying eighth, finishing ninth. It did not go unnoticed that Hill, a dominant winner for Williams the year before, ran as high as fourth in his Arrows.

Frentzen came on song at Imola, however, winning his first grand prix, after Villeneuve had retired, and when he also took pole position at Monaco, it seemed that he bad come through his crisis period. Shortly before the start of the race, though, there was rain, and Williams unfathomably opted to start both cars on dry tyres.

The reasoning was that this was merely a shower, which would swiftly pass, but even had they been right, surely it was obvious that Schumacher, on intermediates and putting his wet weather genius to work, would by then be out of reach. That much, too, should have dawned on the drivers: Schumacher's decision to go with intermediates was taken by Schumacher.

Jacques put things straight again in Barcelona, starting from pole position, and dominating after a supremely intelligent drive. An abrasive track surface and hot weather made for chaotic blistering problems for the Goodyear runners, but Villeneuve, neat and disciplined, took care of his tyres, and that was the difference.

NIGEL ROEBUCK, 50 years old, decided to quit his industrial job and enter journalism at the age of 24. In 1971, he starts writing for the American magazine «Car & Drivers», before joining the British weekly motorracing magazine «Autosport» in 1976. He is covering Formula One since 1977, while working for the «Sunday Times», for «Auto week» and the Japanese magazine «Racing On».

(Left hand page)
Frank Williams listens to Heinz-Harald Frentzen during practice. The rapport between the team boss and his two drivers was not always cordial.
◁

△
«Wait and see Frank, we will crush them.» Patrick Head seems to lose his British stiff upper lip when it comes to the battle with Ferrari.

Montreal, Villeneuve's home race, may have marked some kind of turning-point in his season, however. Earlier he had been highly critical of major technical regulation changes, to be introduced by the FIA in 1998, and as a consequence was summoned to Paris for a dressing-down – four days before the Canadian Grand Prix. The significance of the timing was lost on neither Jacques nor anyone else familiar with the workings of contemporary Formula 1.
The loan of a private jet for the trip from Canada to France and back meant that the travel, at least, was painless, but Villeneuve's prerace routine was necessarily disturbed, and it set the tone for his weekend. Being beaten to pole position by Schumacher was an annoyance, nothing more, but what happened in the race – Jacques spun out of contention on the second lap – affected him profoundly. As he strode away from the car, his body language was eloquent: he couldn't believe what he had done.

«Villeneuve's managers have been busily engaged in trying to set up a new team aimed at beating Williams»

When next we saw him, at Magny-Cours, we couldn't believe what he had done, either, for now his hair was dyed blonde. It was just for fun, he said, but others saw deeper connotations. *«You know what they say about people wholve had a big shock - been made redundant or something,»* murmured one paddock sage. *«They tend to grow a beard, or shave it off if they already had one. It's some psychological thing, a need to change your appearance, to take your mind off whatfs happened to you. Maybe that's why Jacques has done this...»*
Well, maybe. Whatever his motives for going blonde, though, no one doubted that Villeneuve had been profoundly affected by his novice's mistake, not least perhaps because Schumacher had won, returning to the lead of the championship once more.
He won in France, too, leading all the way. Here, anticipating rain, Villeneuve started on compromise settings, which hampered him seriously, for the rain began only very late in the race; he finished fourth, two places behind Frentzen.
Luck was with Jacques at Silverstone, though. Starting from pole position, he led, then lost time with a loose front wheel, but still came through to win, after both Schumacher and Mika Hakkinen had retired from the lead. Frentzen stalled on the grid, had to start from the back, and crashed on the opening lap...
Heinz also went out on the first lap at Hockenheim, after clashing with Irvine, and his team mate spun off later, while engaged in a battle with ... Jarno Trulli.
Neither had been quick in qualifying; all told, this was the most uncompetitive race for Williams in a decade.
It had nothing to do with shortage of power on this flat-out circuit, as Gerhard Berger proved, by dominating in his Renault-powered Benetton.
Simply, neither Villeneuve nor Frentzen could find a set-up that worked.
During qualifying, Frentzen had suggested that the team was not allowing him to use the setup of his choice. Patrick Head jumped on that: *«The whole point is that Heinz is using his own set-up - and that's probably part of the problem. There is no animosity here, between the team and the drivers: it's simply a question of arriving at the best settings, And I happen to think they should be somewhat different from what the drivers consider to be the best...»*
Again, thoughts turned back to Hill, formerly the Williams baseline - and a man who had easily won the German Grand Prix the previous year. By now, members of the team were freely conceding (off the record, of course) that his removal had been a mistake, a view further amplified by events in Hungary, where Villeneuve won - but only after passing Damon's stricken Arrows on the very last lap.
At Spa it rained, which meant that Schumacher won as he liked, his task eased by the fact that - as at Monte Carlo - he started on the right tyrese intermediates, while his major rivals did not. Villeneuve, majestic in qualifying, would have walked the race, had the rain held off, but it did not.
At Monza, a circuit which effectively precludes overtaking, Frentzen and Villeneuve were in the hunt, but not in contention for the win, finishing third and fifth, respectively.
As the end of the season approached, therefore, everything appeared to have gone awry at Williams.
After starting from pole position at each of the first four races, for example, Villeneuve had added only three more in the next nine, and that was a major departure from recent tradition, for qualifying fastest had long been regarded as the Williams norm.
You can cite any number of factors in the team's relative tall from grace in 1997; you can point to the loss of Newey, to the continuing and unwelcome distraction of the Italian legal proceedings against team members, following Ayrton Sennals fatal accident in 1994, to the fact that Villeneuve's managers have been busily engaged in trying to set up a new team aimed at beating Williams, to all manner of things.
In the end, though, what it came down to was this: Villeneuve and Frentzen did not succeed in getting the best out of the best cars in the business. Many times in the past, Hill was initially dissatisfied with the handling balance, then worked methodically with his engineers through the weekend, and went to the grid with a set-up that worked. Sometimes, as at Melbourne, as at Spa, Villeneuve had what he considered a perfect car, but that was a comparative rarity in 1997.
And there's something else, too. No Formula I car is perfect every time out, and the secret of winning championships is to score consistently, even on days when you cannot win. Villeneuve and Frentzen squandered too many points this year, while Schumacher wasted not one. However the World Championship finished, Michael was the man who deserved it.

▷
Frank Williams with Renault Sport Director General, Christian Contzen. The two men enjoyed a social and business relationship since 1989. It came to an end this year with a sixth title for the French constructor.

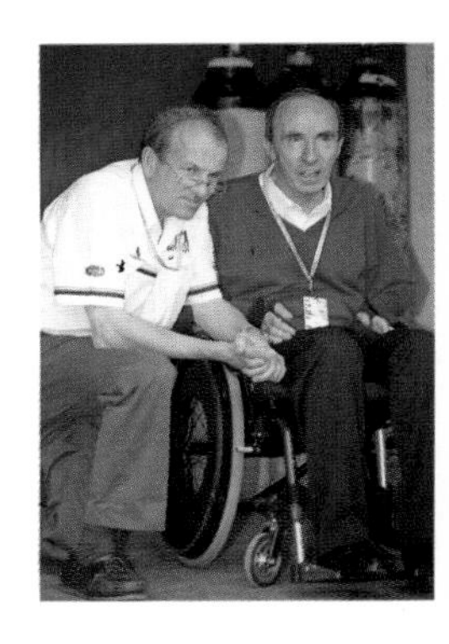

1997 : punto di vista Italiano

Ferrari has finished mutating. The butterfly takes wing

by Christiano Chiavegato
«La Stampa»

For Ferrari, 1998 is above all the year it returns to its roots. The era of the English-based technical centre is over. Gone is the difficult relationship with John Barnard and the era of long faxes and interminable telephone conversations with FD&D at Shalford is now a thing of the past. Gone too are the misunderstandings and the problems that come from waiting too long for a design or from manufacturing a part hundreds of miles from the factory. No one can deny the English designer's brilliance, his good qualities and his clever inventions, like the semi-automatic gearbox which, in 1989, brought Formula 1 a very important technical evolution. However, the situation had become untenable from a practical point of view.
Therefore Jean Todt, as part of the task he was entrusted with by president Luca di Montezemolo found himself faced with the job of bringing back to Maranello all the design work and some elements of the manufacturing process. This mission had already started the previous year when Barnard had been released from his duties. Ross Brawn came on board as technical director, quickly followed by Rory Byrne, who became the Scuderia's chief designer. Yet again it was a case of taking people from the tightly knit Formula 1 market, but these days there can be no national frontiers for this sport which demands the presence of international experts, capable of doing the very best job possible. The important thing for Ferrari is to have restored its level of competence, which had been lacking for some years and to have created the chance to do things off their own bat once again. The plan is now one hundred percent in place thanks to the construction of a new and very advanced wind tunnel, right next to the factory. It is the work of famous Italian architect, Renzo Piano, who created among other projects, the original and much admired Kansai airport in Osaka. *«1997 served to finalise the organisational structure of the race team,»* says Sporting Director Jean Todt. *«In the course of the new season, we will need at the most, some minor adjustments to consolidate it and prepare as best we can to embark on a new period in Ferrari's history, when we must no longer be outsiders, but outright contenders for victory. It is also for this reason that it was preferable to ensure continuity in a team which can count on a driver of Michael Schumacher's ability and that is why we kept Eddie Irvine, so that there would be no new element to cause turbulence and which would have required another period of adaptation. It is clear that we must now aim straight for the world championship, with no half measures. This is our stated objective.*
While last year we were fighting for the title right up to the last race and this meant we had to put in an extra effort to continue the development of the F 310 B, we did not let up in our work on the 1998 car. It is a completely new concept and not just because of the radical changes to the technical regulations. A model of the car was already in the wind tunnel in April and a group of engineers, totally divorced from our current car, continued to study and design the car, which has absolutely nothing in common with the previous model. We want to start with a vehicle which is both reliable and competitive.»
The French boss explained that Ferrari now has a very straightforward structure, divided into three sections.
As previously mentioned, Ross Brawn fills the role of technical director, charged with coordination and organisation, both at the track and in the factory. Rory Byrne is in charge of the design of the car, while Paulo Martinelli oversees the design and development of the engines.
The test team still operates under the direction of Ing. Mazzola, while Ing. Ascanelli is in charge of operations for the race team. *«Our intention is to have a flexible team,»* explains Todt. *«It must react quickly, while at the same time moving development forward in the areas of electronics, mechanics and aerodynamics. We do not intend following the competition, but we will endeavour to lead the way in terms of development. This is not an easy task, given the quality of the opposition, ever more numerous and well armed, but it is the only way forward to be in the forefront of the sport and avoid nasty surprises. All our work must make the best possible use of all our resources, also taking into account the capacity of our external suppliers, with whom we intend to collaborate very closely. In this area, we also intend making the fullest use of other structures which are fully available to us, such as the circuits at Fiorano and Mugello, which are equipped with everything needed to carry out in depth testing in every area.»*
Over the winter season, every area at Ferrari works flat out, both on the track and in the factory. One area of particular effort, at an almost fanatical level, is the development of the 047 engine, which shares practically no common parts with its predecessor. Based on the new technical regulations, which call for a narrower car, Martinelli's men are having to rethink their philosophy when it comes to the construction of the Maranello V10. With this in mind, work began as far back as last summer and a dozen or so prototype engines were built and extensively run on the test bench in a continuously evolving process. The biggest novelty in this area is a supercomputer, which president Montezemolo had already wanted to acquire three years ago. Throughout the development period, this "brain" has been studying data on various materials, on production methods and on every possible element that can be studied. The final result has meant that an entirely new engine has seen the light of day, which is totally integrated as a unit along with the chassis and the car's aerodynamic configuration.

> *«We firmly believe this could be the start of a new era which will bring great satisfaction to Ferrari and to its innumerable tifosi»*

The main aim has been to get the weight of the engine lower down as well as gaining ten percent in terms of its height off the ground. This process has been helped by the use of a new generation of clutch, with a reduced diameter, which has allowed the crankshaft to be lowered in the block.
The other challenge confronted by Ferrari has been to increase engine rotation speed to a level which until recently would have been considered impossible, by working with higher water temperatures, thanks to a better thermal exchange.
This means that the surface area of the radiators can be reduced, bringing with it an obvious aerodynamic benefit. With smaller radiators, the car penetrates the air more effectively and has less effect on maximum speed, which was one of the major problems suffered by the F 310 B during the 1997 season.
Ferrari has set itself the target of having an engine which is more compact, lighter, capable

CHRISTIANO CHIAVEGATO, *56 years old, was introduced very young to journalism. He started at «La Stampa» in 1959, while still attending various sporting events for «La Gazzetta dello Sport» for fifteen years. He has covered about ten Olympic Games, summer and winter, before concentrating on motorsports at the end of the sixties. Since 1976, he has not missed a single GP and has written many books on Ferrari, and a biography of Niki Lauda.*

of superior performance levels, is easy to drive and reliable. Obviously, along with the new engine, a new gearbox is being studied and virtually all the mechanical components will also be new.
Another area to which Maranello has turned its attention is that of the brakes. With the new rules outlawing the use of highly specialised material for the pads and the thickness of

the discs having been reduced, this has involved a great deal of research and testing, carried out at first on the old car and then on the new model.
While it might be true that, unlike other teams, Ferrari did little testing with a laboratory car last season, to fine tune various aspects of the current configuration, it ha to be said that the Maranello engineers made much use of computer simulation, so as to be ready for the moment when the 1998 challenger had to be produced.
It is clear that the area of electronics has not been overlooked, which despite being limited in a none too clear fashion in the regulations, has assumed a fundamental role in the development of cars for the next century. Ferrari's own specialists have worked closely with Magneti-Marelli, who have unparalleled experience in this field, working with several major manufacturers, including Mercedes for whom they have worked in the American CART series. Together with Ferrari, they have done everything to develop systems which will be vital in order to match the very top teams. From programmable hydraulic differentials to fly-by-wire throttle, to various control systems and data acquisition, everything has been studied in depth to ensure there are no surprises lurking around the corner and also to explore new possibilities.
Finally we come to the aerodynamics. The group put at Rory Byrne's disposal is made up of expert engineers as well as promising new talent and it has tried to follow as well as possible, the results of research carried out by the South African designer. Only when it takes to the track will it be known if work in the wind tunnel has produced a car which is capable of allowing the Maranello team to perform at the level of the targets it has set itself for this season. In theory, everything seems to be in place, but the ultimate test can only come on the tracks, face to face with the opposition, in what is proving to be a very close contest. Only one thing is certain: Ferrari has left nothing to chance in its efforts to give Schumacher and Irvine a first class car, capable of beating the opposition fair and square on all and any of the circuits that host rounds of the world championship. Todt and all his men know very well that everything hinges on having a good start to the season. *«This time, let us hope we will not be forced to play second fiddle,»* repeats Jean Todt. *«This time we must assume the role of the team to beat. We know that it will not be easy and that we will have to continue working flat out, with all our strength. The history of Formula 1 shows that a few teams are capable of putting together a winning streak in terms of championships.*
We firmly believe this could be the start of a new era which will bring great satisfaction to Ferrari and to its innumerable tifosi from all around the world, who follow us with unrivalled passion.»

△
Michael Schumacher, out of the blue in his red Ferrari. Hiring the German was the key to the Prancing Horse's return to form.

Ferrari technical director Ross Brawn seems to be enjoying his new role with the Italian team. He has once again teamed up with Rory Byrne and Michael Schumacher. The trio which won the world championship in 1994 and 1995 was back together again.
▽

1997 vu du Canada

Candid Canada...

by Philippe Cantin
«La Presse»

It was one of those balmy June days, when the sun is trying its best and the breeze blows with you. On the Ile Notre-Dame, five minutes drive from downtown Montreal, tens of thousands of spectators were heading for the Gilles Villeneuve Circuit, where the start of the Canadian Grand Prix was but a few hours away.
The atmosphere was electric. Waving huge Quebec flags, the blue and white standard with the four fleur de lys, the Jacques Villeneuve supporters were filled with eager anticipation. This time, their golden boy would not be denied by Damon Hill, as happened in 1996. He would walk away with the race, build on his lead in the world drivers' championship and, above all, he would summarily silence his tormentors at the FIA, who were currently held in very low esteem.
Would you believe it: less than one week before the race, the sport's governing body had the barefaced cheek to summon Villeneuve to its Paris headquarters, to remind him to mind his "Ps and Qs." In the press, on radio and television, the pundits vigorously denounced this meeting. Why force Villeneuve, already preparing himself in Montreal, to make two Atlantic crossings, just days before the grand prix? How could one explain, that the sport of motor racing, a torch bearer for high- technology, could not have organised some form of video conference to interrogate the 26 year old racer?
The trouble had begun a few weeks earlier. Unhappy with the proposed regulation changes for Formula 1, due to come into effect in 1998, Villeneuve had not held back when it came to expressing his displeasure. *«Formula 1 must not be made into a circus,»* he raged. *«If it goes on like this, then a driver who is prepared to take risks, will not gain any advantage. Formula 1 is more safety conscious than ever; too much so. I am well used to the speeds in F1 and I want to go even faster. If any other driver but Senna had died in 1994, there would not have been such a reaction today. I want to stay in F1, on condition that it stays the same and I can have fun.»*
Villeneuve's comments had been reported the world over and the FIA, upset by the tone of his criticism, summoned him to explain his language. In Quebec, this call from the governing body was incomprehensible. The North American mentality could not accept the fact that a man be asked to justify the simple act of expressing an opinion, even if he had used harsh words. It was seen as a deplorable loss of basic freedom. Legal experts questioned on the affair, said there was not even anything libellous in what Villeneuve had said. In short, the whole affair was making waves.
In the end, Villeneuve was given a ticking off and told to choose his words more carefully in future. If anything, the incident had actually increased his popularity in the country of his birth.
It was in this highly charged atmosphere that Villeneuve tackled the Canadian Grand Prix. But by the second lap, he was already out of the race. He lost control of his Williams-Renault at the chicane before the pits and buried the nose of his car into an advertising hoarding which encouraged tourists to visit Quebec! It was a nightmare for Villeneuve and a cold shower for the fans. At the wheel of one of the most reliable cars in the field, he was knocked out, before the crowd even had a chance to vocalise their support. *«It was such a stupid mistake,»* said Villeneuve. *«I was not even pushing hard. I was running behind Michael Schumacher and I was trying to look after my tyres, when the car just got away from me. The track was dusty and I was being cautious. It is the sort of mistake that can be forgiven in Formula 3 or Atlantic, but not in Formula 1.»*

The 15th June was not a good day for French speaking drivers. Even unluckier was Olivier Panis, who suffered a serious accident which brought an end to what had looked like a very promising season.
Despite these disappointments for the local crowd, the grand prix was once again a major commercial success. Over 100,000 spectators turned up on race day and they were all in party mood. Events organised around the grand prix also drew big crowds, notably the rock concerts in Montreal and the jazz and comedy festivals, as well as the traditional firework display, while even cinemas reported increased business. So, if everything went so well, why are Canadian race fans worried about losing their event to some far corner of the Pacific Rim? The answer is the new anti- tobacco laws, which are the subject of much heated debate.
Despite the size of the problem, the basic premise is simple. In April 1997, out of worthy concern for the nation's health, the federal government in Ottawa, passed an anti-tobacco legislation.
One of its clauses limits the rights of cigarette manufacturers from publicising their product through major cultural and sporting activities, which would prompt their removal of support from these events. The law also forbids racing cars from carrying cigarette branding as from 1st October 1998. However there is a get-out clause and the Canadian Prime Minister has promised to soften the blow. This should allow Marlboro, Rothmans and all the others to carrying on putting their names on Formula 1 cars.
Norman Legault, the Canadian race promoter and a good friend of Bernie Ecclestone, was in the front line of this struggle. He told anyone who cared to listen that in the case of Australia, which has strict anti-tobacco laws, Formula 1 is still immensely popular. *«The Health Minister can grant exemptions in line with precise criteria,»* he explained. *«It is not easy, believe me.*

PHILIPPE CANTIN,
38 years old, studied law before turning to journalism in 1984. He has covered the Olympic Games, the Tour de France and many other top-level sporting events in the United States and Europe. He has also been a political correspondent. In addition to Formula 1, he is particularly interested in economics and sport in general.

The organisers must prove that the event is part of an international championship, that foreign competitors are involved, that it will be broadcast worldwide and that the event will attract foreign spectators. They must also prove that, unless an exemption is granted, then the event will not take place. The law has teeth, but the government is being flexible to protect investments.»
Losing the grand prix to Asia would be a hard blow for the Montreal economy, which has been in serious trouble for the past few years. The race attracted thousands of fans from the USA, Europe and Japan. These people spent millions of dollars in hotels, restaurants and shops. They brought in new money. Other sports, although equally popular, do not have the same impact as the vast majority of spectators were local.
Mr. Legault holds the rights to eventually stage a grand prix in China. *«The circuit at Zhuhai is already built at the centre of a triangle made up of Hong Kong, Macau and Canton. All facilities are in place: pits, race control tower and so on. All that is needed is the spectator grandstands.»*

«I've tried something similar. Dior make it in a champagne colour. Nice, isn't it?»

If the Canadian Grand Prix was to leave Montreal, this is the part of the world where it could be replaced. But barring mishaps, this threat should not affect the 1998 race, for which Mr. Legault is planning to improve facilities at the Gilles Villeneuve circuit, most notably in the press office and paddock areas.
Once the Canadian Grand Prix was over, Montreal bade farewell to the big circus for another year. However, Jacques Villeneuve's exploits on the race tracks of Europe continued to dominate the newspapers to the end of the season.
Two weeks after his Montreal mishap, Villeneuve was in Magny-Cours for the French Grand Prix. On the Thursday before the race, he was once again voicing his opinion to a group of English, French and Canadian journalists, on the subject of what he considered to be an over-the-top reaction to Olivier Panis' accident. *«As a racing driver you know the risks,»* he began. *«It is always a shame when a serious accident happens and it is a set-back to a career, especially in the case of Olivier, who was going so well. But you can break both legs skiing for example and then no one gives a damn, or says that skiing is dangerous and should be banned. But, after the accident in Montreal, I read everywhere that we had forgotten how dangerous Formula 1 was and that safety measures had to be increased. Two broken legs is not that serious. It is serious for Olivier of course, but this sort of accident happens to motorcyclists on the road every day.»*
«Compared with 15 years ago, we cannot complain. At the time, anyone having that sort of crash would have lost both legs and every year, drivers got very badly hurt. At least one died every year. We must therefore calm down a bit and stop complaining. If there was no risk in the sport, then people would lose interest in it. When you are keen on racing as a kid, it's because you want to do crazy things.»
Panis' accident caused the Canadian Grand Prix to be stopped, a decision which Villeneuve did not approve of. *«If I died in a grand prix, I would not want the race to be stopped. I know the risks and I enjoy taking them.»*
The candour of his acidic comments, in keeping with his earlier declarations, meant Villeneuve was once again in the media spotlight. He also attracted attention for another reason, entirely unconnected with racing. He arrived in the Magny-Cours paddock with his hair dyed platinum blonde. Why? *«Because it was fun and I felt like it,»* he explained, adding that Frank Williams had found it very funny. In the press office, opinion was divided on the subject of Jacques's fashion statement.
Martine, a French colleague, supported the tonsorial change. *«I've tried something similar. Dior make it in a champagne colour. Nice, isn't it?»*
While Frank Williams might have smiled at his Marilyn Monroe-esque hairdo, he was less impressed with his driver's comments on the way the team set up the cars.
The problem had already arisen the previous year. It is obvious that Villeneuve likes to set up his car in a way that does not always sit well with the Williams engineers, who try and impose their views on him. The driver considered that these pressures were pushing him and his race engineer in a direction which did not suit him.
He felt that, as a consequence of this, he was losing valuable preparation time for the races. Williams technical director, Patrick Head, rejected this interpretation of the facts. As he was leaving Magny-Cours after the French Grand Prix, he said: *«We have never prevented Jacques from setting up the car to his tastes.»*
The atmosphere in the team was tense. Arriving in England ten days later, the rumours were flying: Villeneuve would leave Williams to join his manager Craig Pollock, who was planning to buy an existing team or create a new one. This time, Villeneuve did not say a word. Faced with the press, he settled for the usual cliches and platitudes, avoiding the controversial subject all together.
This seemed to do the trick as, making the most of Mika Hakkinen's misfortune in the final part of the race, he won the event for the second year in a row.
If he came away with the main prize and if this win is talked about more than most, then it is because it illustrates one of Villeneuve's main qualities - tenacity. On lap 23, a win looked out of the question. While Michael Schumacher was sailing on serenely in the lead, Villeneuve was stuck in the pits for a massive 33 seconds, while his mechanics struggled to remove the left front wheel from his car, which had stuck because of a faulty wheel nut. Back on the track, he never gave up and the reward finally came his way.
At the end of the season, despite all the rumours to the contrary, Villeneuve confirmed he would be staying with Williams in 1998. His French-Canadian fans who appreciate his down to earth manner, hope he will finally win the Canadian Grand Prix. Many of them are also getting excited about another Quebecois driver. Patrick Carpentier had his first taste of racing in the CART series in 1997 and there is a fervent hope he might join Villeneuve in F1 in the not too distant future.

Jacques Villeneuve's girlfriend, Sandrine Gros d'Aillon did not attend many grands prix this season. But when she did turn up at the track, she gave her champion all her support.
▽

1997 aus deutscher Sicht

Mercedes has its eye on Michael Schumacher, naturally

by Anno Hecker
«Frankfurter Allgemeine Zeitung»

Hot and sweaty but happy, Norbert Haug was waving about an internal memo which read, *«Do what you can to come to Frankfurt.»* It was not a threat from the Mercedes team, but rather an invitation to all the sports bosses in the company to make the most of their second success of the 1997 season at the international motor show. David Coulthard had just taken his McLaren-Mercedes to victory in the Italian Grand Prix at the famous track set in the royal park of Monza. He owed the victory to a perfectly timed pit-stop. It was easy therefore for Daimler-Benz main board director in charge of passenger cars, Jurgen Hubbert, to draw a strategic significance from this perfectly executed win. *«This victory has come at the best possible moment.»*

Meanwhile, Mario Ilien is sipping quietly on a glass of champagne outside the Mercedes motorhome. The Swiss engine builder is not making much of a fuss, even though his engine is the main talking point in the paddock. *«Yes, our fuel consumption certainly played an important part».*

The man seems as modest as his engine is efficient. The ten cylinder, 775 horsepower engine with Mercedes on the cam covers allows the team to adopt a flexible race strategy, thanks to its excellent fuel economy.

At its one and only pit-stop, McLaren did not have to put in as much fuel as the opposition, making life quicker for the team's 21 strong pit crew.

When France's Jean Alesi, who had been leading the race, spent one second longer in the Benetton pit, Coulthard charged off towards the chequered flag. A few hours later, Hubbert spoke of a victory for the entire team and while it is not in the Mercedes tradition to boast, the men from Stuttgart were delighted with the inscription on Coulthard's T-shirt, which read: *«Thank you for the power.»*

Mercedes had to wait almost five years to make its point. Coulthard's win in the Australian Grand Prix had been considered a lucky one, helped by the high number of retirements. *«But Monza, was a victory we made for ourselves,»* said Hubbert. It was made thanks to the F110F engine, which Ilien had introduced after the first third of the season.

The policy, elaborated with McLaren, of concentrating first and foremost on the machinery and the drivers second, was paying off at last. It was a policy shared with Williams, who have always tried to have the best car to secure the services of the best driver. Mercedes wanted to prepare an offer that Michael Schumacher could not refuse. *«Everyone knows what Michael Schumacher winning the world championship with Mercedes would mean. Nothing could beat that. It would be the tops.»*

After performances from Coulthard and Hakkinen that Mercedes strangely considered to be mediocre, they were on the lookout for fresh talent. Damon Hill seemed to be in with a chance, thanks to his friendship with the team's new aerodynamicist, Adrian Newey. The men from Stuttgart were convinced of the English driver's ability to develop a racing car, but the manner in which Hill approached the engine manufacturer upset the management. *«He tried every possible way and left no stone unturned. But he did not make direct contact with the motor sport department,»* was Mercedes' version of events. Hill might have been forgiven this mistake, if it had not been for his negative comments about the team's existing drivers, Coulthard and Hakkinen. *«This is not the sort of polite English behaviour we had come to expect from him,»* said one Mercedes insider. Neither was it a very bright comment, as Mercedes had been involved in choosing these two so-called bad drivers.

Apart from that, it would have been difficult for Mercedes and McLaren to sack one of its existing drivers to make room for Hill. Ron Dennis always showed fatherly concern for David Coulthard, while Mika Hakkinen was held in high esteem by Mercedes motor sport boss, Norbert Haug.

The reaction to their re-signing at Spa-Francorchamps during the Belgian Grand Prix was telling. They were both relieved rather than happy; pleased to accept a deal after the reigning world champion had felt insulted by the offer Dennis had made him. This was rumoured to be a fee of two million dollars per year and a performance related bonus of one million dollars per race win. Hill did not consider this to be a serious offer and took one final phone call in the paddock when he was informed he had "missed the boat."

According to Hubbert, the only element missing from the master plan was Michael Schumacher. Until now, Mercedes had justified the absence of their favourite son by saying their car was too slow. *«Michael is a good friend of ours. But until we can prove to him that our car is competitive, we are not a viable choice for him.»* This seemed plausible if not entirely true.

When Schumacher had wanted to leave Benetton two years ago, McLaren-Mercedes had a good chance of getting him on board. At the time, Ferrari was no better than the Anglo-German team and the Italians had not put more money on the table. But Ferrari had promised Schumacher a say in which engineers were brought in and how the team would be run. Ron Dennis however, would not countenance a driver having any influence on his organisation. Insiders reckon that, but for this sticking point, Schumacher would have been a Mercedes driver by now.

But even without Schumacher, Mercedes believe they can be in front next season. Hubbert is betting on Adrian Newey's ability, even though he has only been allowed to work for the team since 1st August 1997. After winning at Monza, Mercedes acknowledged that in the space of just five weeks, the former Williams aerodynamicist had already been a great help. *«It is amazing what Adrian has already achieved. We have made a lot of progress,»* said Hubbert. For the forthcoming season, Hubbert was

ANNO HECKER,
33 years old, worked first as a physical education instructor before turning to journalism in 1986. After working as a political correspondent for a Bonn news agency, he joined «Frankfurter Allgemeine Zeitung» in 1991 to cover motor sports. He specialised in stories combining politics and sport.

expecting a major step forward, because of the change to the technical regulations. *«This man has taken Williams to the top and kept it at that level for many years. There is no reason why he should not do the same for us.»*
And sooner rather than later no doubt. Because if Newey makes a go of it in 1998, then Mercedes would happily accept coming a close second to Schumacher in a Ferrari, with the assumption that the German driver would then be looking for a new challenge.

«If it says BMW, then it's got BMW inside»

His current contract expires at the end of 1999, but there are rumours of a get-out clause should a new opportunity arise. This could see Mercedes aligning its dream team one year before embarking on an all-German tussle with BMW, who are due to power the Williams cars starting in 2000. This is something the men at Mercedes are looking forward to, as it justifies their involvement in the highest level of motor sport. *«The competition will be even more attractive and tough from a German angle. It is good to take on the challenge of Formula 1 to try and seduce the buying public.»*
BMW actually announced their return to the sport on the day after McLaren won at Monza and Mercedes, euphoric after their win, had some kind words to say about their future rivals. *«They will not make the same mistakes as us. I hope they will have a better time,»* commented Hubbert, referring to the fact that his board had been unhappy with the three pointed star's slow start in Formula 1. *«After coming back in 1993, we tended to sit on our laurels from the past. The public expected us to succeed immediately, because we were linked to McLaren. We quickly came back down to earth. Past glories are quick to fade.»*
Hubbert was referring to the glory days of the Silver Arrows, run by Alfred Neubauer, to the days of Rudolf Caracciola, Manfred von Brauchitsch and Manuel Fangio. At the time, Mercedes came, saw and conquered. These days it takes three years of trying for an engine supplier to get its act together. *«Building an engine is just a small part of the job. You need special equipment and test beds and above all, you need a lot of experience,»* says Mario Ilien.
The quickest route to glory is through collaboration with a specialist firm which is more flexible than a major manufacturer: a collaboration like the one between Ilmor and Mercedes which owns 25 percent of the British company.
It is therefore with great care that Mercedes use the term Silver Arrows, a symbol of invincibility in motorsport in the Thirties and Fifties. The opposition knows exactly what part Mercedes plays in McLaren's overall scheme of things. *«We will develop our own Formula 1 engines and we will not buy in specialist help from outside,»* explained BMW's motor sport manager, Karl-Heinz Kalbfell, before going on to target the Stuttgart rivals even more clearly. *«If it says BMW, then it's got BMW inside. If we make it, we make all of it. We do not want to wait 50 races for our first win.»* The duel has begun. Kalbfell will now have to live up to his fighting talk and Mercedes is ready to take him on, despite their problems. *«We cannot quit as losers,»* said Hubbert at Monza. *«We cannot allow ourselves to do that.»*

△
The McLaren mechanics' black battle dress is smart enough to draw a crowd. Luckily the public are not allowed in the pit lane...

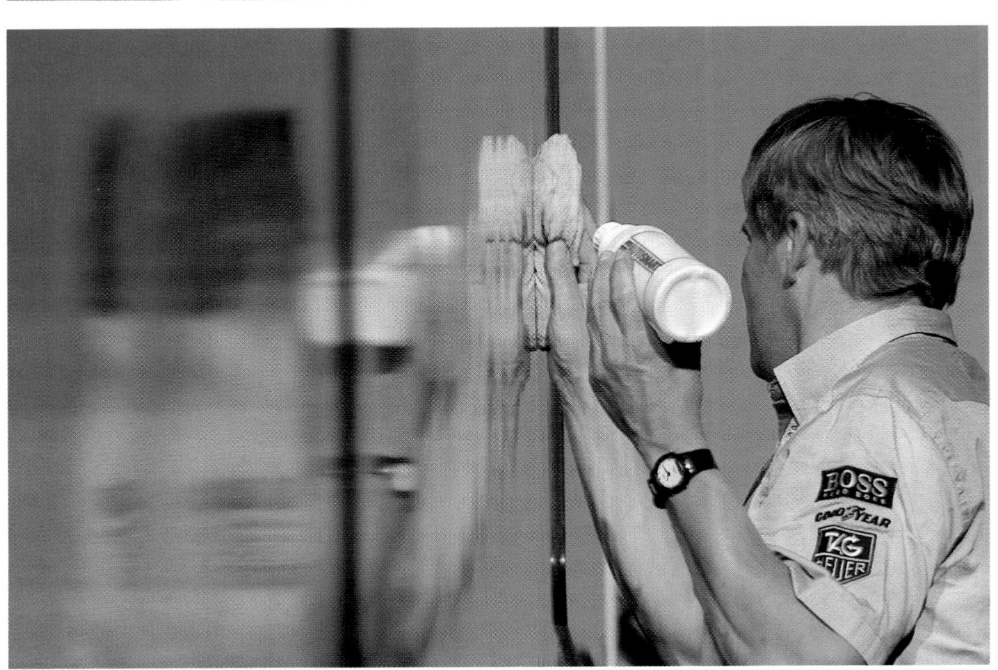

◁
At Mercedes, everything is order and beauty, luxury and calm. Or so it seems. The first job for the team, on arriving at the track, is to go at the motorhome with spit and polish...

◁
(left hand page) Mika Hakkinen retires. An all too familiar sight this season.

1997 wo hurikaeru

In Japan, interest in F1 is growing again. But rather slowly...

by Kunio Shibata
«GPX Press», Tokyo

This year, right from its first steps in Formula 1, Bridgestone has shown a performance level superior to that of its rival Goodyear and there is also talk of Honda coming back to the sport. Despite this fact, the popularity of F1 in Japan is still much lower than in European countries and the Japanese are forced to play only a secondary role in the sport, despite making an important financial and technical contribution. What has gone wrong with the Japanese system?

Japanese drivers

For several years now I have lost my appetite for writing about Formula 1. Although my stories are aimed at the Japanese market, Japanese drivers are not involved in fighting for victory. They make desperate efforts but are usually left to run at the back of the field. That was certainly the case this season.

Ukyo Katayama has been in Formula 1 since 1992. Because of his "kamikaze" driving style he was voted "Bravest driver of the 1994 season," by readers of the Italian magazine "Autosprint."

This year he switched from Tyrrell to Minardi, but he hardly ever finished a race and he has never made it to the podium throughout his career.

Ukyo was forced to announce his retirement at Suzuka. *«I still feel capable of driving and fighting in Formula 1, but I think the time has come,»* said Ukyo after the announcement. *«At the end of the '94 season, Flavio Briatore had asked me to become Michael Schumacher's team-mate. But at the time, I was still under contract to Tyrrell and my personal sponsor, Japan Tobacco, advised me to stay. I should not have obeyed and I was wrong not to have taken my chance. But now the moment has passed.»*

The other Japanese driver, Shinji Nakano, had quite a difficult debut. In qualifying he was always about one second slower than his team-mate, Olivier Panis.

In the races, despite having a very powerful Mugen engine, he seemed to spend most of his time running down with the cars using V8s, while Panis was fighting for the podium. The French driver's accident did not make his life any easier.

Olivier's replacement, Jarno Trulli, was also an F1 debutant, but as soon as he sat in the Prost, he was instantly quicker than Nakano. Shinji finally scored two points, by finishing sixth in both Canada and Hungary, which is not actually too bad for a beginner. But when compared to the performances of other new drivers like Trulli, Fisichella, Ralf Schumacher or Wurz, it has to be said, he was put completely in the shade.

Hirotoshi Honda, son of the founder of Honda Motors and president of Mugen, has supported Nakano since he was in karts. His arrival in F1 was unexpected, as he had never won in F3000 in Japan, but it had Honda's support.

However, his performances have been so disappointing this season, that Mr. Honda did not even try and foist his services on Eddie Jordan, who runs the Mugen engines in 1998. He might find a drive at Minardi, thanks to the backing of some Japanese sponsors, but it is unlikely his results will be any better than this year's.

KUNIO SHIBATA, 41 years old, he left Japan, giving up his job in journalism in 1982 to move to Paris and study Political Science. He became a freelance producer for Japanese television and having always been interested in motor racing, he began covering the grands prix for a press agency in 1987 when Satoru Nakajima arrived on the scene. He has written for the specialist Japanese magazine, Grand Prix Xpress since 1991.

Tyre wars

I am not particularly chauvinistic, but what Bridgestone did this year certainly brought a smile to my lips!

Since Pirelli pulled out of the sport, Goodyear had supplied all the teams for the best part of ten years, and a good job they did of it. But it was a monopoly and it was killing the competition. The arrival of the Japanese company was therefore well received by everyone, including Goodyear. From now on, the American firm did not have to look after the entire field and they could spend less money. Furthermore, they had unique knowledge, accumulated over 30 years in the sport and they had also managed to keep the top four teams – Williams, Ferrari, Benetton and McLaren, on their books. There was no reason for them to worry unduly about the opposition.

However, even during pre-season testing, Bridgestone had shown its impressive potential, especially in the wet: at Magny-Cours on rain tyres, Olivier Panis had lapped 4 seconds quicker than Jacques Villeneuve. Somewhat timid, but determined nevertheless, Technical Director Hamashima said: *«We have come to F1 one year earlier than planned. This will therefore be a learning year. But we hope to be considered a serious rival to Goodyear as soon as possible.»*

They proved competitive right from the start. In Brazil, for the second round of the season, Panis put the company's black and red colours on the podium and two weeks later in Argentina, they missed out on pole position by a whisker.

Of course, these performances were not solely down to Bridgestone, but it was obvious that the tyres had played a significant role. Bridgestone tyres had an advantage and still do, over the Goodyears in two areas. Firstly on a wet track, especially in very heavy rain. Secondly, even when running a softer compound, tyre performance has been more consistent, while the construction seems to cope better under strong side forces, as experienced on slow tracks. This meant that the Japanese rubber was a significant factor in Rubens Barrichello's second place in Monaco, as well as Damon Hill's second place in Budapest.

It seemed that, towards the end of the season, Bridgestone's performance dropped off slightly as none of their drivers made it to the podium after the Hungarian Grand Prix. *«I would have been happier if Bridgestone had won,»* said Hamashima after their poor performance in the Japanese GP, where their best result was Hill's twelfth place. *«However, we have had some good results this season. I had never under- estimated Goodyear's competence and I was not wrong! But I swear, I am very happy with this first season.»*

Lap times were around two seconds quicker than the previous season at every circuit. While chassis and engines have improved, the biggest difference came from the tyres. Cautious to begin with, Bridgestone practically declared war on Goodyear and the American company fought back well, developing new products. The fight between these two companies certainly spiced up the 1997 championship.

Takagi - a new hope?

In the previous edition of this book, I tipped Toranosuke Takagi as a future Japanese star. Now the deed is done and he will drive for Tyrrell in 1998. But one year later, I wonder if I was right.

For several years, Formula Nippon (Japanese F3000) has been an accepted route into F1. Of the 22 drivers who competed in F1 in 1997, eight of them did at least one year in Japan. The last of these was Ralf Schumacher who breezed into Japan and left with the title. Takagi competed against Ralf, won a few races, but was never a threat.

This year, with the departure of the German driver to F1, his natural successor should have been Takagi. But he only won one race and the title was won by the Spaniard, Pedro De la Rosa. Yet another foreigner was the Formula Nippon champion.

There are, naturally, a whole host of excuses. His chassis was not very competitive and Takagi was unable to concentrate on the races because of frequent trips to Europe and so on. But he was supposed to win as he had spent three years in Formula Nippon. If he really was the great white hope, this was not the time to be pussyfooting around in a local series.

His trips to Europe were to fulfill his role as Tyrrell test driver and to compete in the Porsche Supercup.

Why Porsche? Simply because this series used a lot of the Formula 1 circuits and it would help Takagi to learn the tracks. This was the idea of Satoru Nakajima, Japan's first Formula 1 driver and Takagi's Formula Nippon team owner. Each time he made the trip to Europe, Takagi was looked after by one of Nakajima's managers. Everything was done for him; hotel bookings, shopping, finding Japanese restau-

Despite his patent lack of results, Katayama-San is still very popular in Japan. The announcement of his retirement was the cause for national concern. His retirement, early in the race, did not help matters.

rants. He was a star of the future and had to be treated like one.
The results? He never won a Porsche race, nor did he ever make it to the podium. But Takagi was not downhearted. *«The goal was not to win, but to learn the circuits.»*
I really did not have the heart to question him further. A racing driver is a racing driver, whatever the car or the conditions. *«The Porsche is too different to a single seater and it is very heavy,»* he claimed.
But look at Mika Hakkinen at Monaco in 1992. It was his first ever race in a Porsche. He started from pole and was never headed on his way to the chequered flag.

«Either he sat alone in the motorhome or he would leave the track before the grand prix was even over»

Let's skip it and move on to what else the young Japanese driver was doing. Did he spend his time learning English so that he could communicate with the Tyrrell engineers and mechanics? Did he study the driving styles of Schumacher or Villeneuve, his future rivals? The answer is that he did practically nothing. Either he sat alone in the motorhome or he would leave the track before the grand prix was even over (*«So that I can miss the traffic,»* he said.) He has made little effort to get to grips with Formula 1, or to communicate with the people involved.
At the moment, he is proud of being quick, but that will evaporate at the start of the 1998 season.
After this cultural shock, I hope he will get used to the real world as quickly as possible. At 23 years of age, he is still young, the youngest Japanese driver to come into F1. It is the main and only point in his favour right now.

Failure of the Japanese system

It is often said that the Japanese are invisible in the world, even though they are omni-present. The same applies in F1. Honda, Bridgestone, Mild Seven, Pioneer, Showa, PIAA. There are few teams who do not have some Japanese connection, however it is sometimes difficult to remember what they are doing there.
Why? Because the Japanese prefer to work incognito and the star system is frowned on. When they embark on a new project, they first establish a system. Then they install competent people to work within it and provide them with a manual. All you have to do is read the handbook, Japan is a handbook society. Adapting to life in a system - the family, group or community, is a major virtue of Japanese life. Everyone can join in and everyone is replaceable. In F1, most Japanese workers are replaced every three years at the latest.
But Formula 1 is an egocentric environment and of course the driver has the biggest ego of all and it is only recently that the Japanese realised that their system was not conducive to producing good F1 drivers.
Japan has a motor sport history dating back 40 years - not as long as Europe but the same as Brazil, which has produced several champions. Japanese drivers have never won a grand prix, let alone a championship, even though there are driving schools and driver scholarships. But at the moment it is not working. After Takagi, there is not one talented local driver in Formula Nippon or F3. *«It is better to find a young Italian or Brazilian and naturalise them as Japanese, as has been done in soccer for the World Cup!»* say some of my colleagues. It is a sad joke. In my opinion, it is down to the Japanese mentality, which allows people to work as part of a system, but not as individuals. Take them away from their roots and they are lost. The young drivers seem to share this mentality. They are so happy to be racing in their home country that they fail to see the need to go off in search of new experiences and new horizons, as do their South American counterparts. What is more, so long as they stay in Japan, they can earn a comfortable living. Even an F3 driver can pick up 160,000 dollars per year and while they stay in Japan they can be considered as quick drivers. That way they never lose face.
Now you have a better understanding of why Takagi behaves the way he does and why I am pessimistic about his chances of success. But I am still prepared to wait for a miracle...

At Suzuka circuit, the crowd seemed as big as usual. At any rate the Nippon track is as busy as ever and the Grand Prix continues to be a sell-out.

Bridgestone: not bad for a first attempt

The Japanese company came close to winning a grand prix in its first season of Formula 1. We spoke to its two key personnel, Hiroshi Yasukawa and Hirohide Hamashima.

Present day Formula 1 is not just about drivers toughing it out on the track. It also represents a titanic struggle between major companies who are investing ever bigger budgets in the sport.
In this context, one can only take pleasure in the arrival of a new marque in the F1 arena. Variety is the spice of life, so they say and the arrival of Bridgestone this season has certainly confirmed that.
Until last year, Goodyear was the only tyre company in F1 and from that came all the usual scenarios one expects with a monopoly: the Akron engineers were not motivated to research new tyre compounds and they only brought one type of tyre to each race. Even if the teams were not always happy with this situation, they had to accept it.
Then in August 1996, the President of the Bridgestone Corporation officially announced that the company would enter Formula 1 in 1997. This was hardly a major revelation as the Arrows team had already been testing these tyres for several weeks, which had prompted Goodyear to hit back by only supplying them with tyres for the races, but not for private testing.
By diving into Formula 1, Bridgestone was taking a logical step forward as regards its path through the various motor racing disciplines. Founded in 1931, Bridgestone has over 92,000 employees around the world and has the biggest share of the world's passenger car tyre market. *«Three years ago,* said Hiroshi Yasukawa, Bridgestone, *Michelin and Goodyear each had 17 percent of the world market. Today, Bridgestone has 19%, Michelin 18% and Goodyear 15%.»*
Bridgestone had been involved in motor sport until 1973, the year the world had its energy crisis. *«We stopped all sporting activity at that point,»* continued Yasukawa, himself a former touring car driver. *«We came back in 1976, but only at national level. For five years, all we did was the Japanese Formula 2 championship.»*
This was the era when Bridgestone first got involved in Formula 1, albeit on a very limited basis. *«I was appointed head of motor sport in 1976 and my dream had always been to get involved in Formula 1,»* said Yasukawa. *«In fact, in 1976 we did supply Mr. Hoshino's private team for the Japanese Grand Prix at Mount Fuji. It rained a lot that year and for a brief moment "our" car was third, which was an exceptional performance given our lack of experience.»*
The following year, Bridgestone did the same deal but waited until 1980 to come to Europe. *«This coincided with Honda's entry into the European Formula 2 series,»* recalled Yasukawa. *«I had asked Mr. Honda if we could work together and he replied that it was possible as long as we came up to the performance level he was looking for. I therefore headed for Europe with tyres as my luggage, but the team did not try them until the third race. It was a success, as the following season, we were F2 champions with Geoff Lees.»*

Monaco Grand Prix. Rubens Barrichello's Stewart has just finished second, giving Bridgestone its best ever result up to that point.

After this initial success, more followed for Bridgestone. The company stayed in Formula 2 until 1984 and won the title the first time this series became the F3000 championship in 1985, with Christian Danner. In 1986, Bridgestone branched out into Group C, then the DTM in 1991, with Mercedes-Benz, winning the championship the following year.
In 1994, they initiated a test programme for Indy and the following year, Bridgestone won the ITC series and began to turn its attention to F1. The marque won its first Indy title in 1996 with Jimmy Vasser and did it again in '97 with Alessandro Zanardi.
It was time to move into Formula 1. *«We had carried out a market research survey into our brand name,»* explained Yasukawa. *«A specialist company asked the public if they had heard of Bridgestone. In Japan the result was 100%, but in Europe only 15% of the respondents had heard of us. We decided to remedy that situation and we looked at several possible solutions, from television advertising campaigns to sponsorship of soccer clubs. Finally we decided that Formula 1 would best suit our needs. It has to be said that, since we went Indy racing, our sales have increased in the United States.»*
However, the engineers had not waited for last year's decision to begin work. In charge of development at Bridgestone, Hirohide Hamashima explained that F1 related research had begun back in 1989. *«At the time, we only had an F3000 chassis, fitted with a Formula 1 engine lent to us by Mugen. In fact it was Honda who had asked us for F1 tyres, because they were unable to find any in Japan to carry out their own test programmes.»*
In 1988, Bridgestone bought out its old rival Firestone, the second largest American tyre manufacturer. It was a takeover that made waves. *«The first few years were difficult as we had to completely restructure everything,»* remarked Yasukawa. *«This proved very tough and it was not really the right time to think about going motor racing.»*
It was in 1993 that the directors of the company began to turn their thoughts to Formula 1. *«At the time there were only two or three people working full-time on our F1 project, although we could rely on good support from other areas of the company.»*
The first tests, carried out with Arrows in 1996, went very well and Bridgestone Corporation President, Yoichiro Kaizaki therefore decided to take the plunge. Ligier (soon to become Prost,) Arrows, Minardi and Stewart all came on board, as did the short-lived Lola team.
At the end of this first season, the results are very satisfying, as the company made it to the podium on four occasions, two of them thanks to Olivier Panis. Bridgestone even led some races for quite a few laps, in Hungary and Austria.
Given that the top teams are all under contract to Goodyear, it is not so bad. *«I think we can actually be very proud of our first season,»* analysed

Bridgestone brings almost 2000 tyres for its four contracted teams. There are two types of slick tyre and six types of wets.

Hirohide Hamashima. *«This year, our objective was simply to set up the logistics, the technical support, the motorhome and all the necessary infrastructure. That was our first aim and we easily achieved it.»*

«Tyres are responsible for 70% of a Formula 1 car's performance.»

The biggest problem confronting the Bridgestone engineers was the fact that there were many circuits they had never visited before, either in private testing or for GT races (DTM and ITC.) *«This was most noticeable in Australia and Argentina,»* recalled Hamashima. *«Sometimes it was very difficult to decide on the type of compound. We had to take everything into consideration: the outline of the track, its surface and comments from the drivers and engineers. We did a computer simulation and we hoped our results matched the opinions of the engineers from the teams we supplied. If it worked, then all the better, but if not, we had to find a compromise. It was, in fact, a very interesting task.»*

While the general outcome of the 1997 season was a positive one for Bridgestone, it was by no means all roses. *«For us, the hardest thing was to make ourselves understood by our partners,»* said Hamashima. *«In F1, nobody was in the habit of having any competition on the tyre front and the teams did not want to lose too much time fitting in with our requests. They did not understand our needs and we had to fight hard to get our way. It got better towards the end of the season. Once the first good results started to come in, people began to realise that sometimes they had to spend one or two days doing nothing but tyre testing, so that direct back-to-back comparisons could be made.»*

For the company's chief engineer, there was also a cultural problem. *«We found it very difficult to communicate with the engineers from the teams. We had a different job to theirs and we spoke a different language. We therefore had to check constantly that we had understood one another and it was not always easy.»*

In 1997, Bridgestone was known particularly for the performance of its wet weather tyres, which had proved to be very impressive during pre-season testing. Since then, Goodyear has made up some of the performance gap. *«It is true that our grooved tyres are rather good,»* said Hamashima. *«But I do not think there is any big secret about that. It is just the result of us having a lot of experience of running in the rain. Perhaps our logic is simply better than that of the others.»*

Bridgestone actually brought six different types of wet weather tyres to each race, one for very heavy rain, three for "normal" rainfall and two for damp conditions.

As Hamashima explains, these days it is undoubtedly easier to gain tenths of a second by choosing the right tyre than it is by modifying the chassis. *«In my opinion, tyres decide 70% of a car's performance and the rest is down to the chassis. In fact, it is pointless setting up your car until you have decided what type of tyre to use in the race.»*

A modern F1 tyre is made of rubber, but also carbons, oil and numerous other constituents that are part of the secret of its construction; a secret which Hamashima would not divulge. *«We work on the compound, but also on the construction. The two go hand in hand.»*

For Yasukawa, the Formula 1 involvement has already paid off after just one season. *«We will carry out a detailed study, but it seems that the recognition of our brand in Europe has already doubled compared with last year. Our sales are also increasing step by step and we are therefore very happy with what we have achieved from the commercial point of view. Internally, our F1 involvement has also served to motivate the staff.»*

For 1998, the company is naturally working on the new grooved tyres and has set itself higher targets. *«We are getting there gradually. Goodyear has enjoyed a monopoly for so long that it will take us some time to get to their level. But I am not worried and I am very happy with the performance of our four teams to date. They have done an excellent job. I trust these teams, but it is true that several other teams have been in touch about the future.»*

△
In Argentina, Goodyear technicians were spotted scraping rubber samples off the track, no doubt in an attempt to analyse the Bridgestone compounds. Engineers from the Japanese company maintain they have not gone in for this form of industrial espionage. "It does not serve any purpose," says Hirohide Hamashima. "Once the tyre is used and has left rubber on the track, the compound changes. Any analysis would be useless and maybe even dangerous."

(On left) Hiroshi Yasukawa ▷
has worked for Bridgestone since 1972 and has been in charge of motor sport activity since 1976.

(On right) Hirohide Hamashima ▷▷
joined Bridgestone in 1977. He transferred to the company's English office in December 1996 to take control of the company's Formula 1 technical support.

Michael Schumacher wearing the F1 parka, which he also wears skiing.

Clothing a Formula 1 team: marrying style and function

Since January 1994, the Paris couture house of Cerruti has been the official clothing supplier to the Ferrari team. The partnership provided the opportunity to rethink completely the Scuderia's clothing range from the mechanics' travel kit to the their working overalls, as well as various other items.
For the Cerruti designers, Ferrari's demands set them a new challenge to study. Nino Cerruti and Maranello's Sporting Director Jean Todt came up with clothes that were both simple and comfortable, while expressing a sporty elegance. But they also had to meet the requirements of the job and had to be comfortable, strong, light, waterproof and easy to care for. However, before getting down to the manufacturing process, made to measure for each member of the team, several ideas were put forward by the Cerruti design team. *«We came up with several suggestions,»* said Patrick Banville, one of the stylists from the "mens" studio of the Place de la Madeleine couturier. *«Our brief was very precise and we submitted several proposals to Mr. Todt. We did not go to the bother of field testing them as our products would be replacing existing clothing.»*
Cerruti have experience of producing sports clothing and therefore there were no major technical problems. *«In the 70s and 80s, we had a substantial sports range, most notably tennis wear,»* continued Banville. *«We had maintained our contacts with the suppliers we had used back then, particularly a small factory which specialised in reinforced stitiching.»*
According to Patrick Banville, the main criteria for production were dominated by weather conditions. *«The clothing supplied to Ferrari had to be completely waterproof. The guys working in the pit-lane have to be able to work in the rain without getting wet. Fuel spray must not penetrate the garments, but the clothing must be able to breathe in hot conditions. This put a lot of demands on us and the clothing had to suit a variety of conditions: a parka for cold conditions, a sleeveless jacket for warmer conditions and so on. We had to come up with different items for every possible weather condition.»*

A Cerruti gathering: from left to right, David Ginola, Jean Todt, Eddie Irvine, Prince Albert of Monaco and Nino Cerruti.

The Cerruti designers had no problems with the Ferrari collection when it came to the materials used. *«This was quite straightforward,»* said Banville. *«The practical side is very important but we did not want to neglect the aesthetic side. For the mechanics at the track, aesthetics are not really a priority, but for us, it was naturally very important. Our biggest challenge with this project was finding room on the clothes for all the logos! It was not easy pleasing everyone.»*

Nothing has been left to chance in the range of clothing supplied to Scuderia Ferrari. The size and placing of pockets, the shape of the garments; all these factors had to fit in with the needs of the Maranello team.
Since then, Cerruti and Ferrari have collaborated to produce a range of clothing called "Les Authentiques," aimed at providing the general public with clothes based on a sporting theme.

Even under their refuelling helmets, the mechanics wear Cerruti.

△ *Michael Schumacher attacks and gives all four carbon discs a hammering.*

The development of carbon brakes: a very complex science

Carbon brakes are a minor technological miracle. While an engine weighing over 140 kilos can just about manage to get a Formula 1 car to accelerate up to 2 G, four discs, each weighing a mere 1.3 kilos, can put it through almost 5 G of deceleration.
This is an incredible figure for discs with a diameter of just 280 mm, a size more or less corresponding to the brake discs of a normal GTI-type road car.
Up until now, the complex manufacturing process has been something of a black art. The science of braking is not very precise and the Carbone Industrie engineers rely heavily on their past experience. «*The study of friction has no exact mathematical formula as its base,*» explains Philippe Rerat, head of the racing division within the French company. «*We depend to a large extent on our experience and a feeling to decide in which direction to go with our research.*»
All the same, Carbone Industrie has certain weapons in its armoury to deal with this uncertainty and the teams provide the Villeurbanne-based company with a great deal of information on the behaviour of their discs during the races.
«*The teams provide us with diskettes containing all the telemetric data,*» continues Rerat. «*We can find the speed, the deceleration, the pressure in the brake fluid circuit at any moment on a lap and not just when the driver is braking. We normally ask to be supplied this data from the fastest lap, or from a series of laps. Luckily, the teams are getting much more organised in terms of supplying us this information.*»
Carbone Industrie therefore relies heavily on these «field trials» to develop its products. «*We do a lot of private testing with the teams. We sometimes ask them to work exclusively on brake testing, so that nothing can else can interfere with the data. Normally they are happy to oblige and try and fit us into their schedule.*»
The three Carbone Industrie technicians, who cruise the Grand Prix pit lanes have access to all their teams' telemetric data and so must be scrupulously secretive in the way they go about their work. «*This is the price of our credibility,*» continues Rerat. «*If we passed on any information from one team to another, inevitably it would be found out one day, for example when an engineer leaves a team to work for another one. We therefore have to treat all teams on an exactly equal footing.*»
Carbone Industrie – which became a division of Messier Bugatti – has its own test bed to analyse the performance of its discs. «*This bed is unique in the world,*» says Rerat. «*Because it can simulate the braking of any vehicle from a Formula 1 car to a truck. That is to say from a light vehicle with low inertia and high speed, to a heavy goods vehicle with very high inertia and low speed.*» Brakes for high speed trains and aircraft are tested at Paris and Velizy, while the rest of the work is done at the Villeurbanne factory.
The test bed consists of a rotating arm on which weights can be attached. One can then alter the inertia by changing the mass. «*The difficulty with a Formula 1 car is that the inertia varies as the car is braking, because there is a weight transference from the rear to the front and because the aerodynamic forces of the wings are reduced as the speed decreases. At the rear end, the inertia diminishes while it goes up at the front. On our test bed, this variation can be simulated by computer, which drives a motor that simulates an external force.*»
This test bed was first used in September 1996, replacing a more basic version which is now used for material testing. «*With the old system, we did comparison testing,*» continues Rerat. «*With the new one we are learning about the phenomenon itself.*»
For the automotive applications, speeds of up to 400 km/h can be simulated at an inertia of 100 sq.m/kg (equivalent of a 3-tons vehicle). The motor can reproduce 400 horsepower per wheel.
The whole set-up is covered with a huge cooling box for the discs, thus simulating the effect of speed on the car. «*This speed varies during acceleration and deceleration and the wind tunnel reacts to within one tenth of a second. In a matter of tenths it can up the speed from 80 to 350 km/h. The simulated cooling of the discs is very important, as although temperature has little effect on the braking performance it does significantly affect wear, as the discs destroy themselves if not cooled.*»
Carbon Industrie is currently in the process of developing even more sophisticated testing equipment, using computer simulation techniques which allow an even better understanding of the braking process.
«*This equipment should allow us to simulate every conceivable braking situation,*» claims Rerat. «*For example, if there is a rule saying that F1 cars will no longer have front wings in 1999, we must be capable of simulating that effect. This new test computer will be up and running by the middle of 1998.*»
«*Simulation equipment is becoming more and more complex, but it is impossible to make progress without it. Soon we will be able to predict the effect of various cooling ducts as well as the shape of the wings and so forth.*»
In braking, as in so many other areas of motorsport, it would seem that computers hold the key...

◁ *Carbone Industrie's test bed at their Villeurbanne plant. Visible is the enormous wind machine at the level of the platform.*

1998 came early

For Carbone Industrie, the future is already here. Testing for the new 1998 technical regulations started a long time ago. «*Williams were the first to go testing with us,*» explains Philippe Rerat. «*We knew the specification of the 1998 cars and we tried to reproduce their characteristics on the test bed. We tried new materials and construction methods. This experience helped us a great deal in deciding which direction we should work in and the test bed confirmed our expectations.*»
As far as brakes are concerned, the 1998 regulations state that the thickness of the discs will not exceed 28 millimetres as compared to 32 mm in 1997. «*This makes for easier braking, less harsh and with a longer life. The original idea was to restrict the size to one inch (25.4 mm) but we explained this would put the drivers' safety in question and the Federation moved on to 28 millimetres.*»

Alcatel and Prost Grand Prix: the perfect technological partnership

by Dominique Caussanel
«Drapeau à Damier»

Since the 1997 Monaco Grand Prix, Alcatel has been in partnership with the Prost Grand Prix team. This partnership is divided into two areas of activity based around Alcatel's involvement with the team with the famous name. Caroline Mille, Director of Communications for the Alcatel Alsthom Group, explains how it works. *«Most notably, our partnership brings technological benefits in terms of manpower and advanced technologies. These can be of real benefit in helping the team achieve its goal of winning the world championship. Our group, which is present in 130 countries around the world and employs around 180,000 people has found a natural expression for its Hi-Speed Company strategy, through this association with one of the most promising teams in Formula 1.»*
As a French company, it was only natural that Alcatel should align itself with the only French team in grand prix racing, with the aim of flying its colours in all countries hosting a round of the Formula 1 World Championship; countries in which Alcatel is already operational. The aim of the partnership is to show that Alcatel products aimed at the general public can also play a key role in the operations of a grand prix team. To this end, all the prototype products used by the team have their base in a commercially available item. At the same time, Formula 1 provides a challenge and a technical platform for the development of new products, created with the knowledge acquired from its presence at the races.
«This partnership also represents a human challenge,» explains Alcatel sponsorship manager, Laurent Lachaux. *«A crew led by technical manager Gilles Thevenet has been created to efficiently coordinate the group's subsidiary companies as they work with the team. This integrated team, along with the 190,000 employees of Alcatel Alsthom, must prove they have the right sort of response and reaction time to take them into the next millennium. Joel Comtesse works with the team throughout the year to provide, on a full-time basis, the best possible radio communications solutions for the duration of the partnership. Formula 1 is constantly changing its requirements and Alcatel can provide Prost Grand Prix with the very latest technology to help it meet its aims.»*
For Alcatel, this fits in perfectly with its objective of being «The Hi-Speed Company,» in all its areas of activity and the partnership with Prost Grand Prix provides a challenge worthy of the name.
The partnership with Prost has blown a wind of change through the internal relations of Alcatel companies around the world. An in-house Formula 1 Club has been established and it is a unique operation which already has 7500 members from around the world. *«Members of the Formula 1 Fan Club attend every grand prix to support their team,»* says Fabienne Brunet, the company's internal public relations director. *«The «Hi-Speed» spirit quickly latched onto Alcatel's presence in Grand Prix and the Fan Club has proved very popular with 7500 members from 25 countries around the world signing up in three months.»* The Fan Club has generated a great deal of interest within the company with a range of F1 related material available to members. Competitions are organised, tied in to visits to the grands prix and company karting days have also been held. The «Hi-Speed» spirit has actually become reality within the group.

Joel Comtesse, the Alcatel radio communications specialist, is fully integrated as part of the team.

The Alcatel control unit on the pit wall allows the team to keep in permanent contact with their cars on the track.

△
Technical briefing in the Prost Grand Prix team truck: the engineers and drivers are in communication by video-conference with the factory back at Magny-Cours. A state of the art technology, unique in Formula 1.

Gilles Thevenet: Alcatel Project Manager for the Prost Grand Prix team coordinates all the company's activities linked to the team.
▽

A complex job list

Alain Prost and Alcatel had four major technical points on their agenda.

- Communication between the pits and drivers in both cars entered for each grand prix have to be perfect when the cars are running on the track. The importance of this can be seen from the fact that, at the 1997 season opener in Melbourne, Jean Alesi ran out of fuel in the race, as he was unable to hear orders from his pit, begging him to come in and refuel.
  In this area, Alcatel's influence was immediately felt during practice sessions and the races. For 1998, studies are under way to improve the quality of communication even further and the arrival of digital radios should be a help, right from the start of the 1988 season.

- The second area where Alcatel's experience is being brought to bear, is in the domain of communication between the team members themselves during a grand prix weekend, in practice and race conditions. Formula 1 mechanics work in a very noisy environment, with the sound of their own cars, those in the next door garages and the cars passing by the pits on the track and in order to work efficiently, each mechanic must be able to communicate clearly with his colleagues.
  Therefore, Alcatel has developed a special radio channel that can be used exclusively by the Prost Grand Prix engineers and mechanics, without intruding on the airwaves reserved for communication between drivers and team management.

- It is this area of communication between team manager, team director and engineers of Alain Prost's team that is the first priority for next year and while progress has already been made in this area, Alain Prost wants more. The team personnel, Alain Prost, Cesare Fiorio, the engineers, the engine engineers and the Bridgestone technicians must all be able to converse in complete confidence, during practice and the race. Radio frequencies are allocated by the FIA, in conjunction with the local radio licensing authority in each country, so it is not inconceivable that signals can get mixed up and other teams could listen in to confidential conversations. There is an added complication in that Alain Prost has an agreement with French digital TV company Canal + and has to be able to go on air at certain times during sessions and the race. In order to ensure the most efficient radio communication between all concerned, Alain Prost has access to a radio control console on the pit-wall.

Using this, Prost can control all his team's communication in a manner which rules out possible eavesdropping from journalists or personnel from other teams. From this it can be seen that Alcatel is much more than a sponsor and a technical partner; it is at the heart of the decision making processes of the Prost team.

The Alcatel radio in the cockpit of each car must be a perfect fit in the limited space available. It must also withstand the acceleration and vibration of the car in action.

Problems to solve

The final weapon in the Alcatel armoury is the video-conference link it has put at the disposal of the team. Every fifteen days, during the grand prix season, over 60% of the team is away at the races. In order to keep the evolution and development work of the team alive and kicking during these periods, the Prost team has a permanent video link from the track to the factory. This ensures that engineers at the race track can exchange ideas and solutions by sight and sound with staff back at base.
In order to get all these complex facilities working properly the Alcatel engineers have had to confront a whole host of problems born out of the difficult working conditions to be found in Formula 1. To start with, all the equipment to be used at the grands prix must be interchangeable and easily transported. During a qualifying session, a driver might want to switch from his race car to the spare car and it is imperative that the radio link fitted to his helmet is instantly compatible from one car to the other. The wiring loom is linked to the driver's seat and the radio control box must be instantly accessible at all times. On a more general point, all the equipment used at a grand prix must be assembled and dismantled at every race, therefore it has to be exceptionally reliable and easy to modify. It takes an Alcatel engineer just 15 seconds to refit a radio from one car to another without having to touch the driver end of the equipment.
Formula 1 is a great consumer of radio communication, be it the organisers, the emergency services, the media, other teams and even helicopters used by television. This means that the electro-magnetic environment around a grand prix is pretty much saturated, therefore confidential broadcasting is one of the biggest problems facing Alcatel, in its dealings with the Prost team. To ensure the most secure transmissions possible, Alcatel uses Private Mobile Radio technology, which it has perfectly adapted to this specific task.
Gradually, Alcatel is creating a spiders-web network between all the team members. Four double frequencies are used to run the overall communication system in the team and Alain Prost himself is the only member to have access to all four, either separately or at the same time. Alcatel has developed a computer which controls the radio frequencies and that will result in a communications system based on vocal recognition. This will rely on the digital radios which the Prost Grand Prix team will use in Formula 1.

One of the most popular events for the supporters club: the factory visit with Alain Prost himself as the guide.

The supporters club membership card, shown actual size. 7500 members have joined the fan club in 25 countries around the world.

Alain Prost delighted

«The agreement we have with Alcatel is a long term partnership which has a clearly defined timetable. The first priority was driver - pit communication. We have made progress at every race and this is all going in the right direction and working very well. Of course we also have to look to the future and we have several new ideas in the pipeline for 1998. With a partnership like ours with Alcatel, we are looking to gain an advantage over the other teams and we have already introduced several innovative procedures which have proved successful. It is very difficult to communicate with a Formula 1 car from the pit-wall during a race, but this is no longer a problem for us. We now have a video conference link between our trucks at the track and the factory in France. This system has to be improved still further and our partnership with Alcatel will become more and more important to our daily life. For example, they are heavily implicated in the construction of our new factory. Alcatel is an essential part of our future in Formula 1. It is a major contributor as we strive to achieve our goals. In the short term, given the targets we have set ourselves, Alcatel will be a big help in doing better than our competitors.»

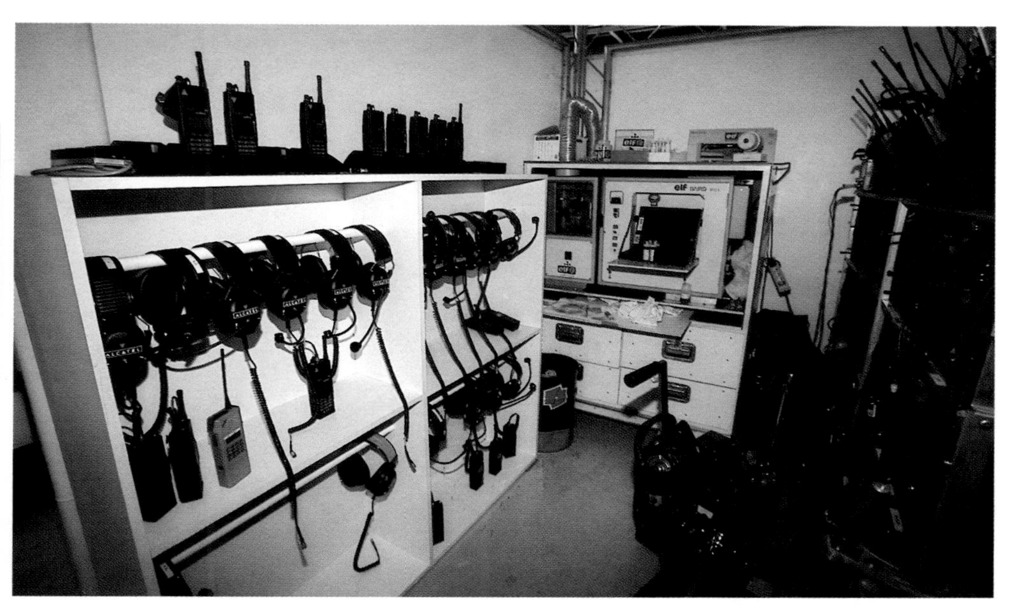

◁
The team uses 50 Alcatel radios and headsets to communicate in the most testing situations.

Alcatel has equipped the Prost factory with the very latest in office telecommunication.
▽

An ultra-modern factory

Finally, Alcatel is also involved in the construction of the new Prost Grand Prix factory, which is now underway near Paris. The factory will have every conceivable communication device required by a modern company. Everything from the telephone system to security and surveillance cameras will all be provided by Alcatel.

When the Alcatel guests leave the circuit, the part of their visit that has made the strongest impression is the trip to the pits to meet the drivers, just prior to the race.
▽ ▽

The Scuderia's fiftieth anniversary

Ferrari and F 1 : half a century to create a legend

by Jacques Vassal
«Auto Passion»

Over 500 grands prix, 112 wins and 22 world championships have helped create the Scuderia Ferrari legend. One that is filled with moments of glory as well as some missed opportunities.

On 14th July 1951, the Argentinian driver. Froilan Gonzalez took a historic victory at Silverstone, at the wheel of a 375 F1. It was the first appearance of a Ferrari in a World Championship Grand Prix and he also beat the formidable Alfetta 159 fair and square. *«On that day, I felt as though I had killed my mother,»* Enzo Ferrari would later write in his memoirs. In saying this, he was evoking the fact that, from 1929 to 1939, he had worked for Alfa Romeo, where he learnt the tricks of his trade. During the war, he built machinery at Maranello and had to wait until 1947 to launch the first car to bear his name, the 125 S sports barchetta with a 1500cc V12 engine. Designed by Gioacchino Colombo, this V12 would serve as the basis for the first Ferrari Formula 1 cars, the 125 F1, but it was soon apparent that they were not up to the job of beating the powerful Alfetta in the new fangled World Championship which had been created in 1950. The Scuderia actually missed the first race at Silverstone where unsurprisingly, victory went to Alfa Romeo.

During this time, Aurelio Lampredi, the young chief engineer who succeeded Colombo, was fine tuning the next generation weapon. The 125 F1 was abandoned in favour of a new generation of normally aspirated V12s of increasing capacity until they reached the maximum allowed in the regulations, 4.5 litres (Tipo 375.) Although these cars gave away 40 horsepower to the Alfetta 159, but the Ferrari's used less fuel than the turbocharged Alfettas, thus saving them precious time in refuelling. At the Nurburgring, then at Monza, the 375 F1 won two more grands prix.

In 1952. Alfa Romeo, having won all there was to win, decided to quite grand prix racing, as did Talbot, who were in financial difficulty. The Maserati 4CLT was no longer competitive and they were looking for something new. In England, the BRM V16 was not ready, while HWM and Cooper-Bristol were not ready either. The same applied to Gordini in France and Veritas in Germany, who could only realistically take part in F2. The CSI (the forerunner to the FIA) was worried that they would be left with depleted grids for the grands prix and therefore decided to switch the Drivers' World Championship to the Formula 2 series, where the cars were limited to 2 litres, normally aspirated. Of the half dozen constructors and the handful of privateers who entered the series, Ferrari was the best by a long chalk. The car, the 500 F2, was well designed, simple, elegant, reliable and strong. It also had the best drivers.

In the winter of 1950-51, the prolific Lampredi started work on a 4 cylinder 2 litre destined for Formula 2. Although less powerful than the 2 litre V12 Tipo 166, it had more torque, was more compact and more reliable. It was fitted with hairpin valve springs and was said to be influenced by the design of the Manx Norton 500cc single cylinder motorcycle. With 185 horsepower on tap it was about as powerful as the Maserati A6GCM, but it was more reliable.

▷ *1956: Juan Manuel Fangio and Enzo Ferrari did not always get on as well as this photo, taken during practice for the Italian GP might suggest. Thanks to the generosity of Peter Collins, who handed over his car, the Argentinian finished second in the race, to take his fourth World Championship. (photo Bernard Cahier)*

22nd June 1952: Ascari wins the Belgian GP ahead of team-mate Nino Farina, driving the 500 F2 at Spa-Francorchamps. (photo Autopresse) ▷ ▽

JACQUES VASSAL, *Journalist, writer and translator, Jacques Vassal is a firm Ferrari enthusiast. Since 1989, he has worked for the magazine Auto Passion, for whom he writes road tests, and interviews and portraits of drivers, including former Ferrari drivers such as Luigi Villoresi, John Surtees and Maurice Trintignant. (photo Gerard Rocroy)*

◁ *1st July 1956: Fangio in the French GP at Reims, at the wheel of a Ferrari 801. He was only fourth, but Collins and Castellotti in similar cars finished first and second. (archives Dominique Pascal)*

Ferrari had one of the best drivers in the shape of Alberto Ascari, son of motorcycle racer Antonio. He was determined, very fast and loyal. Stirling Moss reckoned he was the equal of Fangio and when the Argentinian missed most of the 1952 season after an accident, Ascari had the field to himself for the rest of the year. and took the title. Even his team mates Villoresi, Taruffi and Farina were only left the crumbs. In 1952 and '53 the 500 F2 won 14 grands prix, with Ascari accounting for 11 of them, including 9 in a row. Strangely, one of the few times the Scuderia was beaten fair and square was by the Gordini of Jean Behra at Reims in '52. But that year the event was not in the championship and Ascari won the official French round at Rouen.
Ascari took his second title in 1953. Reims and Monza were two races that eluded him; the French round remembered for the fantastic duel between a young Mike Hawthorn in he Ferrari and the veteran Fangio in a Maserati. The Englishman won, while at Monza, it was Fangio's turn after Ascari collected a spinning car.

1956: Fangio the unhappy champion

Rule changes in 1954 did Ferrari no favours and the cars were unreliable and did not hold the road well. Ascari and Villoresi left for Lancia where engineer Jano was building his original D50 with a V8 engine and side mounted fuel tanks. Ferrari's drivers were Hawthorn, Gonzales, Trintignant, Farina and sometimes Manzon or Maglioli. Although Gonzales won in England and Hawthorn took the honours in Spain, life was too difficult up against the Mercedes W 196 which won first time out at Reims. The Maserati 250 F was also improving. In 1955, Fangio, aided and abetted by Moss took the title for himself and Mercedes. Trintignant saved the Scuderia's honour with a solitary victory in Monaco. But in the summer of 1955, Ferrari had a stroke of luck. Lancia pulled out of racing, leaving all its equipment, including seven cars, many engines and loads of spare parts to Ferrari, who had also just been given financial aid by Fiat to the tune of 50 million lire.
The manna from heaven was well used by the master of Maranello, helped by the fact that Mercedes also pulled out of the sport, which put Fangio on the transfer market. The Argentinian, who was already a three times world champion became the Scuderia's lead driver, supported by several young hopefuls:

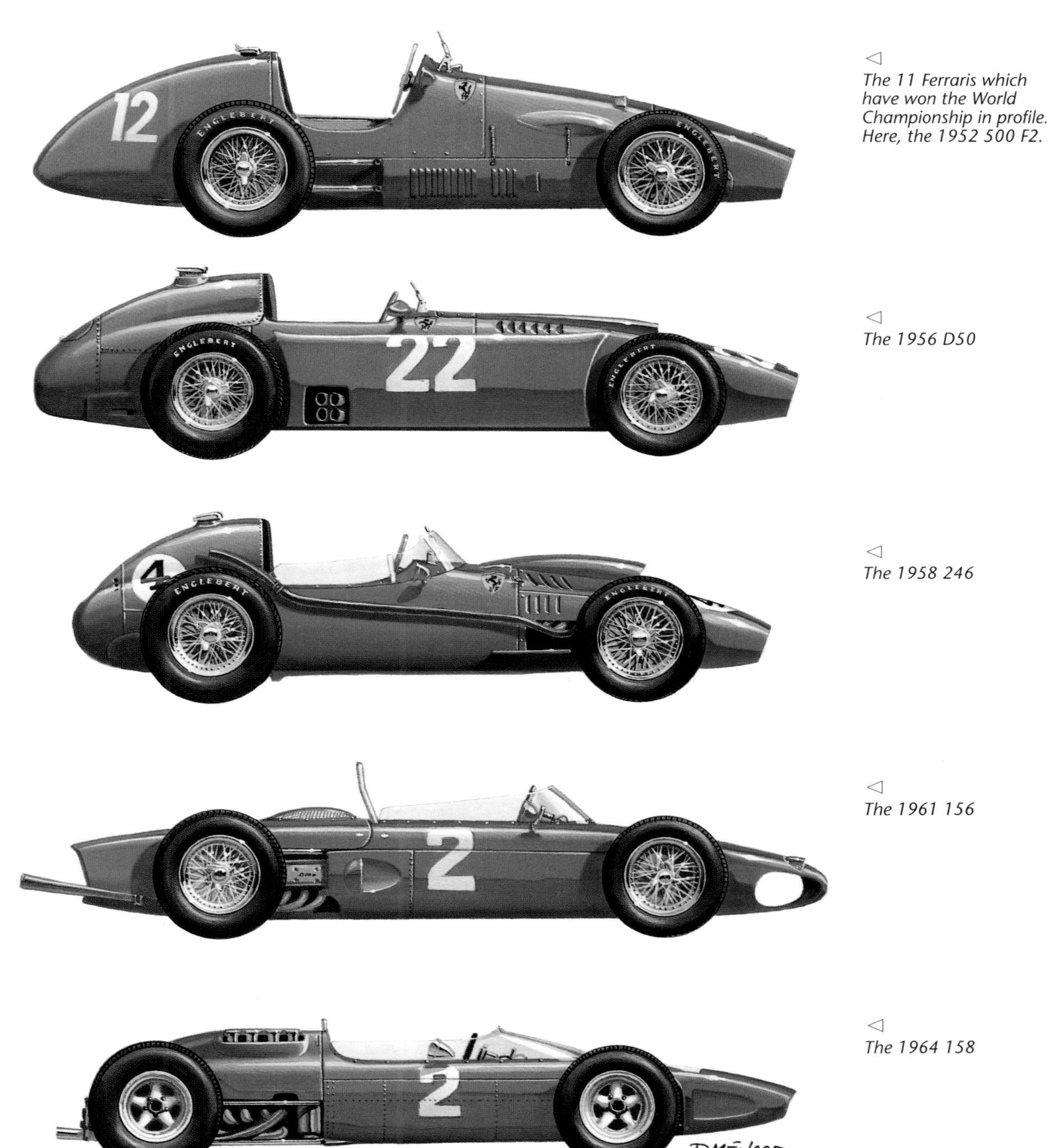

◁ *The 11 Ferraris which have won the World Championship in profile. Here, the 1952 500 F2.*

◁ *The 1956 D50*

◁ *The 1958 246*

◁ *The 1961 156*

◁ *The 1964 158*

6th July 1958: Mike Hawthorn on his way to winning the French GP at Reims at the wheel of a Dino 246. Sadly his team-mate Luigi Musso died in the race. One month later, the same fate would befall his friend Peter Collins at the Nurburgring. (archives Dominique Pascal)

the Italians Luigi Musso and Eugenio Castelloti, the Spaniard Alfonso de Portago and England's Peter Collins. In 1956, they ran in Lancias, renamed as Ferrari 801. These were V8 engined with around 240 horsepower.
Although it brought him his fourth world title, Fangio's only season with Ferrari was not a happy one. On 22nd January he christened his new contract by winning at home in Buenos Aires, having taken over Musso's car. In Monaco, in a bad mood he lost his usual sangfroid and spun off on the third lap, handing victory to Moss in the Maserati 250 F. He only finished second after team manager, Eraldo Sculati, called Collins in to hand over his car. Spa was worse: starting from pole he retired with a broken transmission, allowing Collins and the Belgian journalist Paul Frere to score a Ferrari one-two. In the French GP, Collins and Castellotti assured first and second place for the Scuderia, with Fangio only fourth. Despite great tension between Fangio and Enzo Ferrari, the Argentinian went on to win the British and German races back to back. As they went into the final round in Italy, Fangio and Collins were level pegging on points. Forced to retire with broken steering on lap 20, Fangio could only watch as Moss, Musso and Collins fought it out. On lap 34, when he came in for new tyres, Collins handed the car over to Fangio who took off in pursuit of Moss. The points acquired were enough to give him his fourth World Championship, ahead of Moss and Collins.

1958: Mike Hawthorn and the Dino

Running modified 801, Peter Collins and «mon ami mate» Mike Hawthorn were the crack team for the Scuderia in 1957, but they powerless against Fangio in the Maserati 250 F, who claimed his fifth World Championship. Ferrari also suffered after the deaths of Castellotti in testing at Modena and De Portago in the Mille Miglia, in an accident which also cost the life of co-driver Nelson and several spectators. By 1958, the Scuderia was back on course, with Hawthorn, Collins and Musso driving the new Dino 246, designed by Carlo Chiti a light, compact car with a new V6. It put out 290 bhp at 8500 rpm. The Maseratis were off the pace, but the Vanwalls which had won in England and Italy the previous year looked very strong. This was the first year a Constructors' Championship was also up for grabs and it became a duel between Ferrari and Vanwall, challenged by the nimble Cooper- Climax, the first mid-engined F1 cars. Maurice Trintignant won Monaco for Rob Walker's team in one of these. But Ferrari and Vanwall shared the other victories. Stunned by the deaths of Musso at Reims and Collins at the Nurburgring, Hawthorn, who was to die in January 1959 in a road accident, took one win in the Dino. The Constructors' title went to Vanwall.
1959 and 1960 saw the withdrawal of Maserati and Vanwall, with BRM and Aston Martin making progress, the debut of Lotus, but of all the triumphs of Cooper and Jack Brabham, the Australian who would win two World Championships. The Scuderia won few races with Tony Brooks and Phil Hill as the Dino had not really evolved.

1961-1964: Hill and Surtees crowned champion

1961 saw a Ferrari revival as the English constructors struggled to come to terms with the new 1500cc F1 regulations. However, everything was in place at Maranello where the new 156 had around a 50 horsepower advantage over the best Climax could offer. Thanks to brilliant driving, only Stirling Moss in a Rob Walker Lotus 18, managed to beat Ferrari on two occasions at Monaco and Nurburgring. Von Trips, Phil Hill and Baghetti shared the other wins. The final round in Italy ended in tragedy when von Trips was killed at the start of the race. Hill became World Champion.
In 1962, Ferrari concentrated on endurance racing and their Formula 1 campaign suffe-

The American Phil Hill had started racing in Sports Cars with an MG. He then raced Ferraris at home and joined the Scuderia in 1957, winning Le Mans with Olivier Gendebien the following year in a 250 Testa Rossa. He won the 1960 Italian GP at Monza, the last time a front-engined car won a round of the World Championship. (archives Dominique Pascal)

red. With Chiti and other engineers having left the marque, a 26 year old Mauro Forghieri found himself in charge of technical matters while Eugenio Dragoni was sporting director. BRM and Graham Hill took the championships and 1963 looked like being a hard fight against Jim Clark and the Lotus 25. Ferrari took on former motorcycle world champion John Surtees. This methodical, meticulous Englishman with an interest in the technical side of the sport, squired by Lorenzo Bandini put Ferrari back on the right track. The new 156 was a better car than its predecessor and the team was already working on the 158 V8. Surtees dominated at the Nurburgring but Clark and Lotus took the titles.

1964 saw Ferrari return to its winning ways, albeit with a touch of luck. The 158 Aero won three times, in England and Italy with Surtees and in Austria with Bandini. The 1512 flat twelve engine with 220 horsepower appeared towards the end of the season for Bandini to drive in Italy and Mexico. The championship went down to the last lap in Mexico, with Clark, Hill and Surtees all in the running. Surtees took the title after Bandini ran into the back of Hill on lap 31 and Clark retired with an oil leak, leaving Dan Gurney's Brabham to win. Bandini moved over to let Surtees into second place, which saw him crowned with a one point lead. Ferrari took the Constructors' Championship. Clark and Lotus dominated 1995, the final year of the 1500cc cars, and Ferrari made do with the minor placings.

1966 - 1979: From V12 to Boxer, the apogee of the 3 litre formula

Ferrari were hopeful of winning with the new 3 litre formula. On paper the 312 V12 was a strong force, but it was too heavy. In Monaco, Surtees retired and Bandini finished second in a Dino 246. Surtees had a great win in the wet at Spa ahead of Rindt in a Cooper-Maserati, but the Englishman fell out with Dragoni on the eve of the Le Mans 24 Hours and walked out. He was replaced by Mike Parkes and Ludovico Scarfiotti, who won the Italian GP. Recruited in 1967, the Kiwi Chris Amon suffered innumerable breakages and misfortunes with the new 312 with its central exhaust system and the Scuderia also suffered from the death of Bandini at Monaco. In 1968, the Belgian Jacky Ickx joined the team and won the French GP at Rouen in the rain.

Ickx left to join Brabham in 1969 but returned to Ferrari the following year, where he was joined by the young Italian, Ignazio Giunti. The team introduced a new car with a 465 horsepower flat 12 engine: the 312 B Boxer. This engine evolved over the years and would win many races for Ickx, Andretti and Lauda. In 1974 and '75, a new sporting director was appointed by Fiat. He was a young lawyer called Luca Cordero di Montezemolo. Recruited with the help of Clay Regazzoni, who brought him to Fiorano in the summer of 1973 for secret testing, the Austrian Niki Lauda, nicknamed «the computer» won his first grand prix at Jarama in 1974 in the last of the 312 B3. The spring of 1975 saw the appearance of Forghieri's new baby, the 312 T with transverse gearbox. At the wheel, the Austrian was unbeatable, winning in Monaco, Belgium, Sweden, France and the USA, to take the title, while Regazzoni won at Dijon and Monza to give Ferrari the Constructors' title. In 1976, with new aerodynamics, the 312 T became the T2. Winning in Brazil, South Africa, Belgium, Monaco and even Great Britain, after an appeal, Lauda looked on the way to a second title, when he had a terrible accident, which nearly cost him his life at the Nurburgring. He bravely overcame terrible burns to return for the Italian GP where he finished fourth. But he pulled out of the Japanese race, held in torrential rain and handed the title to James Hunt. Lauda got his revenge in 1977 with three wins and a championship for himself and Ferrari. However, since he pulled out of that Japanese race, the atmosphere had been tense between Lauda and the Scuderia chiefs, Daniele Audetto and Roberto Nosetto. Lauda left, to be replaced in 1978 by Carlos Reutemann and the brilliant Canadian, Gilles Villeneuve, who was regarded as an adopted son by Enzo Ferrari. In 1979, the 312 T3 and then T4 were put in the hands of Villeneuve and the South African Jody Scheckter, who became World Champion with wins in Zolder, Monaco and Monza, the last time a Ferrari driver won the title. With Villeneuve winning in Kyalami, Long Beach and Watkins Glen, Ferrari took the Constructors' Championship again.

◁ *11th May 1975: The Austrian Niki Lauda had a superb Monaco GP, driving an all - conquering 312 T. He led the race from start to finish, watched by Gianni Agnelli, the boss of Fiat. (photo DPPI)*

1981 - 1988: The turbo era

After a very bad 1980 season with the last of the normally aspirated 312, the T5, Ferrari followed Renault's lead, launching the turbocharged 126 CK in 1981. Villeneuve tried this in practice for the 1980 Italian GP. With Scheckter gone, he was joined by Didier Pironi. In the summer of '81, the English designer Harvey Postlethwaite came to fine tune the 126C chassis. It was a turning point for Ferrari, who until then, had always concentrated on the engine and paid little attention to the chassis. Postlethwaite was also the first foreign engineer to work for the team which had always been entirely Italian until then.

1982 should have been a great year for the Scuderia and its young and brilliant drivers, who were locked in an intense personal rivalry. In San Marino, Pironi ignored team order to win from his team- mate, who was killed in

◁ *The 1975 312T*

◁ *The 1976 312T2*

◁ *The 1977 312T2*

9th September 1979: The 312 T4 of Jody Scheckter and Gilles Villeneuve are about to finish first and second in the Italian GP at Monza, in one of those trouble free races which so delighted the tifosi. (photo DPPI)

practice for the Belgian Grand Prix. Pironi won in Holland, but saw his season and indeed his career halted by a huge accident, when he broke both legs in practice for the German GP, which was won by fellow Frenchman Patrick Tambay. He also finished second at Monza, while the returning Mario Andretti's third place there was enough to give Ferrari the title, while the Drivers' Championship went to Finland's Keke Rosberg, although many people, including Enzo Ferrari himself, felt Pironi was the moral winner. In 1983, two Frenchmen drove the new 126 C2: Tambay and Rene Arnoux. Thanks to one win for the former and three for the latter, Ferrari took its last Constructors' title.

In 1984, Postlethwaite developed the 126 C4 and Michele Alboreto became the first Italian to drive for the team since Arturo Merzario in 1973. Alboreto won the Belgian GP and in 1985 added wins in the Canadian and German races. He was second in the championship behind Alain Prost, and with some additional points scored by Stefan Johannsson, Ferrari were second in the Constructors' Championship.

In 1986, Forghieri was replaced by John Barnard, who was given full powers to set up a satellite design base in Guildford, England. After Lauda, Gerhard Berger became the second Austrian to drive for the team, alongside Alboreto in 1987 and 1988. In 1988, less than a month after the death of Enzo Ferrari, they scored an emotional one-two in the Italian Grand Prix at Monza.

The 1979 312T4

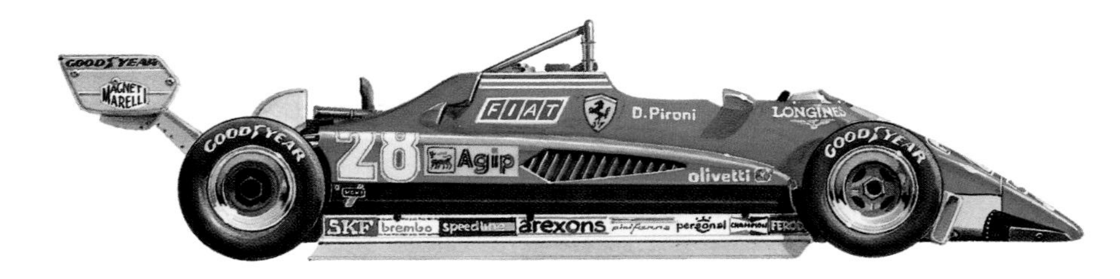

The 1982 126C2

The 1983 126C3

1990: Prost and Ferrari... nearly World Champions

1989 was another transitional year. Cesare Fiorio moved from Lancia to replace Marco Piccinini as Sporting Director, while FISA initiated a new 3.5 litre normally aspirated formula. To meet this challenge, John Barnard produced the 640 chassis, while at Maranello, a new V12 was built with five valves per cylinder, producing 665 horsepower.

The Englishman Nigel Mansell joined Berger, who made way for Alain Prost in 1990. He won five races that year with the 641/2 including Ferrari's 100thvictory at the French GP. He lost out on the World Championship to Ayrton Senna in the McLaren after the two men collided at the Japanese Grand Prix on the very first lap. But for this incident, which a year later Senna admitted was his fault, Prost would doubtless have been champion. With his rigorous and methodical approach, the Frenchman had at least put Maranello back on the right track, to await the arrival of Jean Todt in July 1994, the return to a 3 litre formula in 1995, the creation of Ferrari's first ever V10 and the recruitment in 1996 of a certain Michael Schumacher.

While the German just failed to take the title this season, there is a wind of change rushing through the Scuderia, which should see it return to its winning ways. Why not in 1998?

This year the Tyrrell team celebrated its 400th grand prix. Time for a quick glance in the wing mirror.

400 not out for Uncle Ken

At 73 years of age, the least well off team owner in the pit lane has not lost faith. For him, the good old days are next week. A giant of a man with the walk of a lumberjack (his first job) Ken Tyrrell has been everywhere and done everything there is to do in Formula 1. He first entered a grand prix back in 1969 and almost thirty years later, his team has 402 races to its credit. He has not missed a single one of them and therefore quietly celebrated his 400th at the Luxembourg Grand Prix. Ken Tyrrell's curriculum vitae includes two world championships, 23 wins and 14 pole positions.
Today, those successes seem a long way off, as his last win dates back to 1983, when Michele Alboreto won the United States Grand Prix. The bad times do not seem to have affected Ken Tyrrell too much. He still wears the same smile in the paddock, waiting for better times, which will probably never come.

You have not had much luck these past few years and you have often changed engines: Ford, Renault, Honda, Ilmor, Yamaha, Ford again. This could not have been easy.

Ken Tyrrell: At the beginning of the Seventies, you had the Ford Cosworth DFV engine. It was excellent and not too sophisticated. It was quite simple to build a car around it, get a good driver and go out and win the next grand prix. These days, Formula 1 is mainly about engines. You must have the support of a major manufacturer. We do not have that, which makes our job very difficult. We try to get a deal with a big constructor, but we obviously have not done a good enough job to convince them, even though we have contacted every conceivable name. It is a question of results. This is in fact the hardest part of my job.

You have very little sponsorship on your car and yours is undoubtedly the poorest team in the field. How do you make both ends meet?

Ken Tyrrell: We decide what we can do with the available budget. My principle is not to spend money we do not have in the bank. Without that we would have gone under a long time ago, just like a lot of other small teams have done recently. There were years when we were in the red, but we made up for these in the good years. When everything is going well I do not spend the lot, but I build up reserves for the bad times. This year we should just about manage to balance the books. Our biggest problem is that we cannot get long term sponsorship deals. Indeed, only the top four or five teams manage to do this.

It is said that your team is very well run and that if you had just half the Williams budget you would be world champions.

Ken Tyrrell: If we had half the Williams budget, we would have a lot more than we do now (laughs). But I do not know if that would be enough to be world champion. When I first came into F1 in 1968, I ran chassis supplied by Matra. It was down to me to find and pay for the engine, the transmission, the drivers and to line up the two cars for the races. At the time my budget was ,80,000 for the season, a quarter of which went to pay Jackie (Stewart.) There were six or seven of us in the factory and we got the job done, so you can see I know how to run a budget.

Formula 1 has changed a lot recently, mainly due to the increased importance of television. How do you view these changes?

Ken Tyrrell: No doubt about it, it is very positive. Television has brought Formula 1 to the whole world, where as before the fans had to come to the races. Television has brought the sponsors and wealth. Look at the paddocks today: smart, spacious and clean. Thirty years ago we prepared the cars in terrible pits, under tents and in the pouring rain. When FOCA was formed in the mid-Seventies, each team owner was given a specific task to improve the situation. I was in charge of improving Silverstone. It was so disgusting, I told the organisers F1 would not come back unless they rebuilt the pits. Do you know what Frank Williams' job was? He was in charge of the paddock toilets at every track and had to make sure there were enough of them and that they were clean!

◁
«And do you know what was Frank Williams' responsibility? The paddock toilets...» With 30 years experience behind him, Uncle Ken has a whole host of amusing tales to tell.

Do you not think that F1 is not as much fun as it used to be twenty years ago, particularly for spectators, who can no longer get near the drivers?

Ken Tyrrell: And how do you suggest the public gets to the drivers? There are 100,000 of them out there in the stands. How can they all come and touch Michael Schumacher? It is impossible, just impossible. It is the price of success of the sport.

Do you not miss the good old days?

Ken Tyrrell: What good old days? The good old days is now, or maybe even next week. But it is certainly not yesterday! I am just as motivated as I was 30 years ago. For me, motor racing is a sort of incurable disease, which I will suffer until my death. Some years have been very hard, but my passion for the sport has not faltered. There have been times when it would have been easier just to give it all up, but that is not my style.

The Concorde Agreement: a moral question

Ken Tyrrell is one of three dissident team owners, who have refused to sign the Concorde Agreement, the document which sets out the commercial implications of Formula 1.

Why did you not sign the Concorde Agreement?

Ken Tyrrell: When I started in Formula 1 in 1968, it was very easy to get into the sport. You just had to get hold of the Ford engine, build a car around it, find some money and off you went. Since then, up until last year, that was still the case and I made sure it was. But today, with the 1997 Concorde Agreement that Bernie (Ecclestone) wants us to sign, it is no longer the case. Today, you must first pay the FIA a 24 thousand dollar deposit to come into F1. It is madness. So I did not sign. Because I believe it is my duty to leave F1 in the same way in which I found it. It is a question of moral responsibility. But we are all big boys and we will find some common ground.

What is your relationship with Bernie Ecclestone?

Ken Tyrrell: Oh, it is excellent. Since I have known him, I have regarded him as a true friend. He listens to me, maybe more than to some of the others, because of my age and the time we have known one another. But sometimes, I get the impression that what I tell him goes in one ear and out the other.

Once again this year, the two Tyrrells of Salo and Verstappen line up with virtually no sponsorship. What with that and the fact the team is not entitled to money from the television rights this season, balancing the books has been a minor miracle.
▽

The long road to hell

The Tyrrell team had a fairly flamboyant debut, as it won the championship at its first attempt. *«I did it the same way you can do it today. I hired the best driver. That's all there is to it,»* comments Ken Tyrrell.
Indeed, winning that first championship is still the Englishman's best memory of the sport. Two years later, Jackie Stewart did it again, but at the end of the season, the team was badly affected by the death of Francois Cevert at the United States Grand Prix at Watkins Glen.
Since those days, the Tyrrell team has been on a slippery slope towards the abyss of anonymity, despite some memorable moments, like the 1975 six-wheeler.
«I think the start of our problems dates back to 1973,» recalls Tyrrell. *«Jackie* (Stewart) *had become world champion for the second time. He had decided to retire at the end of the season and Francois Cevert should have replaced him. He was as quick as Jackie. When Francois died, we had nothing and had to start over again with two drivers who did not have enough experience. We never got back to where we were.»*

The 17 Grand Prix

A world championship is not just a tale of a fight between two star drivers. 17 Grand Prix each have their own atmosphere and tales to tell, along with anecdotes and moments of joy and disappointment. Action!

Marlboro
Marlboro
Marlboro
5
Marlboro
Shell
EAGLE
GOODYEAR
05-10

West
BOSS

The return of the silver arrows

A surprise in Melbourne. Confounding all the experts, it was David Coulthard and his McLaren-Mercedes who won the opening round of the season. The English team had been waiting since 1993 for this victory.
Williams should have won, but for Jacques Villeneuve being forced into an error by Eddie Irvine and Heinz-Harald Frentzen sidelined by his team running the wrong size brake discs. For the Grove boys, this was the first in a long line of mistakes.

QANTAS AUSTRALIAN GRAND PRIX MELBOURNE

First cliff hanger

Traditionally, a whole host of winter test sessions at Estoril or other warm weather tracks allowed teams and pundits alike to get a feel for the coming season's pecking order.
However, this year, stricter rules regarding testing meant that the teams had split their activities over several circuits to fine tune their 1997 challengers.
This meant that very few head to head or team to team confrontations had taken place to produce an obvious hierarchy in the run up to the Australian Grand Prix.
Everyone was in the dark, so that the first day of practice in Melbourne was preceded by eager and impatient expectation. Would the Williams-Renaults confirm their positions as favourites? Would Frentzen live up to his reputation? How would the Ferraris and Benettons go?
At lunchtime on Friday, after the first practice session, the order showed that Jean Alesi was in front, ahead of Michael Schumacher, Jacques Villeneuve and Ralf Schumacher. Four different cars in the top four places promised an exciting season ahead.

Wash your mouth out Michael

By the end of the afternoon, Michael Schumacher was credited with the fastest time and the German was going to have to wash his mouth out for lying to us. Over the past few weeks, he had been claiming that his Ferrari was so uncompetitive that he would be unable to make it to the podium in the first half of the season. Looking at the time sheet, it seemed he had been deliberately trying to dupe the opposition as to his car's true potential. *«The car worked a lot better than I expected,»* confessed the double world champion. *«The handling imbalance we suffered from last year has gone completely. For sure it is good to be out in front, but today does not mean much so we should not jump to conclusions.»*
The forty or so German journalists who had made the trip to Melbourne were happy with the day's result as right behind Michael Schumacher came his fellow countryman, Heinz-Harald Frentzen.

Heinz ahead of Jacques

If there was one duel everyone was eagerly awaiting this season, it was the battle between the two Williams-Renault drivers, Heinz-Harald Frentzen and Jacques Villeneuve.
On Friday, Round 1 had gone to the German, who was second fastest just behind Michael Schumacher. He did not seem prepared to gloat. *«I have nothing to get excited about, finishing ahead of Jacques,»* he revealed. *«Especially as I don't know what set-up he was running.»*
Nevertheless, the smile on his face showed that Frentzen was happy with his first day in the office. *«I am starting a new life with Williams and I was rather nervous this morning. What does impress me is that I am so high up the order after putting in the same sort of effort that gave me a mid-grid position last season.»*

△ *Michael Schumacher was third on the grid, but he was a whopping 2.1 seconds behind Jacques Villeneuve. He had taken a pasting. «Of course the tyres could be a factor. The only thing I know about the Williams tyres is that they are black! I am surprised. I expected a one second gap, but not two.»*

The McLarens are coming

Friday had been a nightmare for them. However, come the hour of qualifying on Saturday, the two McLaren-Mercedes were suddenly up the front, with David Coulthard and Mika Hakkinen on the second and third rows of the grid respectively. *«I quickly realised that I could beat Michael's (Schumacher) time,»* claimed the Scotsman. *«But unfortunately I didn't manage to string a good lap together and then I had a slight off on what could have been my quickest lap. That's why he is ahead of me.»*
Traffic was Hakkinen's downfall. *«The split times on my last lap looked excellent, but I was slowed by another car in the final part of the lap. At least the changes we have made to the balance of the car since yesterday are beginning to pay off, but we still have a long way to go.»* It was a good day for Ron Dennis. *«Without the traffic we would have been third and fourth.»* And if they had been the only cars on the track they could have been first and second!

«That's it. If I make a mess of F1, I'll be a rock star.» Jan Magnussen explains his career plan to Paul Stewart and former Beatle, George Harrison (on left.) ▽

«Hi Thierry!» In great good humour, Damon Hill waves at our photographer. For his first grand prix with Arrows, the Englishman was up against it. Either his car broke down or it was going very slowly and the world champion only just managed to qualify it in 20th place in the dying moments of the session. He could take heart from the tumultuous applause which accompanied his efforts. ▽

Jacques Villeneuve demoralises the opposition

Jacques Villeneuve lived up to expectations. Widely tipped as favourite to walk away with the first grand prix, not to mention this year's title, he duly delivered an amazing pole position, over two seconds faster than the rest of the field.

There was no doubt he had put in a fantastic lap, although Villeneuve himself was not convinced. *«Of course I tried as hard as I could,"* he said. *"But the lap could have been better if I hadn't made a mistake. I suppose it's impossible to do a perfect lap when you are pushing as hard as you can.»*

Of course the big question was which of the two tyre compounds the Canadian had used in qualifying, in the knowledge that these were the type of tyre he would have to commit to for the race. *«I cannot tell you that,»* continued Villeneuve. *«But it does not matter, because even if I was on soft tyres, the others might have been doing the same. I have to say that practice is made more difficult and more complicated because of this tyre business. We spend a lot of time comparing the different types of tyre rather than thinking about the chassis and its set- up.»*

The Canadian had no particular worries about the next day's race. *«I don't have any major problems. The car seems to be going well, even if I cannot be sure how it will go tomorrow. I have to do some work on the brakes, because after two laps in practice the pedal is like a sponge.»*

Both happy and sad

Heinz-Harald Frentzen had put up the second fastest time in qualifying, but he had a close shave. With three minutes to go before the end of the session, he was only eighth. *«I was very unlucky this afternoon,»* he said. *«And to be honest, I am not very happy with my second place. On my first set of tyres I ran into a lot of traffic and on my second set, the tyres seemed to die on me, but I do not know why. When I went out again for my third run, the red flag came out. I thought this was not going to be my lucky day, but I got a fourth run in, which was just about acceptable.»*

Despite this tale of woe, the German admitted he would have had a hard time beating Villeneuve's lap. *«I think it would have been impossible to make up 1.7 seconds. Jacques did a very good time and I will be very interested to have a look at his telemetry readings. All the same, second is my best ever qualifying position and I am very happy.»*

◁ *«You will let me have a copy won't you?» On Thursday, Michael Schumacher seems happy to take part in the traditional first day of term photo.*

Five seconds from the promised land

In recent times, we have often seen teams arrive in Formula 1 which have more in common with the Keystone Cops than with motor racing. One only has to think back to the days of Monteverdi, Andrea Moda or Life; all teams who have now passed into oblivion.

One could be forgiven for thinking that F1, 1997 style had evolved and was now serious enough as a sport to escape this type of joke, but here came Lola to prove us all wrong. Despite giving every appearance of having the wherewithal to go the distance and wheeling out two cars which looked well prepared, Lola immediately got a sharp lesson in just how competitive and unforgiving is the world of F1 these days. On Saturday, Vincenzo Sospiri and Riccardo Rosset were a massive five seconds off the pace- not off the pole position time mind you, but five seconds off the 107% barrier. It was bad enough for them to have travelled all the way to Australia and then miss the cut for the grid, but there was far worse to come. The team's title sponsor, Mastercard decided to throw in the towel immediately. This seemed a strange decision in light of the team's brave predictions at the time of its launch when they proclaimed they intended being in a position to challenge for the championship within four years, a period which corresponded to the deal signed between Lola and Mastercard.

The team had folded before it even had time to unpack its bags.

"Riccardo, how on earth could you think we even stood a chance?" Vincenzo Sospiri seems to accept his non-qualification with good grace. He was unaware this was already the end of the line.

STARTING GRID

Left	Row	Right
		Jacques VILLENEUVE 1'29"369
Heinz-H. FRENTZEN 1'31"123	-1-	
		M. SCHUMACHER 1'31"472
David COULTHARD 1'31"531	-2-	
		Eddie IRVINE 1'31"881
Mika HAKKINEN 1'31"971	-3-	
		Johnny HERBERT 1'32"287
Jean ALESI 1'32"593	-4-	
		Olivier PANIS 1'32"842
Gerhard BERGER 1'32"870	-5-	
		R. BARRICHELLO 1'33"075
R. SCHUMACHER 1'33"130	-6-	
		Nicola LARINI 1'33"327
G. FISICHELLA 1'33"552	-7-	
		Ukyo KATAYAMA 1'33"798
Shinji NAKANO 1'33"989	-8-	
		Jarno TRULLI 1'34"120
Mika SALO 1'34"229	-9-	
		Jan MAGNUSSEN 1'34"623
Damon HILL 1'34"806	-10-	
		Jos VERSTAPPEN 1'34"943
Pedro DINIZ 1'35"972	-11-	

△ A surprise win for David Coulthard in this the first grand prix of the season. The Scotsman made the most of his opportunities and had a good strategy.

▷ «And another swig for Mummy.» David Coulthard drank his fill of champagne and more, on the Melbourne podium.

Business as usual in the streets of Melbourne. The capital of the state of Victoria seemed less interested in the grand prix than they had been in 1996. ▽

David Coulthard wakes Ron Dennis from his bad dream

«The colour silver is not ours by right. If the cars happen to be that colour, then they must win to merit the title!» Mercedes Motor Sport Director Norbert Haug did not realise how prescient were his words when he said this at the February launch of the new McLaren livery. The famous Silver Arrows pulled out of F1 in 1955, immediately after winning the Italian Grand Prix. 42 years later, the German marque's favourite colour returned to the track with its winning ways intact. A coincidence which, in the heat of the moment, Norbert Haug interpreted as a sign from the heavens. *«It's incredible, it's sensational!»* he babbled, surrounded by a pack of journalists. *«Everything went perfectly today. Nobody made a single mistake.»*
Indeed, David Coulthard's race had been exemplary and he was undoubtedly the hero of the hour. With Jacques Villeneuve out of the running (see opposite) the Scotsman set off on a charge, finishing the first lap in second place behind Heinz-Harald Frentzen.*«I made a good start,»* he said. *«Then I got more and more confident. I was talking to the team over the radio and gradually we realised we could do something special here today.»*
McLaren made the right choice in deciding to make only pit-stop, as it was only when Frentzen made his second visit to the pits that David Coulthard had the race in the bag. *«It was lucky for us that Williams did not choose the same strategy,»* continued the Scot. *«Because, to be honest, if they had done, then Heinz-Harald would have won.»*
Once in the lead the McLaren driver won as he pleased, keeping an occasional eye in his mirrors for Michael Schumacher in second place. *«I never thought this could happen to me, but as I came up to the finish line, I started to cry with emotion,»* added David. *«We had been under such huge pressure in the team that this result was fantastic.»*

Hakkinen wants more

On the third step of the podium, Mika Hakkinen gave the Anglo-German alliance further cause for celebration. *«Of course I would rather have been standing where David was,»* joked the Finn. *«But I am very happy all the same. This is a great result for the team. You will see that we will be fighting like this all season now. McLaren and Mercedes will surprise you.»*
McLaren had not tasted victory since Ayrton Senna did the business in the 1993 Australian Grand Prix, 49 grands prix ago. However for Mercedes it was their first win in the modern era. *«I think we will have a very good party tonight,»* said Mario Ilien, Swiss engineer and father of the Mercedes V10. A glass of champagne in his hand, a smile that stretched from ear to ear, Ilien was also celebrating his first ever F1 win.
However, without a doubt, the happiest man of all was Ron Dennis. The boss has often admitted he is physically in pain when his team does not win. In Melbourne David Coulthard finally found the right medicine to ease his master's suffering.

Was it down to the track?

This first race of the season had been a Formula 1 feast. In light of the tussles we had witnessed between McLaren, Ferrari and Williams one was entitled to expect 1997 to produce a cracking season of races.
In the past few years, Formula 1 had suffered too often from the dominance of one single team. After Melbourne it seemed that someone had finally given the cards a proper shuffle. Jacques Villeneuve may well have started as favourite, but there were no guarantees that he would have won the race had he survived the first corner, while his team-mate Heinz Harald Frentzen showed the limitations of Williams's two stop strategy and demonstrated that they had brake problems; problems which Villeneuve had already come up against in practise.
With just the Australian Grand Prix to go on, one had every right to expect a close fought season, even though certain expert pundits were adding a note of caution to this suggestion. *»It would be best not draw any hasty conclusions after this race,»* cautioned Renault's chief engineer Bernard Dudot. *«You have to bear in mind that Melbourne is a one-off as a circuit and does not necessarily show where the balance of power will lie on the classic tracks.»*
For the Frenchman, this race had all been done by mirrors, which masked the superiority of the Williams-Renault. It had simply been a bad day for the team. The rest of the season would prove him wrong. The FW19 might well have been the best car, but the team would go on to make enough errors to offset that.

Fate gives Williams a pasting

During practice, everything had gone like clockwork. Jacques Villeneuve had taken pole position and Heinz-Harald Frentzen had qualified alongside him. The signs were good and the race seemed a mere formality for the Williams-Renault team.
However, at the start, Villeneuve got too much wheelspin and messed up his start. With Frentzen having taken the lead, the Canadian found himself at the first corner, wedged between Johnny Herbert's Sauber and Eddie Irvine's Ferrari. The inevitable collision ensued and Villeneuve was out of the race.
Once back in the pits, the Canadian was spitting bullets. *«Irvine came alongside me like a mad man,»* he explained. *«He locked his wheels and we touched. There was no way his move could have worked and I cannot believe he tried it.»* Having said his piece he went off in search of Irvine who simply shrugged his shoulders. *«I was on the inside, Villeneuve was on the outside,»* he explained later. *«I was clearly in front so it was definitely my corner. Jacques should have known it is impossible to overtake on the outside.»*

△ *«Go David go.» The huge crowd surrounding the podium did not seem to care who had won. For them, the grand prix was just an excuse to stage one long party.*

A very rare failure

Heinz-Harald Frentzen might have been able to save the day for Williams and at the start of the race he was comfortably in the lead. *«It was the first time I have ever led a grand prix and I was telling myself that my parents must be watching me on television so I had better not make a mistake! The car was well balanced but I had a big problem with the brakes. I knew they would be on the limit anyway so I tried to look after them by occasionally slowing the pace a bit. But I was on a two stop strategy and when I realised that Coulthard and Schumacher were only stopping once, I had to push again.»*
At his second pit-stop, the right rear wheel on his Williams would not budge and the eight seconds lost were enough to relegate «HH» to third. *«From then on, I had to go flat out if I was to have any chance of winning,»* he continued. *«I tried but suddenly the left front brake disc broke and that was it.»*
A broken brake disc is a very rare occurrence - it only happened once the previous season. As far as Carbone Industrie are concerned, the fault lay with Williams. *«These days, engineers don't give the brakes a second thought,»* reflected Jean-Luc Etcheverry, a technician with the French company. *«Along with Montreal, Melbourne is the toughest track for brakes. It was imperative for the teams to fit our biggest brakes with a 30mm thickness. However, the Williams calipers could only accommodate a 28 mm disc. It is hardly surprising that one of them failed.»* Frentzen was forced to retire just three laps from the flag.

«My dear Jacques, I don't think Eddie Irvine is going to help your cause in the championship battle.» Johnny Herbert and Jacques Villeneuve, having both suffered at the hands of the Irishman, walk back to the pits. Both had missed out on a good chance of a podium finish. ▽

Michael Schumacher already on the pace

Ferrari's Sporting Director Jean Todt had every right to wear his high days and holidays smile after Michael Schumacher finished second and proved that the Scuderia would be a force to be reckoned with this season. *«I could not have wished for more,»* admitted the German. *«These six points are a perfect way to start the season.»*
Michael Schumacher tucked in behind David Coulthard's McLaren right from the start, but never managed to get past him. *«I thought I was quicker than David,»* he said. *«Because every time I dropped back a few metres I was easily able to close the gap again. But it is really impossible to overtake on this track.»*
The Ferrari driver was running second when he was called in to the pits for an unscheduled second stop as a technical problem meant that the full load of fuel had not gone into the tank at the first attempt. *«At first, when the team radioed me to come in, I could not believe it. I asked them if it was me they were talking to! I immediately thought I was going to lose my second place, but in the end, the extra stop did not change anything."*

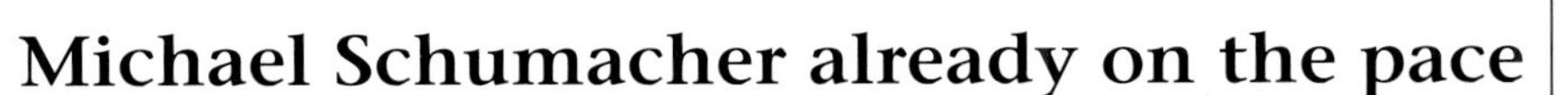

▽ *And they're off for another season. Some however will not get far: Jacques Villeneuve's race ended in Johnny Herbert's Sauber, while out in front, Heinz-Harald leads from the eventual race winner.*

IN THE POINTS

1.	David COULTHARD	West McLaren Mercedes	1 h 30'28"718
2.	M. SCHUMACHER	Scuderia Ferrari Marlboro	at 20"046
3.	Mika HAKKINEN	West McLaren Mercedes	at 22"177
4.	Gerhard BERGER	Mild Seven Benetton Renault	at 22"841
5.	Olivier PANIS	Prost Gauloises Blondes	at 1'00"308
6.	Nicola LARINI	Red Bull Sauber Petronas	at 1'36"040

Fastest lap : H.-H. FRENTZEN, lap 36, 1'30"585, avg. 210,710 km/h

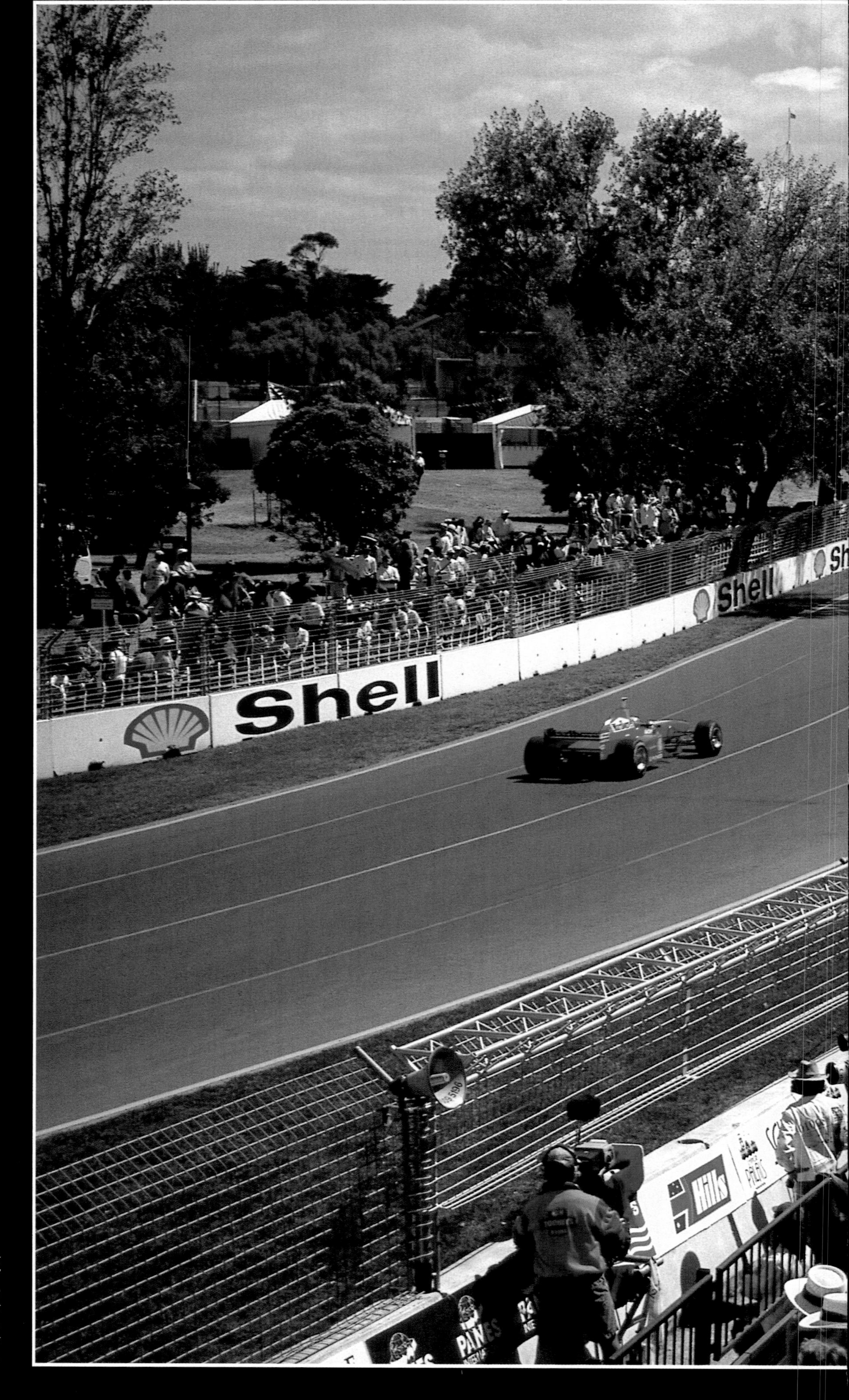

"Enjoy your meal, ladies and gentlemen and please accept our apologies for the dreadful noise from these cars." What passes for High Society in Melbourne had turned out in droves for the Grand Prix at Albert Park. Nothing but the best was good enough for them.
There was something of an old colonial atmosphere, not found at any other race.

Shell

The twelve labours of Alain Prost have begun

▷ Alain Prost with Hirotoshi Honda and the team's general manager, Bruno Michel. This trio were soon to set the sparks flying on a regular basis, starting with fifth place in the Australian Grand Prix.

Running a Formula 1 team is no easy task. In Melbourne, Alain Prost, four times world champion and brand new owner of the team - he took over the reins on 14th February - was beginning to come to terms with the enormity of the task which faced him.
He was not really all smiles. Prost spent his first few days as a team owner running hither and thither, from the garage to the pit wall and from the briefing room to the team's computer screens.
All the while having to deal with questions from his mechanics, his backers or those who wished to be his backers. *«Running a team is very tiring,»* he sighed. *«It might not be noticeable from the outside, but one is under enormous pressure. My heart skipped a beat when I saw the car go out on the track for the first time on Friday and it nearly stopped completely when I saw the same car go off the track a few moments later!»*

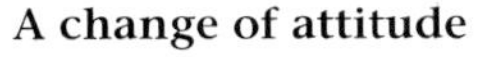

A change of attitude

The Frenchman admitted that, for the moment, his sole aim was to change the team's mental attitude. *«I still have an awful lot to learn,»* he admitted. *«First and foremost I want to turn Prost Grand Prix into a winning team. Changing the team's mentality is a long and arduous process that can only be done step by step. A winning attitude is one that asks itself every day, how it can get better. This might only be a question of words but it is very important all the same.»*
Constantly in demand, with his mobile 'phone ringing incessantly, Alain Prost has not had a moment to plan his future. *«I am exhausted, but at the moment I am not too keen on delegating. I want to be at the centre of every decision. The hardest part is thinking about both the short term and the long term. I have to keep the team going on a day to day basis, but also look to the future.»*
This means, amongst other matters, employing a technical director. Naturally one's thoughts turn to the former Ferrari designer, John Barnard. *«I have to admit I am talking to him,»* confirmed Prost. *«But he is not the only one. In a few weeks time I will be able to say more on the subject.»*

Two points take the pressure off

On Saturday, Olivier Panis qualified his Prost Mugen-Honda in ninth place on the grid. Not bad at a first attempt.
Then on Sunday came the apotheosis. In the morning, Olivier was fourth quickest in the warm-up, which was held in cool conditions and therefore favoured the Bridgestone runners. He then went on to finish fifth that afternoon, behind four Goodyear runners. He was the best placed Bridgestone runner, which was more than enough to please his new boss. *«To be honest, a few points for Olivier with Shinji* (Nakano) *not too far behind, is just what I had hoped for,»* exclaimed Prost after the race. *«Given the circumstances it was my ideal scenario. The team was under terrible pressure this weekend and the mechanics wanted, at all costs, to prove to me their worth. They wanted to prove that the results of winter testing had not been fluked and these two points have given us a bit of breathing space. They will also cement our relationship with Honda and Bridgestone. We could not have asked for more.»*
The fifth place came as a result of a cautious race strategy. *«I did not want to take any risks,»* added Prost. *«We were a bit on the limit as far as the tyres were concerned and I preferred to play it safe by going for two stops. Watching the race from the pit wall was honestly a trial. I was never so stressed in all my time as a driver.»* The result was not enough to tempt Prost to rest on his laurels. *«On the contrary, we are going to push harder now, as it is March and it will soon be time to get the new car under way. Above all, these two points will not change my strategy. We should not get carried away by this quick result and we have to concentrate on the task that lies ahead.»*
Whether behind the wheel or driving the boss' desk, it was clear that Alain Prost was still the Professor.

▷ Jean Alesi on the way to one of the biggest mistakes of his career. Just before his retirement he had moved up from fifth to second in the space of four laps.

Jean Alesi runs out of fuel

The race has just ended. From outside come the echoes of David Coulthard's victory celebrations. But inside the Benetton garage, you can hear a pin drop. Jean Alesi and Flavio Briatore stand facing one another staring at the floor. Neither of them breathes a word.
For both of them, it has been a bitter pill to swallow. On lap 35, while running in second place, the man from Avignon ran out of fuel. He had quite simply not seen the pit-board hung out by his team, telling him to come in and refuel.
The last time he came past the pits, Nick Wirth, already an imposingly tall figure, had actually stood on the pit wall in a vain attempt to attract the driver's attention. It was to no avail. "Once again, I'm going to be taken for an idiot," lamented Alesi after the race. "It is not the case. I was in the middle of a tough fight and I just did not see it. Normally I am told when it is time to pit over the radio, but it had been broken since the start of the race!" The Frenchman could not explain why he had not noticed the warning signs on his dashboard, nor how he could forget to refuel as he saw himself move up the running order as others came in to the pits one after the other.
Flavio Briatore did not want to talk about it. "In any case, we wasted two days trying to find a good set-up. It is a weekend to forget," he muttered between gritted teeth. Evidently, Gerhard Berger's fourth place was not enough to console him.

«At least I cannot crash into Irvine if I am on foot.» On the Wednesday before the race, Jacques Villeneuve does a reconnaissance lap of the track. ▽

PRACTICE TIMES

No	Driver	Make/Engine/Chassis	Practice Friday	Practice Saturday	Qualifying	Warm-up
1.	Damon HIll	Arrows/Yamaha/A18/3 (B)	1'35"073	1'34"640	1'34"806	1'33"394
2.	Pedro Diniz	Arrows/Yamaha/A18/2 (B)	1'38"092	1'33"693	1'35"972	1'33"735
3.	Jacques Villeneuve	Williams/Renault/FW18/1 (G)	1'33"371	1'28"594	1'29"369	1'31"235
4.	Heinz-Harald Frentzen	Williams/Renault/FW18/2 (G)	1'32"910	1'30"026	1'31"123	1'31"353
5.	Michael Schumacher	Ferrari/Ferrari/F310B/174 (G)	1'32"496	1'30"682	1'31"472	1'32"586
6.	Eddie Irvine	Ferrari/Ferrari/F310B/173 (G)	1'34"157	1'30"651	1'31"881	1'32"908
7.	Jean Alesi	Benetton/Renault/B197/5 (G)	1'33"255	1'31"635	1'32"593	1'34"113
8.	Gerhard Berger	Benetton/Renault/B197/4 (G)	1'34"271	1'31"389	1'32"870	1'32"939
9.	Mika Hakkinen	McLaren/Mercedes/MP4/12/2 (G)	1'34"742	1'30"674	1'31"971	1'32"537
10.	David Coulthard	McLaren/Mercedes/MP4/12/3 (G)	1'34"432	1'30"305	1'31"531	1'32"091
11.	Ralf Schumacher	Jordan/Peugeot/197/3 (G)	1'33"437	1'31"071	1'33"130	1'32"704
12.	Giancarlo Fisichella	Jordan/Peugeot/197/2 (G)	1'34"777	1'32"027	1'33"552	1'32"394
14.	Olivier Panis	Prost/Mugen Honda/JS45/3 (B)	1'34"927	1'31"303	1'32"842	1'31"674
15.	Shinji Nakano	Prost/Mugen Honda/JS45/2 (B)	1'39"652	1'33"415	1'33"989	1'33"897
16.	Johnny Herbert	Sauber/Petronas/C16/3 (G)	1'34"593	1'31"197	1'32"287	1'31"512
17.	Nicola Larini	Sauber/Petronas/C16/2 (G)	1'36"223	1'31"281	1'33"327	1'33"109
18.	Jos Verstappen	Tyrrell/Ford/025/2 (G)	1'36"716	1'33"679	1'34"943	1'33"832
19.	Mika Salo	Tyrrell/Ford/025/3 (G)	1'36"142	1'33"194	1'34"229	1'33"339
20.	Ukyo Katayama	Minardi/Hart/M197/3 (B)	1'40"947	1'32"264	1'33"798	1'34"902
21.	Jarno Trulli	Minardi/Hart/M197/2 (B)	1'36"392	1'33"588	1'34"120	1'40"623
22.	Rubens Barrichello	Stewart/Ford/SF1/2 (B)	1'40"002	1'32"826	1'33"075	1'32"989
23.	Jan Magnussen	Stewart/Ford/SF1/3 (B)	1'37"023	1'33"767	1'34"623	1'34"162
24.	Vincenzo Sospiri	Lola/Ford/T95/30/3 (B)	1'42"590	1'44"286	1'40"972	not qualif.
25.	Ricardo Rosset	Lola/Ford/T95/30/2 (B)	1'41"166	1'41"416	1'42"086	not qualif.

LAP CHART

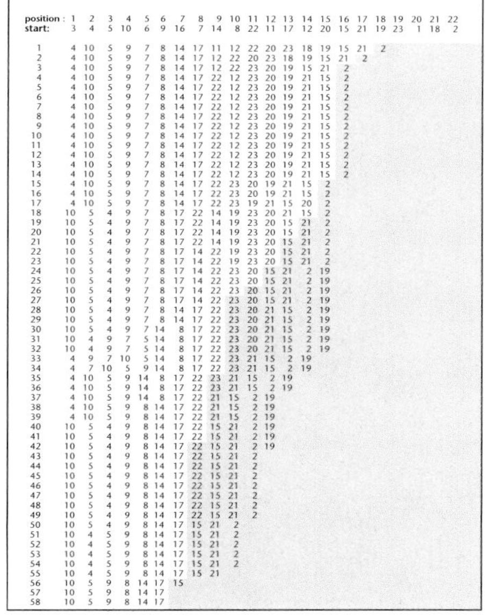

position :	1	2	3	4	5	6	7	8	9	10	11	12	13	14	15	16	17	18	19	20	21	22
start:	3	4	5	10	6	9	16	7	14	8	22	11	17	12	20	15	21	19	23	1	18	2
1	4	10	5	9	7	8	14	17	11	12	22	20	23	18	19	15	21	2				
2	4	10	5	9	7	8	14	17	12	22	20	23	18	19	15	21	2					
3	4	10	5	9	7	8	14	17	12	22	23	20	19	15	21	2						
4	4	10	5	9	7	8	14	17	22	12	23	20	19	21	15	2						
5	4	10	5	9	7	8	14	17	22	12	23	20	19	21	15	2						
6	4	10	5	9	7	8	14	17	22	12	23	20	19	21	15	2						
7	4	10	5	9	7	8	14	17	22	12	23	20	19	21	15	2						
8	4	10	5	9	7	8	14	17	22	12	23	20	19	21	15	2						
9	4	10	5	9	7	8	14	17	22	12	23	20	19	21	15	2						
10	4	10	5	9	7	8	14	17	22	12	23	20	19	21	15	2						
11	4	10	5	9	7	8	14	17	22	12	23	20	19	21	15	2						
12	4	10	5	9	7	8	14	17	22	12	23	20	19	21	15	2						
13	4	10	5	9	7	8	14	17	22	12	23	20	19	21	15	2						
14	4	10	5	9	7	8	14	17	22	12	23	20	19	21	15	2						
15	4	10	5	9	7	8	14	17	22	23	20	19	21	15	2							
16	4	10	5	9	7	8	14	17	22	23	20	19	21	15	2							
17	4	10	5	9	7	8	14	17	22	23	19	21	15	20	2							
18	10	5	4	9	7	8	17	22	14	19	23	20	21	15	2							
19	10	5	4	9	7	8	17	22	14	19	23	20	15	21	2							
20	10	5	4	9	7	8	17	22	14	19	23	20	15	21	2							
21	10	5	4	9	7	8	17	22	14	19	23	20	15	21	2							
22	10	5	4	9	7	8	17	14	22	19	23	20	15	21	2							
23	10	5	4	9	7	8	17	14	22	19	23	20	15	21	2							
24	10	5	4	9	7	8	17	14	22	23	20	15	21	2	19							
25	10	5	4	9	7	8	17	14	22	23	20	15	21	2	19							
26	10	5	4	9	7	8	17	14	22	23	20	15	21	2	19							
27	10	5	4	9	7	8	17	14	22	23	20	15	21	2	19							
28	10	5	4	9	7	8	14	17	22	23	20	21	15	2	19							
29	10	5	4	9	7	8	14	17	22	23	20	21	15	2	19							
30	10	5	4	9	7	14	8	17	22	23	20	21	15	2	19							
31	10	4	9	7	5	14	8	17	22	23	20	21	15	2	19							
32	10	4	9	7	5	14	8	17	22	23	20	21	15	2	19							
33	4	9	7	10	5	14	8	17	22	23	21	15	2	19								
34	4	7	10	5	9	14	8	17	22	23	21	15	2	19								
35	4	10	5	9	14	8	17	22	23	21	15	2	19									
36	4	10	5	9	14	8	17	22	23	21	15	2	19									
37	4	10	5	9	14	8	17	22	21	15	2	19										
38	4	10	5	9	8	14	17	22	21	15	2	19										
39	4	10	5	9	8	14	17	22	21	15	2	19										
40	10	5	4	9	8	14	17	22	15	21	2	19										
41	10	5	4	9	8	14	17	22	15	21	2	19										
42	10	5	4	9	8	14	17	22	15	21	2	19										
43	10	5	4	9	8	14	17	22	15	21	2											
44	10	5	4	9	8	14	17	22	15	21	2											
45	10	5	4	9	8	14	17	22	15	21	2											
46	10	5	4	9	8	14	17	22	15	21	2											
47	10	5	4	9	8	14	17	22	15	21	2											
48	10	5	4	9	8	14	17	22	15	21	2											
49	10	5	4	9	8	14	17	22	15	21	2											
50	10	5	4	9	8	14	17	15	21	2												
51	10	4	5	9	8	14	17	15	21	2												
52	10	4	5	9	8	14	17	15	21	2												
53	10	4	5	9	8	14	17	15	21	2												
54	10	4	5	9	8	14	17	15	21	2												
55	10	4	5	9	8	14	17	15	21													
56	10	5	9	8	14	17	15															
57	10	5	9	8	14	17																
58	10	5	9	8	14	17																

BRIDGESTONE

Best result for a Bridgestone shod runner:

Olivier Panis, Prost Mugen Honda, *5th*

CLASSIFICATION & RETIREMENTS

Pos	Driver	Team	Time
1.	Coulthard	McLaren Mercedes	in 1h30'28"718
2.	Schumacher	Ferrari	at 20"046
3.	Hakkinen	McLaren Mercedes	at 22"177
4.	Berger	Benetton Renault	at 22"841
5.	Panis	Prost Mugen Honda	at 1'00"308
6.	Larini	Sauber Petronas	at 1'36"040
7.	Nakano	Prost Mugen Honda	at 2 laps
8.	Frentzen	Williams Renault	brake
9.	Trulli	Minardi Hart	at 3 laps
10.	Diniz	Arrows Yamaha	at 4 laps

Lap	Driver	Team	Reason
1	Hill	Arrows Yamaha	throttle
1	Herbert	Sauber Petronas	accident
1	Villeneuve	Williams Renault	accident
1	Irvine	Ferrari	puncture
2	Schumacher	Jordan Peugeot	gearbox
3	Vestappen	Tyrrell Ford	off
13	Fisichella	Jordan Peugeot	off
31	Katayama	Minardi Hart	fuel supply
33	Alesi	Benetton Renault	out of fuel
35	Magnussen	Stewart Ford	handling
41	Salo	Tyrrell Ford	engine
48	Barrichello	Stewart Ford	oil pressure

FASTEST LAPS

	Driver	Time	Lap
1.	Frentzen	1'30"585	36
2.	M. Schum.	1'31"067	54
3.	Coulthard	1'31"412	29
4.	Hakkinen	1'31"509	33
5.	Berger	1'31"624	54
6.	Panis	1'31"762	40
7.	Alesi	1'31"976	33
8.	Larini	1'32"784	27
9.	Barrichello	1'33"386	24
10.	Fisichella	1'34"147	14
11.	Nakano	1'34"171	52
12.	Salo	1'34"194	22
13.	Diniz	1'34"465	23
14.	Katayama	1'34"918	14
15.	Magnussen	1'35"257	26
16.	Trulli	1'35"959	21
17.	Verstappen	1'37"038	2
18.	R. Schum.	1'48"323	1

FIRST ROUND

QANTAS AUSTRALIAN GRAND PRIX, MELBOURNE

Date : March 9, 1997
Length: 5302 meters
Distance : 58 laps, 307.516 km
Weather: sunny, 24 degrees

CHAMPIONSHIPS

(after one round)

Drivers:

1. David COULTHARD 10
2. M. SCHUMACHER 6
3. Mika HAKKINEN 4
4. Gerhard BERGER 3
5. Olivier PANIS 2
6. Nicola LARINI 1

Constructors :

1. McLaren / Mercedes 14
2. Ferrari 6
3. Benetton / Renault 3
4. Prost / Mugen Honda 2
5. Sauber / Petronas 1

RACE SUMMARY

- Damon Hill retires on the formation lap.
- At the start, Heinz-Harald Frentzen takes the lead, while Eddie Irvine pushes Jacques Villeneuve and Johnny Herbert onto the grass. All three of them retired.
- In the early stages, Frentzen pulls away from Coulthard, Michael Schumacher, Hakkinen and the two Benettons.
- Frentzen pits as early as lap 18, letting Coulthard into the lead. The German will not regain the lead until lap 33, when the McLarens refuelled.
- On lap 35, while in second place behind Frentzen, Alesi runs out of fuel.
- On lap 40, Coulthard is guaranteed his first place when Frentzen makes his second pit stop.
- Frentzen retires with three laps to go with a broken brake disc. Coulthard wins from Michael Schumacher and Hakkinen.

WEEK-END GOSSIP

- **Ten million lost**

The Melbourne transport Trade Union voted for a total strike over the grand prix weekend, from twelve midnight on Friday to the same time on Sunday. For the race organisers, this meant that the public would not be able to use the free tram service which they had organised and which had carried a record 490,000 people in 1996. On Thursday, there were already one third less spectators than the previous year. On each day they lost 20,000 people, while race day was a catastrophe, with entire grandstands occupied by just five or six people. It was obvious that the organisers were going to make a loss, estimated at ten million Australian dollars, around five million pounds. The loss therefore had to be absorbed by the government of the State of Victoria.

- **The Concorde discord continues**

The Concorde agreement was still in the news. On Saturday, McLaren boss Ron Dennis, explained that his team along with the other dissidents, Frank Williams and Ken Tyrrell, were taking the matter to the civil courts, adding that, *«The whole of Formula 1 would suffer.»* He confirmed that he was ready to reveal the reasons for the disagreement which revolved around the 13 million dollars which the teams receive on an annual basis in exchange for the television rights. It seemed that at the moment, when the FIA asked the teams to sign the relevant agreements, the financial terms were not made clear.

Eight days later, when the final deadline had passed, the teams who had signed were presented with a very good deal, but for Williams, Tyrrell and McLaren it was already too late. *«Normally, you don't sign anything without knowing the details. That is what we were being asked to do. Now that everything is out in the open we cannot get back in on the deal. It's ridiculous,»* complained Frank Williams.

Two weeks before the Australian Grand Prix, the signatory teams could not reach unanimity on letting the rebels back in.

Naturally they did not want to divvy up the kitty into ten parts when they previously thought it was only going to be split seven ways.

- **Williams get all hyped up**

The Williams team announced a new sponsor in the shape of energy drink Hype. They could hardly keep quiet about it as the fluorescent orange and yellow Hype logos on the sides of the FW19 could be seem from the far end of the circuit.

«Ooh that tickles!» Bernie Ecclestone will not let just anyone kiss him on his forehead, but when the person in question is Elle «The Body» McPherson, then why not? The Australian super model was just one of the many celebrities to be seen in the Melbourne paddock, along with Prince Albert of Monaco.

West
COMPUTER ASSOCIATES
Benz
West

From winner to loser

For the McLaren drivers, no two grands prix were the same. After taking victory in Melbourne, the team was completely off the pace in Brazil. David Coulthard could only qualify tenth and Mika Hakkinen, 17th (see photo.)
Jacques Villeneuve seized his opportunity in the second race of the season and took pole position, victory and the fastest lap of the race. The Canadian was never challenged, even though his car was far from perfect. The Brazilian round also gave Olivier Panis cause for celebration, as he finished third. It was his first podium finish since Monaco 1996.
Apart from the McLarens, Interlagos also highlighted some other weaknesses in the pack. Heinz-Harald Frentzen looked lost and finished ninth. At Ferrari, Michael Schumacher was never on the pace and took just two points for fifth place.

Giving it plenty, Giancarlo Fisichella qualified seventh at Interlagos. In Australia, the Italian had been beaten by his team-mate Ralf Schumacher, but here he had the upper hand. It looked as though competition would be fierce between these two young lions.

Panis by 8.5 centimetres

This qualifying session was one of the closest in the history of F1, with eight drivers in the same second and the top five drivers in five different makes of car.
Overall, just three seconds barely separated the Williams of Jacques Villeneuve on pole from Mika Salo in the tail-end Charlie position.
In some instances the gaps were incredibly small. In fifth place on the grid, Olivier Panis had beaten Jean Alesi by just one thousandth of a second.
At the speed these cars were crossing the start/finish line (approximately 305 km/h) the difference equated to a distance of 8.5 centimetres! As best placed Bridgestone runner, Panis' time was still remarkable. *«I've never seen anything like it,»* said Gerhard Berger, commenting on how close it had been, after the session. *«It is really good for the spectators, even if I would have preferred the Benettons to be one second clear of the field!»* At the moment, that looked unlikely, as the Austrian had qualified in third place.

Frank Williams was evidently not too happy with Heinz-Harald Frentzen's poor performance. While Jacques Villeneuve was on pole, the German was only eighth.

Schumacher surprised at his performance

Villeneuve - Schumacher - Berger: the top three in qualifying in Sao Paulo was much more unexpected than the one in Melbourne.
Indeed, Jacques Villeneuve was the only one to have pulled out a semblance of a gap on this extraordinarily tight grid. *«I have to say it is quite difficult to make a difference on this type of circuit»*, he explained. *«It is hard to find a good set-up and to do a good lap, the way you could in Australia. I do not particularly like this track and my car is not perfect, so I am happy to find myself on pole position.»*
A water leak on his car had forced the Canadian to finish the session in the spare car, which was set up for Frentzen.
Despite this, Villeneuve did a quicker time than the German, which put a big smile on his face.
Michael Schumacher, in second place, had not expected to do so well. *«The gap surprises me, as I thought we would be further back. We have made some progress since Australia and this is the result, although we still have big problems over the bumps.»* As for his team-mate, down in 14th place, Michael Schumacher had nothing to say. *«I don't know what happened to him, but I know at least one person who will be happy about it,»* he added, glancing across at Villeneuve sitting next to him, alluding to his coming together with the Irishman in Melbourne.
Gerhard Berger was third for Benetton. *«At least we are back to a more usual situation than we were in Australia,»* rejoiced the Austrian. *«This is the position we expected to be in, taking into account our performance in winter testing. In Melbourne, it was impossible to get the tyres up to a working temperature. The problem is that we have a lot of engineers and each one comes up with a different solution.»*
Berger admitted nevertheless that the situation was not as clear as it seemed. *«The gap between the top ten is so close that you could easily end up second or tenth with an almost identical time.»*

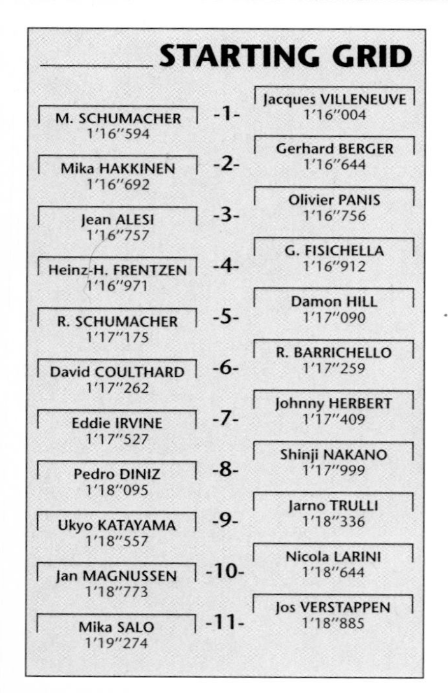

STARTING GRID

	Row	
		Jacques VILLENEUVE 1'16"004
M. SCHUMACHER 1'16"594	-1-	
		Gerhard BERGER 1'16"644
Mika HAKKINEN 1'16"692	-2-	
		Olivier PANIS 1'16"756
Jean ALESI 1'16"757	-3-	
		G. FISICHELLA 1'16"912
Heinz-H. FRENTZEN 1'16"971	-4-	
		Damon HILL 1'17"090
R. SCHUMACHER 1'17"175	-5-	
		R. BARRICHELLO 1'17"259
David COULTHARD 1'17"262	-6-	
		Johnny HERBERT 1'17"409
Eddie IRVINE 1'17"527	-7-	
		Shinji NAKANO 1'17"999
Pedro DINIZ 1'18"095	-8-	
		Jarno TRULLI 1'18"336
Ukyo KATAYAMA 1'18"557	-9-	
		Nicola LARINI 1'18"644
Jan MAGNUSSEN 1'18"773	-10-	
		Jos VERSTAPPEN 1'18"885
Mika SALO 1'19"274	-11-	

Despite his problems, Jacques Villeneuve does the Interlagos grand slam

△ Jacques Villeneuve is caught out by Michael Schumacher when the lights went out. Thanks to his superior top speed, the Canadian passed the German before the end of the first lap.

Sunday follows Sunday, but no two are ever the same for Jacques Villeneuve. Having retired at the first corner in the Australian Grand Prix, three weeks earlier, the Canadian dominated the Brazilian weekend. His Williams-Renault was never really troubled, even if Gerhard Berger closed the gap in the final stages of the race. *«I was worried before the start you know, as I had never won a grand prix from pole position,»* he joked as he came off the podium. Villeneuve had plenty to celebrate, having notched up pole position, victory and the race fastest lap.

While the Canadian came away with every prize here, there could be no denying the fact he had a less than perfect race.
At the first start he had once again got it wrong and Michael Schumacher made the most of it to push him off onto the grass at the first corner.
It was Melbourne all over again. *«What Michael did was not very nice, but I fell for his trap and nearly threw it all away,»* he said. *«When I found myself on the grass I was really angry. That really was a beginner's mistake.»*

Luckily for him, the race was stopped to clear away Magnussen's Stewart, which had stalled. *«That was a lucky break, because not only was I down in ninth place, but also some gravel had got into my seat. It would have made for a very uncomfortable time if the race had carried on.»*
At the re-start, Villeneuve wisely let Schumacher lead round the first corner, before overtaking him down the pit straight. From then on, the man from Quebec pulled out a lead, though not quite as easily as was expected of him. *«I had a lot of problems at the start of the race. We had decided to start with a bit less wing to improve our straight line speed and it made the car difficult to drive through the corners. It got better as the race went on.»*
Despite this fact, the Canadian was being caught by Berger's Benetton in the final stages of the race. *«That was because my third set of tyres was not good,»* explained Jacques. *«The car was sliding a lot. If Gerhard had caught me, I would have been in trouble.»*

First start, first corner: Jacques Villeneuve went onto the grass and it was mayhem at the back of the class.

«Job done!» Villeneuve takes his first win of the season in Sao Paulo. ▽

IN THE POINTS

	Driver	Team	Time
1.	Jacques VILLENEUVE	Rothmans Williams Renault	1 h 36'06"990
2.	Gehard BERGER	Mild Seven Benetton Renault	at 4"190
3.	Olivier PANIS	Prost Gauloises Blondes	at 15"870
4.	Mika HAKKINEN	West McLaren Mercedes	at 33"033
5.	M. SCHUMACHER	Scuderia Ferrari Marlboro	at 33"731
6.	Jean ALESI	Mild Seven Benetton Renault	at 34"020

Fastest lap : J. VILLENEUVE, lap 28, 1'18"397, avg. 197.089 km/h

«HH» hardly has an excuse

The biggest disappointment of the weekend was the performance of Heinz-Harald Frentzen. In practice, the German was unable to match the pace of team-mate Jacques Villeneuve, but his race was even more of a disaster, as he spent most of his time wallowing around the tenth place mark. Towards the end, he was even passed by Giancarlo Fisichella in the Jordan.
After the race he looked far from happy as he explained his problems. *«I made a complete mess of my start,»* he said. *«Then I found myself stuck behind the Jordans. There was nothing I could do about it and to make matters worse, my gearbox was not working properly from around the halfway point onwards. The gears would not go in cleanly and I could not maintain a decent pace.»*
These are just the sort of excuses that the Williams management find hard to swallow. The cynics in the paddock were already saying that the German was not as good as his reputation would have people believe.
This was something of a hasty judgement as we were only at race two of a 17 grands prix season.

TOTAL
B&H
BENSON &
HEDGES

Ralf Schumacher on the Brazilian skyline. The young German was only on his second grand prix, but he had already fixed his target for the season: to do better than team-mate Giancarlo Fisichella at all costs. It was rumoured that Ralf did not sleep if "Fisico" was even one thousandth of a second quicker.
In the race, he had passed the Roman during the pit-stops and that was enough to keep him happy. He would retire on lap 53 however, with an electrical problem.

△
A thoughtful Gerhard Berger. All the same, this Brazilian Grand Prix had gone quite well for him, as he finished second, just over 4 seconds behind Villeneuve.

«That's much better, thank you,» says Berger

On the second step of the podium, Gerhard Berger admitted he had tried everything to catch the Williams of Jacques Villeneuve, but it was in vain. *«Towards the end, I was pushing hard, but it was difficult to get past the back markers. It was that difficult situation, where you want to be sure of second place as the team needs the points and at the same time you know you have to keep the pressure up if you want to win. My only chance was to push Jacques into making a mistake. I hope that at least the spectators enjoyed our dice.»*

The Austrian had no complaints when it came to his Benetton B197. *«The car was going quite well, even if it is still definitely not on a par with the Williams.*
We know that winter testing went quite well for us and I think this second place is a more accurate reflection of what we can do, than the disaster we went through in Melbourne.
Everything went well in the race and the mechanics did a perfect job. I just had a few problems with lack of grip on my second set of tyres. But nothing serious.»

▷ △
«Whoops!» Michael Schumacher holds a superb slide in his Ferrari F 310 B. At Interlagos, the German had a quiet race. Starting from the front, he gradually dropped back to finish an unspectacular fifth.

A Prost sort of weekend

Without a doubt, Olivier Panis was the happiest of the three men on the podium. Fresh as a daisy after the race, he was immediately and inevitably quizzed as to the relative merits of this podium and his win in Monaco the previous year. This opening question in the press conference took him somewhat by surprise. *«Monaco had nothing to do with this,»* he replied. *«There are a lot of new things in the team and I am very happy with third place. Our decision to make only one pit-stop was the right one and the Bridgestones worked very well. The Mugen engine was even better and the car was easy to drive. I am very happy.»* When he announced the creation of his new team on 14th February, Alain Prost would not have believed one of his cars could finish third in only its second grand prix. At Interlagos, the Frenchman was in seventh heaven as he watched his driver spraying the champagne in the company of Jacques Villeneuve and Gerhard Berger.
Modestly, Prost preferred the anonymity of the garage to the hustle and bustle of the scene around the podium. *«Of course this is a fantastic result,"* he said. *"In Melbourne, our two points owed a lot to luck, but here we did it purely on merit and this podium is well deserved.»*
Prost being Prost, he even managed to find something to complain about. *«It's a shame there was a second start, because the way the race got underway the first time, we might have been able to finish second.»* He even admitted in all seriousness that the team: *«Had missed the boat!»* The Interlagos podium certainly augured well for the rest of the season. *«I think we have every right to expect further good results this season,»* concluded Alain Prost. *«We will not win the next grand prix, but I am quite optimistic. We have a solid base and we must make the most of that as soon as possible.»*

Ferrari and McLaren come trailing home

The pecking order had changed radically compared to the one established in Melbourne: bye-bye McLaren and Frentzen, hello Panis, Hill and Villeneuve.
Melbourne winner David Coulthard was completely off the pace in Brazil. While his teammate Mika Hakkinen finished fourth in this grand prix, the Scotsman had to settle for tenth place, having spent most of his race stuck behind Damon Hill in the Arrows. Deeply disappointed he had little to say about his afternoon's work. *«The car was going well, but I lost a lot of time behind Hill. The problem was that very few cars retired. Normally here, you just have to finish to score points.»*
This poor performance at Interlagos seemed to have had little effect on Mercedes motorsport boss, Norbert Haug. *«After two races, we are leading the drivers' and constructors' championships. That is encouraging,»* he said. Ostriches and heads in the sand spring to mind.

Michael off the pace

Michael Schumacher had been flattering to deceive in practice. Having qualified on the front row, he was off the pace in the race. The German was giving away 10 km/h to the Williams at the end of the straight. *«Frankly, I was hoping for better than fifth place. But the two points I picked up today, might come in useful when it is time to add up the final scores. We have a problem with lack of traction. What is more, as I expected, our tyres would not last the distance, even with two stops.»*

▷
The first podium of a new partnership is something to celebrate. Alain Prost only had to wait until his second grand prix as team boss. Once again, the Frenchman wasted no time, just as in the days when he lived his life at 200 mph.

PRACTICE TIMES

No	Driver	Mkae/Engine/Chassis	Practice Friday	Practice Saturday	Qualifying	Warm-up
1.	Damon Hill	Arrows/Yamaha/A18/3 (B)	1'18"978	1'17"490	1'17"090	1'17"973
2.	Pedro Diniz	Arrows/Yamaha/A18/2 (B)	1'19"573	1'17"795	1'18"095	1'19"664
3.	Jacques Villeneuve	Williams/Renault/FW19/4 (G)	1'17"829	1'16"030	1'16"004	1'17"421
4.	Heinz-Harald Frentzen	Williams/Renault/FW19/2 (G)	1'17"506	1'16"611	1'16"971	1'17"866
5.	Michael Schumacher	Ferrari/Ferrari/F310B/174 (G)	1'18"488	1'16"720	1'16"594	1'18"316
6.	Eddie Irvine	Ferrari/Ferrari/F310B/173 (G)	1'20"787	1'17"635	1'17"527	1'18"879
7.	Jean Alesi	Benetton/Renault/B197/5 (G)	1'18"000	1'16"588	1'16"757	1'18"034
8.	Gerhard Berger	Benetton/Renault/B197/4 (G)	1'18"437	1'16"517	1'16"644	1'18"358
9.	Mika Hakkinen	McLaren/Mercedes/MP4/12/2 (G)	1'19"271	1'16"205	1'16"692	1'17"642
10.	David Coulthard	McLaren/Mercedes/MP4/12/3 (G)	1'18"818	1'16"820	1'17"262	1'18"313
11.	Ralf Schumacher	Jordan/Peugeot/197/3 (G)	1'18"479	1'16"833	1'17"175	1'18"630
12.	Giancarlo Fisichella	Jordan/Peugeot/197/2 (G)	1'19"326	1'17"192	1'16"912	1'18"563
14.	Olivier Panis	Prost/Mugen Honda/JS45/3 (B)	1'19"408	1'18"069	1'16"756	1'17"800
15.	Shinji Nakano	Prost/Mugen Honda/JS45/2 (B)	1'20"520	1'18"283	1'17"999	1'19"406
16.	Johnny Herbert	Sauber/Petronas/C16/3 (G)	1'18"261	1'17"587	1'17"409	1'17"843
17.	Nicola Larini	Sauber/Petronas/C16/2 (G)	1'21"120	1'17"934	1'18"644	1'19"401
18.	Jos Verstappen	Tyrrell/Ford/025/2 (G)	1'20"076	1'18"473	1'18"885	1'19"690
19.	Mika Salo	Tyrrell/Ford/025/3 (G)	1'19"546	1'18"161	1'19"274	1'19"088
20.	Ukyo Katayama	Minardi/Hart/M197/3 (B)	1'19"963	1'18"316	1'18"557	1'19"218
21.	Jarno Trulli	Minardi/Hart/M197/2 (B)	1'20"521	1'18"043	1'18"336	1'19"102
22.	Rubens Barrichello	Stewart/Ford/SF1/2 (B)	1'19"613	1'17"148	1'17"259	1'18"743
23.	Jan Magnussen	Stewart/Ford/SF1/3 (B)	1'21"864	1'18"630	1'18"773	1'19"282

LAP CHART

position :	1	2	3	4	5	6	7	8	9	10	11	12	13	14	15	16	17	18	19	20	21	22
start:	3	5	8	9	14	7	12	4	1	11	22	10	16	6	15	2	21	20	17	23	18	19
1	3	5	9	8	7	14	1	10	12	11	16	22	4	21	6	2	17	15	19	18	20	
2	3	5	9	8	7	14	1	10	12	11	16	4	22	6	2	17	21	15	19	18	20	
3	3	5	9	8	7	14	1	10	12	11	4	16	22	6	2	17	15	21	19	18	20	
4	3	5	8	9	7	14	1	10	12	11	4	16	22	6	2	17	15	21	19	18	20	
5	3	5	8	9	7	14	1	10	12	11	4	16	22	6	2	17	15	21	19	18	20	
6	3	5	8	9	7	14	1	10	12	11	4	16	22	6	2	17	15	21	19	18	20	
7	3	5	8	9	7	14	1	10	12	11	4	16	22	6	2	17	15	21	19	18	20	
8	3	5	8	9	7	14	1	10	12	11	4	16	22	2	6	17	15	21	19	18	20	
9	3	5	8	9	7	14	1	10	12	11	4	16	22	2	6	17	15	21	19	18	20	
10	3	5	8	9	7	14	1	10	12	11	4	16	22	2	6	17	15	21	19	18	20	
11	3	5	8	9	7	14	1	10	12	11	4	16	22	2	6	17	15	21	19	18	20	
12	3	8	5	9	7	14	1	10	12	11	4	16	22	2	17	6	15	21	19	18	20	
13	3	8	5	9	7	14	1	10	12	11	4	16	22	2	17	6	15	21	19	18	20	
14	3	8	5	9	7	14	1	10	12	11	4	16	22	2	17	6	15	21	19	18	20	
15	3	8	5	9	7	14	1	10	12	11	4	16	22	17	2	6	15	21	19	18	20	
16	3	8	5	9	7	14	1	10	12	11	4	16	17	6	15	21	19	22	18	20		
17	3	8	5	9	7	14	1	10	12	11	4	17	16	6	15	21	19	18	20			
18	3	8	5	9	7	14	1	10	12	11	4	17	6	15	21	18	19	16	20			
19	3	8	5	9	7	14	1	10	12	11	4	17	6	15	21	18	16	19	20			
20	3	8	5	9	7	14	1	10	12	11	4	17	6	15	21	16	18	19	20			
21	3	8	5	9	7	14	1	12	11	4	17	10	6	15	21	16	18	19	20			
22	3	8	5	9	7	14	1	12	11	4	6	17	15	21	16	10	19	18	20			
23	3	5	9	14	7	8	1	12	11	4	6	15	21	16	10	17	19	18	20			
24	3	5	14	9	8	1	12	11	4	7	6	15	16	21	10	17	19	18	20			
25	3	5	14	8	1	11	4	9	7	12	15	16	10	21	17	6	19	18	20			
26	3	5	14	8	1	4	9	7	16	10	15	21	11	17	12	6	19	18	20			
27	3	14	8	1	4	9	5	7	16	10	15	21	11	17	12	6	19	18	20			
28	3	14	8	1	9	5	7	4	16	10	11	15	21	17	12	6	19	18	20			
29	3	14	8	1	9	5	7	16	10	11	4	15	12	17	21	6	19	18	20			
30	3	14	8	1	9	5	7	16	10	11	4	15	12	17	21	6	19	18	20			
31	3	14	8	9	1	5	7	16	10	11	4	12	15	17	21	6	19	18	20			
32	3	14	8	9	1	5	7	16	10	11	4	12	15	17	21	6	19	18	20			
33	3	14	8	9	1	5	7	16	10	11	4	12	15	17	21	6	19	18	20			
34	3	14	8	9	1	5	7	16	10	11	4	12	15	17	21	6	19	18	20			
35	3	8	14	9	1	5	7	16	10	11	4	12	17	15	21	6	19	18	20			
36	3	8	9	1	5	7	14	16	10	11	4	12	17	15	19	21	18	6	20			
37	3	8	9	1	5	7	14	16	10	11	4	12	17	15	19	21	18	6	20			
38	3	8	9	5	7	14	16	10	1	11	4	12	17	19	21	18	15	6	20			
39	3	8	9	5	7	14	16	10	4	12	11	17	1	19	21	18	15	6	20			
40	3	8	5	7	14	16	4	9	10	12	17	1	11	19	21	18	15	6	20			
41	3	8	5	7	14	4	16	9	12	17	1	10	11	19	21	18	15	6	20			
42	3	8	5	7	14	4	9	12	17	16	1	10	11	19	21	18	15	6	20			
43	3	8	5	7	14	4	9	12	17	16	1	10	11	21	19	18	15	6	20			
44	3	8	5	7	14	4	9	12	17	16	1	10	11	21	18	19	15	6	20			
45	3	8	7	5	14	4	9	16	17	1	10	12	11	21	18	19	15	6	20			
46	8	3	14	7	4	9	5	16	1	10	12	11	17	21	18	18	15	6	20			
47	8	3	14	4	9	5	7	16	1	10	12	11	17	21	19	15	6	18	20			
48	8	3	14	9	5	4	7	16	1	12	10	11	17	21	19	15	6	18	20			
49	3	8	14	9	5	7	16	4	1	12	10	11	17	21	19	15	6	18	20			
50	3	8	14	9	5	7	16	4	12	1	10	11	17	21	19	6	15	18	20			
51	3	8	14	9	5	7	16	4	12	1	10	11	17	21	19	6	15	18	20			
52	3	8	14	9	5	7	16	4	12	1	10	11	17	21	19	15	6	18	20			
53	3	8	14	9	5	7	16	4	12	1	10	17	21	19	15	18	6	20				
54	3	8	14	9	5	7	16	4	12	1	10	17	21	19	15	18	6	20				
55	3	8	14	9	5	7	16	4	12	10	1	17	21	19	15	18	6	20				
56	3	8	14	9	5	7	16	4	12	10	1	17	21	19	15	18	6	20				
57	3	8	14	9	5	7	16	4	12	10	1	17	21	19	15	18	6	20				
58	3	8	14	9	5	7	16	4	12	10	1	17	21	19	15	18	6	20				
59	3	8	14	9	5	7	16	4	12	10	1	17	21	19	15	18	6	20				
60	3	8	14	9	5	7	16	4	12	10	1	17	21	19	15	18	6	20				
61	3	8	14	9	5	7	16	4	12	10	1	17	21	19	15	18	6	20				
62	3	8	14	9	5	7	16	4	12	10	1	17	21	19	15	18	6	20				
63	3	8	14	9	5	7	16	4	12	10	1	17	21	19	15	18	6	20				
64	3	8	14	9	5	7	16	12	4	10	1	17	21	19	15	18	6	20				
65	3	8	14	9	5	7	16	12	4	10	1	17	21	19	15	18	6	20				
66	3	8	14	9	5	7	16	12	4	10	1	17	21	19	15	18	6	20				
67	3	8	14	9	5	7	16	12	4	10	1	17	21	19	15	18	6	20				
68	3	8	14	9	5	7	16	12	4	10	17	1	21	19	15	18	6					
69	3	8	14	9	5	7	16	12	4	10	17	21	19	15	18	6						
70	3	8	14	9	5	7	16	12	4	10	17	21	19	15	18	6						
71	3	8	14	9	5	7	16	12	4	10	17	21	19	15								
72	3	8	14	9	5	7	16	12	4													

BRIDGESTONE

Best result for a Bridgestone shod runner:

Olivier Panis, Prost Mugen Honda, *3rd*

CHAMPIONSHIPS

(after two rounds)

Drivers:

1.	David COULTHARD	10
	Jacques VILLENEUVE	10
3.	Gerhard BERGER	9
4.	M. SCHUMACHER	8
5.	Mika HAKKINEN	7
6.	Olivier PANIS	6
7.	Nicola LARINI	1
	Jean ALESI	1

Constructors :

1.	McLaren / Mercedes	17
2.	Williams / Renault	10
	Benetton / Renault	10
4.	Ferrari	8
5.	Prost / Mugen Honda	6
6.	Sauber / Petronas	1

CLASSIFICATION & RETIREMENTS

Pos	Driver	Team	Time
1.	Villeneuve	Williams Renault	in 1h36'06"990
2.	Berger	Benetton Renault	at 4"190
3.	Panis	Prost Mugen Honda	at 15"870
4.	Hakkinen	McLaren Mercedes	at 33"033
5.	Schumacher	Ferrari	at 33"731
6.	Alesi	Benetton Renault	at 34"020
7.	Herbert	Sauber Petronas	at 50"912
8.	Fisichella	Jordan Peugeot	at 1'00"639
9.	Frentzen	Williams Renault	at 1'15"402
10.	Coulthard	McLaren Mercedes	at 1 lap
11.	Larini	Sauber Petronas	at 1 lap
12.	Trulli	Minardi Hart	at 1 lap
13.	Salo	Tyrrell Ford	at 1 lap
14.	Nakano	Prost Mugen Honda	at 1 lap
15.	Verstappen	Tyrrell Ford	at 2 laps
16.	Irvine	Ferrari	at 2 laps
17.	Hill	Arrows Yamaha	gearbox
18.	Katayama	Minardi Hart	at 5 laps

Lap	Driver	Team	Reason
	Magnussen	Stewart Ford	did not start
16	Diniz	Arrows Yamaha	spin
17	Barrichello	Stewart Ford	suspensions
53	Schumacher	Jordan Peugeot	electrics

FASTEST LAPS

	Driver	Time	Lap
1.	Villeneuve	1'18"397	28
2.	R. Schum.	1'18"441	29
3.	Berger	1'18"509	25
4.	Fisichella	1'18"611	39
5.	Hakkinen	1'18"649	34
6.	Frentzen	1'18"707	30
7.	Larini	1'18"730	45
8.	Alesi	1'18"754	25
9.	M. Schum.	1'18"773	44
10.	Coulthard	1'18"925	35
11.	Herbert	1'19"008	19
12.	Panis	1'19"094	57
13.	Irvine	1'19"275	41
14.	Nakano	1'19"657	39
15.	Hill	1'19"910	41
16.	Katayama	1'19"960	42
17.	Trulli	1'20"105	55
18.	Verstappen	1'20"274	43
19.	Salo	1'20"376	61
20.	Diniz	1'20"406	10
21.	Barrichello	1'20"788	14

SECOND ROUND

GRANDE PRÊMIO DO BRASIL, INTERLAGOS

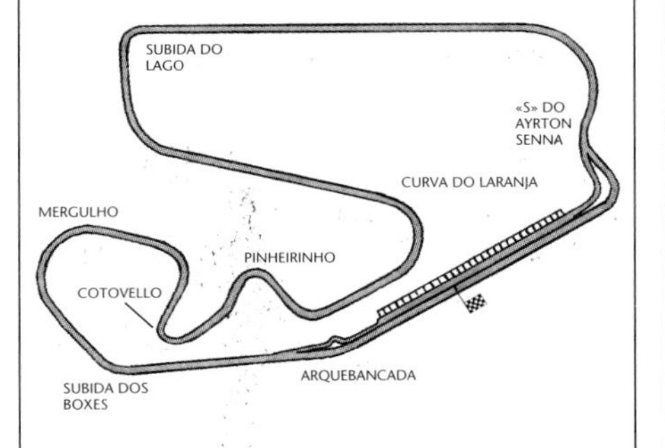

Date : March 30, 1997
Length: 4325 meters
Distance : 72 laps, 309.024 km
Weather: cloudy, 23 degrees

RACE SUMMARY

- At the start, Schumacher hustles Villeneuve onto the grass. Behind them, Fisichella gets out of shape, causing mayhem at the first chicane, resulting in a pile-up.
- The race is stopped as Magnussen's Stewart is blocking the track.
- At the second start, Schumacher heads Villeneuve, who then passes the German at the end of the first lap.
- Villeneuve quickly pulls away in the lead. Schumacher holds off Berger but is forced to let him pass on lap 12.
- While the leaders all refuel, Panis takes second place on lap 26.
- As the main players all stop twice, Panis makes do with one pit-stop, which gives him third place.
- Hill retires on lap 69 when his car catches fire in the pits.
- At the front, Berger is catching Villeneuve but cannot pass him. The Austrian finishes in second place.

WEEK-END GOSSIP

• Penalties by the bucket load

The Brazilian Stewards were merciless on many counts. This year, the white line marking the entrance to the pit lane had been repainted.

It was very long and encroached on the racing line. On Friday, all the drivers crossed it at least once.

So on Saturday morning, the Stewards put out an edict stating that any driver who put so much as a tyre over the line would be penalised.

A team of observers was sent out to keep an eye on it and the penalties rolled in.

By the end of Saturday, the times set by Heinz-Harald Frentzen, David Coulthard, Jan Magnussen and Pedro Diniz were all disallowed.

Olivier Panis was the only one capable of providing a good enough explanation for his actions to avoid all penalty.

To add to the confusion, at six thirty on Sunday morning, whereas no one was aware of it, the Stewards issued yet another statement, authorising the drivers to cross the line, "Because of the bumps on the track at the level of the white line."

Those who had been penalised were delighted with the news.

• A Villeneuve team?

It appeared that a major coup was being prepared by Jacques Villeneuve as the Canadian driver was said to be at the centre of a project to create a new team, which would make its Formula 1 debut in 1999.

The project apparently involved the British racing car builder, Adrian Reynard, who had built the chassis Villeneuve used to win the Indycar Championship and the Indy 500 – although Newey was linked to McLaren-Mercedes.

The project would see all parties involved in this previous episode reunited, as the main sponsor was supposed to be cigarette company Players, the Canadian brand which had supported Jacques Villeneuve during his years racing in the United States.

• A good deal

The Prost team continued to swell its coffers.

In Brazil it announced the signing of a four year deal with Bic, makers of pens and lighters. The company's yellow logo was already much in evidence on the car.

• TAG Heuer with Fisichella

The Swiss watch company, TAG Heuer announced in Sao Paulo that it had just signed a five year deal with young Italian hotshot, Giancarlo Fisichella, the Jordan Peugeot driver.

TAG Heuer already sponsored both McLaren drivers Mika Hakkinen and David Coulthard, as well as Gerhard Berger and Ukyo Katayama.

The spectators had to go through strict security controls before entering the Interlagos circuit. Because of this, the queue at the gates had to wait for several hours on Sunday morning. But the Paulistas seemed prepared to put up with the inconvenience with good grace. ▽

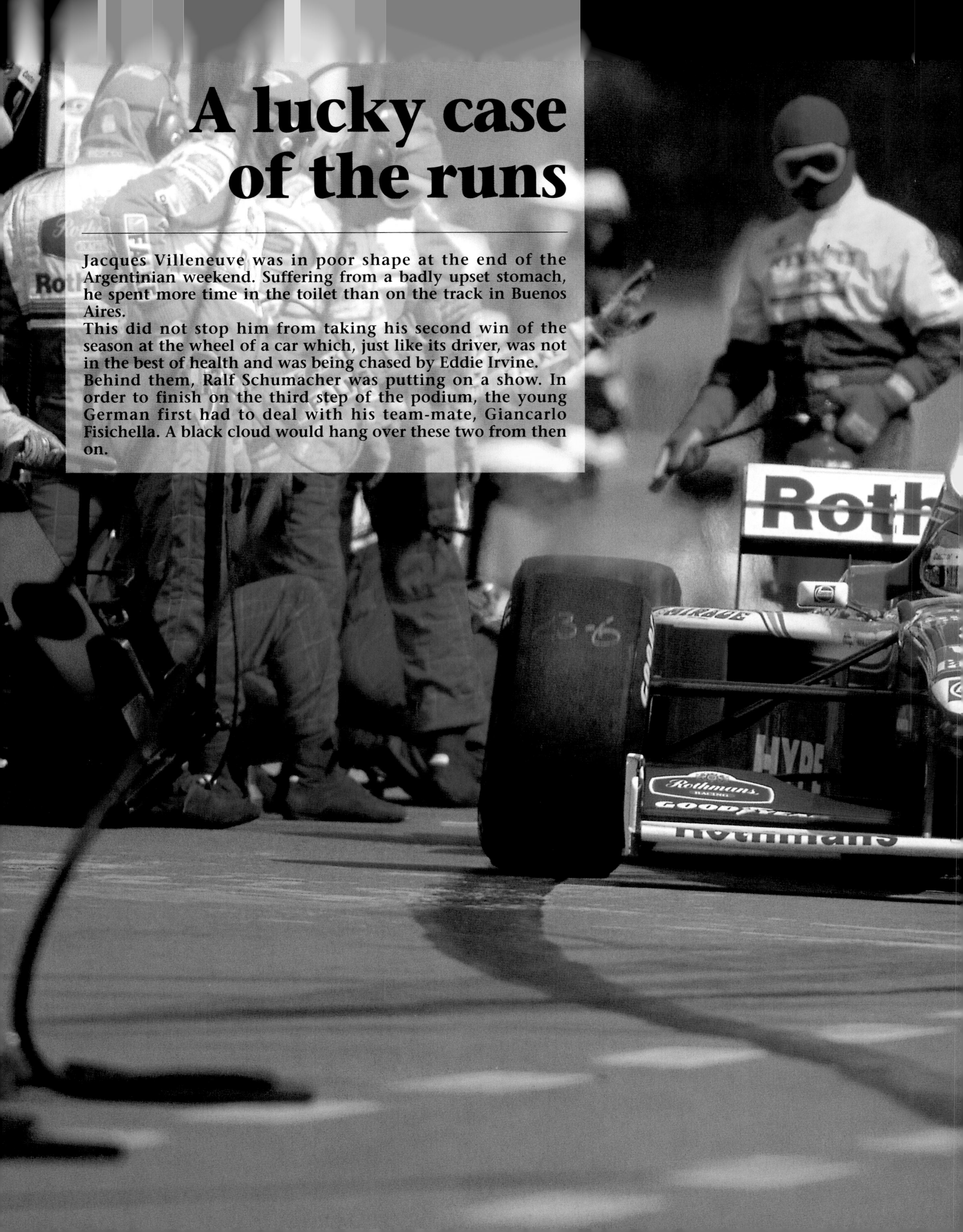

A lucky case of the runs

Jacques Villeneuve was in poor shape at the end of the Argentinian weekend. Suffering from a badly upset stomach, he spent more time in the toilet than on the track in Buenos Aires.

This did not stop him from taking his second win of the season at the wheel of a car which, just like its driver, was not in the best of health and was being chased by Eddie Irvine.

Behind them, Ralf Schumacher was putting on a show. In order to finish on the third step of the podium, the young German first had to deal with his team-mate, Giancarlo Fisichella. A black cloud would hang over these two from then on.

GRAN PREMIO MARLBORO DE ARGENTINA
BUENOS AIRES

Williams 100th pole position in pain

Jacques Villeneuve was not in good shape. He had taken a quick holiday in Salvador de Bahia, between the Brazilian and Argentinian races and had swallowed a piece of Brazilian beef that disagreed with him.
The Canadian arrived at the track with a bad case of what is politely referred to as the «Turista», an ailment that meant long hours sitting on a toilet seat. Despite his troubles, he still posted the quickest time on Friday, thanks to fitting a new set of tyres right at the end of the session. *«I should be alright for qualifying,»* he stated. *«But we still have a lot of work to do to the set-up for the race.»*
On Saturday, Villeneuve took pole position, despite still suffering with stomach problems. *«The car is perfect, but I'm not,»* admitted the man from Quebec. *«I thought it would have cleared up by now, but it has not. In qualifying you only have to do a few laps, but I am not sure if I can last a race distance.»*

Hospital ward

The Williams garage was like a hospital ward as Heinz-Harald Frentzen had a fever, having caught a cold the previous week. *«It is my fault,»* he confessed. *«That will teach me to sleep without a blanket.»* Despite running a temperature, Frentzen still set the second fastest time, somewhat making up for his miserable time in the Brazilian Grand Prix. *«I have completely changed the way I set up the car and it is beginning to pay off,»* he explained.
It was the Williams team's 100th pole, a fact that Jacques Villeneuve did not seem at all concerned about.

△
«And then, bingo, I overtake him on the inside.» Jacques Villeneuve explains his strategy to race engineer, Jock Cleare.

▷ △
An aerial view of the Buenos Aires circuit. A «Monaco style»" track, without the buildings.

Third on the grid

Olivier Panis in fine form

Alain Prost is biting his fingernails more than usual. Sitting on the pit-wall, the Frenchman follows the progress of his cars with even more interest than when he was driving himself. On Saturday, he got even more excited when Olivier Panis set the third fastest time in qualifying for the Argentinian Grand Prix. *«Yes, I think Alain is much more excited than I am,»* laughed the man from Grenoble at the end of the session. *«As the team owner, he is under much more pressure. He gets completely involved in everything and he even sort of works as my engineer. We work together on the set-up and then it is down to me to try it out on the track.»*

New tyre compound

Bridgestone arrived in Argentina with a new tyre compound which seemed particularly effective on the Buenos Aires circuit and this helped Panis secure the best qualifying position of his career. *«It is true that Bridgestone did a lot of work here,»* admitted frankly the Frenchman. *«But I have to say, apart from that, the car is very well balanced. So I am totally confident when I go into a corner and I can push hard without any worries. It is the best car I have ever driven by a long chalk.»*

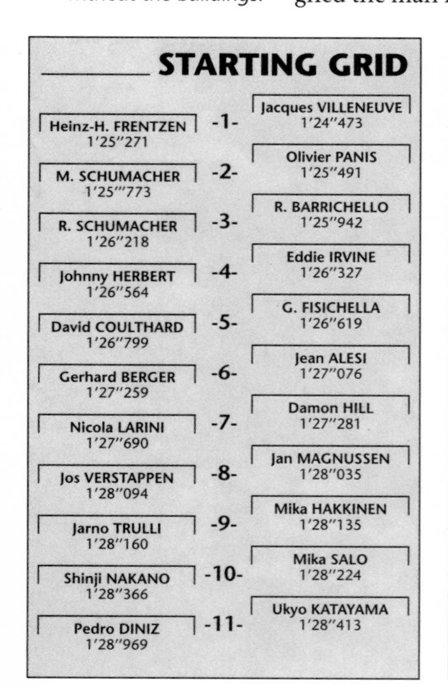

STARTING GRID

	Pos.	
		Jacques VILLENEUVE 1'24"473
Heinz-H. FRENTZEN 1'25"271	-1-	
		Olivier PANIS 1'25"491
M. SCHUMACHER 1'25"'773	-2-	
		R. BARRICHELLO 1'25"942
R. SCHUMACHER 1'26"218	-3-	
		Eddie IRVINE 1'26"327
Johnny HERBERT 1'26"564	-4-	
		G. FISICHELLA 1'26"619
David COULTHARD 1'26"799	-5-	
		Jean ALESI 1'27"076
Gerhard BERGER 1'27"259	-6-	
		Damon HILL 1'27"281
Nicola LARINI 1'27"690	-7-	
		Jan MAGNUSSEN 1'28"035
Jos VERSTAPPEN 1'28"094	-8-	
		Mika HAKKINEN 1'28"135
Jarno TRULLI 1'28"160	-9-	
		Mika SALO 1'28"224
Shinji NAKANO 1'28"366	-10-	
		Ukyo KATAYAMA 1'28"413
Pedro DINIZ 1'28"969	-11-	

A painful victory

«This was, without a doubt, the most difficult race of my entire career.» While looking drawn and haggard, Jacques Villeneuve had a mile wide smile on his face after the race. Struggling with his stomach bug, he had a agonising drive and won the race in considerable discomfort.

The day had begun rather badly. Villeneuve had hoped he would have been cured before the race, but instead his condition deteriorated over Saturday night and Sunday morning, to the point where he had to spend part of race day in the circuit's medical centre. It was a wrecked Jacques Villeneuve who clambered into his cockpit on the starting grid.

Despite his troubles, Villeneuve made a magnificent getaway.

The early stages went according to plan, but after his first refuelling stop, he began to encounter problems. *«We chose to run on the soft tyres and it was a mistake,»* he said. *«At the start of the race it was not too bad. But after my first visit to the pits, the team realised that Ferrari and Jordan were not going to do the same as us and stop three times. At the same time, my gearbox started to play up, jumping out of gear. It would change up or down all on its own and I had to be very careful.»*

This was not his only problem as the Williams' road holding began to deteriorate at the same time, allowing Eddie Irvine to close right up on him. *«I was having difficulty holding him off, because my right front tyre was finished. As the race progressed and it got hotter, so my tyres picked up more rubber off the track.»*

At the finish, Villeneuve's engineer Jock Cleare could not believe the state his car was in. *«It's not a car, it's a wreck,»* he said with surprise. *«It is absolutely incredible that Jacques managed to win in this.»*

The hardships endured made the win all the more enjoyable. *«It was really very tough here,»* said the Canadian. *«I had to drive at qualifying speed for at least one third of the race. It was the most satisfying win of my whole career.»*

A big mistake from Michael Schumacher in Buenos Aires. «I had so much oil on my visor at the first corner, that I could see nothing at all. I hit Barrichello under full acceleration and it was all over.» It was also over for «Rubinho» who had qualified fifth and had hoped to pull off a surprise. ◁▽

A superb fourth place for Johnny Herbert and his Sauber-Petronas. ▽

IN THE POINTS

	Driver	Team	Time
1.	Jacques VILLENEUVE	Rothmans Williams Renault	1 h 52'01"715
2.	Eddie IRVINE	Scuderia Ferrari Marlboro	at 0"979
3.	Ralf SCHUMACHER	B&H Total Jordan Peugeot	at 12"089
4.	Johnny HERBERT	Red Bull Sauber Petronas	at 29"919
5.	Mika HAKKINEN	West McLaren Mercedes	at 30"351
6.	Gerhard BERGER	Mild Seven Benetton Renault	at 31"393

Fastest lap : Gerhard BERGER, lap 63, 1'27"981, avg. 174.269 km/h

Eddie Irvine renews his driving license

Eddie Irvine gives the impression of being one of the strangest people in the paddock; one day capable of committing monumental errors, the next of making outrageous statements and the next of putting in a truly great drive.

After his suicide bombing attack on Jacques Villeneuve in Australia, the Irishman more than made amends in Buenos Aires, by finishing second. *«I made a very good start,»* he said, although Olivier Panis was not of the same opinion as he was pushed onto the grass by the Ferrari driver. *«Then at the first corner, I lost a bit of ground and found myself fourth,»* continued Irvine. *«From then, I just drove my own race. We knew the car was good enough here to let us do something special.»*

In the closing stages of the race, Irvine profited from Villeneuve's problems to put him seriously under threat and he finished less than a second behind the Williams. *«I was quicker than him, but unfortunately there was not enough difference in performance between the two of us for me to get past,»* regretted Irvine who had behaved impeccable and had not tried anything stupid. *«Second place was good enough for me. I think it shows we are beginning to solve our problems.»*

Ralf drives into Giancarlo and into third place

Naturally, Ralf Schumacher was all smiles after the race. In only his third Grand Prix, the little brother was already on the podium. It was a great effort for a driver who had barely turned 22 years of age. However, he was the only one smiling in the Jordan camp. When he crossed the line and took the chequered flag, not one of his mechanics made the trip to the pit wall to give him the welcome that this sort of performance normally deserves. The Jordan boys had not been impressed with the way in which Ralf had dispensed with his team-mate Giancarlo Fisichella on the twenty fourth lap. The German had well and truly punted the Italian off the track, but still refused to admit he was at fault. *«I do not really know what happened with Giancarlo,»* he dared to say after the race. *«I was following him, he got closer to me and we touched. I admit this sort of thing should not happen between team-mates. It is a real shame.»*

This racing incident did little to enhance Ralf Schumacher's image in the paddock, where he was already considered to be too cocky for his own good.

For his part, Giancarlo Fisichella would not calm down after the race. It was understandable, as he had just missed out on the chance of his first ever F1 podium. *«Everyone saw what happened. Okay, so Ralf might have apologised, which shows he knows he was in the wrong. I am very angry, but we will talk about it again.»* Fisichella was wrong on that last point, as from then on, the two men hardly exchanged a word for several months.

To complete this tale and to make matters worse, it seems that the mechanics' actions in not going to the pit wall were directed not only at Ralf, but also at team boss Eddie Jordan, who this year, had reduced their bonus payments made in relation to points scored by the team.

▷
Mika Hakkinen's Black Magic refuelling. In Buenos Aires, the Finn managed to bring home two points for fifth place having started from way back in 17th spot on the grid - he had spun during qualifying.

Olivier Panis had set out to win. «At the start, Michael Schumacher ran into me, which bent a steering arm, but I was still able to keep pace with Villeneuve quite comfortably.» Having planned one pit-stop less than the others, he could have won if his engine had not cut out without warning.
▷ ▽

In Buenos Aires, even the marshals love to tango. Panic on the track after the first corner crash.
▽

Heinz-Harald cancels his holidays

Heinz-Harald Frentzen's dismal performance in Brazil earned him a real pasting in the press. This criticism piled on the pressure for Frentzen, whose engineers felt that since he had joined Williams he had been an inconsistent performer. *«I knew Heinz-Harald would take a bit of time to settle in and get used to our way of working, but I must admit it is taking a bit longer than I had expected,»* said Williams technical director, Patrick Head, in Buenos Aires. *«I think his problem is that he believes a bit too much in his own talent.»*

In between the two South American grands prix, Frentzen had originally planned to take a few days holiday in Brazil.

However, after his disastrous Interlagos interlude, he cancelled these plans. *«I flew back to England, to spend a few days at the Williams factory. I was asking myself a serious question. Why was my driving style so unsuited to the car? I had several meetings with my race engineer, Tim Preston and with Patrick Head. We worked on the problem, using computers as no track testing was planned, but we simulated several set-up changes which might suit my style better.»* The result of all this work was, that on Saturday, HH qualified on the front row. On Sunday, he might have won, but for a clutch problem which sidelined him in the early stages of the race, forcing to watch the event from the side of the track.

«If I had crossed the track I would have been given a 10,000 dollar fine,» he sighed, once back at the pits. *«Things were already going badly enough as it was.»*

The tyres are getting hot

«Goodyear: 347 Grand Prix wins. Bridgestone: 0 Grand Prix wins. It is good to know the competition is behind us.» The Argentinian Goodyear importer obviously did not feel the need to pull any punches when it came to publicity. The advertising campaign they ran on the day after the Argentinian Grand Prix certainly captured the mood of the Akron-based tyre manufacturer, who has ruled the roost in F1 for several decades. Now it seemed the situation might change.

In Buenos Aires it was obvious that the Bridgestone tyres were performing better than their American opposite numbers. They helped Panis in the Prost and Barrichello in the Stewart to qualify on the second and third rows respectively. The two drivers admitted this performance would have been impossible if they had been on American rubber.

In the Goodyear camp, the situation was making waves. On Saturday night, the Akron engineers were spotted out on the circuit scraping rubber samples left on the track after qualifying.

«We will now have to react very quickly.»

The intention was to analyse the samples in order to work out what compound Bridgestone was using. *«We have already faced competition in the past, but obviously the arrival of another company changes a lot of things for us,»* admitted Stuart Grant, Goodyear's competitions manager. *«We will now have to react very quickly.»*

Several experts were predicting a Bridgestone victory before the end of the 1997 season. The Argentinian Goodyear importer might yet have to change its advertising strategy, before the year is out.

PRACTICE TIMES

No	Driver	Make/Engine/Chassis	Practice Friday	Practice Saturday	Qualifying	Warm-up
1.	Damon Hill	Arrows/Yamaha/A18/3 (B)	1'28"932	1'28"654	1'27"281	1'28"737
2.	Pedro Diniz	Arrows/Yamaha/A18/2 (B)	1'30"727	1'28"853	1'28"969	1'29"341
3.	Jacques Villeneuve	Williams/Renault/FW19/4 (G)	1'25"755	1'25"704	1'24"473	1'27"425
4.	Heinz-Harald Frentzen	Williams/Renault/FW19/2 (G)	1'27"169	1'24"874	1'25"271	1'27"438
5.	Michael Schumacher	Ferrari/Ferrari/F310B/174 (G)	1'27"052	1'26"359	1'25"773	1'27"957
6.	Eddie Irvine	Ferrari/Ferrari/F310B/173 (G)	1'28"137	1'27"468	1'26"327	1'28"601
7.	Jean Alesi	Benetton/Renault/B197/5 (G)	1'27"979	1'26"835	1'27"076	1'27"941
8.	Gerhard Berger	Benetton/Renault/B197/4 (G)	1'27"017	1'26"703	1'27"259	1'29"083
9.	Mika Hakkinen	McLaren/Mercedes/MP4/12/2 (G)	1'29"426	1'28"086	1'28"135	1'28"464
10.	David Coulthard	McLaren/Mercedes/MP4/12/3 (G)	1'28"163	1'27"496	1'26"799	1'28"451
11.	Ralf Schumacher	Jordan/Peugeot/197/3 (G)	1'27"823	1'26"455	1'26"218	1'28"252
12.	Giancarlo Fisichella	Jordan/Peugeot/197/2 (G)	1'27"129	1'26"789	1'26"619	1'27"748
14.	Olivier Panis	Prost/Mugen Honda/JS45/3 (B)	1'26"983	1'26"772	1'25"491	1'27"824
15.	Shinji Nakano	Prost/Mugen Honda/JS45/2 (B)	1'30"069	1'27"885	1'28"366	1'29"490
16.	Johnny Herbert	Sauber/Petronas/C16/3 (G)	1'27"702	1'26"494	1'26"564	1'28"459
17.	Nicola Larini	Sauber/Petronas/C16/2 (G)	1'29"153	1'29"118	1'27"690	1'28"052
18.	Jos Verstappen	Tyrrell/Ford/025/2 (G)	1'29"302	1'27"423	1'28"094	1'29"269
19.	Mika Salo	Tyrrell/Ford/025/3 (G)	1'29"893	1'27"768	1'28"224	1'30"045
20.	Ukyo Katayama	Minardi/Hart/M197/3 (B)	1'30"546	1'28"600	1'28"413	1'29"920
21.	Jarno Trulli	Minardi/Hart/M197/2 (B)	1'31"269	1'29"140	1'28"160	1'28"842
22.	Rubens Barrichello	Stewart/Ford/SF1/2 (B)	1'26"693	1'27"229	1'25"942	1'27"605
23.	Jan Magnussen	Stewart/Ford/SF1/3 (B)	1'30"376	1'28"710	1'28"035	1'29"508

LAP CHART

position :	1	2	3	4	5	6	7	8	9	10	11	12	13	14	15	16	17	18	19	20	21	22
start:	3	4	14	5	22	11	6	16	12	10	7	8	1	17	23	18	9	21	19	15	20	2
1	3	4	14	6	12	1	16	11	7	2	18	20	9	21	19	8	17	15	23	22		
2	3	4	14	6	12	1	23	16	11	7	2	18	9	20	21	19	8	17	15	22		
3	3	4	14	6	12	1	16	11	7	2	18	9	20	21	19	8	17	15	22	23		
4	3	4	14	6	12	1	16	11	7	2	18	9	20	21	19	8	17	15	22	23		
5	3	4	14	6	12	1	16	11	7	2	18	9	20	21	8	19	22	17	15	23		
6	3	14	6	12	1	16	11	7	2	18	9	20	21	8	19	22	17	15	23			
7	3	14	6	12	1	11	16	7	2	18	9	20	21	8	22	19	17	15	23			
8	3	14	6	12	11	16	1	7	2	18	9	20	21	8	22	19	17	15	23			
9	3	14	6	12	11	16	1	7	2	18	9	20	21	22	8	19	23	17	15			
10	3	14	6	12	11	16	1	7	2	18	9	20	22	21	8	19	23	17	15			
11	3	14	6	12	16	11	1	7	2	18	9	22	20	8	19	21	23	17	15			
12	3	14	6	12	16	11	1	7	2	18	9	22	8	20	19	23	21	17	15			
13	3	14	6	12	16	11	1	7	2	18	9	22	8	23	20	19	17	21	15			
14	3	14	6	12	16	11	1	7	2	18	9	22	8	23	20	19	17	21	15			
15	3	14	6	12	16	11	1	7	2	18	9	22	8	23	19	20	17	21	15			
16	3	14	6	12	16	11	1	7	2	18	9	22	8	23	19	17	20	21	15			
17	3	14	6	12	16	11	1	7	2	18	9	22	8	23	19	17	21	15	20			
18	3	14	6	12	16	11	2	18	9	22	1	7	8	23	19	17	21	15	20			
19	3	6	12	16	11	2	18	9	22	1	7	8	23	19	17	21	15	20				
20	3	6	12	16	11	2	18	9	22	1	7	8	23	19	17	21	15	20				
21	3	6	16	12	11	2	18	22	9	7	1	8	23	19	17	21	15	20				
22	3	6	12	11	16	2	18	9	7	1	8	23	19	17	22	21	15	20				
23	3	6	12	11	16	18	2	9	7	1	8	23	19	17	22	21	15	20				
24	3	12	11	6	16	2	9	7	1	8	23	17	19	18	22	21	15	20				
25	3	11	6	16	9	2	7	1	8	17	19	18	23	21	15	20						
26	3	11	6	16	9	2	7	1	8	19	18	23	21	15	20	17						
27	3	11	6	16	9	7	2	8	1	19	18	23	21	20	15	17						
28	3	11	6	16	9	7	2	8	1	18	23	21	19	20	15	17						
29	3	11	6	16	9	7	8	2	1	18	23	21	19	20	15	17						
30	3	11	6	16	9	7	8	2	1	18	23	21	19	20	15	17						
31	3	11	6	16	9	7	8	1	2	18	23	21	19	20	15	17						
32	3	11	6	16	9	7	8	1	2	18	23	21	19	20	15	17						
33	3	11	6	16	9	7	8	1	2	18	23	21	19	20	15	17						
34	3	11	6	16	9	7	8	18	23	21	19	20	17	15	2							
35	3	6	16	9	7	11	8	18	23	21	19	17	20	15	2							
36	3	6	16	9	11	8	7	18	23	21	19	17	20	15	2							
37	3	6	16	9	11	7	18	8	23	21	19	17	20	15	2							
38	3	6	16	9	11	7	18	8	23	21	19	17	15	2								
39	6	16	3	9	11	7	18	8	23	19	17	21	15	2								
40	6	3	9	11	16	7	18	8	23	19	17	21	15	2								
41	6	3	11	16	9	7	18	8	23	19	17	21	15	2								
42	6	3	11	16	9	7	18	8	23	17	19	21	15	2								
43	6	3	11	16	9	7	18	8	23	17	19	21	15	2								
44	6	3	11	16	9	7	8	23	17	19	21	15	2									
45	3	6	11	16	9	7	8	23	17	21	19	15	2									
46	3	6	11	16	9	7	8	23	17	21	19	15	2									
47	3	6	11	16	9	7	8	17	23	21	19	15	2									
48	3	6	11	16	9	7	8	23	21	19	15	2	17									
49	3	6	11	16	9	7	8	23	21	19	15	2	17									
50	3	6	11	16	9	7	8	23	21	19	2	17										
51	3	6	11	16	9	7	8	23	21	19	17											
52	3	6	11	16	9	7	8	23	21	19	17											
53	3	6	11	16	9	7	8	23	21	19	17											
54	3	6	11	16	9	7	8	23	21	19	17											
55	3	6	11	16	9	7	8	23	21	19	17											
56	3	6	11	16	9	8	7	23	21	19	17											
57	3	6	11	16	9	8	7	23	21	19	17											
58	3	6	11	16	9	8	7	23	19	21	17											
59	3	6	11	16	9	8	7	23	19	21	17											
60	3	6	11	16	9	8	7	23	19	21	17											
61	3	6	11	16	9	8	7	23	19	21	17											
62	3	6	11	16	9	8	7	23	19	21	17											
63	3	6	11	16	9	8	7	23	19	21	17											
64	3	6	11	16	9	8	7	23	19	21												
65	3	6	11	16	9	8	7	23	19	21												
66	3	6	11	16	9	8	7	23	19	21												
67	3	6	11	16	9	8	7	19	21													
68	3	6	11	16	9	8	7	19	21													
69	3	6	11	16	9	8	7	19	21													
70	3	6	11	16	9	8	7	19	21													
71	3	6	11	16	9	8	7	19	21													
72	3	6	11	16	9	8	7															

BRIDGESTONE

Best result for a Bridgestone shod runner:

Jarno Trulli, Minardi Hart, 9th

CHAMPIONSHIPS

(after three rounds)

Drivers:

1.	Jacques VILLENEUVE	20
2.	David COULTHARD	10
	Gerhard BERGER	10
4.	Mika HAKKINEN	9
5.	M. SCHUMACHER	8
6.	Eddie IRVINE	6
	Olivier PANIS	6
8.	R. SCHUMACHER	4
9.	Johnny HERBERT	3
	Nicola LARINI	1
	Jean ALESI	1

Constructors :

1.	Williams / Renault	20
2.	McLaren / Mercedes	19
3.	Ferrari	14
4.	Benetton / Renault	11
5.	Prost / Mugen Honda	6
6.	Jordan / Peugeot	4
7.	Sauber / Petronas	4

CLASSIFICATION & RETIREMENTS

Pos	Driver	Team	Time
1.	Villeneuve	Williams Renault	in 1h52'01"715
2.	Irvine	Ferrari	at 0"979
3.	Schumacher	Jordan Peugeot	at 12"089
4.	Herbert	Sauber Petronas	at 29"919
5.	Hakkinen	McLaren Mercedes	at 30"351
6.	Berger	Benetton Renault	at 31"393
7.	Alesi	Benetton Renault	at 46"359
8.	Salo	Tyrrell Ford	at 1 lap
9.	Trulli	Minardi Hart	at 1 lap
10.	Magnussen	Stewart Ford	oil pressure

Lap	Driver	Team	Reason
1	Schumacher	Ferrari	accident
1	Coulthard	McLaren Mercedes	accident
6	Frentzen	Williams Renault	clutch
19	Panis	Prost Mugen Honda	engine
25	Barrichello	Stewart Ford	hydraulics
25	Fisichella	Jordan Peugeot	accident
34	Hill	Arrows Yamaha	engine
38	Katayama	Minardi Hart	spin
44	Verstappen	Tyrrell Ford	engine
50	Nakano	Prost Mugen Honda	engine
51	Diniz	Arrows Yamaha	engine
64	Larini	Sauber Petronas	spin

FASTEST LAPS

	Driver	Time	Lap
1.	Berger	1'27"981	63
2.	Villeneuve	1'28"028	54
3.	R. Schum.	1'28"382	56
4.	Larini	1'28"410	46
5.	Irvine	1'28"473	63
6.	Alesi	1'28"827	33
7.	Hakkinen	1'29"076	58
8.	Panis	1'29"090	8
9.	Herbert	1'29"296	62
10.	Verstappen	1'29"541	43
11.	Magnussen	1'29"834	48
12.	Nakano	1'29"865	40
13.	Barrichello	1'29"913	23
14.	Salo	1'29"931	62
15.	Fisichella	1'30"278	19
16.	Trulli	1'30"593	53
17.	Hill	1'30"649	23
18.	Diniz	1'31"111	42
19.	Frentzen	1'31"832	5
20.	Katayama	1'31"869	29

THIRD ROUND

GRAN PREMIO MARLBORO DE ARGENTINA, BUENOS AIRES

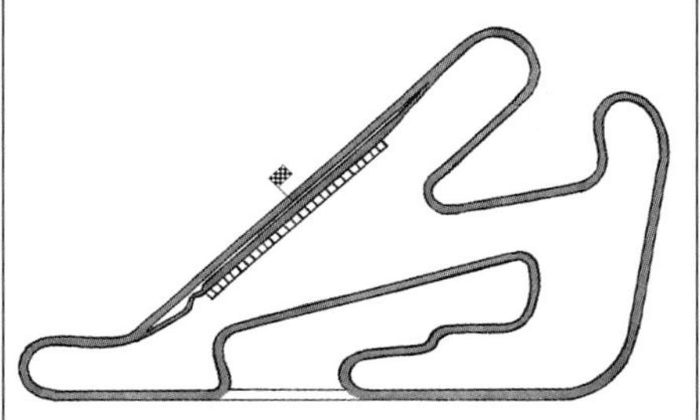

Date :	April 13, 1997
Length:	4257 meters
Distance :	72 laps, 306.502 km
Weather:	sunny, 21 degrees

RACE SUMMARY

- At the first corner, Villeneuve leads from Frentzen. Further back, Schumacher tangles with Barrichello and Coulthard is also knocked out of the race, trying to avoid them.
- The safety car is brought out to control the field, while the three cars are pulled off the track.
- The race gets underway again on lap 5, with Villeneuve leading Frentzen and Panis.
- Frentzen retires on lap 6 with a gearbox problem.
- Panis, in second place, under seven seconds behind Villeneuve, retires on lap 19 with hydraulic failure.
- Villeneuve makes his first pit-stop on lap 22 and rejoins, still in the lead, ahead of Irvine.
- After Irvine refuels, Fisichella finds himself in second spot. On lap 25, his team-mate Ralf Schumacher pushes him off the track and helps himself to second place.
- Villeneuve makes his second pit-stop on lap 38 and does not inherit the lead again, until Irvine makes his second stop.
- Villeneuve makes his third visit to the pitt

WEEK-END GOSSIP

• Alain Prost at the last minute

The agreement signed before the Brazilian Grand Prix between Prost Grand Prix and BIC gave the company's Argentinian office a few headaches. On Friday, the sign writers were hard at work, painting two enormous advertising hoardings at the side of the Autopista 35, the road which leads from the town centre to the track. «Alain Prost Grand Prix corre con BIC.» The work was completed just in time to attract the attention of Saturday's crowd.

• Television crazy

The Argentinians have two obsessions: motor racing and television and in Buenos Aires one can tune in to no less than 65 different channels. Several of them show American films in the original version, another shows non-stop tango 24 hours a day and then there is a huge choice of sports programmes, which naturally enough, devoted masses of air time to the grand prix. On the Sunday before the race, one could watch no less than five programmes showing various races, from the first Indycar race of the year at Surfers Paradise to dozens of local races from stock cars to Formula 3.

• Uncle Ken's retro look

The Tyrrell team stops at nothing to come up with something original. The proof of this was the new and ugly cross wings mounted alongside the cockpit on Uncle Ken's cars in Buenos Aires.

This, so called, "slow track" configuration is supposed to generate extra downforce on tighter circuits like Buenos Aires, Monaco and Budapest.

Biscuits for Damon

In Buenos Aires, Damon Hill's car carried the logos of an Argentinian savoury biscuit called «Rex». It was hardly a major deal and would probably only serve to keep the team in biscuits for the year, as it was just a one off deal for this race.

• BAT reveals its plans

The rumour had already done the rounds in Brazil, but it was pretty much confirmed in Argentina, according to the quality newspaper, the «Times» of London.

According to the paper, the board of BAT, which owns several cigarette brands, had decided to finance the creation of a new F1 team, with a budget of 25 million pounds per year. This was a big enough sum of money to allow for the creation of a top team, which BAT wanted to see win races right from its very first season. The cars, nicknamed BAT-mobiles would be designed and built by Reynard. Adrian Newey, who had left Williams in November, was also linked to the project.

▷ *You can't beat a quick Tango to round off your daily four hour training session. On Thursday before the race, Michael Schumacher enters into the spirit of the thing when a Ferrari sponsor organised a little dancing lesson for him.*

Rothman
thmans
http://www.icnsports

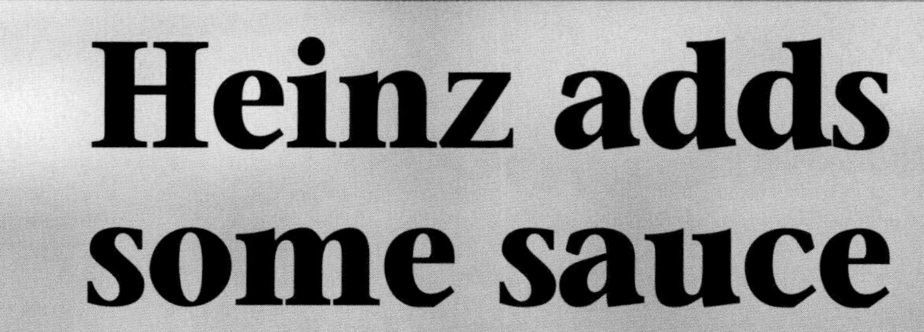

Heinz adds some sauce

In England and in Germany they were saying he was all washed up. The specialist press could not hide their disappointment with Heinz-Harald Frentzen's performance so far this season.
At Imola, the German silenced his critics with a faultless performance, which resulted in the first win of his career. Jacques Villeneuve was forced to retire with gearbox problems, while Michael Schumacher was catching him in the championship, thanks to his second place.

GRAN PREMIO DI SAN MARINO IMOLA

The two Williams fought over pole

△
Third place on the grid for Michael Schumacher. Imola was the inaugural race for the Scuderia's Step 2 engine.

Another good practice session for Olivier Panis, who qualified fourth, much to the delight of Alain Prost.
▷ ▽

The Heinz-Harald season starts here

Heinz-Harald Frentzen had finally found his bearings. In the first three races of the season, the German was overshadowed by his team mate Jacques Villeneuve and seemed hard pushed to match the Canadian's pace.
If you believed the Williams driver, those days were now over.
At Imola on Saturday, «HH» proved his point and showed he was that time definitely in the groove. In the morning's free practice session, the German was quickest. Then, in the afternoon, he made life difficult for Villeneuve, eventually having to settle for second place, just over three tenths of a second slower than his team-mate. *«I think that my problems are finally coming to an end,»* said Frentzen, congratulating himself on his achievement. *«Last week in private testing, I landed on a new way of setting up my car, which suits me much better. This morning, I went even further down that route and everything was almost perfect. I thought I could get pole, but a Prost kicked up some sand when I was on my quickest lap and I was forced to lift off.»*
At the end of this duel at the head of the field, it was finally Jacques Villeneuve who took pole, for the fourth time in four races! *«I must say it was not easy today,»* admitted the man from Quebec. *«This was the hardest fight I have had so far with Heinz-Harald. It was good fun.»*
In the race, the biggest danger to the Williams would come from their brakes, rather than any of the other competitors. *«We have solved the problem we had in Melbourne,»* explained Villeneuve, *«But the brakes still have a hard time here. The car is quite stiff this year and we are applying up to 150 kilos of pressure to the brake pedal. Over ten laps this is not a problem. But over a race distance I wonder if I will last to the end.»* With Frentzen alongside the Canadian, the stage was set for a season long battle between the two...or so we thought. *«I knew the first three grands prix would be tough,»* said «HH». *«And I always felt my season would begin in Imola.»*
This late start meant the German was 20 points down on the Canadian.

STARTING GRID

Row		
-1-	Heinz-H. FRENTZEN 1'23"646	Jacques VILLENEUVE 1'23"303
-2-	Olivier PANIS 1'24"075	M. SCHUMACHER 1'23"955
-3-	G. FISICHELLA 1'24"596	R. SCHUMACHER 1'24"081
-4-	Mika HAKKINEN 1'24"812	Johnny HERBERT 1'24"723
-5-	David COULTHARD 1'25"077	Eddie IRVINE 1'24"861
-6-	Nicola LARINI 1'25"544	Gerhard BERGER 1'25"371
-7-	Jean ALESI 1'25"729	R. BARRICHELLO 1'25"579
-8-	Jan MAGNUSSEN 1'26"192	Damon HILL 1'25"743
-9-	Shinji NAKANO 1'26"712	Pedro DINIZ 1'26"253
-10-	Jarno TRULLI 1'26"960	Mika SALO 1'26"852
-11-	Ukyo KATAYAMA 1'28"727	Jos VERSTAPPEN 1'27"428

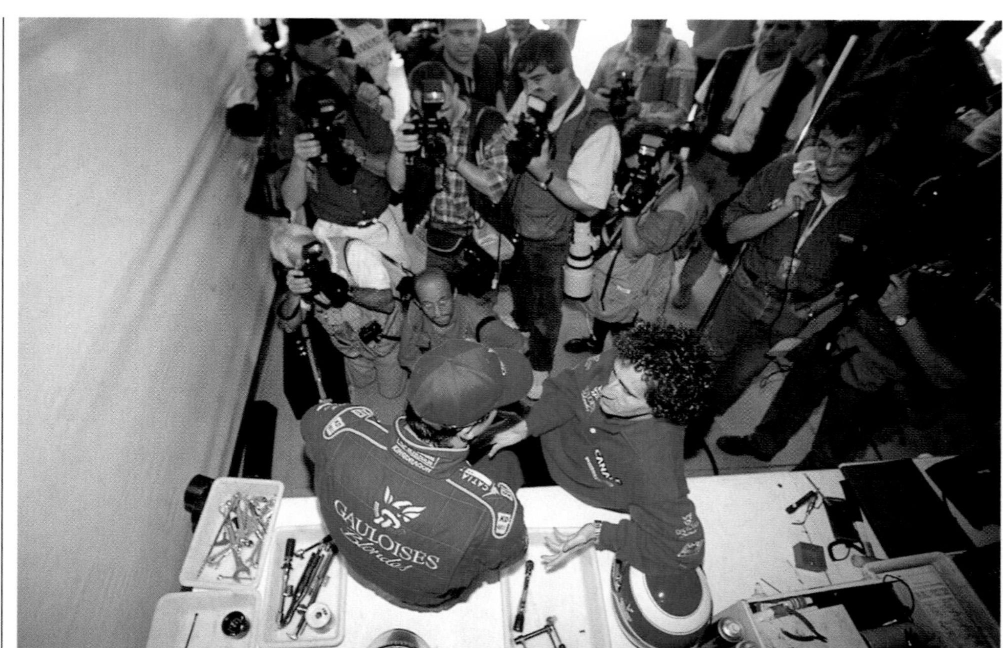

Full marks for «HH»

△
Lights out to start the fourth Grand Prix of the season. Frentzen lets Schumacher squeeze through and finishes the first lap in third place. 62 laps later he would be drinking champagne on the podium. (photo on left)

They said he was inconsistent on the track. They said he lacked mental toughness. He was driving a Williams-Renault, reputed to be the best car of the field and yet he had failed to score a single point so far this season. For many, Heinz-Harald Frentzen was a lost cause. The time had come to stem the tide of disapproval. Mission accomplished. In Imola, he never put a foot wrong. Third at the end of the first lap, «HH» took the chequered flag just over one second ahead of the Ferrari to take the first grand prix win of his career at his 51st attempt. It was an emotional moment. *«I am speechless. It is impossible to describe what I feel at this moment,»* he said as he stepped down from the podium. *«It is an extraordinary feeling, as though oil is running in my heart.»* Quite a poet really.
Heinz-Harald had to fight right to the bitter end for this win. *«At the end of the race, I was trying above all to maintain my concentration. I was thinking about a thousand things at once: about the rain, which had started to leave drops on my visor; about the brakes, which we were not sure would hold until the end and about Michael, whom I had to fend off.»*
The German created his chance of victory during the pit-stops. *«When Jacques and Michael stopped, my engineer told me over the radio that it was down to me now. I did two laps at qualifying pace and was about one second quicker than my usual pace.»* This resulted in «HH» popping out of the pits, after his own stop, ahead of Michael Schumacher and Jacques Villeneuve. *«I had to zig-zag a bit to keep Michael behind me,»* admitted «HH». *«But after all he had done the same to me at the start of the race. Today, it was my day.»*

IN THE POINTS

	Driver	Team	Time
1.	Heinz-H. FRENTZEN	Rothmans Williams Renault	1 h 31'00"673
2.	Michael SCHUMACHER	Scuderia Ferrari Marlboro	at 1"237
3.	Eddie IRVINE	Scuderia Ferrari Marlboro	at 1'18"343
4.	Giancarlo FISICHELLA	B&H Total Jordan Peugeot	at 1'23"388
5.	Jean ALESI	Mild Seven Benetton Renault	at 1 lap
6.	Mika HAKKINEN	West McLaren Mercedes	at 1 lap

Fastest lap : H.-H. FRENTZEN, lap 42, 1'25"531, avg. 207.503 km/h

The Ferraris signal their intentions

For the ranks of tifosi massed around the Imola circuit, Sunday's race could be filed away as a failure.
Of course, both «their» cars finished on the podium, which was something to be pleased about, but victory, the only acceptable result in their eyes, had eluded them.
However, for Michael Schumacher, the result of the San Marino Grand Prix gave cause for optimism, because for the first time this season, the Ferraris had managed to match the cracking pace set by the Williams.
The German might not have won, but he was only a few car lengths behind. Victory could not be too far off. *«I never thought I could finish second,»* he confessed after the race. *«Given our performance in practice, I was expecting third place at best. But I have to say the car was absolutely fantastic today, even though we had chosen an intermediate set- up, just in case it started to rain during the race.»*
Right from the start, the German had slotted in close behind Jacques Villeneuve and seemed to have no trouble in keeping up. *«My speed was very similar to his in the most important sections of the track,»* he explained. *«This is very encouraging, when I think of the various improvements we have in the pipeline.»*
The Scuderia's Sporting Director, Jean Todt shared his driver's enthusiasm. *«It is clear that we are still slightly lagging behind the Williams, but not by much,»* was his analysis of the situation. *«We have a few modifications still to come, which should allow us to move ahead, starting from the French Grand Prix. The critical thing is not to lose too much ground in the championship until then.»*
In third place, Eddie Irvine confirmed that the Scuderia was in good shape. *«I made quite a good start»*, explained the Irishman, *«But there was nowhere for me to pass and I had to back off* (it is good to know he can do that after all!) *Then I realised that the four in front were pulling away, as was Panis, so I decided to take it easy.»* Eddie even went so far as to describe the end of his race as «boring».

△
The gentle Emilia Romagna countryside. Sandwiched between the urban landscapes of Buenos Aires and Monaco, the San Marino leg of the championship is always much appreciated by the Formula 1 circus.

At Imola, many were the drivers who only saw the back end of Eddie Irvine's car, as he made the most of Ferrari's progress to take third spot.
◁

Jacques Villeneuve dances in the rain. After two days of fine weather, the heavens opened over the Emilia region on Sunday morning and the warm-up provided a few graceful skating moments.
The Canadian was sixth in the half hour session, while an on-form Heinz-Harald Frentzen was quickest.

Rothmans
RENAULT
Rothmans
Rothmans

△
David Coulthard waits for the good times. After winning in Melbourne, the Scotsman seemed to have lost his way. In Imola, he would retire on lap 39 with an engine problem.

Three years after the death of «Magic» Senna, a statue of him was unveiled near the Tamburello corner, where the accident took place.
▷ ▽

Jacques Villeneuve gives 1998 rules a pasting

Everyone in Formula 1 was agreed that there is not enough overtaking in grand prix racing. In 1996 therefore, the FIA decided to tackle the problem.
The end result, arrived at with the help and expertise of several engineers, was a new set of regulations to be introduced for the 1998 season.
The main points of the new rules were that the width of the cars would be reduced to 180 centimetres (a reduction of 20 cms) and that grooved tyres would replace the slicks (see pages 218 - 219.) The aim was to reduce cornering speeds and to increase braking distances, thus making for closer racing.
In the week prior to Imola, the Williams team went to Barcelona, where they were the first to run a test car built to these new regulations. While their test driver, Jean- Christophe Boullion ran the narrow car, it fell to Jacques Villeneuve to try the grooved tyres. He was definitely not impressed. *«It's a joke»*, he told anyone who cared to listen, when he arrived at Imola. *«It is like driving a Formula Ford, but with a lot more power. You can brake as hard as before with these tyres, but you lose all feeling for the car. F1 is supposed to be the pinnacle of the sport, but if this is what it will be like, then I would rather quit. It's ridiculous.»*

Original aim not going to happen

According to the Canadian, the original aim of increasing overtaking opportunities by increasing braking distances was not going to happen. *«I do not understand why overtaking is supposed to be easier if the braking distance is longer,»* he continued. *«In any case, everyone brakes on the limit and it is difficult to do any better, whether the braking distance is long or not.»*
Asked on Thursday for his views on Villeneuve's opinion, FIA President, Max Mosley said that a single Williams test session would not be enough to invalidate the 1998 rules. *«We must wait,»* he remarked.
Supporting this view, Ferrari made it clear at Imola, that it would not agree to go back on the changes, or at least on the width reduction of the monocoque.
The Scuderia claimed it had already invested too much in the 1998 chassis to throw all its drawings in the bin.

First points for «Fisico»

The Jordans were definitely in cracking form. After Ralf Schumacher finished on the podium in Argentina, it was Giancarlo Fisichella's turn to shine, as he finished fourth at Imola.
One hour after the end of the race, «Fisico» was still in the garage, sweating inside his race suit as he signed autographs.
He was obviously savouring the moment of his first F1 points. *«I am very excited with this result,»* he exclaimed. *«I might have been able to finish on the podium, because my car was exceptional today. My biggest mistake was to have made a bad start and I ended up stuck behind Panis and Irvine.»*
Ralf Schumacher, in the other Jordan, had made a very good start, matching Frentzen's pace, before having to retire on lap 18 with a broken half-shaft.

PRACTICE TIMES

No	Driver	Make/Engine/Chassis	Practice Friday	Practice Saturday	Qualifying	Warm-up
1.	Damon Hill	Arrows/Yamaha/A18/3 (B)	1'27"334	1'26"034	1'25"743	1'50"824
2.	Pedro Diniz	Arrows/Yamaha/A18/2 (B)	1'29"117	1'27"042	1'26"253	1'52"171
3.	Jacques Villeneuve	Williams/Renault/FW19/4 (G)	1'26"499	1'23"739	1'23"303	1'50"727
4.	Heinz-Harald Frentzen	Williams/Renault/FW19/5 (G)	1'26"600	1'23"477	1'23"646	1'48"505
5.	Michael Schumacher	Ferrari/Ferrari/F310B/174 (G)	1'25"997	1'24"982	1'23"955	1'49"160
6.	Eddie Irvine	Ferrari/Ferrari/F310B/173 (G)	1'25"981	1'24"719	1'24"861	1'48"528
7.	Jean Alesi	Benetton/Renault/B197/5 (G)	1'26"382	1'25"586	1'25"729	1'51"315
8.	Gerhard Berger	Benetton/Renault/B197/4 (G)	1'26"259	1'25"027	1'25"371	1'52"927
9.	Mika Hakkinen	McLaren/Mercedes/MP4/12/2 (G)	1'27"184	1'24"980	1'24"812	1'51"772
10.	David Coulthard	McLaren/Mercedes/MP4/12/4 (G)	1'26"549	1'26"226	1'25"077	1'48"605
11.	Ralf Schumacher	Jordan/Peugeot/197/3 (G)	1'28"091	1'24"626	1'24"081	1'50"483
12.	Giancarlo Fisichella	Jordan/Peugeot/197/4 (G)	1'27"612	1'24"325	1'24"596	1'50"807
14.	Olivier Panis	Prost/Mugen Honda/JS45/3 (B)	1'26"779	1'24"586	1'24"075	1'48"547
15.	Shinji Nakano	Prost/Mugen Honda/JS45/2 (B)	1'29"021	1'27"709	1'26"712	1'52"581
16.	Johnny Herbert	Sauber/Petronas/C16/1 (G)	1'26"842	1'24"766	1'24"723	1'51"904
17.	Nicola Larini	Sauber/Petronas/C16/2 (G)	1'26"831	1'25"650	1'25"544	1'51"953
18.	Jos Verstappen	Tyrrell/Ford/025/2 (G)	1'29"736	1'27"383	1'27"428	1'51"094
19.	Mika Salo	Tyrrell/Ford/025/3 (G)	1'29"087	1'27"004	1'26"852	1'53"344
20.	Ukyo Katayama	Minardi/Hart/M197/3 (B)	1'29"974		1'28"727	1'50"994
21.	Jarno Trulli	Minardi/Hart/M197/2 (B)	1'30"820	1'27"970	1'26"960	1'53"771
22.	Rubens Barrichello	Stewart/Ford/SF1/2 (B)	1'26"679	1'25"586	1'25"579	1'50"754
23.	Jan Magnussen	Stewart/Ford/SF1/3 (B)	1'28"177	1'25"791	1'26"192	1'50"556

CLASSIFICATION & RETIREMENTS

Pos	Driver	Team	Time
1.	Frentzen	Williams Renault	in 1h31'00"673
2.	Schumacher	Ferrari	at 1"237
3.	Irvine	Ferrari	at 1'18"343
4.	Fisichella	Jordan Peugeot	at 1'23"388
5.	Alesi	Benetton Renault	at 1 lap
6.	Hakkinen	McLaren Mercedes	at 1 lap
7.	Larini	Sauber Petronas	at 1 lap
8.	Panis	Prost Mugen Honda	at 1 lap
9.	Salo	Tyrrell Ford	at 2 laps
10.	Verstappen	Tyrrell Ford	at 2 laps
11.	Katayama	Minardi Hart	at 3 laps

Lap	Driver	Team	Reason
1	Trulli	Minardi Hart	pompe hydraul.
3	Magnussen	Stewart Ford	off
5	Berger	Benetton Renault	spin
12	Hill	Arrows Yamaha	off
12	Nakano	Prost Mugen Honda	accident
18	Schumacher	Jordan Peugeot	transmission
19	Herbert	Sauber Petronas	electrics
33	Barrichello	Stewart Ford	oil pressure
39	Coulthard	McLaren Mercedes	engine
41	Villeneuve	Williams Renault	gearbox
54	Diniz	Arrows Yamaha	gearbox

FASTEST LAPS

	Driver	Time	Lap
1.	Frentzen	1'25"531	42
2.	M. Schum.	1'25"537	61
3.	Villeneuve	1'25"997	21
4.	Coulthard	1'26"067	33
5.	Fisichella	1'26"620	23
6.	Larini	1'26"753	43
7.	Hakkinen	1'26"791	29
8.	Irvine	1'26"811	45
9.	Alesi	1'27"091	30
10.	R. Schum.	1'27"217	17
11.	Herbert	1'27"594	17
12.	Barrichello	1'27"741	28
13.	Diniz	1'27"793	45
14.	Panis	1'28"064	27
15.	Salo	1'28"189	32
16.	Verstappen	1'28"886	54
17.	Hill	1'29"237	8
18.	Katayama	1'29"554	59
19.	Nakano	1'30"554	11
20.	Berger	1'33"513	4
21.	Magnussen	1'36"710	2

WEEK-END GOSSIP

- **Death threat for Irvine**

Who says Formula 1 cares nothing for frontiers and nationalities? After their little lad got on the podium in Argentina, Eddie Irvine's parents received death threats. The flag raised behind Irvine on the podium was the Irish one, but Irvine comes from Northern Ireland and is therefore a British citizen. *«I had asked for a neutral flag that would offend no one,»* said Irvine in Imola. *«But they told me that was not possible.»*

- **Newey to McLaren**

Adrian Newey, considered to be one of the best aerodynamicists in F1 has found refuge at McLaren. Because of contractual clauses with Williams involving a ban on working for other teams, he would not be starting until 1st August and would therefore have little influence on the grey team's 1998 car according to Ron Dennis. Believe this if you want. He was reputed to be on a salary of .2 million, which should have satisfied the man who was unhappy with his pay at Williams.

- **Bye Bye Lola**

After its brief F1 appearance in the Australian Grand Prix, the Lola team had pulled out of the sport, «in order to find new sponsors.» But any hope of ever seeing the team again had gone. The team went bankrupt on 28th April and its equipment had been sold at auction. To avoid similar fiascos in the future, Bernie Ecclestone planned to change the rules for entry into the sport. Up until now, a new team who wanted to take part in the championship, had to pay a $500,000 deposit to the FIA, which was refundable if the team took part in every race of its first season. This was obviously too small a sum, as many new teams were able to find the money, so Mr. E decided to up the ante to 24 million pounds! paid back to the teams at the rate of two million pounds per month plus interest, over the first two years. This would effectively weed out the less than serious players.

- **Hill in trouble**

The days of victory seemed a long way back in the past. Since the start of the season, Damon Hill was reduced to fighting hard for minor places in the race order. It was unworthy of his talent and his world championship crown. It was during one of these unnoticed duels at Imola, that the Englishman collided with Shinji Nakano's Prost, while the two men were fighting for the honour of being second from last! *«I had been stuck behind him for over a lap,»* explained Hill when he got back to the pits. *«He kept shutting the door on me and I finally lost my patience.»* Hill had been forced to start from the pit lane in the team's spare car, after an oil leak was discovered on his race car.

LAP CHART

position:	1	2	3	4	5	6	7	8	9	10	11	12	13	14	15	16	17	18	19	20	21	22
start:	3	4	5	14	11	12	16	9	6	10	8	17	22	7	1	23	2	15	19	21	18	20
1	3	5	4	11	16	14	6	12	10	9	7	22	17	2	23	18	19	15	8	20	1	
2	3	5	4	11	16	14	6	12	10	9	7	22	17	2	23	18	19	15	8	20	1	
3	3	5	4	11	16	14	6	12	10	9	7	22	17	2	18	19	15	8	20	1		
4	3	5	4	11	16	14	6	12	10	9	7	22	17	2	18	19	15	8	20	1		
5	3	5	4	11	16	14	6	12	10	9	7	22	17	2	18	19	15	1	20			
6	3	5	4	11	16	14	6	12	10	9	7	22	17	2	18	19	15	1	20			
7	3	5	4	11	16	14	6	12	10	9	7	22	17	2	18	19	15	1	20			
8	3	5	4	11	16	14	6	12	10	9	7	22	17	2	18	19	15	1	20			
9	3	5	4	11	16	14	6	12	10	9	7	22	17	2	18	19	15	1	20			
10	3	5	4	11	16	14	6	12	10	9	7	22	17	2	18	19	15	1	20			
11	3	5	4	11	16	14	6	12	10	9	7	22	17	2	18	19	15	1	20			
12	3	5	4	11	16	14	6	12	10	9	7	17	22	2	18	19	20					
13	3	5	4	11	16	14	6	12	10	9	7	17	22	2	18	19	20					
14	3	5	4	11	16	14	6	12	10	9	7	17	22	2	18	19	20					
15	3	5	4	11	16	14	6	12	10	9	7	17	22	2	18	19	20					
16	3	5	4	11	16	14	6	12	10	9	7	17	22	2	18	19	20					
17	3	5	4	11	16	14	6	12	10	9	7	17	22	2	18	19	20					
18	3	5	4	16	6	12	14	10	9	7	17	22	18	19	2	20						
19	3	5	4	6	12	14	10	9	7	17	22	18	19	2	20							
20	3	5	4	6	12	10	9	7	17	14	22	18	19	2	20							
21	3	5	4	6	12	10	9	7	17	22	14	18	19	2	20							
22	3	5	4	6	12	10	9	7	17	22	14	18	19	2	20							
23	3	5	4	6	12	10	9	7	17	22	14	18	19	2	20							
24	3	4	5	6	12	10	9	7	17	22	14	18	19	2	20							
25	3	4	5	10	9	7	6	12	22	14	17	18	19	2	20							
26	4	3	5	10	9	7	6	12	22	14	17	18	19	2	20							
27	4	5	3	10	9	7	6	12	22	14	17	18	19	2	20							
28	4	5	3	10	9	7	6	12	22	14	17	18	19	2	20							
29	4	5	3	10	9	7	6	12	22	14	17	18	19	2	20							
30	4	5	3	10	9	7	6	12	22	14	17	18	19	2	20							
31	4	5	3	10	9	7	6	12	22	14	17	19	2	18	20							
32	4	5	3	10	9	7	6	12	22	14	17	19	2	18	20							
33	4	5	3	10	9	6	12	7	14	17	2	19	18	20								
34	4	5	3	10	9	6	12	7	17	14	2	19	18	20								
35	4	5	3	10	6	12	9	7	17	14	2	19	18	20								
36	4	5	3	10	6	12	7	9	17	14	2	19	18	20								
37	4	5	3	10	6	12	7	9	17	14	2	19	18	20								
38	4	5	3	10	12	6	7	9	17	14	2	19	18	20								
39	4	5	3	12	6	7	9	17	14	2	19	18	20									
40	4	5	3	12	6	7	9	17	14	2	19	18	20									
41	4	5	12	6	7	9	17	14	19	18	2	20										
42	4	5	12	6	7	9	17	14	19	18	2	20										
43	4	5	12	6	7	9	17	14	19	18	2	20										
44	5	4	6	12	7	9	17	14	19	18	2	20										
45	4	5	6	12	7	9	17	14	19	18	2	20										
46	4	5	6	12	7	9	17	14	19	18	2	20										
47	4	5	6	12	7	9	17	14	19	18	2	20										
48	4	5	6	12	7	9	17	14	19	18	2	20										
49	4	5	6	12	7	9	17	14	19	18	2	20										
50	4	5	6	12	7	9	17	14	19	18	2	20										
51	4	5	6	12	7	9	17	14	19	18	2	20										
52	4	5	6	12	7	9	17	14	19	18	2	20										
53	4	5	6	12	7	9	17	14	19	18	2	20										
54	4	5	6	12	7	9	17	14	19	18	20											
55	4	5	6	12	7	9	17	14	19	18	20											
56	4	5	6	12	7	9	17	14	19	18	20											
57	4	5	6	12	7	9	17	14	19	18	20											
58	4	5	6	12	7	9	17	14	19	18	20											
59	4	5	6	12	7	9	17	14	19	18	20											
60	4	5	6	12	7	9	17	14	19	18												
61	4	5	6	12	7	9	17	14														
62	4	5	6	12																		

FOURTH ROUND

GRAN PREMIO DI SAN MARINO, IMOLA

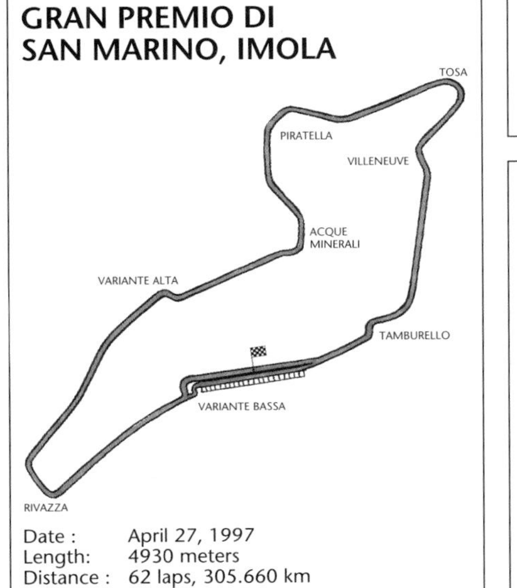

Date : April 27, 1997
Length: 4930 meters
Distance : 62 laps, 305.660 km
Weather: cloudy, 17 degrees

All results

Best result for a Bridgestone shod runner:

Olivier Panis, Prost Mugen Honda, *8th*

CHAMPIONSHIPS

(after four rounds)

Drivers:

	Driver	Points
1.	Jacques VILLENEUVE	20
2.	M. SCHUMACHER	14
3.	David COULTHARD	10
	Heinz-H. FRENTZEN	10
	Eddie IRVINE	10
	Gerhard BERGER	10
	Mika HAKKINEN	10
8.	Olivier PANIS	6
9.	R. SCHUMACHER	4
10.	Johnny HERBERT	3
	Giancarlo FISICHELLA	3
	Jean ALESI	3
12.	Nicola LARINI	1

Constructors :

	Constructor	Points
1.	Williams / Renault	30
2.	Ferrari	24
3.	McLaren / Mercedes	20
4.	Benetton / Renault	13
5.	Jordan / Peugeot	7
6.	Prost / Mugen Honda	6
7.	Sauber / Petronas	4

RACE SUMMARY

- Villeneuve makes the best start, ahead of Michael Schumacher and Frentzen. Panis is overtaken by Ralf Schumacher and Herbert.
- In the early stages, the Villeneuve-M. Schumacher-Frentzen-R. Schumacher pack pulls away. Further back, Panis is holding up Irvine, Fisichella and the two McLarens.
- On lap 12, Hill tangles with Nakano and both have to retire.
- On lap 18, Irvine and Fisichella pass Panis, while ahead of them, Ralf Schumacher retires.
- Schumacher pits on lap 24, as does Villeneuve two laps later, before re-joining behind the Ferrari.
- Frentzen pits on the following lap and then takes the lead, ahead of Schumacher and Villeneuve.
- On lap 39 Coulthard goes out with a broken engine and Fisichella makes the

Return of the tightrope walker

In a class of his own, Michael Schumacher was once again the author of a legendary drive in the sumptuous surroundings of Monaco.
In the rain, he ran away from the field to take victory and the lead in the world championship. Williams made a complete mess of things, deciding to start on slick tyres, despite the pouring rain. The mistake would cost them dear in the championship.

arexons
GRAND PRIX DE MONACO
MONTE-CARLO

△ Johnny Herbert in the lavish setting of Monaco. On Thursday, the local boy, who along with 13 other F1 drivers lives in the Principality, set the fastest time in practice.

In the aftermath of his win in Imola

Heinz-Harald's first pole

It is what is known as the state of grace. That condition where success just flows and Heinz-Harald Frentzen was enjoying his moment of glory. After winning in Imola, two weeks earlier, the German followed it up by securing pole position for the Monaco Grand Prix.
In Monte Carlo everything is more expensive, including the best seats on the starting grid. As every overtaking move in the race requires a degree of irresponsibility, a good grid position is vital if you have any plans of winning the race. Heinz-Harald Frentzen on Saturday, was therefore more than pleased with himself for notching up his first ever pole position on this circuit, in the last few minutes of the session. *«I did not think I would be able to match Michael's time,»* revealed the Williams driver. *«Especially as I was not completely happy with my car as I had no grip at the front end. With Tim, my engineer, we decided to make a complete change to my set-up for my last run. It was a bit of gamble but it payed off as the car was perfect! When the team told me over the radio what my time was, they said Michael still had one run left, so I had to sit and wait until I could celebrate.»*
The pole position gave «HH» the feeling that he might win another race. *«Of course I am ideally placed. I will do everything I can to be ready for it. I will get a good night's sleep and I certainly will not touch a drop of alcohol this evening!»*

«HH» in action. His efforts were to be rewarded with pole position. ▽

Benetton lose the plot and are shooting in the dark

There were a lot of disappointed people after Monaco qualifying this year. That was certainly the case at Prost, as Olivier Panis was only 12th and admitted he had never found a good set-up.
But Benetton were in even bigger trouble. The root of the problem was a badly balanced car, which never let its tyres reach their optimum working temperature in qualifying. *«As soon as we run the car with a light fuel load and push the car to its limits, the differential plays tricks on us,»* explained Gerhard Berger. *«In the same corner, you can go from full understeer to complete oversteer without any warning.»*
The problem was a real mystery to the team engineers. *«We don't really know what to do about it,»* confessed Benetton's chief engineer, Nick Wirth. *«At the moment we are shooting in the dark. We are taking educated guesses and we hope to land on the right solution!»*
Benetton arrived with a new aerodynamic package for this race and a new electronic differential. Sadly on Saturday, all these new modifications, efforts and promises came to nought as the Benettons only qualified 9th (Alesi) and way down in 17th (Berger.)

In Monaco, the number of people with the right accreditation is inversely proportional to the space available in the pit-lane. This results in the sort of queues you see at the local supermarket on a Saturday morning. ▽

Herbert is quickest on Thursday. The Saubers are on top form

△
Michael Schumacher squeezed onto the starting grid between the two Williams. To his great surprise, the German topped the time sheet for most of the one hour session, until he was knocked off his perch in the dying moments by Heinz-Harald Frentzen.

«Go Johnny Go.» On Thursday, squeezed into the spectator area on the slope leading to the Grimaldi Palace, a group of Johnny Herbert fans were frantically waving their banners, every time their hero in Sauber No. 16 went by. Johnny Herbert probably never saw them and on this day he did not seem to need any encouragement. In top form, the Englishman put up the quickest time of the day, impudently quicker than the Ferraris and Williams. *«I love Monaco,»* he declared, just minutes after doing his time. *«It's not just because I live here. It is definitely the toughest track on the calendar.»* With a schoolboy smile, Herbert added he was not surprised by his performance as his car had been so good since the start of the season. To cap it all, the Sauber team had come up with a new aerodynamic package for this race, which had been tested the previous week in Barcelona and seemed to be very effective. *«With these modifications we have managed to keep the car well balanced, while improving the downforce,»* added Herbert. *«That is particularly important here and anyway the car is very good in the three slowest corners on this track. If we can get rid of some of its understeer it would be almost perfect.»*
Quickest time or no, Peter Sauber was as phlegmatic as ever. *«It's only Thursday,»* he said, chewing on his cigar. *«I am very happy, but I would be just as happy if we qualified in the front three rows on Saturday.»*
The boss was write to sound a note of caution, as on Saturday, Johnny Herbert could do no better than seventh place and thus missed out on the objective of the top three rows.
It was a close thing as he missed out on sixth place, which eventually went to Ralf Schumacher, by just 16 hundredths of a second. *«Unfortunately the track conditions changed this afternoon,»* regretted the English driver. *«This morning, we took off some of the downforce on the front wing and this afternoon we had to go back to Thursday's settings. At times it felt as though the car was split in two and I had to hold it together. It was a shame. At the end, the car was a bit better but it still had too much understeer to hope for anything better.»*

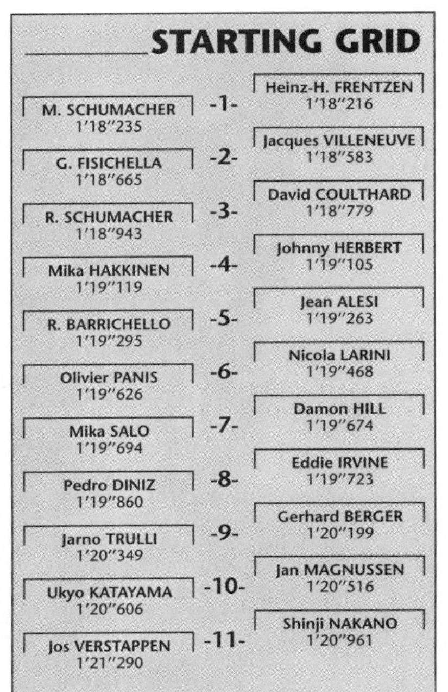

STARTING GRID

Row		
-1-	M. SCHUMACHER 1'18"235	Heinz-H. FRENTZEN 1'18"216
-2-	G. FISICHELLA 1'18"665	Jacques VILLENEUVE 1'18"583
-3-	R. SCHUMACHER 1'18"943	David COULTHARD 1'18"779
-4-	Mika HAKKINEN 1'19"119	Johnny HERBERT 1'19"105
-5-	R. BARRICHELLO 1'19"295	Jean ALESI 1'19"263
-6-	Olivier PANIS 1'19"626	Nicola LARINI 1'19"468
-7-	Mika SALO 1'19"694	Damon HILL 1'19"674
-8-	Pedro DINIZ 1'19"860	Eddie IRVINE 1'19"723
-9-	Jarno TRULLI 1'20"349	Gerhard BERGER 1'20"199
-10-	Ukyo KATAYAMA 1'20"606	Jan MAGNUSSEN 1'20"516
-11-	Jos VERSTAPPEN 1'21"290	Shinji NAKANO 1'20"961

A fantastic win for Michael Schumacher

△ In a class of his own, Michael Schumacher put on an incredible display of race craft and car control in the pouring rain that fell on the Monaco Grand Prix. Here, he tackles the port chicane.

The photo that proves the error of their ways. At the end of lap 2, Heinz-Harald Frentzen, who had started from pole, on slicks, tries to fend off Jean Alesi who was ninth on the grid. It is what is known as getting it wrong. ▷

The tightrope walker returns

The race has just ended. Michael Schumacher parks his car under the royal box, undoes his belts and steps out of his Ferrari. The winner of the Monaco Grand Prix looks as though he has been on a Sunday afternoon drive. *«Yes, I feel fine,»* he confirmed a few minutes later. *«I must say that driving in the rain is not very demanding, physically. The steering wheel turns with very little effort and you are going so slowly in the corners that there are none of the usual lateral G-forces. In fact, it is very easy.»*
This was surprising given the treacherous conditions which reigned throughout the day. After three days of sunshine, the rain fell on the Principality just half an hour before the start. It was too late for the rules to allow an extra fifteen minutes of practice, to give the teams an opportunity to set up the cars for the wet.

Wisdom and anticipation at Ferrari

At Ferrari, they had prepared for this eventuality. Three minutes before the pit-lane closed prior to the start, Michael Schumacher switched cars and jumped into the spare. *«We had prepared one car for the dry and another for the wet. After one reconnaissance lap I decided to go for the latter.»* It was a wise choice, as the rain did not stop for the entire race. Once the lights went out, no one ever saw the Ferrari again, except when it lapped them. He had a six second lead at the end of the first lap. *«Everything was going well,»* said Schumacher. *«The only place I had a problem was the section from Mirabeau to Le Portier. I had to dip the clutch, because the engine was pushing too hard for the conditions. Other than that, I was keeping up a steady pace so as not to lose concentration. That was the hardest part.»*

A sad memory

Michael Schumacher's race was exemplary on all counts and was the perfect antidote to his race here in 1996, when the German got it all wrong at le Portier corner on the first lap, when the race was also run in the rain. *«I think that today, I have made up for last year's mistake,»* he remarked. *«I thought about that moment for the entire race. Every time I went through the corner, I told myself to be careful and I slowed down.»*
This year in Monaco, the German made just one error, when he went straight on at the Ste. Devote chicane. *«I had quite a few problems with my brakes. On that lap one of my front wheels locked. I might have been able to get round all the same, but I preferred to play it safe and take the escape road. I had a big enough lead for it not to matter.»*
With this, his first victory of the season, Schumacher took the lead in the championship, which gave him cause for optimism. *«Until now, I was lucky that the Williams had problems. We will still have a difficult race in Barcelona. After that, we stand a good chance. We must wait and see.»*
On Sunday night Jean Todt promised that the Scuderia would pull out all the stops to get the new version of the F 310 B ready as soon as possible.
He added that the Monaco win was more valuable in terms of the boost it gave team morale rather than because of the ten points it brought them in the championship.
It was clear that Michael Schumacher's Ferrari was a much more competitive mount than the 1996 car. Nevertheless, since the start of the season he declared he hoped he would not lose out on too many points before the arrival of the new version of the car.
In Monaco, he certainly had not lost ground. Indeed he positively walked on water on the Monegasque circuit. Michael Schumacher proved beyond doubt that he deserved a third world title.

IN THE POINTS

	Driver	Team	Time
1.	Michael SCHUMACHER	Scuderia Ferrari Marlboro	2 h 00'05"654
2.	Rubens BARRICHELLO	Stewart Ford	at 53"306
3.	Eddie IRVINE	Scuderia Ferrari Marlboro	at 1'22"108
4.	Olivier PANIS	Prost Gauloises Blondes	at 1'44"402
5.	Mika SALO	Tyrrell Ford	at 1 lap
6.	Giancarlo FISICHELLA	B&H Total Jordan Peugeot	at 1 lap

Fastest lap : M. SCHUMACHER, lap 26, 1'53"315, avg. 106.937 km/h

▷
Formation lap in Monaco. The only good thing about the terrible conditions is that they make for good photographs.

Williams soak up the criticism

With the atrociously wet conditions at the start, all the cars lined up on the grid on rain tyres; all except the two Williams and Mika Hakkinen's McLaren, which started on slicks. *«We had weather reports indicating that the rain would stop after 30 minutes. We therefore started on slick tyres and dry settings. But obviously it was a big mistake,»* admitted Jacques Villeneuve after the race. *«The car was still very difficult to drive, even after I changed to wets and I ended up hitting the barrier and bending my suspension.»* Starting from pole position, Heinz-Harald Frentzen suffered a similar fate. Williams had thrown away the race by taking exactly the same gamble as the one that brought them victory with Keke Rosberg in 1983. That time, the rain stopped early on, but not this time.
«Our drivers were not responsible for the choice of slick tyres. It was the team alone that took the decision,» regretted Frank Williams. *«We just took a gamble based on the information at our disposal. If it had payed off, we would have been heroes.»*
For the time being however, Williams, the World Champions, were the laughing stock of the paddock. *«We also had a weather forecast which predicted the rain would end after ten minutes,»* mocked the Prost team's sporting director, Cesare Fiorio. *«But you only had to look at the sky to know it was not about to dry out. Williams simply made a very big mistake.»*
If the rain was not falling heavily enough for them on the start line, Williams only needed to have a man stationed at Mirabeau to know it was raining cats and dogs there and that slicks were an unthinkable option. This mistake might cost the reigning world champions dear, when the final points tally was added up.

Monaco gets bigger

While extremely popular with the fans, the Monaco track is certainly not a big favourite with the drivers, nor the mechanics who face difficult working conditions. It is a narrow, dangerous anachronism, which owes its place on the calendar to the legend which surrounds the event.
All the same, the organisers attempt the impossible to improve their circuit. This year, they resurfaced a good third of the track, from the tunnel exit to the start/finish line, which did a good job of smoothing out some of the terrible bumps. However, the biggest change was carried out to the «S» before the swimming pool. This used to be a blind corner and the exit was hidden from the drivers' line of sight by a concrete wall. For this year, much to the drivers' delight, these walls were replaced by flat kerbs, which much improved the visibility. *«It's definitely better,»* confirmed Heinz-Harald Frentzen. *«Before, if a car was sideways across the track, you would be going straight for it. Now, we can approach the corner with more confidence. But it is also quicker. What with this and the new surface, I reckon we will be lapping three seconds quicker.»*
This modification to the chicane was carried out by extending part of the port out into the sea. The solution certainly met with approval from Prince Rainier, as the surface area of his tiny Principality had just been increased by around 450 square metres!

GAULOISES
avex group
BiC
elf
14

Olivier Panis was unable to repeat his race-winning form of 1996. This year, he could not find a good set up for his car in practice and qualified down in 12th place. Nevertheless, in the race he managed to climb through the field, one place at a time, to finish a brilliant fourth.

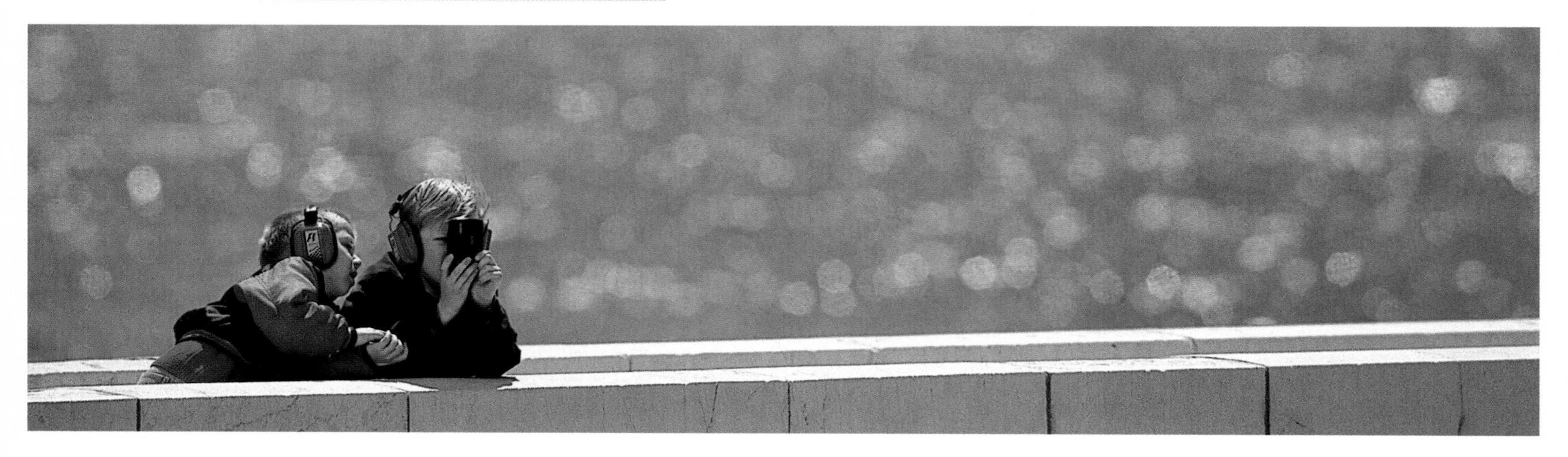

△ «Set the shutter speed at 1/125th and the aperture to F8.0, because I'm worried it might be underexposed.» Quality of photography knows no age barrier.

Formula 1 goes under the hammer

Friday is normally a day of rest at the Monaco GP, but this year there was no time for an afternoon nap. At half past three, an auction of Formula 1 memorabilia had been organised by Brooks in the Yacht Club; a swanky building at one end of the harbour. Prince Albert 1st of Monaco, a self-confessed Formula 1 fan did not want to miss out on the event, the profits from which went to the Princess Grace Orphanage in Sri Lanka.
There were over 50 lots put up for auction by the F1 teams and drivers, including gloves, helmets and even bits of bodywork. Everything sold like hot cakes to the 200 or so people present and telephone bidders from London and Tokyo.
The sale provided a useful barometer of a driver's reputation. Ukyo Katayama's overalls therefore, went for 8500 francs, while those worn by Jacques Villeneuve, when he won his first grand prix in Spain last year, went for 46,000 francs.
The suit that Michael Schumacher had worn in practice the previous day fetched 42,000 francs, while the nose of his 1996 Ferrari, complete with wing went for 52,000FF.
The most expensive item of the day was not even there. Bernie Ecclestone took it upon himself to offer the helmet worn by the driver who would claim pole position in the following day's session. The bids went through the roof until the hammer came down at 78,000 francs.
The event generated a total income of 810,000 francs (around £82,000.)

The Crying Scotsmen

«I have never been so happy in my whole career. Never!» In Monaco, Jackie Stewart would not stop going on about how happy he was after the race, as his team celebrated Barrichello's second place at a motorhome party. *«I was never very emotional when I was driving. But here, Paul and I were standing together for the duration of the race and when Rubens crossed the line, we both burst into tears. It was......fantastic!»*
It has to be said that this result was totally unexpected. Until now, no Stewart had managed to get to the end of a race since the season had started. While the car occasionally shone in a practice session, it seemed to suffer too many reliability problems to ever get to see a chequered flag.
However, on Sunday in Monaco, nothing untoward happened and while Rubens Barrichello was on the second step of the podium, Jan Magnussen finished seventh. This was the best ever result achieved by a team in its first F1 season. «This is a very big moment for me,» claimed «Rubinho». *«My car was set up for the dry, but the car was fantastic, thanks to the Bridgestone tyres, especially in the early part of the race, when I managed to overtake Herbert and the two Jordans.»*
Having taken just six laps to move into second place, the Brazilian had even tried to close on Schumacher! *«I stepped up the pace, but there was nothing I could do. Then I made a mistake at the chicane, my car went over the kerb and my car started to hit the bumps. From then on, I decided to make sure of my second place.»*
For the Stewart team, this result meant they could look forward to the rest of the season in a new light. *«You bet,»* added Rubens. *«I have to say that we have not yet done a single day of testing since the start of the season. It is not that we do not have the money, but simply because the car never managed more than ten laps before stopping with a problem. There was no point going all the way to somewhere like Estoril, for something like that to happen. Now we know the car can go the distance, we can finally start developing it.»*
Thus the team planned to go testing in Barcelona for four days, immediately after Monaco and Jackie Stewart no doubt hoped he would be getting his hankie out again for the forthcoming grands prix.

▷ «It could be you!» On Saturday, it seemed that Paul and Jackie Stewart knew their number would come up at the Monaco GP.

Thanks to Bridgestone

The post race partying in the wake of Barrichello's second place was not restricted to the Stewart motorhome. At the opposite end of the paddock, another party was going on, under the awning of the Bridgestone motorhome. You would have been hard pressed to notice mind you, as this was a Japanese style bash and therefore a quiet affair. *«I am lost for words,»* said the company's technical director, Hirohide Hamashima. *«This is our first experience of a Formula 1 race in the wet. It has shown us that we can go still further in producing a more competitive wet weather tyre.»* The Bridgestones did not seem that bad to begin with and it is unlikely that Rubens Barrichello would have finished second without the Bridgestone advantage. *«Without a doubt, our tyres gave us an advantage,»* said Olivier Panis after finishing fourth in the Prost. *«I could have had a good result here, but my settings were not perfect and I had to fight my car the whole way.»*

results

PRACTICE TIMES

No	Driver	Make/Engine/Chassis	Practice Friday	Practice Saturday	Qualifying	Warm-up
1.	Damon Hill	Arrows/Yamaha/A18/3 (B)	1'21"962	1'20"287	1'19"674	1'23"561
2.	Pedro Diniz	Arrows/Yamaha/A18/2 (B)	1'22"622	1'19"947	1'19"860	1'23"776
3.	Jacques Villeneuve	Williams/Renault/FW19/4 (G)	1'21"445	1'18"612	1'18"583	1'21"657
4.	Heinz-Harald Frentzen	Williams/Renault/FW19/5 (G)	1'21"885	1'18"370	1'18"216	1'21"794
5.	Michael Schumacher	Ferrari/Ferrari/F310B/174 (G)	1'21"330	1'19"265	1'18"235	1'21"843
6.	Eddie Irvine	Ferrari/Ferrari/F310B/173 (G)	1'22"072	1'19"563	1'19"723	1'23"322
7.	Jean Alesi	Benetton/Renault/B197/5 (G)	1'22"010	1'18"950	1'19"263	1'23"349
8.	Gerhard Berger	Benetton/Renault/B197/4 (G)	1'21"573	1'19"788	1'20"199	1'22"974
9.	Mika Hakkinen	McLaren/Mercedes/MP4/12/2 (G)	1'21"675	1'18"748	1'19"119	1'21"480
10.	David Coulthard	McLaren/Mercedes/MP4/12/3 (G)	1'22"020	1'19"192	1'18"779	1'22"141
11.	Ralf Schumacher	Jordan/Peugeot/197/3 (G)	1'21"939	1'19"380	1'18"943	1'23"442
12.	Giancarlo Fisichella	Jordan/Peugeot/197/4 (G)	1'21"463	1'18"560	1'18"665	1'22"555
14.	Olivier Panis	Prost/Mugen Honda/JS45/3 (B)	1'23"096	1'22"008	1'19"626	1'21"683
15.	Shinji Nakano	Prost/Mugen Honda/JS45/2 (B)	1'25"530	1'21"923	1'20"961	1'24"656
16.	Johnny Herbert	Sauber/Petronas/C16/1 (G)	1'21"188	1'20"976	1'19"105	1'22"233
17.	Nicola Larini	Sauber/Petronas/C16/2 (G)	1'22"383	1'20"459	1'19"468	1'23"958
18.	Jos Verstappen	Tyrrell/Ford/025/2 (G)	1'23"056	1'21"124	1'21"290	1'23"334
19.	Mika Salo	Tyrrell/Ford/025/3 (G)	1'23"483	1'20"516	1'19"694	1'23"380
20.	Ukyo Katayama	Minardi/Hart/M197/3 (B)	1'39"353	1'22"076	1'20"606	1'22"982
21.	Jarno Trulli	Minardi/Hart/M197/2 (B)	1'25"178	1'21"849	1'20"349	1'23"875
22.	Rubens Barrichello	Stewart/Ford/SF1/2 (B)	1'22"370	1'20"338	1'19"295	1'23"453
23.	Jan Magnussen	Stewart/Ford/SF1/3 (B)	1'23"810	1'20"764	1'20"516	1'24"035

CLASSIFICATION & RETIREMENTS

Pos	Driver	Team	Time
1.	Schumacher	Ferrari	in 2h00'05"654
2.	Barrichello	Stewart Ford	at 53"306
3.	Irvine	Ferrari	at 1'22"108
4.	Panis	Prost Mugen Honda	at 1'44"402
5.	Salo	Tyrrell Ford	at 1 lap
6.	Fisichella	Jordan Peugeot	at 1 lap
7.	Magnussen	Stewart Ford	at 1 lap
8.	Verstappen	Tyrrell Ford	at 2 laps
9.	Berger	Benetton Renault	at 2 laps
10.	Katayama	Minardi Hart	at 2 laps

Lap	Driver	Team	Reason
1	Diniz	Arrows Yamaha	spin
2	Hill	Arrows Yamaha	accident
2	Hakkinen	McLaren Mercedes	accident
2	Coulthard	McLaren Mercedes	accident
8	Trulli	Minardi Hart	off
10	Herbert	Sauber Petronas	off
11	Schumacher	Jordan Peugeot	spin
17	Villeneuve	Williams Renault	accident
17	Alesi	Benetton Renault	spin
25	Larini	Sauber Petronas	puncture
37	Nakano	Prost Mugen Honda	spin
40	Frentzen	Williams Renault	off

FASTEST LAPS

	Driver	Time	Lap
1.	M. Schum.	1'53"315	26
2.	R. Schum.	1'53"430	10
3.	Barrichello	1'53"495	10
4.	Frentzen	1'53"504	22
5.	Irvine	1'54"202	48
6.	Fisichella	1'54"806	9
7.	Salo	1'54"968	22
8.	Verstappen	1'55"045	23
9.	Villeneuve	1'55"218	14
10.	Magnussen	1'55"303	27
11.	Panis	1'55"309	18
12.	Alesi	1'55"451	9
13.	Herbert	1'55"840	8
14.	Berger	1'55"841	8
15.	Katayama	1'56"101	24
16.	Nakano	1'56"906	19
17.	Larini	1'56"940	19
18.	Trulli	2'00"038	7
19.	Coulthard	2'11"201	1
20.	Hakkinen	2'15"786	1
21.	Hill	2'17"648	1

LAP CHART

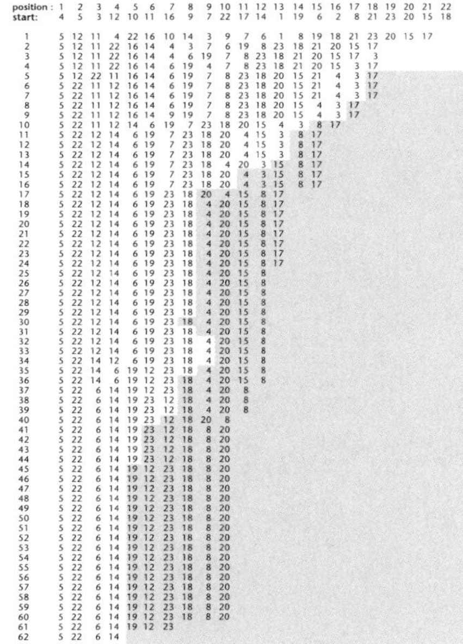

position:	1	2	3	4	5	6	7	8	9	10	11	12	13	14	15	16	17	18	19	20	21	22
start:	4	5	3	12	10	11	16	9	7	22	17	14	1	19	6	2	8	21	23	20	15	18
1	5	12	11	4	22	16	10	14	3	9	7	6	1	8	19	18	21	23	20	15	17	
2	5	12	11	22	16	14	4	3	7	6	19	8	23	18	21	20	15	17				
3	5	12	11	22	16	14	4	6	19	7	8	23	18	21	20	15	17	3				
4	5	12	11	22	16	14	6	19	4	7	8	23	18	21	20	15	3	17				
5	5	12	22	11	16	14	6	19	7	8	23	18	20	15	21	4	3	17				
6	5	22	11	12	16	14	6	19	7	8	23	18	20	15	21	4	3	17				
7	5	22	11	12	16	14	6	19	7	8	23	18	20	15	21	4	3	17				
8	5	22	11	12	16	14	6	19	7	8	23	18	20	15	4	3	17					
9	5	22	11	12	16	14	9	19	7	8	23	18	20	15	4	3	17					
10	5	22	11	12	14	6	19	7	23	18	20	15	4	3	8	17						
11	5	22	12	14	6	19	7	23	18	20	4	15	3	8	17							
12	5	22	12	14	6	19	7	23	18	20	4	15	3	8	17							
13	5	22	12	14	6	19	7	23	18	20	4	15	3	8	17							
14	5	22	12	14	6	19	7	23	18	4	20	3	15	8	17							
15	5	22	12	14	6	19	7	23	18	20	4	3	15	8	17							
16	5	22	12	14	6	19	7	23	18	20	4	3	15	8	17							
17	5	22	12	14	6	19	23	18	20	4	15	8	17									
18	5	22	12	14	6	19	23	18	4	20	15	8	17									
19	5	22	12	14	6	19	23	18	4	20	15	8	17									
20	5	22	12	14	6	19	23	18	4	20	15	8	17									
21	5	22	12	14	6	19	23	18	4	20	15	8	17									
22	5	22	12	14	6	19	23	18	4	20	15	8	17									
23	5	22	12	14	6	19	23	18	4	20	15	8	17									
24	5	22	12	14	6	19	23	18	4	20	15	8	17									
25	5	22	12	14	6	19	23	18	4	20	15	8										
26	5	22	12	14	6	19	23	18	4	20	15	8										
27	5	22	12	14	6	19	23	18	4	20	15	8										
28	5	22	12	14	6	19	23	18	4	20	15	8										
29	5	22	12	14	6	19	23	18	4	20	15	8										
30	5	22	12	14	6	19	23	18	4	20	15	8										
31	5	22	12	14	6	19	23	18	4	20	15	8										
32	5	22	12	14	6	19	23	18	4	20	15	8										
33	5	22	12	14	6	19	23	18	4	20	15	8										
34	5	22	14	12	6	19	23	18	4	20	15	8										
35	5	22	14	6	19	12	23	18	4	20	15	8										
36	5	22	14	6	19	12	23	18	4	20	15	8										
37	5	22	6	14	19	12	23	18	4	20	8											
38	5	22	6	14	19	23	12	18	4	20	8											
39	5	22	6	14	19	23	12	18	4	20	8											
40	5	22	6	14	19	23	12	18	20	8												
41	5	22	6	14	19	23	12	18	8	20												
42	5	22	6	14	19	23	12	18	8	20												
43	5	22	6	14	19	23	12	18	8	20												
44	5	22	6	14	19	23	12	18	8	20												
45	5	22	6	14	19	12	23	18	8	20												
46	5	22	6	14	19	12	23	18	8	20												
47	5	22	6	14	19	12	23	18	8	20												
48	5	22	6	14	19	12	23	18	8	20												
49	5	22	6	14	19	12	23	18	8	20												
50	5	22	6	14	19	12	23	18	8	20												
51	5	22	6	14	19	12	23	18	8	20												
52	5	22	6	14	19	12	23	18	8	20												
53	5	22	6	14	19	12	23	18	8	20												
54	5	22	6	14	19	12	23	18	8	20												
55	5	22	6	14	19	12	23	18	8	20												
56	5	22	6	14	19	12	23	18	8	20												
57	5	22	6	14	19	12	23	18	8	20												
58	5	22	6	14	19	12	23	18	8	20												
59	5	22	6	14	19	12	23	18	8	20												
60	5	22	6	14	19	12	23	18	8	20												
61	5	22	6	14	19	12	23															
62	5	22	6	14																		

FIFTH ROUND

GRAND PRIX DE MONACO, MONTE CARLO

ANTONY NOGHÈS
SAINTE-DÉVOTE
«S» DE LA PISCINE
LA RASCASSE
BUREAU DE TABAC
MONTÉE DE L'AVENUE D'OSTENDE
CHICANE DU PORT
CASINO
MIRABEAU
LOEWS
TUNNEL
PORTIER

Date : May 11, 1997
Length: 3366 meters
Distance : 62 laps, 208.692 km
Weather : rain, 16 degrees

BRIDGESTONE

Best result for a Bridgestone shod runner:

Rubens Barrichello, Stewart Ford, *2nd*

CHAMPIONSHIPS

(after five rounds)

Drivers:

1.	M. SCHUMACHER	24
2.	Jacques VILLENEUVE	20
3.	Eddie IRVINE	14
4.	David COULTHARD	10
	Heinz-H. FRENTZEN	10
	Gerhard BERGER	10
	Mika HAKKINEN	10
8.	Olivier PANIS	9
9.	Rubens BARRICHELLO	6
10.	Ralf SCHUMACHER	4
	Giancarlo FISICHELLA	4
12.	Johnny HERBERT	3
	Jean ALESI	3
14.	Mika SALO	2
15.	Nicola LARINI	1

Constructors :

1.	Ferrari	38
2.	Williams / Renault	30
3.	McLaren / Mercedes	20
4.	Benetton / Renault	13
5.	Prost / Mugen Honda	9
6.	Jordan / Peugeot	8
7.	Stewart / Ford	6
8.	Sauber / Petronas	4
9.	Tyrrell / Ford	2

WEEK-END GOSSIP

- **The stars come out in the daytime!**

The Monaco Grand Prix always attracts the biggest crowd of poseurs and celebrities and this year was no exception. We had famous models from Eva Herzigova to Claudia Schiffer and sports stars like Max Biaggi and Luc Alphand.

- **The Max Mosley counter-attack**

Over the previous few weeks, several drivers, including Jacques Villeneuve, had attacked the new F1 technical regulations, due to come into effect at the start of the 1998 season.

On Saturday, FIA President Max Mosley came down from the mountain in Monaco to fight his corner and defend the new rules. He was apparently surprised that the teams had not spoken out in his defence. *«These modifications were arrived at after consultation with a group of engineers from all the teams,»* he thundered. *«At the time, they were unanimous in their support, whereas it now seems that some of them have changed their mind, even though nothing has been changed since. I do not want to hear any argument and these decisions will be implemented, come what may.»* He was certainly stamping his authority.

The FIA President appeared to have been put out by Jacques Villeneuve's opinions, which held that the new cars would be harder to drive, that it would level out the drivers' abilities and that it would make Formula 1 more dangerous. *«He is wrong and I can prove it,»* continued Mosley. *«Slick tyres allow a car to travel more quickly and the force of impact in an accident is entirely dependent on speed. We have seen, over the past few years, that the increase in speeds owes more to the tyres than to any other factor. We reduced their width to 20 inches a few years ago and then to 15 inches four years ago. We should have gone further, which would have allowed us to keep some of the best corners. If we do nothing on the tyre front, then we will end up racing for the whole season on go-kart tracks, as they are the only type of circuit which would keep the speeds down to an acceptable level. I recall that all the great drivers, from Fangio to Moss, made their name at a time when levels of grip were much lower than they are today. So I do not see how those conditions levelled out the driver's ability.»*

According to Max Mosley therefore, Jacques Villeneuve was wrong on all counts. *«A driver always wants more downforce and more power, but is not interested in safety. It is my job to ensure that Jacques will be 50 one day and will come and see me to tell me that I was probably right. Jacques is wrong when he says that grooved tyres will make driving easier. You cannot just dismiss the whole of motor racing's history like that. In fact, Jacques is suggesting that no racing drivers were any good, until he came along.»*

RACE SUMMARY

- At the start, Schumacher disappears into the distance, ahead of Fisichella, who leads Frentzen and Ralf Schumacher. All the cars are on rain tyres, except for the two Williams and Hakkinen's McLaren.
- On lap 2, Coulthard spins at the chicane. Alesi, in the Benetton, brakes to avoid him and is hit by Hakkinen. Hill runs into the back of Irvine and along with the two McLarens, is forced to retire.
- After two laps, Schumacher has an 11 second lead over Fisichella. Behind them Barrichello has got past Frentzen.
- Villeneuve pits on lap 4 to fit rain tyres and re-joins in 17th spot.
- On lap 5, Barrichello passes Ralf Schumacher and on the next lap he disposes of Fisichella to take second place, 25 seconds behind Schumacher.
- Frentzen is living a nightmare on his slick tyres. He changes to wets on lap 6th and finds himself in 16th place, ahead of Villeneuve.
- Herbert goes straight on and out of the race at Ste. Devote on lap 9. He had been fifth.
- On lap 10, Berger spins, breaking the front wing. After having it replaced he is in second from last position.
- On lap 17, Alesi spins at Le Portier. Stalling his engine, he is forced to retire as does Villeneuve after slamming into a barrier.
- Panis and Irvine finally get past Fisichella, who finishes sixth after a long dog fight.
- After his one and only pit stop, Irvine finds he is ahead of Panis and makes it to the

«Pass the pate». The Benetton mechanics make the most of a lunchtime break to admire the yachts in the Monaco harbour. There is no harm in dreaming.

RENAULT
Rothmans
ANDERSEN
CONSULTING
Rothmans
RACING
Rothmans
Rothmans
RENAULT

Jacques on top form

After two barren grands prix, Jacques Villeneuve was back on track in Barcelona.

But while the Canadian took his third win of the season, Heinz-Harald Frentzen was once again left floundering far behind in eighth place.

Olivier Panis continued his sensational improvement to finish second. A win could not be too far off.

GRAN PREMIO MARLBORO DE ESPAÑA BARCELONA

△ Jacques Villeneuve in superb form. In Barcelona, the Canadian was convincingly quickest in an FW17 which seemed unbeatable.

The Williams-Renaults fight it out

There was no mercy shown between the two Williams drivers on Saturday. Heinz- Harald Frentzen and Jacques Villeneuve were alone in battling for pole position and they were way ahead of the rest.

The duel finally turned in the Canadian's favour. *«I am really satisfied with my day,»* commented Villeneuve at the end of the session. *«After two difficult grands prix, I knew everything would go better here. We have done a lot of private testing on this track, but it has not been easy. There was pressure and a lot of stress, because I could not get the car to handle the way I wanted. We changed a lot of small things throughout the session. They were only detail changes, but in fact they radically affected the car's behaviour. We are not far off having a perfect car. We are almost there.»*

In the last few minutes of the session, Frentzen had one last attempt at beating his teammate, but it failed. *«I was not completely happy with the balance of my car and on top of that, the wind had changed direction. On this track, with its long straight, that was enough to make it impossible to go any faster.»*

Coulthard third

In third spot was the surprising David Coulthard. *«Yes, it is a surprise for me also. It seems we have cut back the gap to the Williams and that is partly due to the new «F specification» Mercedes engine. But it is also down to the track conditions, which suit our car. The balance is quite good.»* The Scotsman said he was reasonably optimistic for the race.

«Shame there isn't a photographer to immortalise our handshake!» The footballer Ronaldo, who the previous evening had played one of his last matches for Barcelona, paid Michael Schumacher a visit on Saturday morning. ▷

STARTING GRID

	Row	
		Jacques VILLENEUVE 1'16"525
Heinz-H. FRENTZEN 1'16"791	-1-	
		David COULTHARD 1'17"521
Jean ALESI 1'17"717	-2-	
		Mika HAKKINEN 1'17"737
Gerhard BERGER 1'18"041	-3-	
		M. SCHUMACHER 1'18"313
G. FISICHELLA 1'18"385	-4-	
		R. SCHUMACHER 1'18"423
Johnny HERBERT 1'18"494	-5-	
		Eddie IRVINE 1'18"873
Olivier PANIS 1'19"157	-6-	
		Gianni MORBIDELLI 1'19"323
Mika SALO 1'20"079	-7-	
		Damon HILL 1'20"089
Shinji NAKANO 1'20"103	-8-	
		R. BARRICHELLO 1'20"255
Jarno TRULLI 1'20"452	-9-	
		Jos VERSTAPPEN 1'20"582
Ukyo KATAYAMA 1'20"672	-10-	
		Pedro DINIZ 1'21"029
Jan MAGNUSSEN 1'21"060	-11-	

Third victory of the season for Jacques Villeneuve

△
The start. Jacques Villeneuve gets the better of Michael Schumacher and David Coulthard. Behind them, Olivier Panis is engulfed in the pack. This is the second start as the first one was aborted after Ralf Schumacher stalled on the grid.

Jacques delighted, Heinz deflated

With a quick spray of the champagne bottle in Barcelona, Jacques Villeneuve wiped out the memory of his two consecutive failures at Imola and Monaco and was more than pleased with himself as he stepped off the podium. *«Winning here partly makes up for the stupidity in Monaco.»* Villeneuve led from start to finish, apart from a couple of laps after his refuelling stops. While Michael Schumacher had chosen to stop three times, the Williams driver opted for just two stops. *«It is always a bit of a risky gamble to stop three times,»* he claimed. *«It is imperative to start from the front and push very hard from start to finish. Stopping only twice, I was able to maintain a more sensible pace and look after my tyres.»* This win was all the more welcome, as it preceded the Canadian Grand Prix by three weeks. *«It is a great satisfaction to go to Montreal as leader of the world championship,»* he agreed. *«It gives me a bit of breathing space, because I will be under a lot of pressure there. It will be my most important race of the season.»*

«HH» incurs the wrath of the Williams team

Jacques Villeneuve's obvious joy was in sharp contrast with Heinz-Harald Frentzen's black mood. Having changed out of his overalls into his customary denim shirt, the German looked downcast when he had to face the press who wanted to hear about his race and why he could do no better than finish ninth. *«To be honest, it's a mystery to me,»* he complained. *«Everything had gone well in practice and the tyres never gave any sign of trouble. Again this morning, in the warm-up, everything was fine. And then in the race, after two laps I started to get blisters on my tyres. I just don't understand it.»*

The Williams team did not seem to agree with Heinz-Harald. Patrick Head's Number Two, James Robinson vented his anger. *«Heinz-Harald knows exactly what he did wrong,»* he declared. *«After the warm-up, he decided to start with his spare car, even though he had only tried it for three laps. Evidently, he only discovered during the race that this chassis was wearing out the tyres very rapidly. We warned him against his choice, but he insisted. This is the result of his decision.»*

Olivier second, Alain stressed out

Ever onward would seem to be the Prost team's motto.

After coming third in Brazil, Olivier Panis was on the podium again in Barcelona, this time in second place, less than six seconds behind Jacques Villeneuve's Williams. Not bad for someone who came around at the end of the first lap in thirteenth spot!

Looking as though he had just driven down to the shops, the man from Grenoble recounted his race in his usual down to earth fashion. *«I made a bad start, but after that everything went well. The car was perfectly balanced and the tyres seemed indestructible. We had already discovered that in the warm-up and we were hoping for some points. But I would not have dared hope for second place.»*

Under the motorhome awning, Alain Prost was in seventh heaven. Smiling for the cameras, answering questions fired at him from all sides, he did not stint from praising his driver and his team. Later, having got over the emotion of the moment, he even admitted that he thought victory might have been on the cards. *«We knew the tyres would last and we were confident,»* was his analysis of the situation. *«In fact the race went 100% according to plan. After 20 laps we could see the way Olivier was dealing wih the opposition. I turned to Cesare Fiorio (the team's sporting director) and I said: 'This time we can do it. Today, we have to win.' We might have needed a bit of luck, but it was not impossible.»*

For the Frenchman, watching from the pit wall, it had been an exhausting race. *«It was horrible,»* he added. *«It was one of the most exciting races of my career. When you are a driver, you concentrate on yourself and have no notion of what is going on around you. But from here, I can see everything and it is unbearably stressful. I had a knot in my stomach which never happened to me as a driver. A good thing too, as I could never have been world champion if I had been in such a state.»*

Lap 36. Mika Salo sees his left rear tyre give up, just as he was about to come into the pits to have them changed.
▽

IN THE POINTS

	Driver	Team	Time
1.	Jacques VILLENEUVE	Rothmans Williams Renault	1 h 30'35"896
2.	Olivier PANIS	Prost Gauloises Blondes	at 5"804
3.	Jean ALESI	Mild Seven Benetton Renault	at 12"534
4.	Michael SCHUMACHER	Scuderia Ferrari Marlboro	at 17"979
5.	Johnny HERBERT	Red Bull Sauber Petronas	at 27"986
6.	David COULTHARD	West McLaren Mercedes	at 29"744

Fastest lap : G. FISICHELLA, lap 20, 1'22'242, avg. 206.960 km/h

△ Ferrari re-fuelling. Only 4th place awaited them.

Morbidelli replaces Larini

Italian transfer at Sauber

In the Formula 1 paddock, Peter Sauber comes across as a bit of a softie. With his permanent smile, the man from Zurich seems almost too laid back for the unforgiving world of grand prix.
However, in Barcelona, he proved he is also capable of taking hard decisions when circumstances demand it. On Wednesday, he announced that his second driver, Nicola Larini was sacked, to be replaced by another Italian, Gianni Morbidelli, the Ferrari test driver. Larini only drove five grands prix for the Swiss team, but he blotted his copybook so indelibly with numerous off-track excursions that Peter Sauber lost all confidence in him. The decision was taken quickly and with full support from Ferrari, who thus made life easier for Sauber. Gianni Morbidelli would therefore drive the second Sauber for the rest of the season. *«Up until now, I have only driven one day in the C16,»* he explained. *«But it has been enough for me to tell that the team is really professional. I settled in quickly and was able to form an impression of the car, although I will keep that to myself. I think that my experience with Ferrari will allow me to makes some useful suggestions to the Sauber engineers.»*

Morbidelli makes his F1 comeback after one year away ▽

Irvine in trouble again

Once again, Eddie Irvine's dubious etiquette on the track got him into trouble in Barcelona. In the closing stages of the race, the Irishman repeatedly and obviously blocked Olivier Panis as the Frenchman tried to lap him. This unsporting behaviour did not escape the attention of the stewards who albeit, rather belatedly, gave him a ten second penalty.
Many believed the Irishman was simply obeying orders from Ferrari, who saw this as an opportunity for Michael Schumacher to catch the cars ahead of him. *«What Ferrari did is completely unacceptable,»* fumed Alain Prost. *«This is not my idea of how the sport should run.»*

«See over there. The little man with the glasses and the white shirt. He is the king around here!» Jackie Stewart explains the F1 monarchy to King Juan Carlos, at the Spanish Grand Prix. ▽

△ *Jean Alesi heading for the podium.*
In Barcelona, Formula One's francophone family could compliment itself on a 100% French-speaking podium, thanks to Jacques Villeneuve, Olivier Panis and Jean Alesi. Nevertheless the post-race press conference was held in English.

PRACTICE TIMES

No	Driver	Make/Engine/Chassis	Practice Friday	Practice Saturday	Qualifying	Warm-up
1.	Damon Hill	Arrows/Yamaha/A18/3 (B)	1'23"592	1'20"768	1'20"089	1'22"499
2.	Pedro Diniz	Arrows/Yamaha/A18/2 (B)	1'25"049	1'21"365	1'21"029	1'23"057
3.	Jacques Villeneuve	Williams/Renault/FW19/4 (G)	1'19"766	1'17"664	1'16"525	1'19"961
4.	Heinz-Harald Frentzen	Williams/Renault/FW19/5 (G)	1'21"887	1'17"457	1'16"791	1'20"335
5.	Michael Schumacher	Ferrari/Ferrari/F310B/177 (G)	1'21"319	1'18"734	1'18"313	1'21"302
6.	Eddie Irvine	Ferrari/Ferrari/F310B/176 (G)	1'21"423	1'20"907	1'18"873	1'22"327
7.	Jean Alesi	Benetton/Renault/B197/5 (G)	1'19"566	1'18"476	1'17"717	1'20"697
8.	Gerhard Berger	Benetton/Renault/B197/2 (G)	1'20"933	1'19"213	1'18"041	1'21"150
9.	Mika Hakkinen	McLaren/Mercedes/MP4/12/6 (G)	1'21"421	1'18"757	1'17"737	1'20"296
10.	David Coulthard	McLaren/Mercedes/MP4/12/3 (G)	1'21"312	1'18"056	1'17"521	1'20"823
11.	Ralf Schumacher	Jordan/Peugeot/197/3 (G)	1'20"198	1'19"419	1'18"423	1'20"276
12.	Giancarlo Fisichella	Jordan/Peugeot/197/4 (G)	1'20"537	1'18"901	1'18"385	1'20"814
14.	Olivier Panis	Prost/Mugen Honda/JS45/4 (B)	1'21"636	1'20"412	1'19"157	1'20"852
15.	Shinji Nakano	Prost/Mugen Honda/JS45/2 (B)	1'23"191	1'20"561	1'20"103	1'21"937
16.	Johnny Herbert	Sauber/Petronas/C16/5 (G)	1'21"379	1'18"692	1'18"494	1'22"019
17.	Gianni Morbidelli	Sauber/Petronas/C16/2 (G)	1'23"451	1'20"151	1'19"323	1'21"484
18.	Jos Verstappen	Tyrrell/Ford/025/4 (G)	1'23"209	1'21"599	1'20"582	1'23"686
19.	Mika Salo	Tyrrell/Ford/025/3 (G)	1'22"849	1'20"849	1'20"079	1'23"549
20.	Ukyo Katayama	Minardi/Hart/M197/3 (B)	1'22"892	1'20"829	1'20"672	1'23"259
21.	Jarno Trulli	Minardi/Hart/M197/2 (B)	1'25"064	1'21"582	1'20"452	1'23"748
22.	Rubens Barrichello	Stewart/Ford/SF1/4 (B)	1'23"246	1'20"336	1'20"255	1'23"613
23.	Jan Magnussen	Stewart/Ford/SF1/2 (B)	1'22"839	1'20"602	1'21"060	1'23"439

CLASSIFICATION & RETIREMENTS

Pos	Driver	Team	Time
1.	Villeneuve	Williams Renault	in 1h30'35"896
2.	Panis	Prost Mugen Honda	at 5"804
3.	Alesi	Benetton Renault	at 12"534
4.	Schumacher	Ferrari	at 17"979
5.	Herbert	Sauber Petronas	at 27"986
6.	Coulthard	McLaren Mercedes	at 29"744
7.	Hakkinen	McLaren Mercedes	at 48"785
8.	Frentzen	Williams Renault	at 1'04"139
9.	Fisichella	Jordan Peugeot	at1'04"767
10.	Berger	Benetton Renault	at 1'05"670
11.	Verstappen	Tyrrell Ford	at 1 lap
12.	Irvine	Ferrari	at 1 lap
13.	Magnussen	Stewart Ford	at 1 lap
14.	Morbidelli	Sauber Petronas	at 2 laps
15.	Trulli	Minardi Hart	at 2 laps

Lap	Driver	Team	Reason
12	Katayama	Minardi Hart	hydraul. system
19	Hill	Arrows Yamaha	engine
35	Nakano	Prost Mugen Honda	gearbox
36	Salo	Tyrrell Ford	tyre
39	Barrichello	Stewart Ford	engine
51	Schumacher	Jordan Peugeot	engine
54	Diniz	Arrows Yamaha	engine

FASTEST LAPS

	Driver	Time	Lap
1.	Fisichella	1'22"242	20
2.	M. Schum.	1'22"295	44
3.	Coulthard	1'22"430	22
4.	Panis	1'22"422	29
5.	Villeneuve	1'22"534	9
6.	R. Schum.	1'22"784	14
7.	Irvine	1'22"839	30
8.	Frentzen	1'22"841	54
9.	Alesi	1'23"096	20
10.	Berger	1'23"106	42
11.	Herbert	1'23"178	54
12.	Hakkinen	1'23"241	30
13.	Nakano	1'23"516	21
14.	Barrichello	1'23"564	23
15.	Diniz	1'23"716	24
16.	Hill	1'23"761	12
17.	Trulli	1'24"213	45
18.	Verstappen	1'24"517	43
19.	Morbidelli	1'24"647	24
20.	Salo	1'24"775	4
21.	Magnussen	1'25"300	40
22.	Katayama	1'26"273	4

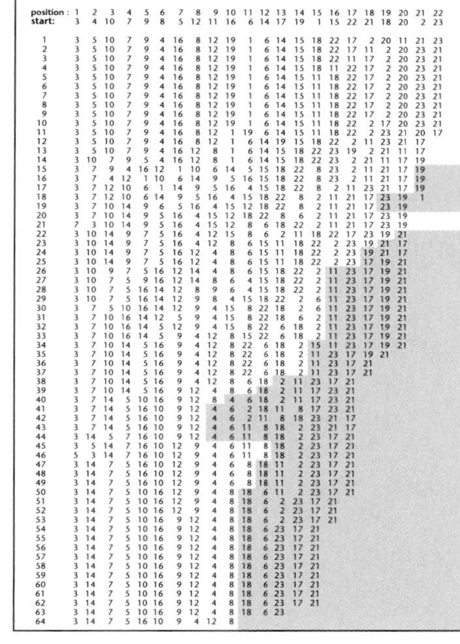

LAP CHART

position :	1	2	3	4	5	6	7	8	9	10	11	12	13	14	15	16	17	18	19	20	21	22
start:	3	4	10	7	9	8	5	12	11	16	6	14	17	19	1	15	22	21	18	20	2	23
1	3	5	10	7	9	4	16	8	12	19	1	6	14	15	18	22	17	2	20	11	21	23
2	3	5	10	7	9	4	16	8	12	19	1	6	14	15	18	22	17	11	2	20	23	21
3	3	5	10	7	9	4	16	8	12	19	1	6	14	15	18	22	11	17	2	20	23	21
4	3	5	10	7	9	4	16	8	12	19	1	6	14	15	18	11	22	17	2	20	23	21
5	3	5	10	7	9	4	16	8	12	19	1	6	14	15	11	18	22	17	2	20	23	21
6	3	5	10	7	9	4	16	8	12	19	1	6	14	15	11	18	22	17	2	20	23	21
7	3	5	10	7	9	4	16	8	12	19	1	6	14	15	11	18	22	17	2	20	23	21
8	3	5	10	7	9	4	16	8	12	19	1	6	14	15	11	18	22	17	2	20	23	21
9	3	5	10	7	9	4	16	8	12	19	1	6	14	15	11	18	22	17	2	20	23	21
10	3	5	10	7	9	4	16	8	12	19	1	6	14	15	11	18	22	2	17	20	23	21
11	3	5	10	7	9	4	16	8	12	1	19	6	14	15	11	18	22	2	23	21	20	17
12	3	5	10	7	9	4	16	8	12	1	6	14	19	15	18	22	2	11	23	21	17	
13	3	5	10	7	9	4	16	12	8	1	6	14	15	18	22	23	19	2	21	11	17	
14	3	10	7	9	5	4	16	12	8	1	6	14	15	18	22	23	2	21	11	17	19	
15	3	7	9	4	16	12	1	10	6	14	5	15	18	22	8	23	2	11	21	17	19	
16	3	7	4	12	1	10	6	14	9	5	16	15	18	22	8	23	2	11	21	17	19	
17	3	7	12	10	6	1	14	9	5	16	4	15	18	22	8	2	11	23	21	17	19	
18	3	7	12	10	6	14	9	5	16	4	15	18	22	8	2	11	21	17	23	19	1	
19	3	7	10	14	9	6	5	16	4	15	12	18	22	8	2	11	21	17	23	19		
20	3	7	10	14	9	5	16	4	15	12	18	22	8	6	2	11	21	17	23	19		
21	7	3	10	14	9	5	16	4	15	12	8	6	18	22	2	11	21	17	23	19		
22	3	10	14	9	7	5	16	4	12	15	8	6	2	11	18	22	17	23	19	21		
23	3	10	14	9	7	5	16	4	12	8	6	15	11	18	22	2	23	19	21	17		
24	3	10	14	9	7	5	16	12	4	8	6	15	11	18	22	2	23	19	21	17		
25	3	10	14	9	7	5	16	12	4	8	6	15	11	18	22	2	23	17	19	21		
26	3	10	9	7	5	16	12	14	4	8	6	15	18	22	2	11	23	17	19	21		
27	3	10	7	5	9	16	12	14	8	6	4	15	18	22	2	11	23	17	19	21		
28	3	10	7	5	16	14	12	8	9	6	4	15	18	22	2	11	23	17	19	21		
29	3	10	7	5	16	14	12	9	8	4	15	18	22	2	6	11	23	17	19	21		
30	3	7	5	10	16	14	12	9	4	15	8	22	18	2	6	11	23	17	19	21		
31	3	7	10	16	14	12	5	9	4	15	8	22	18	6	2	11	23	17	19	21		
32	3	7	10	16	14	5	12	9	4	15	8	22	6	18	2	11	23	17	19	21		
33	3	7	10	16	14	5	9	4	12	8	15	22	6	18	2	11	23	17	19	21		
34	3	7	10	14	5	16	9	4	12	8	22	6	18	2	15	11	23	17	19	21		
35	3	7	10	14	5	16	9	4	12	8	22	6	18	2	11	23	17	19	21			
36	3	7	10	14	5	16	9	4	12	8	22	6	18	2	11	23	17	21				
37	3	7	10	14	5	16	9	4	12	8	22	6	18	2	11	23	17	21				
38	3	7	10	14	5	16	9	4	12	8	6	18	2	11	23	17	21					
39	3	7	10	14	5	16	9	12	4	8	6	18	2	11	17	23	21					
40	3	7	14	5	10	16	9	12	8	4	6	18	2	11	17	23	21					
41	3	7	14	5	16	10	9	12	4	6	2	18	11	8	17	23	21					
42	3	7	14	5	16	10	9	12	4	6	2	11	8	18	23	21	17					
43	3	7	14	5	16	10	9	12	4	6	11	8	18	2	23	21	17					
44	3	14	5	7	16	10	9	12	4	6	11	8	18	2	23	17	21					
45	3	5	14	7	16	10	12	9	4	6	11	8	18	2	23	17	21					
46	5	3	14	7	16	10	12	9	4	6	11	8	18	2	23	17	21					
47	3	14	7	5	16	10	12	9	4	6	8	18	11	2	23	17	21					
48	3	14	7	5	16	10	12	9	4	6	8	18	11	2	23	17	21					
49	3	14	7	5	16	10	12	9	4	6	8	18	11	2	23	17	21					
50	3	14	7	5	10	16	12	9	4	8	18	6	11	2	23	17	21					
51	3	14	7	5	10	16	12	9	4	8	18	6	2	23	17	21						
52	3	14	7	5	10	16	12	9	4	8	18	6	2	23	17	21						
53	3	14	7	5	10	16	9	12	4	8	18	6	2	23	17	21						
54	3	14	7	5	10	16	9	12	4	8	18	6	23	17	21							
55	3	14	7	5	10	16	9	12	4	8	18	6	23	17	21							
56	3	14	7	5	10	16	9	12	4	8	18	6	23	17	21							
57	3	14	7	5	10	16	9	12	4	8	18	6	23	17	21							
58	3	14	7	5	10	16	9	12	4	8	18	6	23	17	21							
59	3	14	7	5	10	16	9	12	4	8	18	6	23	17	21							
60	3	14	7	5	10	16	9	12	4	8	18	6	23	17	21							
61	3	14	7	5	10	16	9	12	4	8	18	6	23	17	21							
62	3	14	7	5	10	16	9	12	4	8	18	6	23	17	21							
63	3	14	7	5	10	16	9	12	4	8	18	6	23									
64	3	14	7	5	16	10	9	4	12	8												

SIXTH ROUND

GRAN PREMIO MARLBORO DE ESPAÑA, BARCELONA

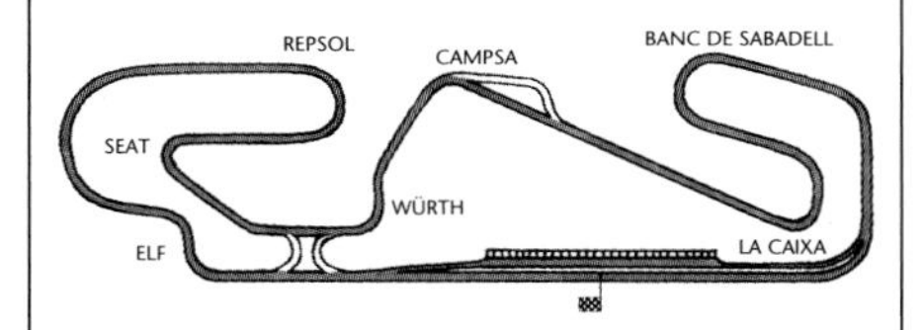

Date : May 25, 1997
Length: 4726 meters
Distance : 64 laps, 302.469 km
Weather : sunny, 22 degrees

BRIDGESTONE

Best result for a Bridgestone shod runner:

Olivier Panis, Prost Mugen Honda, *2nd*

CHAMPIONSHIPS

(after six rounds)

Drivers:

1. Jacques VILLENEUVE 30
2. Michael SCHUMACHER 27
3. Olivier PANIS 15
4. Eddie IRVINE 14
5. David COULTHARD 11
6. Heinz-H. FRENTZEN 10
   Gerhard BERGER 10
   Mika HAKKINEN 10
9. Jean ALESI 7
10. Rubens BARRICHELLO 6
11. Johnny HERBERT 5
12. Ralf SCHUMACHER 4
    Giancarlo FISICHELLA 4
14. Mika SALO 2
15. Nicola LARINI 1

Constructors :

1. Ferrari 41
2. Williams / Renault 40
3. McLaren / Mercedes 21
4. Benetton / Renault 17
5. Prost / Mugen Honda 15
6. Jordan / Peugeot 8
7. Stewart / Ford 6
   Sauber / Petronas 6
9. Tyrrell / Ford 2

RACE SUMMARY

- Ralf Schumacher stalls on the grid and the start is delayed for eight minutes.
- Frentzen makes a mess of his start and finds himself in sixth place. At the front. Villeneuve takes the lead ahead of Coulthard and Michael Schumacher.
- Michael Schumacher passes Coulthard on the first lap and attacks Villeneuve, before rapidly losing ground as his tyres deteriorate.
- Schumacher is definitely holding up Coulthard, Alesi and Hakkinen who are all trying to get by. Frentzen is finding it hard to keep up with these four.
- Hill retires in front of the pits, his car smoking heavily on lap 19. His team-mate Diniz will do exactly the same on lap 54.
- After the first series of pit-stops, Villeneuve heads Coulthard and Hakkinen. The Scotsman is closing on the Canadian.
- Having chosen a three stop strategy, Coulthard soon pits again. Alesi inherits second place ahead of Panis.
- Panis makes the most of his second refuelling stop, to take second place
- After Villeneuve stops for the second time, he slows the pace down and lets Panis close the

WEEK-END GOSSIP

- **Schumi won't play anymore**

On the Sunday before the Spanish Grand Prix, Michael Schumacher played a game of football for Aubonne, a Swiss third division side.
Aubonne is a village a few kilometres from Vufflens-le-Chateau, home to the Ferrari driver. The directors of the club were short of funds and they had written to all and sundry in the area, trying to find someone to pay for the team's kit. Michael replied he would happily pay for the kit, but he also wanted to play for the team.
He therefore took part in several training sessions, without any of the other players giving the game away. He applied for a license and obtained it on Friday 16th May and on the Sunday, he was playing in his first official third division game! The match did not go unnoticed.
Photos quickly whizzed round the globe and they were the main talking point in the Barcelona paddock on the Thursday.
«Schumi» confirmed he had taken part, simply for the fun of it. *«It was good fun,»* he said. *«This match confirmed that I should stick to being a driver rather a footballer! Unfortunately, I was not playing in my usual position on the pitch. I was a sweeper and I hardly touched the ball for the whole game. I prefer to play as a forward. All the same, I got a shot at goal, but I missed.»* For the record, the match was a humiliating 1 - 6 defeat for his team at the hands of Genolier and their only goal came from a penalty. Aubonne was bottom of the division and was fighting against relegation to the fourth division. This meant Michael did not feel too upset about not being up to the mark.
Playing football is not without its risks and one wonders what the Ferrari management would have said if he had come away from Aubonne with a broken ankle. *«My contract does not forbid me to do anything; all it asks is that I am careful,»* continued the double world champion. *«But that is why I do not think I will play again. Aubonne has some good attacking players and I am worried I might take a bad knock. In training there is no problem as they know who I am and they are careful. But in a match, the guys don't care that I am Michael Schumacher and I have watch out, which means I am not free to play quite the way I want to. I like the game and if the opportunity arises, then why not, but I will have to be discrete about it.»*
Indeed he will, otherwise Aubonne can expect to see 500 photographers turn up for the game, with a German TV helicopter flying overhead, with the entire match monitored by a submarine parked in a Swiss lake!

▽ *Barcelona's monumental Gaudi cathedral. The splendour of the Catalan city is timeless.*

A big scare on lap 52

He had set off with the intention of winning the Canadian Grand Prix. The Goodyear runners were in trouble and Olivier Panis on his Bridgestones had every chance of getting to the finish without having to stop and change his tyres every five laps.
But destiny decided otherwise. On lap 52, the Frenchman's Prost suddenly went out of control and hit a tyre wall with a huge force. The race was stopped and Michael Schumacher was declared the winner. However, still waiting for news as to Olivier's condition, the German was in no mood for celebrating.

GRAND PRIX PLAYER'S DU CANADA
MONTREAL

Schumi, by a 13 thousandths whisker from Jacques

Michael Schumacher hard at work on Montreal's Gilles Villeneuve circuit. Much to the disgust of the crowd, the German was about to claim his first pole position of the season.

An artistic shot of Jacques Villeneuve. Under pressure from the fans and under close scrutiny from the FIA, which had summoned him to Paris on the eve of practice, the local boy was going to have a difficult weekend in Montreal.

The huge crowd in the grandstand was holding its collective breath. The chequered flag has already been waved to mark the end of the session, but Jacques Villeneuve and Michael Schumacher are still out on the track. The Canadian crosses the line first, without improving his time. He is still fastest.

Then Schumacher comes into view, his Ferrari in a controlled slide. The crowd cannot believe it; he is quickest and the local hero has been beaten by just 13 thousandths of a second! At the speeds these cars cross the line, that represents a difference of 103 centimetres, a gnats hair over four kilometres. This was Villeneuve's second consecutive failure in Montreal, after Damon Hill had out- qualified him last year.

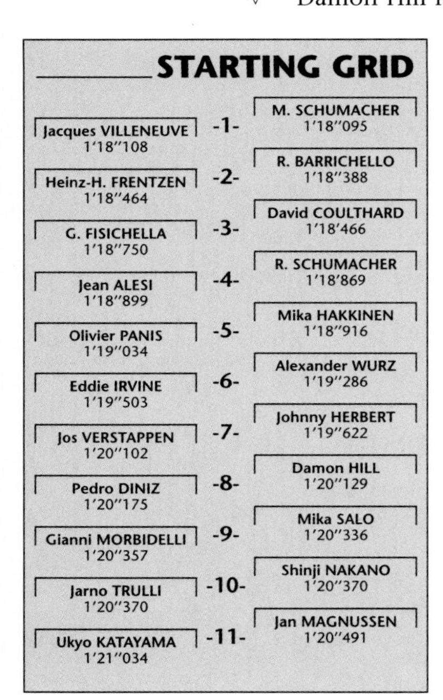

STARTING GRID

		M. SCHUMACHER 1'18"095
Jacques VILLENEUVE 1'18"108	-1-	
		R. BARRICHELLO 1'18"388
Heinz-H. FRENTZEN 1'18"464	-2-	
		David COULTHARD 1'18'466
G. FISICHELLA 1'18"750	-3-	
		R. SCHUMACHER 1'18'869
Jean ALESI 1'18"899	-4-	
		Mika HAKKINEN 1'18"916
Olivier PANIS 1'19"034	-5-	
		Alexander WURZ 1'19"286
Eddie IRVINE 1'19"503	-6-	
		Johnny HERBERT 1'19"622
Jos VERSTAPPEN 1'20"102	-7-	
		Damon HILL 1'20"129
Pedro DINIZ 1'20"175	-8-	
		Mika SALO 1'20"336
Gianni MORBIDELLI 1'20"357	-9-	
		Shinji NAKANO 1'20"370
Jarno TRULLI 1'20"370	-10-	
		Jan MAGNUSSEN 1'20"491
Ukyo KATAYAMA 1'21"034	-11-	

«It's frustrating, especially in front of my fans,» conceded the Canadian. *«But as we have two grands prix in Germany this year, I still have two more opportunities to get my revenge on Michael.»* Nevertheless, Villeneuve felt that all was not lost for the race. *«We knew we would not have the best car on this track. It prefers long fast corners and there aren't any here, so I am not surprised Michael is ahead of us. But I am still confident for the race as we always go better then.»*

It was no surprise that Michael Schumacher was saying the same thing. *«I have every reason to be optimistic,»* was his analysis of the situation. *«Because since the start of the season, we have seen that our car goes better with a heavy fuel load.»* The German attributed this first pole position to the modifications, albeit unseen ones, that had been introduced to the car since the Spanish Grand Prix. *«We are currently revising the chassis from top to bottom. My chances of winning the championship this season are entirely dependent on the effectiveness of these modifications. We must wait and see.»*

Road rage revives Rubinho

The biggest surprise on the starting grid was to find Rubens Barrichello's Stewart- Ford in third place.

Apart from his Monaco Grand Prix podium, which owed much to the tricky weather conditions, the Brazilian had never gone so well all season. *«To be honest, I was hoping to qualify in the top ten, but never as high up as this,»* he exclaimed. *«Our car is very good aerodynamically. We practically took the wings off completely here, but the car still brakes very well.»*

«Rubinho» also admitted that Damon Hill had given him an added boost. *«Damon literally blocked me on my first two runs. I got very upset and that was definitely worth an extra tenth of a second on my third run, which is the equivalent of two places.»*

Olivier intended winning

He had made a complete hash of practice, but his race looked like being a cracker. On Sunday morning, Olivier Panis set a very quick time in the warm-up session, which put him at the top of the time sheet. The performance was down to his Bridgestone tyres, the Prost chassis and renewed optimism.
On lap 52, Panis is going for broke at the wheel of his Prost Mugen-Honda. Having made a bad start and then losing even more time with a pit-stop to change a wing, the Frenchman is straining every sinew to score a few points. Running on Bridgestone, he has every chance of doing so, as the Goodyear runners are all in trouble. From seventh spot, he passes Heinz-Harald Frentzen in the Williams and overtakes Michael Schumacher to un-lap himself. Two laps later it was all over. The rear of his Prost suddenly breaks away, bounces off a concrete wall, crosses the track out of control and slams into a tyre barrier, which ends his race with a huge impact. The Prost's carbon fibre monocoque is shattered and the driver cannot extricate himself from the cockpit. Eventually he is lifted out by marshals. The race is stopped and Olivier is flown to hospital by helicopter.
It is Monday afternoon in a northern suburb of Montreal. At 5400 Boulevard Gouin sits the Sacre-Coeur Hospital, which with its red brick facade, looks more like a cathedral set amidst green lawns. It his here, on the fifth floor in Room 599A of the intensive care unit, that Olivier Panis is recovering from the previous evening's operation aimed at reducing the fractures he suffered as a result of his Canadian Grand Prix accident.
«Mr. Panis is completely knocked out by the operation. He will sleep all day,» says a nurse who appears to be on guard duty. She waves a pile of faxes and get well notes, which have been sent to the driver since his admission. *«They are coming in from everywhere,»* she says. *«Nearly all the teams have written. Even Jacques Chirac has sent a message of sympathy.»*

△ *Lap 55. The race is red flagged and total confusion reigned on the grid. The drivers are keen to know about Panis and for a few minutes, no one is sure if the race will start again.*

Panis appears to be in good hands. At any rate, the operation has been a success. *«It took three and half hours,»* says Pierre Ranger, the orthopaedic surgeon who performed the operation. *«Mr. Panis has a displaced fracture of the tibia and fibula of the right leg and a small simple fracture of the left tibia. As he wanted to make as quick a recovery as possible, we have not put the legs in plaster but we have operated to screw in plates.»*

«He told me not to worry»

In the corridor outside, a Prost team mechanic is on the phone to the factory at Magny-Cours, informing them as to their driver's state of health. *«Having Olivier out of action is a real blow for the team,»* regretted Alain Prost on Sunday evening. *«He had become the cornerstone of the operation. I am thinking of him rather than of the future. I spoke to him for about ten minutes in the medical centre at the circuit, before he was taken off in the helicopter. He seemed to be in good shape mentally and he told me not to worry.»*
Alain Prost admitted that this set-back would be a difficult stage in Olivier's career. *«But given the impact he survived and the state of the monocoque, he is lucky to have come away with two broken legs,»* concluded the owner of Prost Grand Prix. *«The accident could have been a lot worse.»*
According to the Canadian doctors, the Frenchman would probably be well enough to fly back to Paris by the end of the week. It would take at least four months before he would be able to get behind the wheel of his Prost again. *«Maybe less, if he is tough,»* according to Dr. Ranger.

First corner. Olivier Panis is involved in a collision, which damages the front wing. He is forced to pit for a new one and rejoins the race in last position. All the same, he could have won, thanks to his Bridgestone tyres, if the accident had not clipped his wings on lap 52. ◁

Broken suspension

Alain Prost was in no doubt as to the cause of the accident. *«When I saw Olivier in the medical centre, he told me something happened to the car, just before the accident. And the television pictures lead me to believe that something broke in the rear suspension. It is very rare for a component to break unless it was damaged before and in fact, Olivier's car was hit twice before the impact. The first time was the collision at the start and the second time was when he hit the barrier with his right rear wheel, at the time of his second pit-stop. That is possibly what caused the problem, nine laps later.»*
In the opinion of the four times world champion, Olivier would have been powerless to do anything in this type of situation. *"You can usually correct a driving error and you hardly ever make one in a straight line. A mechanical failure however, usually occurs on a fast section, without warning. The car then has a life of its own and the impact is usually serious. Olivier could do nothing about it.»*

No champagne on the podium

There was no party atmosphere on the podium. At the time, there was no news of Olivier Panis and the traditional champagne ceremony seemed out of place to the three drivers. Therefore the corks stayed in place. *«As soon as I got down from the podium, I was told Olivier was out of danger, but I refused to believe it until I could talk to him, face to face,»* said Jean Alesi.
After Panis' accident, the Safety Car was brought out and the cars followed behind for four laps, before the race was stopped after 54 of the scheduled 69 laps. Michael Schumacher's win put him back in the lead of the world championship. *«Naturally it is good to have won, but it was not easy as we had a lot of tyre problems.»*
Although Ferrari had started on a two stop strategy, the German had to make three visits to the pits. *«The car was not too bad on the first set of tyres, but on the second, I had to push hard so that Coulthard would not get away and I had blisters after just five laps. It was incredible.»*

◁ *«We did it!» After the post race press conference, Michael Schumacher returned to his garage to congratulate his team. In the background, Ross Brawn observes the scene with his usual laid back look.*

IN THE POINTS

1.	Michael SCHUMACHER	Scuderia Ferrari Marlboro	1 h 17'40"646
2.	Jean ALESI	Mild Seven Benetton Renault	at 2"565
3.	Giancarlo FISICHELLA	B&H Total Jordan Peugeot	at 3"219
4.	Heinz-H. FRENTZEN	Rothmans Williams Renault	at 3"768
5.	Johnny HERBERT	Red Bull Sauber Petronas	at 4"716
6.	Shinji NAKANO	Prost Gauloises Blondes	at 36"701

Fastest lap : D. COULTHARD, lap 37, 1'19"635, avg. 199.856 km/h

Jean Alesi cannot keep count of his fans in Quebec; a place he is particularly fond of, as the venue of the one and only win of his F1 career in 1995. This time, he finished second, having started from eighth place on the grid. "The car worked quite well in the race," he said. "But I am really waiting for Magny-Cours as the car seems perfect on that track."

MILD SEVEN
MILD SEVEN
MILD SEVEN
MILD SEVEN
AKAI
GOODYEAR

△
Third place in Montreal was a landmark for Giancarlo Fisichella. «A podium finish has been my aim since the start of the season. Of course I am very happy.» He could no doubt have finished second, if his mechanics had not lost vital seconds during his pit-stop.

Another debacle at Williams

For the first time in its history, the Canadian Grand Prix was a sell out. No less than 105,000 fans had turned up at the Ile Notre-Dame in the hope of seeing Jacques Villeneuve triumph.
Bitter disappointment awaited them. It was the at the end of the second lap, that the Canadian got it all wrong at the chicane before the pit straight.
Approaching too quickly, the back end got out of shape, hit the cone on top of the kerb, before parking itself in the concrete wall on the outside of the corner.
Bashing his crash helmet in rage, it was a distraught Jacques Villeneuve who returned to his garage. *«This is the worst mistake of my whole career,»* he admitted with some honesty after the race. *«It was even a beginner's mistake. I was going too quickly, that's all. The track was dusty and I slid off. But the conditions were the same for everyone. I have no excuses, especially as I was not pushing too hard and was biding my time.»*
The disappointment was just as great for the spectators, many of whom began to leave their seats just half an hour after the start of the race.
Without their hero, they had no interest in the grand prix.
Heinz-Harald Frentzen brought the other Williams home in fourth place, after a lack-lustre race and three pit-stops.

A new Berger is among us

▷
With Berger off sick, test driver Alexander Wurz lined up for Benetton. The team had no regrets, as the Austrian kept pace with the best in the race, until his transmission let him down on lap 35.

The big surprise on Thursday was the absence of Gerhard Berger. He had arrived in North America, but his doctor decided he should not race in the Canadian Grand Prix, because of a serious sinus infection.
Alexander Wurz was brought in to drive in his place and made a strong impression. Relaxed, happy and amusing, Wurz proved on the stop watch that he has talent aplenty. Winner of last years Le Mans 24 Hours, the 1986 BMX world champion had been employed as Benetton's test driver for this year.
This meant he had already done hundreds of miles at the wheel of the B 197. *«I am very relaxed,»* he said the day before practice. *«The team is not expecting me to win the race, so I am not under any pressure. I will simply try and do my best and then we will see.»*
On Saturday, we did see. He qualified 11th, three tenths of a second behind his team-mate. Although he made a few driving errors over the course of the weekend, the quick and clever Wurz gave notice he will be a talent to be reckoned with in the future.

The scenic Ile Notre Dame. A combination of greenery and tarmac. The atmosphere at the Canadian Grand Prix is one of the most enjoyable on the calendar.
▽

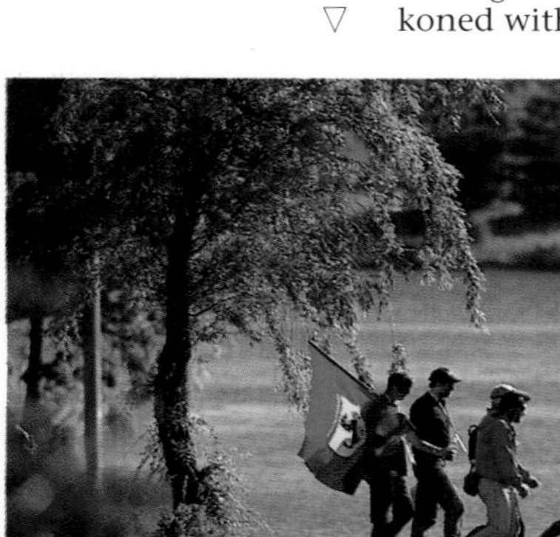

PRACTICE TIMES

No	Driver	Make/Engine/Chassis	Practice Friday	Practice Saturday	Qualifying	Warm-up
1.	Damon Hill	Arrows/Yamaha/A18/3 (B)	1'22"460	1'19"957	1'20"129	1'22"721
2.	Pedro Diniz	Arrows/Yamaha/A18/2 (B)	1'21"777	1'20"366	1'20"175	1'22"110
3.	Jacques Villeneuve	Williams/Renault/FW19/4 (G)	1'20"552	1'18"953	1'18"108	1'19"940
4.	Heinz-Harald Frentzen	Williams/Renault/FW19/5 (G)	1'20"289	1'18"871	1'18"464	1'20"507
5.	Michael Schumacher	Ferrari/Ferrari/F310B/177 (G)	1'21"201	1'18"034	1'18"095	1'20"489
6.	Eddie Irvine	Ferrari/Ferrari/F310B/176 (G)	1'20"987	1'18"829	1'19"503	1'21"469
7.	Jean Alesi	Benetton/Renault/B197/5 (G)	1'20"624	1'18"563	1'18"899	1'19"727
8.	Alexander Wurz	Benetton/Renault/B197/4 (G)	1'21"315	1'19"189	1'19"286	1'20"989
9.	Mika Hakkinen	McLaren/Mercedes/MP4/12/6 (G)	1'21"372	1'19"053	1'18"916	1'19"829
10.	David Coulthard	McLaren/Mercedes/MP4/12/3 (G)	1'21"468	1'19"087	1'18"466	1'19"594
11.	Ralf Schumacher	Jordan/Peugeot/197/3 (G)	1'20"930	1'19"540	1'18"869	1'19"854
12.	Giancarlo Fisichella	Jordan/Peugeot/197/4 (G)	1'20"416	1'18"651	1'18"750	1'19"645
14.	Olivier Panis	Prost/Mugen Honda/JS45/4 (B)	1'20"727	1'18"514	1'19"034	1'19"477
15.	Shinji Nakano	Prost/Mugen Honda/JS45/2 (B)	1'22"930	1'20"089	1'20"370	1'21"850
16.	Johnny Herbert	Sauber/Petronas/C16/3 (G)	1'20"876	1'18"883	1'19"622	1'20"457
17.	Gianni Morbidelli	Sauber/Petronas/C16/4 (G)	1'21"415	1'19"366	1'20"357	1'21"802
18.	Jos Verstappen	Tyrrell/Ford/025/4 (G)	1'22"550	1'19"812	1'20"102	1'21"005
19.	Mika Salo	Tyrrell/Ford/025/3 (G)	1'21"848	1'19"744	1'20"336	1'20"863
20.	Ukyo Katayama	Minardi/Hart/M197/3 (B)	1'22"708	1'21"134	1'21"034	1'22"359
21.	Jarno Trulli	Minardi/Hart/M197/2 (B)	1'24"131	1'19"929	1'20"370	1'21"516
22.	Rubens Barrichello	Stewart/Ford/SF1/2 (B)	1'21"269	1'18"833	1'18"388	1'20"929
23.	Jan Magnussen	Stewart/Ford/SF1/3 (B)	1'23"826	1'20"084	1'20"491	1'20"903

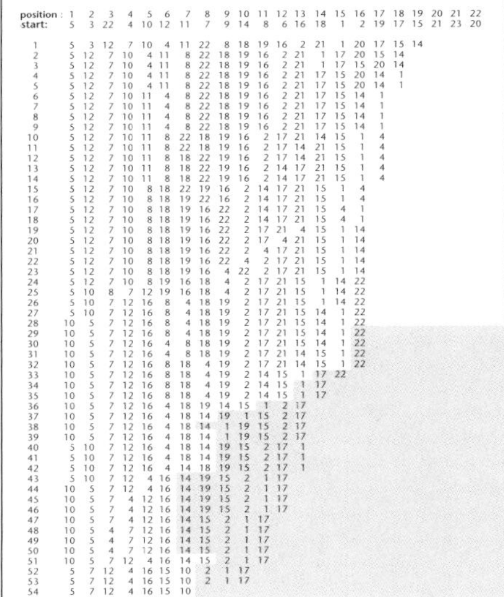

LAP CHART

position:	1	2	3	4	5	6	7	8	9	10	11	12	13	14	15	16	17	18	19	20	21	22
start:	5	3	22	4	10	12	11	7	9	14	8	6	16	18	1	2	19	17	15	21	23	20
1	5	3	12	7	10	4	11	22	8	18	19	16	2	21	1	20	17	15	14			
2	5	12	7	10	4	11	8	22	18	19	16	2	21	1	17	20	15	14				
3	5	12	7	10	4	11	8	22	18	19	16	2	21	1	17	15	20	14				
4	5	12	7	10	4	11	8	22	18	19	16	2	21	17	15	20	14	1				
5	5	12	7	10	4	11	8	22	18	19	16	2	21	17	15	20	14	1				
6	5	12	7	10	11	4	8	22	18	19	16	2	21	17	15	14	1					
7	5	12	7	10	11	4	8	22	18	19	16	2	21	17	15	14	1					
8	5	12	7	10	11	4	8	22	18	19	16	2	21	17	15	14	1					
9	5	12	7	10	11	4	8	22	18	19	16	2	21	17	15	14	1					
10	5	12	7	10	11	8	22	18	19	16	2	17	21	14	15	1	4					
11	5	12	7	10	11	8	22	18	19	16	2	17	14	21	15	1	4					
12	5	12	7	10	11	8	18	22	19	16	2	17	14	21	15	1	4					
13	5	12	7	10	11	8	18	22	19	16	2	14	17	21	15	1	4					
14	5	12	7	10	11	8	18	22	19	16	2	14	17	21	15	1	4					
15	5	12	7	10	8	18	22	19	16	2	14	17	21	15	1	4						
16	5	12	7	10	8	18	19	22	16	2	14	17	21	15	1	4						
17	5	12	7	10	8	18	19	16	22	2	14	17	21	15	4	1						
18	5	12	7	10	8	18	19	16	22	2	14	17	21	15	4	1						
19	5	12	7	10	8	18	19	16	22	2	17	21	4	15	1	14						
20	5	12	7	10	8	18	19	16	22	2	17	4	21	15	1	14						
21	5	12	7	10	8	18	19	16	22	2	4	17	21	15	1	14						
22	5	12	7	10	8	18	19	16	22	4	2	17	21	15	1	14						
23	5	12	7	10	8	18	19	16	4	22	2	17	21	15	1	14						
24	5	12	7	10	8	19	16	18	4	2	17	21	15	1	14	22						
25	5	10	8	7	12	19	16	18	4	2	17	21	15	1	14	22						
26	5	10	7	12	16	8	4	18	19	2	17	21	15	1	14	22						
27	5	10	7	12	16	8	4	18	19	2	17	21	15	14	1	22						
28	10	5	7	12	16	8	4	18	19	2	17	21	15	14	1	22						
29	10	5	7	12	16	8	4	18	19	2	17	21	15	14	1	22						
30	10	5	7	12	16	4	8	18	19	2	17	21	15	14	1	22						
31	10	5	7	12	16	4	8	18	19	2	17	21	14	15	1	22						
32	10	5	7	12	16	8	18	4	19	2	17	21	14	15	1	22						
33	10	5	7	12	16	8	18	4	19	2	14	15	1	17	22							
34	10	5	7	12	16	8	18	4	19	2	14	15	1	17								
35	10	5	7	12	16	8	18	4	19	2	14	15	1	17								
36	10	5	7	12	16	4	18	19	14	15	1	2	17									
37	10	5	7	12	16	4	18	14	19	1	15	2	17									
38	10	5	7	12	16	4	18	14	1	19	15	2	17									
39	10	5	7	12	16	4	18	14	1	19	15	2	17									
40	5	10	7	12	16	4	18	14	19	15	2	17	1									
41	5	10	7	12	16	4	18	14	19	15	2	17	1									
42	5	10	7	12	16	4	14	18	19	15	2	17	1									
43	5	10	7	12	4	16	14	19	15	2	1	17										
44	10	5	7	12	4	16	14	19	15	2	1	17										
45	10	5	7	4	12	16	14	19	15	2	1	17										
46	10	5	7	4	12	16	14	19	15	2	1	17										
47	10	5	7	4	12	16	14	15	2	1	17											
48	10	5	4	7	12	16	14	15	2	1	17											
49	10	5	4	7	12	16	14	15	2	1	17											
50	10	5	4	7	12	16	14	15	2	1	17											
51	10	5	7	12	4	16	14	15	2	1	17											
52	5	7	12	4	16	15	10	2	1	17												
53	5	7	12	4	16	15	10	2	1	17												
54	5	7	12	4	16	15	10															

Best result for a Bridgestone shod runner:

Shinji Nakano, Prost Mugen Honda, *6th*

CHAMPIONSHIPS

(after seven rounds)

Drivers :

1. Michael SCHUMACHER 37
2. Jacques VILLENEUVE 30
3. Olivier PANIS 15
4. Eddie IRVINE.................................14
5. Heinz-H. FRENTZEN......................13
   Jean ALESI.....................................13
7. David COULTHARD 11
8. Gerhard BERGER...........................10
   Mika HAKKINEN 10
10. Giancarlo FISICHELLA 8
11. Johnny HERBERT.............................7
12. Rubens BARRICHELLO.....................6
13. Ralf SCHUMACHER..........................4
14. Mika SALO.......................................2
15. Nicola LARINI 1
    Shinji NAKANO 1

Constructors :

1. Ferrari..51
2. Williams / Renault.........................43
3. Benetton / Renault.........................23
4. McLaren / Mercedes.......................21
5. Prost / Mugen Honda.....................16
6. Jordan / Peugeot 12
7. Sauber / Petronas 8
8. Stewart / Ford 6
9. Tyrrell / Ford...................................2

CLASSIFICATION & RETIREMENTS

Pos	Driver	Team	Time
1.	Schumacher	Ferrari	in 1h17'40"646
2.	Alesi	Benetton Renault	at 2"565
3.	Fisichella	Jordan Peugeot	at 3"219
4.	Frentzen	Williams Renault	at 3"768
5.	Herbert	Sauber Petronas	at 4"716
6.	Nakano	Prost Mugen Honda	at 36"701
7.	Coulthard	McLaren Mercedes	at 37"753
8.	Diniz	Arrows Yamaha	at 1 lap
9.	Hill	Arrows Yamaha	at 1 lap
10.	Morbidelli	Sauber Petronas	at 1 lap
11.	Panis	Prost Mugen Honda	off

Lap	Driver	Team	Reason
1	Magnussen	Stewart Ford	accident
1	Hakkinen	McLaren Mercedes	accident
1	Irvine	Ferrari	accident
2	Villeneuve	Williams Renault	off
6	Katayama	Minardi Hart	off
15	Schumacher	Jordan Peugeot	off
33	Trulli	Minardi Hart	engine
34	Barrichello	Stewart Ford	gearbox
36	Wurz	Benetton Renault	transmission
43	Verstappen	Tyrrell Ford	gearbox
47	Salo	Tyrrell Ford	engine

FASTEST LAPS

	Driver	Time	Lap
1.	Coulthard	1'19"635	37
2.	Frentzen	1'19"997	49
3.	M. Schum.	1'20"171	27
4.	Alesi	1'20"679	50
5.	Herbert	1'20"709	33
6.	Panis	1'20"945	47
7.	Fisichella	1'21"013	27
8.	Wurz	1'21"048	25
9.	Salo	1'21"622	24
10.	Verstappen	1'21"902	21
11.	Nakano	1'22"077	48
12.	Barrichello	1'22"366	26
13.	R. Schum.	1'22"372	14
14.	Diniz	1'22"434	34
15.	Hill	1'22"435	6
16.	Morbidelli	1'22"659	32
17.	Trulli	1'22"712	29
18.	Katayama	1'24"294	5
19.	Villeneuve	1'28"356	1

SEVENTH ROUND

GRAND PRIX PLAYER'S DU CANADA, MONTRÉAL

COURBE SAINT-LAURENT
ÉPINGLE DES STANDS
ÉPINGLE DE L'ÎLE

Date : June 15, 1997
Length: 4421 meters
Distance : 54 laps, 238.734 km
Weather : sunny, 21 degrees

RACE SUMMARY

- Michael Schumacher makes the best start and swerves in front of Alesi and Villeneuve.
- At the first corner, Irvine tangles with Panis and Magnussen. The Prost driver is the only who carries on.
- At the end of the second lap, Villeneuve goes straight on into the wall and retires.
- On lap 7, the Safety Car is brought out after Katayama has an accident.
- Ralf Schumacher has a high speed crash on lap 15 but is unhurt.
- David Coulthard and Michael Schumacher twice take turns at leading the race, as they both make their pit-stops.
- On lap 52, Panis has a big shunt and the race is finally stopped. With more than two thirds distance having been run, full points are awarded.

WEEK-END GOSSIP

- **Villeneuve in the dock**

Jacques Villeneuve is not in the habit of keeping his thoughts to himself. Coming from the American school of thought, a free thinker and something of a rebel, he is no respecter of the order of things in Formula 1, which has only been his home since 1996. On Thursday 24th April at Imola, the Canadian let rip about the new 1998 Formula 1 technical regulations (see page 112.)

His comments were not appreciated by the Williams team. The news only came through on the Wednesday morning before the Canadian Grand Prix, that Jacques Villeneuve had been summoned that day to appear before the FIA World Council, to explain his outburst.

The Canadian company, Bombardier, who make Learjet private aircraft, made one of their craft available to the driver, along with two crews, who flew him to Paris, waited during the hearing and then flew him back to Montreal in record time.

All this for a meeting which eventually only took about ten minutes, after which the driver was given a warning and no further action was taken.

Over the past few years, two other famous drivers had also been hauled over the coals for daring to question the wisdom of the FIA: in 1991, Ayrton Senna openly criticised the then FIA President, Jean-Marie Balestre. The Brazilian was forced to write a letter of apology before being allowed to take part in the 1992 championship. In 1993, Alain Prost was in the dock, before the season had even started, after accusing the FIA of incompetence.

In order to take part in grands prix, the driver must have a super-license, granted after fulfilling certain criteria in terms of their racing achievements. But the license also requires its holders to sign a document stating, among other things, that the driver will not publically criticise the championship, or the FIA itself.

This clause had caused an outcry among the drivers, when it was introduced three years ago, but eventually everyone signed it.

When he came out of the Hotel Crillon, where the Council held the meeting, Villeneuve seemed as relaxed as usual. *«It was just a discussion,»* he explained briefly. *«I was called here because of the language I had used. I am not being asked to change my opinion and I have no intention of doing so. I am aware though, that I must choose my words more carefully when talking to the press.»*

Jacques Villeneuve added he thought it was "a shame" that he had to travel all the way to Paris, two days before practice started for the Canadian Grand Prix.

▽ *In Montreal, even the fire engines are works of art.*

The red tornado

Michael Schumacher did not hang about in Magny-Cours. Starting from pole position, his Ferrari tore off into the lead at the start and stayed there, untroubled by anyone else, all the way to the flag. While rain affected the end of the race, it had no effect on the German.
His skill had given him a 14 point lead in the championship over Jacques Villeneuve.
At Magny-Cours, the Canadian did not feature strongly and finished fourth after spinning at the final corner.

GRAND PRIX DE FRANCE
MAGNY-COURS

Win or place, they are all German

△
Frentzen, Big Schumi and Little Schumi. On Saturday at Magny-Cours it was a case of «Deutschland Über Alles».

«HH» had the time

This weekend, Frentzen had the upper hand over his team mate Villeneuve in practise, and he was the only one who could come close to challenging Michael Schumacher's masterclass. «HH» admitted that: *«he was beginning to get the hang of getting on with his team,»* eight months after first sitting in a Williams-Renault. It seemed rather a long learning curve. *«I don't think so. It is what I expected,»* replied Patrick Head. *«You have to let these things happen in their own time. In fact, I said before the start of the year, that we would have to wait until halfway through the season, before Heinz felt comfortable. We are just about at that point now. He is the one who wanted to walk before he could run, not us. Heinz is now third in the championship, which is not too bad.»*

STARTING GRID

Position	Driver	Driver
-1-	Heinz-H. FRENTZEN 1'14"749	M. SCHUMACHER 1'14"548
-2-	Jacques VILLENEUVE 1'14"800	R. SCHUMACHER 1'14"755
-3-	Jarno TRULLI 1'14"957	Eddie IRVINE 1'14"860
-4-	Jean ALESI 1'15"228	Alexander WURZ 1'14"986
-5-	Mika HAKKINEN 1'15"339	David COULTHARD 1'15"270
-6-	Shinji NAKANO 1'15"857	G. FISICHELLA 1'15"453
-7-	Johnny HERBERT 1'16"018	R. BARRICHELLO 1'15"876
-8-	Pedro DINIZ 1'16"536	Jan MAGNUSSEN 1'16"149
-9-	Jos VERSTAPPEN 1'16"941	Damon HILL 1'16"729
-10-	Norberto FONTANA 1'17"538	Mika SALO 1'17"256
-11-	Tarso MARQUES 1'18"280	Ukyo KATAYAMA 1'17"563

Damon Hill splashes through a puddle. It rained a lot on Friday in the Nievre. For the Englishman, qualifying had not gone well. He was only 17th on the grid and was beaten by his team mate, Pedro Diniz, for the first time this season.
▽

«I can tell you, I am more surprised than anyone to be on pole.»
Having banged on all day Friday about how he would be powerless against the Williams unless it rained, Michael Schumacher was under pressure to explain how he could have fooled everyone and stuck his Ferrari on pole position in sunny weather on Saturday afternoon. *«We will have to look at the telemetry read outs to see what happened,»* he continued in the pole position press conference. *«But I really cannot explain why the car worked so well. Last week, on this same track, we had to fight the car to do a 1m 15.6s. Today I did a 1m 14.5s. It's an incredible and inexplicable difference. We fitted a new front wing this morning, but I do not think it can make such a big difference, especially as we are still not going well in the first two corners.»*
As to his chances in the race itself, Schumacher would not commit himself to make a prediction. *«I don't think we will have an easy time in the race. I think we might even have some serious problems,»* he added.
Sitting next to him, Heinz-Harald Frentzen could contain himself no longer. *«Michael is always saying he has to fight against his car, but he still manages to qualify ahead of everyone!»* pointed out the Williams driver. *«It is the same for the race, when Michael says he is going to have a hard time, it is his way of taking the pressure off his shoulders and putting it on ours.»*
Ralf Schumacher, who was third, continued along the same lines. *«I should not say this, because Michael is my brother, but Heinz is right. Michael is always underestimating his chances.»*
Jacques Villeneuve was fourth on the grid and admitted he was very disappointed. In the morning he had crashed heavily, so he was forced to use the spare, which did not suit him at all.

Ralf wanted pole

The qualifying session ended with an all-German top three; Michael Schumacher ahead of Heinz-Harald Frentzen and brother Ralf. The Jordan driver, just two tenths behind the Ferrari, felt he could have done the pole time. *«The car was well balanced, but I lost fuel pressure on my last lap, so I will never know if I could have got pole position.»*
uckily he did not, as he was already bigheaded enough as it was. Any bigger and his helmet would not have come off, which would have made eating and sleeping a bit difficult.
Indeed, the latest joke doing the rounds in the Magny-Cours paddock was about Ralf. What is the difference between Ralf and God? God knows he is not Ralf.

After several trials and long periods of deliberation, Alain Prost chose Jarno Trulli to replace Olivier Panis. In Magny-Cours, the Italian proved worthy of the task, qualifying on the third row. It seems almost certain, that if Panis had been there, then the Prost team would have started from pole.
▽

The red tornado destroys everything in its path

Michael Schumacher said it again on Saturday. If the rains did not come and flood the Magny-Cours track, then he would be powerless against the two Williams- Renaults.
On Sunday, the first sixty laps of the French Grand Prix were run in perfectly dry conditions. This however, did not stop the Ferrari driver from completely dominating the race, without ever being troubled. He stormed off into the lead, ahead of Frentzen who finished second.
In the early stages, the French Grand Prix was nothing more than a dull procession. The gaps between the cars grew steadily longer and Michael Schumacher was able to pull away to such an extent that even he was surprised. *«I certainly was not expecting this,»* he said in amazement, when it was over. *«I had opted for compromise settings, in case it rained and they worked fantastically in the dry. The new front wing we have introduced here really makes a big difference.»*
Around lap 60, Schumacher had about a thirty second lead over Frentzen, when the rain started to fall on the Nevers region. Hesitating as to what he should do, the leader finally decided to stay out on slicks. He almost regretted it when he went for a long trip through the gravel on lap 63. *«I felt the car go and I simply tried to steer it gently back onto the track. It was a worrying moment,»* he recalled. *«But we made the right choice, in staying on slicks. There were only about ten laps to go and the clouds seemed to be clearing. It was very slippery though. Basically the team were waiting to see what Heinz-Harald would do. If he had pitted, I would have done the same.»*

Williams beaten

On paper, the Williams looked like the cars to beat in this French Grand Prix, as they had easily dominated private testing on the Magny-Cours circuit the previous week. However, after the race, when it was time to study the score sheet, the world champion team had only garnered nine points, split between Frentzen's second place and Villeneuve's fourth. It was a long way off the expected one-two finish. *«I am very happy to be second,»* said Frentzen all the same. *«Until today I had only finished in the points twice and my main aim was to score some more.»*
Heinz-Harald Frentzen would not hear a word spoken against his Williams, even though he had patently been unable to match the pace of Michael Schumacher's Ferrari. *«I have to say I was very surprised by Michael's speed,»* admitted «HH». *«At the start of the race, he was going so quickly, I was convinced he was stopping three times, so I let him get away, as I was on a two stop strategy.»*
When the rain began to fall, the Williams driver was not sure what to do about his tyres. *«Talking to the pits on the radio, we were hesitating between slicks and two different types of grooved tyre. Finally, I decided to stay with slicks and it was a mistake. With wet tyres, I could have gained four seconds a lap and pushed Michael in the closing stages of the race.»*

△
«P1, +19FRENT, +31IRVINE, L39». There are 39 laps separating Michael Schumacher from victory and he has a 19 second lead over Frentzen. With this victory, the Ferrari driver reached the midway point of the season, with a 14 point lead over Villeneuve, while Ferrari, thanks to Eddie Irvine's third place, led Williams-Renault by 13 points in the Constructors' Championship.

△
Peugeot boss Jacques Calvet, came to inspect his troops at Magny-Cours, a few weeks before his retirement.

Villeneuve summoned

At the last corner, on the last lap, Jacques Villeneuve attempts one final desperate move in trying to pass Eddie Irvine, who is suffering with blistered tyres. He fails. The Canadian locks his wheels and starts to spin, wiping out the plastic bollards, marking the entrance to the pit lane. He keeps the engine running and rejoins the track by driving in the opposite direction to the flow of the track. He gets on line just ahead of Jean Alesi, chops in front of him and straight lines the final corner by driving through the gravel trap.
His crazy actions saw the Canadian summoned to appear before the Stewards, who finally decided to let him off without a penalty.

With Jarno Trulli deputising at Prost, Tarso Marques found himself promoted to the role of second Minardi driver. He lasted only six laps, before his Hart engine let go.

IN THE POINTS

	Driver	Team	Time
1.	Michael SCHUMACHER	Scuderia Ferrari Marlboro	1 h 38'50"492
2.	Heinz-H. FRENTZEN	Rothmans Williams Renault	at 23"537
3.	Eddie IRVINE	Scuderia Ferrari Marlboro	at 1'14"801
4.	Jacques VILLENEUVE	Rothmans Williams Renault	at 1'21"784
5.	Jean ALESI	Mild Seven Benetton Renault	at 1'22"735
6.	Ralf SCHUMACHER	B&H Total Jordan Peugeot	at 1'29"871

Fastest lap : M. SCHUM., lap 37, 1'17"910, avg. 196.380 km/h

With Olivier Panis injured and out of action for several weeks, Alain Prost had to find a worthy replacement for him. After long deliberation, he plumped for Jarno Trulli, who until then, had been driving for Minardi, in only his first ever Formula 1 season.
In practice, the Italian fulfilled his obligations, by qualifying sixth. He was tenth in the race.

Surprise at Magny-Cours. Jacques Villeneuve had decided to dye his hair. For someone who claims not to seek publicity, it worked rather well.

The sparks fly between Villeneuve and Williams

You could cut the atmosphere with a knife at the Williams motorhome at Magny- Cours. Jacques Villeneuve had unburdened his heart and his honesty did little to endear him to the Williams management.

It had all begun on the Thursday and people were asking themselves if Jacques was on the wacky baccie. He arrived in the Magny-Cours paddock with platinum blonde hair. *«When I woke up on Wednesday, I decided I wanted to change my hairstyle and I did it. It's as simple as that,»* explained the blonde bombshell. He then went on to share his thoughts on Olivier Panis' accident. *«Formula 1 has become politically correct, with the result that when someone has an accident, everyone walks around looking sad. When in fact, they don't give a damn! As for the driver, we know the risks involved. If I die during a grand prix, I would not want the race to be stopped.»*

On Saturday, the Canadian continued in similar vein, this time complaining about his working conditions. *«Along with my engineer Jock Cleare, we are forced into setting up the car in a way that does not suit us,»* he claimed. *«We have less freedom in our work and we are losing precious time.»* In 1996, Villeneuve had made the same complaint, before things improved towards the end of the year.

This outburst earned the man from Quebec a summons from Frank Williams and the team's technical director Patrick Head, so that he could explain himself. Would a win on Sunday have appeased his masters. *«A win? You're joking,»* replied Villeneuve. *«To please those two, you would need a string of one-two finishes with a 50 second lead over the rest of the field.»*

On Sunday evening, several hours after the race, Patrick Head was still upset by their conflict. *«I do not know why Jacques pretends we prevent him from setting up the car the way he likes. He is wrong on that score,»* boomed the English engineer. *«Jock Cleare and he are very close and I have never stopped them from doing what they want, even if I think he is not setting up the car the way he should.»*

The outcome of the French Grand Prix did nothing to soothe the temper of the Williams management. *«Jacques was a little bit optimistic in attempting his final corner manouevre,»* was Head's analysis. *«But we have also made mistakes this year, notably at Monaco.»*

At Sauber, the young Argentinian, Norberto Fontana, the team's test driver, replaced Gianni Morbidelli, who had broken his wrist in private testing. Fontana did not impress his boss during the race, as he retired after going off the track on lap 41.

Olivier Panis wants to come back in September

It is five o'clock on Thursday afternoon. Olivier Panis seems to be on top form. At least that is the impression one gets, watching the video conference linking the Prost factory at Magny-Cours with the Douarnenez sports rehabilitation centre in Finistere, where the driver is recovering from his Canadian accident, which he admits remembering perfectly well. *«I heard a loud noise at the rear,»* he recalled, *«And suddenly the car was freewheeling. It went sideways and I knew it was going to hit hard. Once everything stopped, I felt a lot of pain in my legs and I immediately realised they were broken. But when I felt that my spine and arms were fine, I was reassured. My first thought was for my wife and my parents, who were watching the race on television at home and must have been worried.»*

The Frenchman had not wanted to see the TV footage of his accident. *«It does not interest me,»* he claimed. *«I want to forget about it and concentrate on my future. I know difficult times lie ahead. I will need patience, which is not one of my strong points.»*

By his side, Dr. Gilles Sauleau, who runs the Douarnenez centre, confirmed that the driver's rehabilitation would take some time. *«Olivier will start walking in the swimming pool next week. But I can tell we will have to slow him down so that he does not try and do too much too soon.»* While the doctor refused to be drawn on a date, Panis reckoned he would be back on the track by the beginning of September. *«I would like to get back in a car tomorrow, but I want to be 150% fit before coming back.»*

Eleven points at once

Even at the moment of winning a grand prix, Michael Schumacher still finds time to think of his little brother. At Magny-Cours, the German can therefore claim the credit for adding an eleventh point to the ten that come with winning the race.

It is thanks to him that his little brother Ralf managed to finish sixth. "I had seen on the giant screens that Ralf had gone off the track and that he was fighting for a place," explained Michael. "I thought that if I let him pass me, he would be able to do an extra lap and move up a place. I opened the door for him at the last corner and he did indeed score a point. If I had not done it, he would have been shown the chequered flag just after me and his race would have ended there." What brotherly love!

Jean Alesi's Benetton, neatly parked in a quiet corner of the circuit. In the race, the only Frenchman competing at Magny-Cours, finished fifth. He had a hard time getting there, as his B197 lacked any traction and wore out the bottom of the monocoque. Apart from that, he also collided with David Coulthard.

PRACTICE TIMES

No	Driver	Make/Engine/Chassis	Practice Friday	Practice Saturday	Qualifying	Warm-up
1.	Damon Hill	Arrows/Yamaha/A18/3 (B)	1'24"494	1'17"280	1'16"729	1'34"061
2.	Pedro Diniz	Arrows/Yamaha/A18/4 (B)	1'26"108	1'17"174	1'16"536	1'36"257
3.	Jacques Villeneuve	Williams/Renault/FW19/4 (G)	1'20"225	1'14"596	1'14"800	1'32"916
4.	Heinz-Harald Frentzen	Williams/Renault/FW19/5 (G)	1'20"469	1'14"987	1'14"749	1'33"314
5.	Michael Schumacher	Ferrari/Ferrari/F310B/177 (G)	1'18"339	1'15"313	1'14"548	1'31"613
6.	Eddie Irvine	Ferrari/Ferrari/F310B/173 (G)	1'31"193	1'15"184	1'14"860	1'30"456
7.	Jean Alesi	Benetton/Renault/B197/5 (G)	1'21"742	1'16"320	1'15"228	1'34"697
8.	Alexander Wurz	Benetton/Renault/B197/2 (G)	1'31"943	1'15"885	1'14"986	1'33"789
9.	Mika Hakkinen	McLaren/Mercedes/MP4/12/6 (G)	1'20"014	1'16"243	1'15"339	1'32"307
10.	David Coulthard	McLaren/Mercedes/MP4/12/4 (G)	1'27"460	1'15"443	1'15"270	1'32"369
11.	Ralf Schumacher	Jordan/Peugeot/197/5 (G)	1'20"020	1'16"232	1'14"755	1'32"573
12.	Giancarlo Fisichella	Jordan/Peugeot/197/4 (G)	1'19"838	1'15"452	1'15"453	1'34"284
14.	Jarno Trulli	Prost/Mugen Honda/JS45/3 (B)	1'29"600	1'16"162	1'14"957	1'34"514
15.	Shinji Nakano	Prost/Mugen Honda/JS45/2 (B)	1'23"839	1'15"858	1'15"857	1'35"929
16.	Johnny Herbert	Sauber/Petronas/C16/5 (G)	1'22"206	1'16"523	1'16"018	1'34"425
17.	Norberto Fontana	Sauber/Petronas/C16/6 (G)	1'27"905	1'17"263	1'17"538	1'33"910
18.	Jos Verstappen	Tyrrell/Ford/025/4 (G)	1'21"512	1'16"941	1'16"941	1'37"212
19.	Mika Salo	Tyrrell/Ford/025/3 (G)	1'25"449	1'17"085	1'17"256	1'35"174
20.	Ukyo Katayama	Minardi/Hart/M197/3 (B)	1'23"469	1'19"469	1'17"563	1'35"569
21.	Tarso Marquès	Minardi/Hart/M197/2 (B)	1'24"535	1'18"109	1'18"280	1'34"786
22.	Rubens Barrichello	Stewart/Ford/SF1/2 (B)	1'23"232	1'16"609	1'15"876	1'31"986
23.	Jan Magnussen	Stewart/Ford/SF1/1 (B)	1'34"357	1'17"008	1'16"149	1'33"972

CLASSIFICATION & RETIREMENTS

Pos	Driver	Team	Time
1.	Schumacher	Ferrari	in 1h38'50"492
2.	Frentzen	Williams Renault	at 23"537
3.	Irvine	Ferrari	at 1'14"801
4.	Villeneuve	Williams Renault	at 1'21"784
5.	Alesi	Benetton Renault	at 1'22"735
6.	Schumacher	Jordan Peugeot	at 1'29"871
7.	Coulthard	McLaren Mercedes	off
8.	Herbert	Sauber Petronas	at 1 lap
9.	Fisichella	Jordan Peugeot	at 1 lap
10.	Trulli	Prost Mugen Honda	at 2 laps
11.	Katayama	Minardi Hart	at 2 laps
12.	Hill	Arrows Yamaha	at 3 laps

Lap	Driver	Team	Reason
6	Marquès	Minardi Hart	engine
8	Nakano	Prost Mugen Honda	spin
16	Verstappen	Tyrrell Ford	brakes
19	Hakkinen	McLaren Mercedes	engine
34	Magnussen	Stewart Ford	brakes
37	Barrichello	Stewart Ford	engine
41	Fontana	Sauber Petronas	off
59	Diniz	Arrows Yamaha	spin
61	Wurz	Benetton Renault	off
62	Salo	Tyrrell Yamaha	electronics

FASTEST LAPS

	Driver	Time	Lap
1.	M. Schum.	1'17"910	37
2.	Frentzen	1'18"136	46
3.	Villeneuve	1'18"649	27
4.	Wurz	1'18"684	35
5.	Barrichello	1'18"781	27
6.	Irvine	1'19"029	20
7.	Alesi	1'19"055	20
8.	R. Schum.	1'19"225	27
9.	Fisichella	1'19"225	34
10.	Coulthard	1'19"317	37
11.	Trulli	1'19"417	32
12.	Fontana	1'19"849	35
13.	Magnussen	1'19"912	32
14.	Hakkinen	1'20"153	14
15.	Salo	1'20"385	31
16.	Hill	1'20"434	42
17.	Katayama	1'20"534	26
18.	Diniz	1'20"557	55
19.	Nakano	1'20"662	7
20.	Herbert	1'20"845	40
21.	Verstappen	1'22"034	15
22.	Marquès	1'22"325	4

LAP CHART

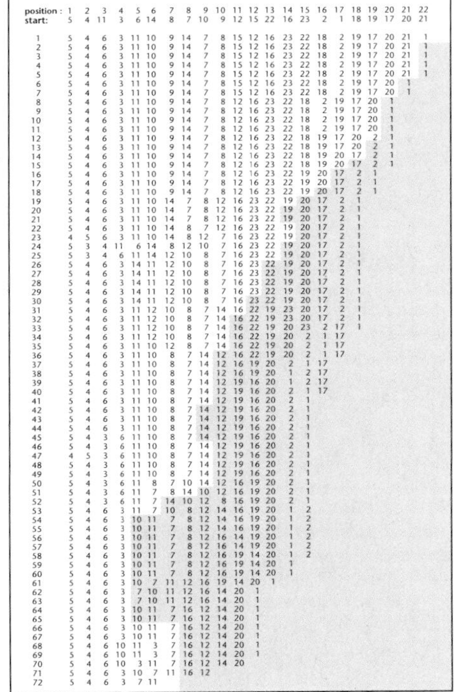

position :	1	2	3	4	5	6	7	8	9	10	11	12	13	14	15	16	17	18	19	20	21	22
start:	5	4	11	3	6	14	8	7	10	9	12	15	22	16	23	2	1	18	19	17	20	21
1	5	4	6	3	11	10	9	14	7	8	15	12	16	23	22	18	2	19	17	20	21	1
2	5	4	6	3	11	10	9	14	7	8	15	12	16	23	22	18	2	19	17	20	21	1
3	5	4	6	3	11	10	9	14	7	8	15	12	16	23	22	18	2	19	17	20	21	1
4	5	4	6	3	11	10	9	14	7	8	15	12	16	23	22	18	2	19	17	20	21	1
5	5	4	6	3	11	10	9	14	7	8	15	12	16	23	22	18	2	19	17	20	21	1
6	5	4	6	3	11	10	9	14	7	8	15	12	16	23	22	18	2	19	17	20	1	
7	5	4	6	3	11	10	9	14	7	8	15	12	16	23	22	18	2	19	17	20	1	
8	5	4	6	3	11	10	9	14	7	8	12	16	23	22	18	2	19	17	20	1		
9	5	4	6	3	11	10	9	14	7	8	12	16	23	22	18	2	19	17	20	1		
10	5	4	6	3	11	10	9	14	7	8	12	16	23	22	18	2	19	17	20	1		
11	5	4	6	3	11	10	9	14	7	8	12	16	23	22	18	2	19	17	20	1		
12	5	4	6	3	11	10	9	14	7	8	12	16	23	22	18	19	17	20	2	1		
13	5	4	6	3	11	10	9	14	7	8	12	16	23	22	18	19	17	20	2	1		
14	5	4	6	3	11	10	9	14	7	8	12	16	23	22	18	19	20	17	2	1		
15	5	4	6	3	11	10	9	14	7	8	12	16	23	22	18	19	20	17	2	1		
16	5	4	6	3	11	10	9	14	7	8	12	16	23	22	19	20	17	2	1			
17	5	4	6	3	11	10	9	14	7	8	12	16	23	22	19	20	17	2	1			
18	5	4	6	3	11	10	9	14	7	8	12	16	23	22	19	20	17	2	1			
19	5	4	6	3	11	10	14	7	8	12	16	23	22	19	20	17	2	1				
20	5	4	6	3	11	10	14	7	8	12	16	23	22	19	20	17	2	1				
21	5	4	6	3	11	10	14	7	8	12	16	23	22	19	20	17	2	1				
22	5	4	6	3	11	10	14	8	7	12	16	23	22	19	20	17	2	1				
23	4	5	6	3	11	10	14	8	12	7	16	23	22	19	20	17	2	1				
24	5	3	4	11	6	14	8	12	10	7	16	23	22	19	20	17	2	1				
25	5	3	4	6	11	14	12	10	8	7	16	23	22	19	20	17	2	1				
26	5	4	6	3	14	11	12	10	8	7	16	23	22	19	20	17	2	1				
27	5	4	6	3	14	11	12	10	8	7	16	23	22	19	20	17	2	1				
28	5	4	6	3	14	11	12	10	8	7	16	23	22	19	20	17	2	1				
29	5	4	6	3	14	11	12	10	8	7	16	23	22	19	20	17	2	1				
30	5	4	6	3	14	11	12	10	8	7	16	23	22	19	20	17	2	1				
31	5	4	6	3	11	12	10	8	7	14	16	22	19	23	20	17	2	1				
32	5	4	6	3	11	12	10	8	7	14	16	22	19	23	20	17	2	1				
33	5	4	6	3	11	12	10	8	7	14	16	22	19	20	23	2	17	1				
34	5	4	6	3	11	12	10	8	7	14	16	22	19	20	2	1	17					
35	5	4	6	3	11	10	12	8	7	14	16	22	19	20	2	1	17					
36	5	4	6	3	11	10	8	7	14	12	16	22	19	20	2	1	17					
37	5	4	6	3	11	10	8	7	14	12	16	19	20	2	1	17						
38	5	4	6	3	11	10	8	7	14	12	16	19	20	1	2	17						
39	5	4	6	3	11	10	8	7	14	12	19	16	20	1	2	17						
40	5	4	6	3	11	10	8	7	14	12	19	16	20	2	1	17						
41	5	4	6	3	11	10	8	7	14	12	19	16	20	2	1							
42	5	4	6	3	11	10	8	7	14	12	19	16	20	2	1							
43	5	4	6	3	11	10	8	7	14	12	19	16	20	2	1							
44	5	4	6	3	11	10	8	7	14	12	19	16	20	2	1							
45	5	4	3	6	11	10	8	7	14	12	19	16	20	2	1							
46	5	4	3	6	11	10	8	7	14	12	19	16	20	2	1							
47	4	5	3	6	11	10	8	7	14	12	19	16	20	2	1							
48	5	4	3	6	11	10	8	7	14	12	19	16	20	2	1							
49	5	4	3	6	11	10	8	7	14	12	19	16	20	2	1							
50	5	4	3	6	11	8	7	10	14	12	16	19	20	2	1							
51	5	4	3	6	11	7	8	14	10	12	16	19	20	2	1							
52	5	4	3	6	11	7	14	10	12	8	16	19	20	2	1							
53	5	4	6	3	11	7	10	8	12	14	16	19	20	1	2							
54	5	4	6	3	10	11	7	8	12	14	16	19	20	1	2							
55	5	4	6	3	10	11	7	8	12	14	16	19	20	1	2							
56	5	4	6	3	10	11	7	8	12	16	14	19	20	1	2							
57	5	4	6	3	10	11	7	8	12	16	14	19	20	1	2							
58	5	4	6	3	10	11	7	8	12	16	19	14	20	1	2							
59	5	4	6	3	10	11	7	8	12	16	19	14	20	1								
60	5	4	6	3	10	11	7	8	12	16	19	14	20	1								
61	5	4	6	3	10	7	11	12	16	19	14	20	1									
62	5	4	6	3	7	10	11	12	16	14	20	1										
63	5	4	6	3	7	10	11	12	16	14	20	1										
64	5	4	6	3	10	11	7	16	12	14	20	1										
65	5	4	6	3	10	11	7	16	12	14	20	1										
66	5	4	6	3	10	11	7	16	12	14	20	1										
67	5	4	6	3	10	11	7	16	12	14	20	1										
68	5	4	6	10	11	3	7	16	12	14	20	1										
69	5	4	6	10	11	3	7	16	12	14	20	1										
70	5	4	6	10	3	11	7	16	12	14	20											
71	5	4	6	3	10	7	11	16	12													
72	5	4	6	3	7	11																

EIGHTH ROUND

GRAND PRIX DE FRANCE, MAGNY-COURS

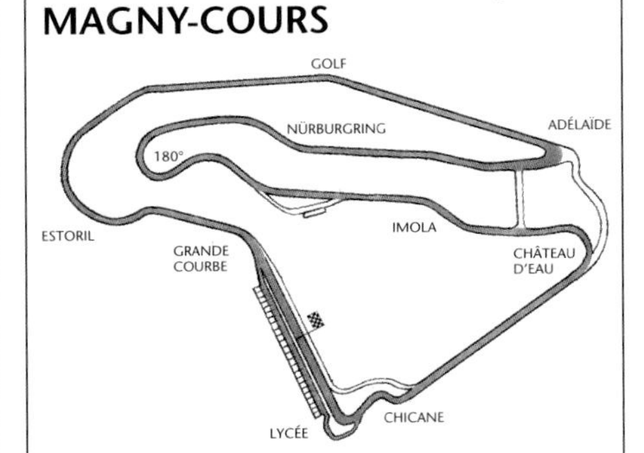

Date : June 29, 1997
Length : 4247 meters
Distance : 72 laps, 305.814 km
Weather : cloudy, then rainy, 23 degrees

Best result for a Bridgestone shod runner:

Jarno Trulli, Prost Mugen Honda, *10th*

CHAMPIONSHIPS

(after eight rounds)

Drivers :

1.	Michael SCHUMACHER	47
2.	Jacques VILLENEUVE	33
3.	Heinz-Harald FRENTZEN	19
4.	Eddie IRVINE	18
5.	Olivier PANIS	15
	Jean ALESI	15
7.	David COULTHARD	11
8.	Gerhard BERGER	10
	Mika HAKKINEN	10
10.	Giancarlo FISICHELLA	8
11.	Johnny HERBERT	7
12.	Rubens BARRICHELLO	6
13.	Ralf SCHUMACHER	5
14.	Mika SALO	2
15.	Nicola LARINI	1
	Shinji NAKANO	1

Constructors :

1.	Ferrari	65
2.	Williams / Renault	52
3.	Benetton / Renault	25
4.	McLaren / Mercedes	21
5.	Prost / Mugen Honda	16
6.	Jordan / Peugeot	13
7.	Sauber / Petronas	8
8.	Stewart / Ford	6
9.	Tyrrell / Ford	2

RACE SUMMARY

- Michael Schumacher makes the best start, leading Frentzen, Irvine and Villeneuve.
- Third in practice, Ralf Schumacher makes a mess of his start and is down in fifth place at the end of the first lap.
- At the start of the race, the gaps get bigger lap by lap. Michael Schumacher is the first to refuel, at the same time as Alesi who is eighth at the time.
- On lap 43, the first drops of rain start to fall and a heavy downpour hits the track on lap 60.
- Behind the leading four, Coulthard is holding off Ralf Schumacher and Alesi for fifth place.
- Michael Schumacher stays on slicks, as do Frentzen, Coulthard, Ralf and Alesi.
- Irvine and Villeneuve both change onto rain tyres. The Canadian drops two places to sixth.
- In the last two laps, Villeneuve moves back up to fourth place and tries to pass Irvine at the last corner. He spins and only just manages to hang onto fourth place.

WEEK-END GOSSIP

• Farewell France

On Sunday evening, there were several long faces in the race organisers' office. Events this weekend had confirmed everyone's worst fears, that 1997 might turn out to be the final running of the French Grand Prix. The previous day, former FIA President Jean-Marie Balestre, had angrily leaked the news that this event did not even feature on the provisional calendar for 1998.

The root of the problem was something called the «Bredin Law», which guarantees the right of information to all media. This meant that TV companies, France 2 and France 3 had to be allowed into the circuit, even though FOA (Formula One Administration, formerly known as FOCA) has a contract with TF1. Bernie Ecclestone immediately claimed that the Bredin Law stopped the French Grand Prix organisers from respecting their exclusive contracts with television companies and had therefore decided to scrub the event from the calendar.

Until now, Guy Drut, the minister for sport and youth had turned a blind eye to the law. But on the eve of the June legislative elections, he was replaced by a communist minister, Mrs. Buffet, who insisted that the Bredin law had to be enforced at Magny-Cours. The good woman did not attend the grand prix, for which she declared her disdain. It seemed that politics and sport were about to mix... badly.

• Renault to return in 2001?

It was just one year ago that Renault announced they would pull out of the sport at the end of 1997. At the time, the constructor wanted to go out with a bang, with two world titles, drivers' and constructors, as well as reaching the symbolic target of 100 grand prix victories.

On the Friday of practise, Renault Sport president, Patrick Faure, was forced to admit these would be difficult targets to meet. At the time, Renault had 90 wins with ten races left to run. *«Nevertheless, we will do all in our power to win the championship,»* he insisted. *«As for the 100 victories, we can look at that later. Renault will not be involved in competition at the highest level for the next three years, but we still have the 21st century.»*

• Bruno Michel leaves

On Thursday of practice, a press release announced that the Prost team's general manager, Bruno Michel was leaving. *«The plan had been for Bruno Michel to stay with us for a few months to ensure a smooth transition. This has now been done. His excellent work has allowed me to take over a company in a good state of health,»* explained Alain Prost.

What this meant in English was that Michel and Prost could not reach an agreement o the former's role in the new team.

The Magny-Cours grandstands were full to bursting point for the race, despite menacing skies and a refreshing summer shower ▽ *towards the end of the race.*

Oh Lucky Jacques!

Jacques Villeneuve should never have won at Silverstone. But out in front, Michael Schumacher suffered his first mechanical failure of the season and the Mercedes engine in Mika Hakkinen's McLaren let go when the Finn was just six laps away from his first grand prix win.

This left the Canadian to pick up the pieces and revive his championship campaign.

Alexander Wurz was the sensation of the day, bringing his Benetton home in third place. Gerhard Berger was almost a thing of the past.

THE 1997 RAC BRITISH GRAND PRIX
SILVERSTONE

«I prefer Billy Idol.» Jacques Villeneuve and his race engineer Jock Cleare locked in serious discussion at the Renault motorhome.

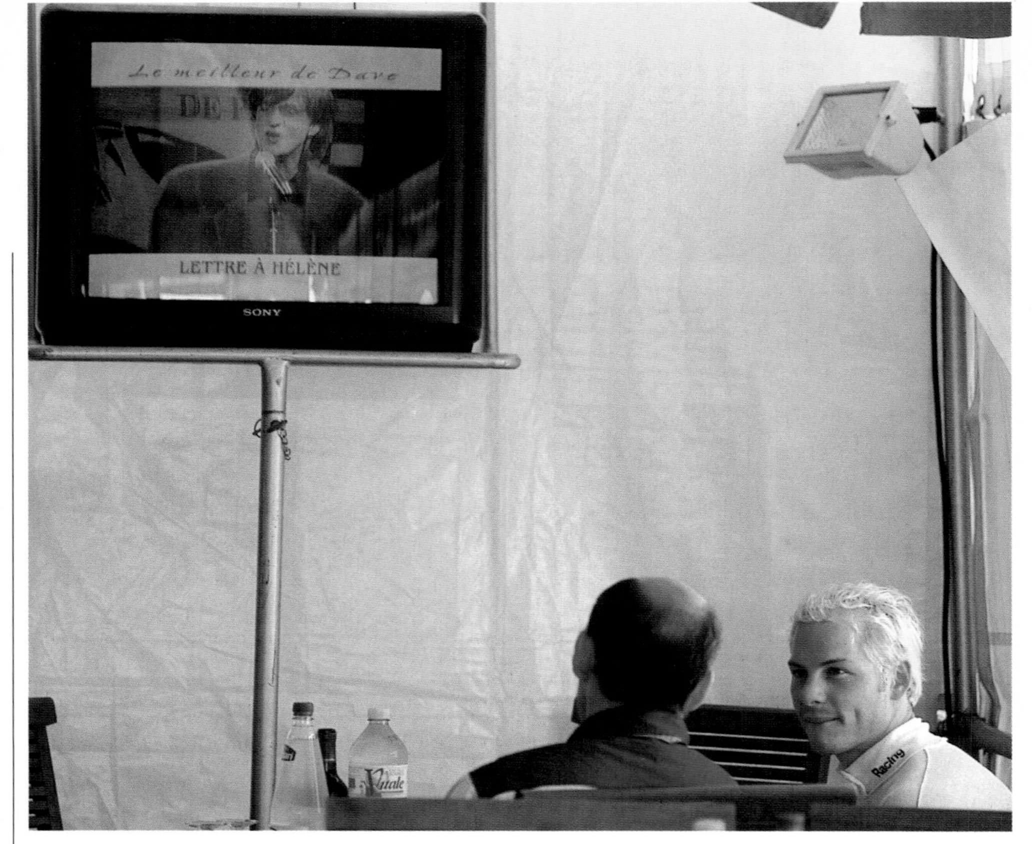

Pole position for Jacques Villeneuve

On track answer to off track critics

The week had got off to a bad start for Jacques Villeneuve. On Monday, Frank Williams said the Canadian had to win at all costs at Silverstone to have any chance of still winning the championship.

For his part, at a press conference in Berne, Jacques Villeneuve had accused his team of having stopped development work on this year's chassis and that was why Ferrari had taken the lead in the championship. *«There are good reasons why Ferrari are ahead of us, but they are not the ones that Jacques puts forward,»* was Frank Williams' reply on the Friday of practice. *«In any case, Jacques does not come to the factory often enough to know what we are working on. He is wrong when he says we are not working on the car.»*

Renault's chief engineer, Bernard Dudot fanned the flames by claiming that if Damon Hill was still at Williams, then the Englishman would be leading the championship. It was yet another slap in the face for Jacques Villeneuve. With seemingly the whole world against him, Villeneuve needed to pull something out of the hat to silence his critics. He did not have to wait long.

On Saturday, he claimed pole position in style, in the dying moments of the session, when the climatic conditions were slightly more favourable. *«It is very difficult to overtake on this track and so I am delighted to be at the front,»* he said at the end of the session.

However, as far as Villeneuve was concerned, pole position did not necessarily mean the race was in the bag. *«The gaps between the cars are so small, that you can quite easily have a good race and still finish outside the points. I think it will be one of the toughest grands prix of the season, especially as on the engine front we no longer have an advantage over our rivals,»* added the Canadian, firing a broadside across Dudot's Friday criticism.

In second place on the grid, Heinz-Harald Frentzen had decided to be sure of a good place, rather than go for pole at all costs. *«I had traffic on my first two runs. That is why I decided to go out again, eight minutes from the end, rather than wait for the rush in the last couple of minutes, even though I could see a cloud was going to hide the sun, which would make the track quicker at the end.»*

It had rained quite heavily in practice and even during the race morning warm-up, which allowed for some great photographic opportunities.

STARTING GRID

	Row	
		Jacques VILLENEUVE 1'21"598
Heinz-H. FRENTZEN 1'21"732	-1-	
		Mika HAKKINEN 1'21"797
M. SCHUMACHER 1'21"977	-2-	
		R. SCHUMACHER 1'22"277
David COULTHARD 1'22"279	-3-	
		Eddie IRVINE 1'22"342
Alexander WURZ 1'22"344	-4-	
		Johnny HERBERT 1'22"366
G. FISICHELLA 1'22"371	-5-	
		Jean ALESI 1'22"392
Damon HILL 1'23"271	-6-	
		Jarno TRULLI 1'23"366
Shinji NAKANO 1'23"887	-7-	
		Jan MAGNUSSEN 1'24"067
Pedro DINIZ 1'24"239	-8-	
		Mika SALO 1'24"478
Ukyo KATAYAMA 1'24"553	-9-	
		Jos VERSTAPPEN 1'25"010
Tarso MARQUES 1'25"154	-10-	
	-11-	R. BARRICHELLO 1'25"525

«Don't you recognise me? My name is Bond, James Bond.» Pierce Brosnan grapples with the swipe car paddock entry system.

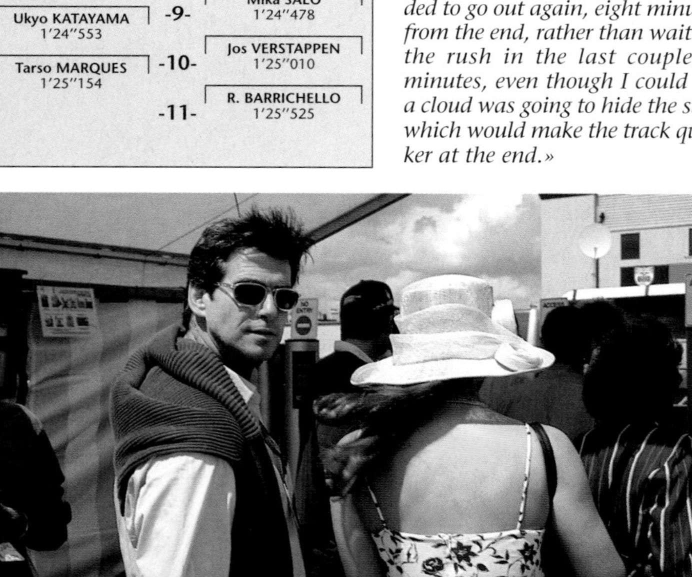

Then came the Schumacher brothers

After two successive poles in Montreal and Magny-Cours, Michael Schumacher found himself back in fourth place at Silverstone. *«I am not too disappointed,»* analysed the German. *«The car is already a lot better than on Friday. In the race, I will settle for scoring as many points as possible.»*

With ten grands prix to go however, it seemed a bit premature to be settling for scraps. The following day's race would prove this.

Eddie Irvine was seventh in the other Ferrari. He probably might have done a bit better if he had not collided with, of all things, a hare on his first flying lap. *«I had to come into the pits to have the front wing checked and to change tyres. Then my car tended to go light in the fast corners and we had to put on more downforce. I think it will be difficult to maintain a good pace in the race.»*

Ralf Schumacher was happy to be fifth as he was ahead of his team-mate, Giancarlo Fisichella and that seemed to be all it took to keep him satisfied. *«I was hoping for better, after all the private testing we have done here,»* he complained all the same, alluding to the fact that the Jordan factory is on the Silverstone doorstep. *«But the other teams must have improved to close the gap, as our car is almost perfect. We have managed to fix our understeer problem.»* «Fisico» could do no better than tenth place and he was fuming. *«It is all the more frustrating as the times are so close and it would have been very easy to be much higher up the grid. But I had some problems with traffic and I made a few mistakes.»*

Villeneuve throws the championship open again

Tifosi the world over were beginning to think that Michael Schumacher was going to dominate the championship in the manner of a latter day Ben Hur. The British Grand Prix pulled them up short and reminded them that they should not underestimate Jacques Villeneuve and the Williams-Renault.
However, this British Grand Prix did not start too auspiciously for the Canadian. Having made a good start, he was immediately chased down by Schumacher, whom he could not shake off. *«I had a serious problem with my left front wheel, which started to come loose around ten laps before my pit-stop,»* admitted Villeneuve. *«I had to really pull on the steering wheel to get the front wheels to react and the steering got very heavy.»*

Tough nut

When he made his first pit-stop, the wheel in question did not want to come off, because of its damaged nut and the Canadian was stationery for 33 seconds, before re-joining the race in seventh place. *«I had mixed feelings at that moment,»* he recalled after the race. *«Of course I was very angry, but at the same time I knew this problem with the wheel could have had much more serious consequences. I might never have got out of the pits at all.»*
Setting off in pursuit of his rivals, Villeneuve was stuck for a long time behind the two Benettons, which had opted for a one stop strategy, while out in front, Michael Schumacher was establishing a comfortable lead. The Ferrari would no doubt have carried off the spoils, if it too had not suffered with a wheel problem.
Having dealt with the Benettons, Villeneuve was now second behind Mika Hakkinen's McLaren. *«I had noticed that Mika had a blistered rear tyres and I think I could have passed him,»* claimed the Canadian. Hakkinen did not agree with this assessment and reckoned he could have kept ahead of the Williams without any bother. Villeneuve eventually took a lucky win, thanks in part to the retirement of his rivals. *«It's true that luck played a part. But we have also had our fair share of mechanical problems this season. I think it is fair that Ferrari should have their turn.»*

△ *Champagne for Jacques Villeneuve. With this, his fourth victory of the season, the Canadian was now just four points behind championship leader Schumacher.*

A furz podium for Alexander Wurz

Jean Alesi was all smiles at the finish. He seemed overjoyed with his second place. *«I am very happy, because I have been pushing the team a lot. This second place is a deserved reward.»*
Having qualified down in 11th place on the grid, Jean owed his podium to a one stop race strategy. *«We had to go for only stopping once, as this was our only chance of getting ahead of the others. The car had such a heavy fuel load that I was very slow. But bit by bit, I could see on my pitboard that I was making up places.»*
Jean Alesi spent most of the race pursued by his team-mate, Alexander Wurz. The Austrian finished third, thus making it onto the podium at only his third attempt. *«Well, er, I'm very happy,»* he stammered. *«I had prepared some words for such an occasion, but now I have forgotten them. Most of all, I would like to thank my team for giving me the chance to drive in a grand prix.»*
He did not have much to say about his race. *«It all went smoothly. At the start, on full tanks, the car was sliding a lot and Fisichella managed to get past me. But after the pit-stop, everything got better. I think I could have passed Jean* (Alesi) *coming out of the pits, but it would have been a bit dangerous and I did not want to take any risks.»*
It seemed certain that Gerhard Berger would be back behind the wheel in Hockenheim, as his insurance company was paying Benetton half a million pounds per race and they did not want to prolong the agony. *«Of course I want to drive,»* said Wurz. *«But this is Gerhard's seat and I will hand it over to him without question. All the same, I feel I have shown my potential.»*

◁ *«No, I did not choose the wrong shoes this morning.» Like so many of the drivers, Alexander Wurz has a little superstition. This mix of colours dates back to his Formula Ford days, when he won a race with similar footwear, as the result of a practical joked played on him by friends.*

IN THE POINTS

	Driver	Team	Time
1.	Jacques VILLENEUVE	Rothmans Williams Renault	1 h 28'01"665
2.	Jean ALESI	Mild Seven Benetton Renault	at 10"205
3.	Alexander WURZ	Mild Seven Benetton Renault	at 11"296
4.	David COULTHARD	West McLaren Mercedes	at 31"229
5.	Ralf SCHUMACHER	B&H Total Jordan Peugeot	at 31"880
6.	Damon HILL	Danka Arrows Yamaha	at 1'13"552

Fastest lap : M. SCHUM., lap 34, 1'24"475, avg. 219.047 km/h

Frentzen: failed again

Heinz-Harald Frentzen's performance was somewhat wide of the mark in the British Grand Prix, as he did not even complete the first lap.
It all began to turn pear shaped when he stalled his Williams-Renault on the grid. *«Heinz-Harald did not follow the procedure that allows you to select neutral,»* explained Williams technical supremo, Patrick Head. *«It seems that he pressed the button which changes down the gears at the same time as the one that selects neutral and that stalled the engine.»* Frentzen's race engineer later explained that «HH» could not have known the effect of pressing both these buttons at the same time.
The start was thus delayed by five minutes and «HH» was shunted to the back of the grid, as demanded by the regulations. Once the race was underway, he had already made up five places, when he was punted off the track at the third corner by Jos Verstappen's Tyrrell.

Mobil 1
Mercedes Benz

Mika Hakkinen had qualified on the second row and was leading the British Grand Prix with seven laps to go. Unfortunately for the Finn, his engine chose to rob him of his maiden grand prix win
A scenario that would be repeated at the Nurburgring.

▷
Tom Walkinshaw's comments about his Number One driver had been splashed all over the English tabloids. The Mirror's headline: «I'll sack flop Hill,» being typical of the genre. The world champion was having a hard time.

«Whoops!» Giancarlo Fisichella gives himself a fright as he attempts a rather unorthodox method of getting around Copse Corner. The Roman would need all his skill to keep it on the island, but it was not enough to stop the Benettons getting past.
▽
▽

John Surtees is back. The Englishman, who won the world championship in 1964 for Ferrari, was taking part in an historic car race at Silverstone.
▽

Stormy weather at Arrows

It all began on the Thursday, when Damon Hill candidly admitted to the press, that he was finding it difficult to maintain his concentration this season. *«When the results are not there, it is always difficult to give your best. I have to fight to stay awake and get on with my job.»*
Having moved from Williams to Arrows in the winter, Hill knew that he would not really be in a position to defend his world championship crown. However, he still harboured hopes of winning one or two races, in part thanks to his Bridgestone tyres.
Unfortunately, by the halfway point in the season, the Englishman was a long way off target. Apart from the retirements due to mechanical problems, there had been several driving errors. To cap it all, Hill was occasionally out-paced by his young and inexperienced team-mate, Pedro Diniz. Had the world champion given up?

Walkinshaw explodes

For his part, Arrows boss Tom Walkinshaw was less than impressed with his driver's performance.
However, he had always kept his thoughts to himself. Up until now that is, up until Hill's remarks about his motivation.
These were enough to make Tom flip his lid. *«When Damon says he lacks motivation, I am horrified,»* said the Scotsman. *«I don't believe any professional sportsman has any difficulty in motivating himself. Damon is one of the best drivers in the world. It is up to him to push the team forward and not the other way around. He is not trying hard enough this year and the result is that the car seems worse than it is. It is true that at the start of the season, we had reliability problems, but these days the responsibility is split equally between him and us.»*

Evidently very angry, the Arrows boss made it clear that he might even get rid of his star driver. *«The current rumour is that Damon is leaving us for a better team. But the opposite situation could well be the truth. If he continues not to do his job properly, then he could be losing us. Up until now, I have been very friendly towards him, but now I might have to try a more direct approach.»* Walkinshaw was paying his driver about 4.8 million pounds in 1997 and he seemed to feel he was not getting his money's worth. *«If the money I pay Damon is not enough to motivate him, then I would have thought that fear of failure would do the trick,»* he concluded.
Damon Hill took his boss' comments like a slap in the face. Somewhat disconcerted, he immediately tried to play things down. *«I am very disappointed by what Tom has said,»* he offered on Friday, after a long chat with Walkinshaw. *«I can understand his frustration, but I do not agree with him. I am doing my best and trying to be as professional as possible.»*

Mika and Michael both happy and sad

There were no Ferraris running at the end of the race. For the Scuderia, the British Grand Prix turned to disaster on lap 39. While comfortably leading the race, Michael Schumacher was forced to retire with a seized wheel bearing on the left rear wheel. Six laps later, it was Eddie Irvine's turn to park his car with a broken right half-shaft. Despite this cruel blow, Schumacher showed no sign of disappointment as he stepped from his cockpit. *«These things can happen. It's all part of racing,»* he mused philosophically. *«It is my first mechanical problem of the season. I prefer to look on the positive side. Today, I was leading comfortably, when my problem happened, which proves we have now caught up to the Williams. In my opinion, this is not so much a day to forget, as a day to celebrate.»*
Mika Hakkinen was another who almost claimed what could have been the first grand prix win of his career. That Sunday, with only six laps to go, the Finn was in the lead, when he had to retire with a broken engine.

McLaren on the same level as Williams

While it was naturally disappointing, McLaren had shown that its MP4/12 was now almost on the same level as the Williams and Ferraris. *«I have really mixed feelings,»* said Mika later that evening. *«On the one hand, I really wanted to win this race. My left rear tyre was blistered, but I am sure I could have stayed ahead of Jacques to the chequered flag. That would be cause for celebration enough. Now I cannot wait for Hockenheim.»*

PRACTICE TIMES

No	Driver	Make/Engine/Chassis	Practice Friday	Practice Saturday	Qualifying	Warm-up
1.	Damon HIll	Arrows/Yamaha/A18/5 (B)	1'26"810	1'23"871	1'23"271	1'38"031
2.	Pedro Diniz	Arrows/Yamaha/A18/3 (B)	1'26"797	1'24"961	1'24"239	1'41"751
3.	Jacques Villeneuve	Williams/Renault/FW19/4 (G)	1'23"266	1'22"063	1'21"598	1'38"507
4.	Heinz-Harald Frentzen	Williams/Renault/FW19/5 (G)	1'23"327	1'23"022	1'21"732	1'39"756
5.	Michael Schumacher	Ferrari/Ferrari/F310B/177 (G)	1'24"132	1'22"586	1'21"977	1'38"670
6.	Eddie Irvine	Ferrari/Ferrari/F310B/173 (G)	1'24"424	1'23"614	1'22"342	1'38"061
7.	Jean Alesi	Benetton/Renault/B197/5 (G)	1'23"785	1'23"607	1'22"392	1'38"876
8.	Alexander Wurz	Benetton/Renault/B197/4 (G)	1'24"203	1'23"161	1'22"344	1'41"489
9.	Mika Hakkinen	McLaren/Mercedes/MP4/12/6 (G)	1'22"935	1'22"000	1'21"797	1'39"074
10.	David Coulthard	McLaren/Mercedes/MP4/12/7 (G)	1'25"360	1'22"712	1'22"279	1'39"846
11.	Ralf Schumacher	Jordan/Peugeot/197/6 (G)	1'24"948	1'23"647	1'22"277	1'42"261
12.	Giancarlo Fisichella	Jordan/Peugeot/197/4 (G)	1'23"883	1'22"962	1'22"371	1'38"993
14.	Jarno Trulli	Prost/Mugen Honda/JS45/4 (B)	1'24"946	1'24"172	1'23"366	1'43"612
15.	Shinji Nakano	Prost/Mugen Honda/JS45/2 (B)	1'26"270	1'23"823	1'23"887	1'41"920
16.	Johnny Herbert	Sauber/Petronas/C16/5 (G)	1'23"581	1'23"131	1'22"368	1'38"707
17.	Norberto Fontana	Sauber/Petronas/C16/6 (G)	1'26"640	1'24"181	1'23"790	1'39"693
18.	Jos Verstappen	Tyrrell/Ford/025/4 (G)	1'27"923	1'25"195	1'25"010	1'41"039
19.	Mika Salo	Tyrrell/Ford/025/3 (G)	1'26"035	1'25"015	1'24"478	1'40"652
20.	Ukyo Katayama	Minardi/Hart/M197/4 (B)	1'26"446	1'24"716	1'24"553	1'41"781
21.	Tarso Marquès	Minardi/Hart/M197/2 (B)	1'27"066	1'25"725	1'25"154	1'43"088
22.	Rubens Barrichello	Stewart/Ford/SF1/2 (B)	1'26"785	1'23"577	1'25"525	1'39"868
23.	Jan Magnussen	Stewart/Ford/SF1/3 (B)	1'25"136	1'24"181	1'24"067	1'39"498

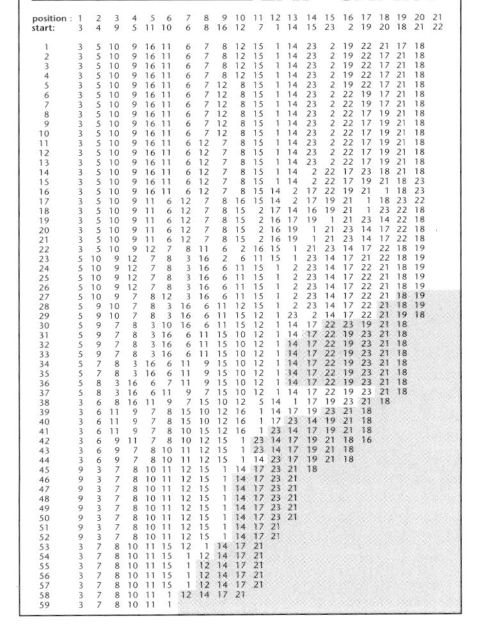

LAP CHART

position :	1	2	3	4	5	6	7	8	9	10	11	12	13	14	15	16	17	18	19	20	21
start:	3	4	9	5	11	10	6	8	16	12	7	1	14	15	23	2	19	20	18	21	22
1	3	5	10	9	16	11	6	7	8	12	15	1	14	23	2	19	22	21	17	18	
2	3	5	10	9	16	11	6	7	8	12	15	1	14	23	2	19	22	17	21	18	
3	3	5	10	9	16	11	6	7	8	12	15	1	14	23	2	19	22	17	21	18	
4	3	5	10	9	16	11	6	7	8	12	15	1	14	23	2	19	22	17	21	18	
5	3	5	10	9	16	11	6	7	12	8	15	1	14	23	2	19	22	17	21	18	
6	3	5	10	9	16	11	6	7	12	8	15	1	14	23	2	22	19	17	21	18	
7	3	5	10	9	16	11	6	7	12	8	15	1	14	23	2	22	19	17	21	18	
8	3	5	10	9	16	11	6	7	12	8	15	1	14	23	2	22	17	19	21	18	
9	3	5	10	9	16	11	6	7	12	8	15	1	14	23	2	22	17	19	21	18	
10	3	5	10	9	16	11	6	7	12	8	15	1	14	23	2	22	17	19	21	18	
11	3	5	10	9	16	11	6	12	7	8	15	1	14	23	2	22	17	19	21	18	
12	3	5	10	9	16	11	6	12	7	8	15	1	14	23	2	22	17	19	21	18	
13	3	5	10	9	16	11	6	12	7	8	15	1	14	23	2	22	17	19	21	18	
14	3	5	10	9	16	11	6	12	7	8	15	1	14	2	22	17	23	18	21	18	
15	3	5	10	9	16	11	6	12	7	8	15	1	14	2	22	17	19	21	18	23	
16	3	5	10	9	16	11	6	12	7	8	15	14	2	17	22	19	21	1	18	23	
17	3	5	10	9	11	6	12	7	8	16	15	14	2	17	19	21	1	18	23	22	
18	3	5	10	9	11	6	12	7	8	15	2	17	14	16	19	21	1	23	22	18	
19	3	5	10	9	11	6	12	7	8	15	2	16	17	19	1	21	23	14	22	18	
20	3	5	10	9	11	6	12	7	8	15	2	16	19	1	21	23	14	17	22	18	
21	3	5	10	9	11	6	12	7	8	15	2	16	19	1	21	23	14	17	22	18	
22	3	5	10	9	12	7	8	11	6	2	16	15	1	21	23	14	17	22	18	19	
23	5	10	9	12	7	8	3	16	2	6	11	15	1	23	14	17	21	22	18	19	
24	5	10	9	12	7	8	3	16	6	11	15	1	2	23	14	17	22	21	18	19	
25	5	10	9	12	7	8	3	16	6	11	15	1	2	23	14	17	22	21	18	19	
26	5	10	9	12	7	8	3	16	6	11	15	1	2	23	14	17	22	21	18	19	
27	5	10	9	7	8	12	3	16	6	11	15	1	2	23	14	17	22	21	18	19	
28	5	9	10	7	8	3	16	6	11	12	15	1	2	23	14	17	22	21	18	19	
29	5	9	10	7	8	3	16	6	11	15	12	1	23	2	14	17	22	21	19	18	
30	5	9	7	8	3	10	16	6	11	15	12	1	14	17	22	23	19	21	18		
31	5	9	7	8	3	16	6	11	15	10	12	1	14	17	22	19	23	21	18		
32	5	9	7	8	3	16	6	11	15	10	12	1	14	17	22	19	23	21	18		
33	5	9	7	8	3	16	6	11	15	10	12	1	14	17	22	19	23	21	18		
34	5	7	8	3	16	6	11	9	15	10	12	1	14	17	22	19	23	21	18		
35	5	7	8	3	16	6	11	9	15	10	12	1	14	17	22	19	23	21	18		
36	5	8	3	16	6	7	11	9	15	10	12	1	14	17	22	19	23	21	18		
37	5	8	3	16	6	11	9	7	15	10	12	1	14	17	22	19	23	21	18		
38	3	6	8	16	11	9	7	15	10	12	5	14	1	17	19	23	21	18			
39	3	6	11	9	7	8	15	10	12	16	1	14	17	19	23	21	18				
40	3	6	11	9	7	8	15	10	12	16	1	17	23	14	19	21	18				
41	3	6	11	9	7	8	10	15	12	16	1	23	14	17	19	21	18				
42	3	6	9	11	7	8	10	12	15	1	23	14	17	19	21	18	16				
43	3	6	9	7	8	10	11	12	15	1	23	14	17	19	21	18					
44	3	6	9	7	8	10	11	12	15	1	14	23	17	19	21	18					
45	9	3	7	8	10	11	12	15	1	14	17	23	21	18							
46	9	3	7	8	10	11	12	15	1	14	17	23	21								
47	9	3	7	8	10	11	12	15	1	14	17	23	21								
48	9	3	7	8	10	11	12	15	1	14	17	23	21								
49	9	3	7	8	10	11	12	15	1	14	17	23	21								
50	9	3	7	8	10	11	12	15	1	14	17	23	21								
51	9	3	7	8	10	11	12	15	1	14	17	21									
52	9	3	7	8	10	11	12	15	1	14	17	21									
53	3	7	8	10	11	15	12	1	14	17	21										
54	3	7	8	10	11	15	1	12	14	17	21										
55	3	7	8	10	11	15	1	12	14	17	21										
56	3	7	8	10	11	15	1	12	14	17	21										
57	3	7	8	10	11	15	1	12	14	17	21										
58	3	7	8	10	11	1	12	14	17	21											
59	3	7	8	10	11	1															

BRIDGESTONE

Best result for a Bridgestone shod runner:

Damon Hill, Arrows-Yamaha, 6th

CLASSIFICATION & RETIREMENTS

Pos	Driver	Team	Time
1.	Villeneuve	Williams Renault	in 1h28'01"665
2.	Alesi	Benetton Renault	at 10"205
3.	Wurz	Benetton Renault	at 11"296
4.	Coulthard	McLaren Mercedes	at 31"229
5.	Schumacher	Jordan Peugeot	at 31"880
6.	Hill	Arrows Yamaha	at 1'13"552
7.	Fisichella	Jordan Peugeot	at 1 lap
8.	Trulli	Prost Mugen Honda	at 1 lap
9.	Fontana	Sauber Petronas	at 1 lap
10.	Marquès	Minardi Hart	at 1 lap
11.	Nakano	Prost Mugen Honda	engine

Lap	Driver	Team	Reason
1	Katayama	Minardi Hart	off
1	Frentzen	Williams Renault	accident
30	Diniz	Arrows Yamaha	engine
38	Barrichello	Stewart Ford	engine
39	Schumacher	Ferrari	roulement de roue
43	Herbert	Sauber Petronas	electronics
45	Salo	Tyrrell Ford	engine
45	Irvine	Ferrari	transmission
46	Verstappen	Tyrrell Ford	engine
51	Magnussen	Stewart Ford	engine
53	Hakkinen	McLaren Mercedes	engine

FASTEST LAPS

	Driver	Time	Lap
1.	M. Schum.	1'24"475	34
2.	Villeneuve	1'24"082	42
3.	Irvine	1'25"236	43
4.	R. Schum.	1'25"872	35
5.	Hakkinen	1'25"988	38
6.	Fisichella	1'26"119	57
7.	Herbert	1'26"232	34
8.	Alesi	1'26"260	50
9.	Wurz	1'26"429	51
10.	Hill	1'26"471	57
11.	Coulthard	1'26"475	57
12.	Trulli	1'26"610	57
13.	Nakano	1'26"778	24
14.	Diniz	1'27"111	25
15.	Magnussen	1'27"586	32
16.	Fontana	1'27"783	17
17.	Barrichello	1'27"877	35
18.	Salo	1'28"053	35
19.	Marquès	1'29"100	32
20.	Verstappen	1'29"137	25

NINTH ROUND

RAC BRITISH GRAND PRIX, SILVERSTONE

MAGOTTS CURVE
CHAPEL CURVE
COPSE CORNER
BECKETTS
STOWE CORNER
PRIORY
ABBEY CURVE
VALE
LUFFIELD
BRIDGE CORNER
WOODCOTE
CLUB CORNER

Date : July 13, 1997
Length : 5140 meters
Distance : 59 laps, 303.260 km
Weather : sunny, 18 degrees

CHAMPIONSHIPS

(after nine rounds)

Drivers :

1. Michael SCHUMACHER 47
2. Jacques VILLENEUVE 43
3. Jean ALESI 21
4. Heinz-H. FRENTZEN......................19
5. Eddie IRVINE 18
6. Olivier PANIS 15
7. David COULTHARD 14
8. Gerhard BERGER 10
   Mika HAKKINEN 10
10. Giancarlo FISICHELLA 8
11. Ralf SCHUMACHER 7
    Johnny HERBERT 7
13. Rubens BARRICHELLO 6
14. Alexander WURZ 4
15. Mika SALO 2
16. Nicola LARINI 1
    Shinji NAKANO 1
    Damon HILL 1

Constructors :

1. Ferrari 65
2. Williams / Renault 62
3. Benetton / Renault 35
4. McLaren / Mercedes 24
5. Prost / Mugen Honda 16
6. Jordan / Peugeot 15
7. Sauber / Petronas 8
8. Stewart / Ford 6
9. Tyrrell / Ford 2
10. Arrows / Yamaha 1

WEEK-END GOSSIP

- **Jordan with Mugen**

It was a fruitful weekend for the Jordan team. On Monday it announced a deal with Mugen-Honda for a supply of Japanese engines in 1988 and 1989 and on Thursday, Eddie Jordan announced that his title sponsor, Benson & Hedges had signed on for a further three years. The next day, Jordan put out yet another press release to announce a deal with MasterCard Latin America and Carribean, thus picking up on the deal that had fallen apart between MasterCard and the Lola team.

- **Quick delivery**

More money in the Benetton piggy bank. Starting with the British Grand Prix, the most heavily stickered car in the paddock now bore additional logos, having signed a deal with Federal Express, which had become one of its major sponsors. From now on they would be responsible for transporting the Benetton cars and equipment all over the world in record time.

- **Nostalgia**

Souvenirs and memories were revived by Renault. They brought to Silverstone their first F1 car, which had made its debut at this track, twenty years ago. It was good to see once again, the car and engine which had introduced turbo-charging to the sport, even if the car in question had been cruelly nicknamed «The FlyingTeapot» at the time.

- **Irvine out**

It seemed that Ferrari planned to dump Eddie Irvine, whose performance and manner did not suit the Scuderia. At Silverstone, the management of the Italian team asked David Coulthard if he would like the job, but the Scotsman turned them down.

- **Lotus return**

The Lotus team, which had gone belly up at the end of 1994, was planning to rise from the ashes in 1999.
At least that was the gist of a press release put out at Silverstone by David Hunt, brother of World Champion James Hunt and now the owner of the famous team. There were no details available as to which engine it wold run, nor where the money would come from.

- **A Frenchman guaranteed**

Fredric Saint-Geours is obviously a master of the administrative arts and during a very convoluted speech, the President of Peugeot Sport explained at Silverstone why the Lion was abandoning Jordan to concentrate on the Prost team. *«We wanted to work exclusively with one team,»* he claimed. *«With Prost we will be more than just an engine supplier. We will be part of the foundation of the team.»*
Saint-Geours added that Peugeot was insisting on at least one of the two drivers being French.

RACE SUMMARY

- Frentzen stalls on the grid and is made to go to the back of the class for the re-start.
- Villeneuve gets away first from Schumacher, who leads the two McLarens and Herbert.
- Frentzen is out on the first lap after colliding with Verstappen. Katayama slams his Minardi into a wall, forcing the race director to bring out the safety car.
- The race is underway again on lap 4 and the Villeneuve-Schumacher tandem pulls out a gap over the McLarens and Herbert.
- At the first round of pit-stops, Villeneuve's left front wheel sticks and the Canadian loses over 30 seconds in the pits.
- Michael Schumacher has a comfortable lead, but is forced to retire shortly after his second pit-stop with a broken wheel bearing.
- On lap 45, Eddie Irvine suffers a similar fate. He was second, but has to retire with a broken half shaft.
- The McLaren and Benetton drivers have chosen a one stop strategy, which sees Hakkinen take the lead shortly before the end of the race.
- Closely followed by Villeneuve, Hakkinen's Mercedes engine lets go, handing victory to the Canadian, ahead of the two Benettons.

▽ *Silverstone, the former wartime airfield is well and truly the home of British motor racing.*

BENETTON
RENAULT
A1
mobilkom
KicKers

Life in the old dog yet

A winning comeback. Having been absent from Formula 1 since the Spanish Grand Prix, because of a sinus infection, Gerhard Berger returned to dominate the Hockenheim event in astonishing fashion.
It was a surprising race in many ways, as it highlighted the talent of Giancarlo Fisichella, who should have finished second. The championship leaders Ferrari, as well as their nearest rivals Williams, did not make a good showing here.

GROSSER MOBIL 1 PREIS VON DEUTSCHLAND HOCKENHEIM

△
The Red Sea comes to Hockenheim. Since Michael Schumacher joined Ferrari, the German fans thought they were tifosi.

▷
A pensive Jean Alesi. He was only sixth on the grid and admitted he would have to work on his set-up, comparing it to Gerhard Berger's.

Giancarlo Fisichella straining for those last hundredths. Guaranteed a Benetton seat for 1998, the Italian was under no pressure and let rip at Hockenheim.
▷ ▽

Gerhard Berger in pole position

Triumphal return

The expected duel between Williams and Ferrari did not materialise. On Saturday, to the surprise of one and all, it was Austria's Gerhard Berger who put his Benetton- Renault on pole position.
Even more surprising was Giancarlo Fisichella's second place, which made for a most unusual grid that held the promise of a very exciting race.
For Gerhard Berger, making his return to the sport (see page 60,) this pole could not have come at a better time. *«I must admit it is a great feeling to be back on pole position,»* beamed the Austrian after the session. *«And I am also very pleased for everyone at Benetton. Last year we suffered with a bad car. But this season, the B197 is excellent and I was unable to get the most out of it through illness and my absence. Today, I have finally managed to give the team the result they deserve.»*
The Austrian's only concern was his state of health. *«I am fit enough,»* he reassured his inquisitors. *«But I would feel better after a winter's skiing. I realise I will have to build up my muscles before the next grand prix.»*

«Fisico» at over 350 km/h

We knew he was talented, but Giancarlo Fisichella continued to surprise the paddock. On Saturday, the little Italian set the second fastest time of the qualifying session and he was only 23 thousandths of a second off the pole position time. *«I don't know what to say. It's incredible, it's fantastic,»* exclaimed «Fisico» after qualifying.
At the start of the session, the Roman's Jordan-Peugeot was really flying, recording the fastest straight line speed of 349.5 km/h before the first chicane.
For the race, Giancarlo had worked out a very simple strategy. *«Just fill it up with petrol, don't touch the settings and go flat out!»*

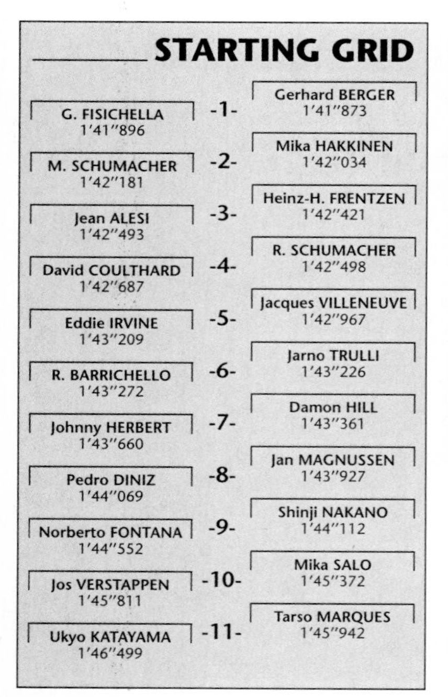

STARTING GRID

	Row	
G. FISICHELLA 1'41"896	-1-	Gerhard BERGER 1'41"873
M. SCHUMACHER 1'42"181	-2-	Mika HAKKINEN 1'42"034
Jean ALESI 1'42"493	-3-	Heinz-H. FRENTZEN 1'42"421
David COULTHARD 1'42"687	-4-	R. SCHUMACHER 1'42"498
Eddie IRVINE 1'43"209	-5-	Jacques VILLENEUVE 1'42"967
R. BARRICHELLO 1'43"272	-6-	Jarno TRULLI 1'43"226
Johnny HERBERT 1'43"660	-7-	Damon HILL 1'43"361
Pedro DINIZ 1'44"069	-8-	Jan MAGNUSSEN 1'43"927
Norberto FONTANA 1'44"552	-9-	Shinji NAKANO 1'44"112
Jos VERSTAPPEN 1'45"811	-10-	Mika SALO 1'45"372
Ukyo KATAYAMA 1'46"499	-11-	Tarso MARQUES 1'45"942

Gerhard with a little help from above

He had never been in such good form. At Hockenheim, Gerhard Berger was the master of his craft after an enforced absence due to a sinus operation and the ensuing period of convalescence, which had forced him to miss the three previous grands prix. Three races where the team had replaced him with Alexander Wurz, who had performed so well that Berger had to come up with something special at Hockenheim to justify his place in the Benetton team.
He certainly more than fulfilled the obligation.

Having secured pole position on Saturday, Gerhard Berger dominated the Hockenheim race with panache. Alone among the front runners to opt for a two pit-stop strategy, the Austrian disconcertingly appeared to win the German Grand Prix, pretty much as he pleased. He only vacated the number one slot for a handful of laps, when Giancarlo Fisichella led the race.
Berger did not look as though the race had taken much out of him as he stepped down from the podium. *«I feel fine,»* confirmed the veteran of the pack. *«I feel as though I had a special extra help from somewhere,»* he added, possibly referring to the fact his father had died a matter of days before. The pleasure the Austrian took from winning was all the greater as it was his first victory in three years. *«I find it difficult to describe my emotions. It is really a very special day for me. And I am also very happy for all the Benetton team. Since Michael left them at the end of 1995, they have gone through difficult times and we have all been under a lot of pressure. But this year's car has enormous potential and it was about time I proved it.»*
Berger's race went like a dream. *«Everything went according to plan, except that after my second pitstop, I was behind Fisichella. I thought I would have trouble overtaking him, but he made a small mistake and I slipped by.»*
Happy and smiling, it was a revitalised Berger who dominated the Hockenheim weekend. *«We have shown we are ahead of the others.»*

△
«A good day's work.» One hour and twenty minutes after the start, Gerhard Berger waves to the crowd. The Austrian's win had wiped out the memory of three missed grands prix.

1, 2, 3, Go. Or how to lead into the first corner, when starting from pole.
◁

«Take it easy Jarno, you're already fourth!» Jarno Trulli put on a superb performance to spend almost his entire 45 laps tailing Jacques Villeneuve.
▽

IN THE POINTS

	Driver	Team	Time
1.	Gerhard BERGER	M. Seven Benetton Renault	1 h 20'59"046
2.	M. SCHUMACHER	Scuderia Ferrari Marlboro	at 17"527
3.	Mika HAKKINEN	West McLaren Mercedes	at 24"770
4.	Jarno TRULLI	Prost Gauloises Blondes	at 27"165
5.	Ralf SCHUMACHER	B&H Total Jordan Peugeot	at 29"995
6.	Jean ALESI	Mild Seven Benetton Renault	at 34"717

Fastest lap : Gerhard BERGER, lap 9, 1'45"747, avg. 232.278 km/h

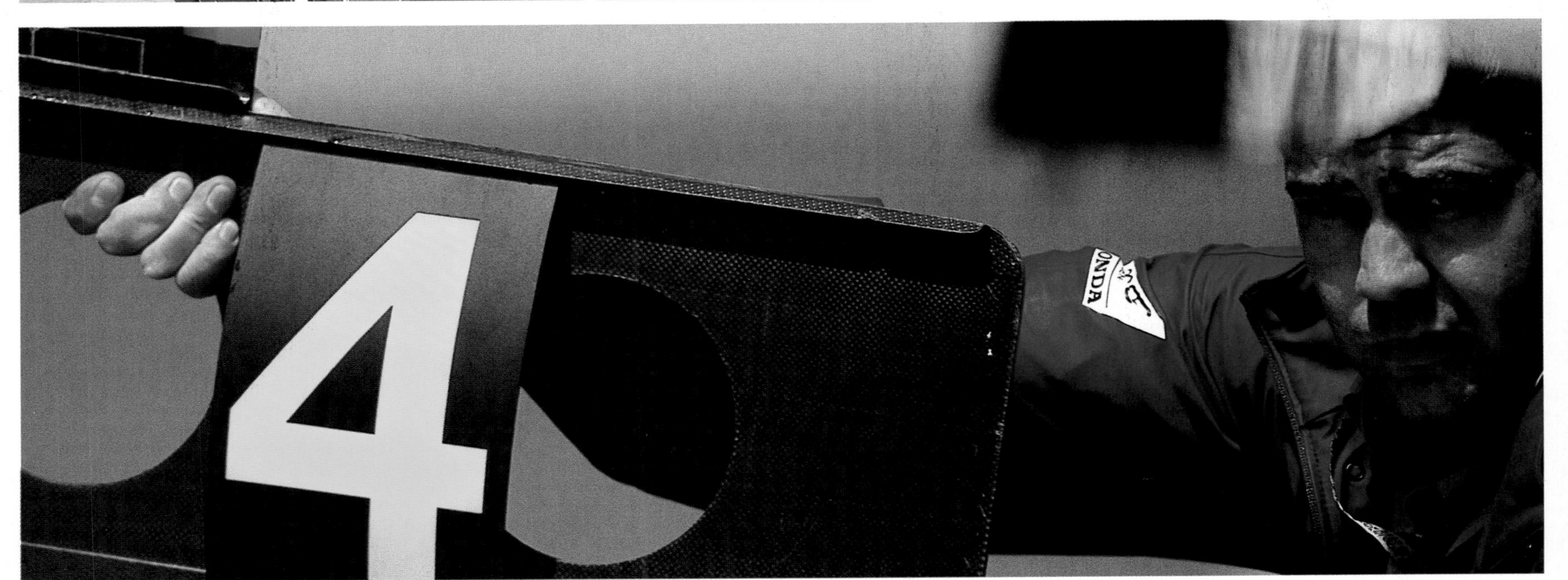

Failed again. "Heinzi's" season was turning into a nightmare, as having crashed out on the first lap at Silverstone, Heinz-Harald Frentzen played the same cards at Hockenheim, where he tangled with Eddie Irvine at the first chicane.

But the best of it was he admitted he had done it on purpose! "I was level with Eddie. As I did not want to go off on the grass and let him get away, I chose to hit him." It turned out to be a one hit wonder, as they both retired.

Racing
RENAULT
Castrol
http://www.icnsportsweb.com
BURG

△ Mika Hakkinen hard at work in the Hockenheim stadium. Third in qualifying, the Finn had the same result in the race, during which he spent his time fighting off the attentions of Jean Alesi and Jacques Villeneuve.

Three grands prix on the Subs. bench and time to think about the future

Gerhard Berger looks healthy enough. After missing three grands prix and spending most of the time in an Austrian hospital, undergoing various operations, no one expected to see him in such sparkling form on the Thursday in the Hockenheim paddock. *«Physically, I feel fine. I have done a lot of training and put back the muscle I had lost. Last week's testing at Monza went very well. I was on the pace after about fifteen laps and I loved it immediately.»*
Despite this resolutely positive statement, the Austrian was not smiling. Choosing his words carefully, it was evident he had done a lot of thinking during his enforced lay-off and most of it about his future. But what future? *"In hospital, I only had a few stupid magazines and four white walls to stare at,"* he said. *«Then I lived through difficult times after the death of my father. I had a lot of time to think about my life and what I wanted to do with it. I am interested in many things and I have a lot of possibilities, not all of them linked to racing. In my own mind, I think I know which way I want to go, but I feel it would be wrong to make a decision after these few weeks of doing nothing. I will give myself two or three races to see how I feel. Only then will I decide on my future.»*
The Austrian, who not that long ago, had said he would like to spend another ten years in Formula 1 had never looked so close to retirement.

Season destroyed

His season had started well, but at the Argentinian Grand Prix he caught a cold. *«My head was hurting. I went to see a doctor who told me I had a bad case of sinusitis and that my sinuses were too small to fix the problem without an operation. But before I could have surgery, the infection had to be cleared up. That is when my problems started, because I reacted badly to the antibiotics. The infection spread. To begin with, at Imola, Monaco and in Spain, I drove with antibiotics, but by Montreal it had got too serious. The doctors forbade me to race and I had to go to hospital. It is the sort of thing that can happen to anyone, but in my case, it completely destroyed my season.»*

Ralf «Rottweiler» Schumacher with Willi Weber, the «Mr. 20%» who manages both the Schumachers. In Germany, Jordan announced they would be keeping him on in 1998. His team-mate Fisichella was more sought after, as Benetton and Jordan were fighting over his services. ▽

High tension at Williams

The German Grand Prix ended more than two hours ago. Under the awning of his motorhome, Frank Williams is upright in his standing frame. With black and white chequered flag trousers and his hair a mess, Jacques Villeneuve comes to say goodbye to his boss, before leaving the circuit. Frank Williams pulls a face and with good reason. Hockenheim ended with yet another fiasco for his team.
Who is to blame? At Williams, they are not in the habit of questioning their abilities. With eight Constructors' World Championships under his belt, Frank Williams reckons he knows how to captain his ship, so it is the drivers who are under suspicion. Heinz-Harald Frentzen is growing his sideburns and Jacques Villeneuve has dyed his hair blonde. They are now known as «Elvis Frentzen» and «Billy Idol» in the paddock. It would seem they need to rehearse more, to stop playing so many wrong notes.
At Hockenheim, both men made driving errors, which did nothing for their standing in the team. The previous week, Frank Williams declared that he would, *«in all probability run his existing driver line-up in 1998.»* But the negotiations were dragging on and Heinz-Harald Frentzen, despite the fact he was on a two year contract, looked very nervous every time the subject of his seat at Williams for 1998 was brought up. Villeneuve's contract had not been formalised either.
At Hockenheim, the Canadian lost ground in the championship, but he remained optimistic. *«Ten points down with seven races to go is not so bad,»* he remarked. *«At any rate, it is a better situation than the one I was in at this time last year. At least this time, I do not have to fight against my team mate.»*
In Germany, the Williams were pale shadows of their former selves. Indeed on Saturday, Mika Hakkinen dared to say out loud what others had been thinking: *«The problem with Williams? It's the drivers,»* he let slip. Encouraging words for his two friends, Heinz and Jacques.

After retiring in the forests. Giancarlo Fisichella is given a lift back to the pits by Michael Schumacher at the end of the race. «Fisico» had been the hero of the day, leading the race for seven laps and looking set to finish a brilliant second until his hopes and a tyre were punctured. ▷

PRACTICE TIMES

No	Driver	Make/Engine/Chassis	Practice Friday	Practice Saturday	Qualifying	Warm-up
1.	Damon Hill	Arrows/Yamaha/A18/5 (B)	1'47"542	1'44"875	1'43"361	1'45"347
2.	Pedro Diniz	Arrows/Yamaha/A18/4 (B)	1'46"873	1'45"454	1'44"069	1'46"477
3.	Jacques Villeneuve	Williams/Renault/FW19/4 (G)	1'48"639	1'44"291	1'42"967	1'45"006
4.	Heinz-Harald-Frentzen	Williams/Renault/FW19/5 (G)	1'48"958	1'43"646	1'42"421	1'45"483
5.	Michael Schumacher	Ferrari/Ferrari/F310B/177 (G)	1'46"322	1'43"628	1'42"181	1'46"662
6.	Eddie Irvine	Ferrari/Ferrari/F310B/173 (G)	1'47"594	1'44"988	1'43"209	1'47"502
7.	Jean Alesi	Benetton/Renault/B197/2 (G)	1'48"455	1'43"257	1'42"493	1'46"448
8.	Gerhard Berger	Benetton/Renault/B197/4 (G)	1'47"887	1'43"428	1'41"873	1'45"497
9.	Mika Hakkinen	McLaren/Mercedes/MP4/12/5 (G)	1'47"386	1'42"989	1'42"034	1'46"258
10.	David Coulthard	McLaren/Mercedes/MP4/12/7 (G)	1'48"648	1'43"579	1'42"687	1'46"138
11.	Ralf Schumacher	Jordan/Peugeot/197/6 (G)	1'46"196	1'42"987	1'42"498	1'45"782
12.	Giancarlo Fisichella	Jordan/Peugeot/197/4 (G)	1'49"010	1'43"349	1'41"896	1'45"403
14.	Jarno Trulli	Prost/Mugen Honda/JS45/3 (B)	1'47"784	1'44"328	1'43"226	1'46"560
15.	Shinji Nakano	Prost/Mugen Honda/JS45/2 (B)	1'47"143	1'44"741	1'44"112	1'46"655
16.	Johnny Herbert	Sauber/Petronas/C16/5 (G)	1'46"517	1'45"082	1'43"660	1'46"919
17.	Norberto Fontana	Sauber/Petronas/C16/6 (G)	1'46"706	1'44"927	1'44"552	1'46"376
18.	Jos Verstappen	Tyrrell/Ford/025/4 (G)	1'47"720	1'46"548	1'45"811	1'49"418
19.	Mika Salo	Tyrrell/Ford/025/1 (G)	1'49"831	1'45"983	1'45"372	1'48"420
20.	Ukyo Katayama	Minardi/Hart/M197/4 (B)	1'51"058	1'46"569	1'46"499	1'50"614
21.	Tarso Marquès	Minardi/Hart/M197/2 (B)	1'49"563	1'46"800	1'45"942	1'47"775
22.	Rubens Barrichello	Stewart/Ford/SF1/1 (B)	1'46"526	1'44"096	1'43"272	1'46"797
23.	Jan Magnussen	Stewart/Ford/SF1/3 (B)	1'47"769	1'45"446	1'43"927	1'50"058

LAP CHART

position :	1	2	3	4	5	6	7	8	9	10	11	12	13	14	15	16	17	18	19	20	21	22
start:	8	12	9	5	4	7	11	10	3	6	14	22	1	16	23	2	15	17	19	18	21	20
1	8	12	5	9	7	3	14	22	16	11	1	23	2	17	19	15	18	20	10	4	6	
2	8	12	5	9	7	3	14	22	11	16	1	23	2	17	15	19	18	20				
3	8	12	5	9	7	3	14	22	11	16	1	23	2	17	15	19	18	20				
4	8	12	5	9	7	3	14	11	22	16	1	2	23	17	15	19	18	20				
5	8	12	5	9	7	3	14	11	22	16	1	2	23	17	15	19	18	20				
6	8	12	5	9	7	3	14	11	22	16	1	2	23	17	15	19	18	20				
7	8	12	5	9	7	3	14	11	22	16	1	2	23	17	15	19	18	20				
8	8	12	5	9	7	3	14	11	22	1	16	2	23	17	15	19	18	20				
9	8	12	5	9	7	3	14	11	22	1	23	17	15	19	18	20						
10	8	12	5	9	7	3	14	11	22	1	23	17	15	19	18	20						
11	8	12	5	9	7	3	14	11	22	1	23	17	15	19	18	20						
12	8	12	5	9	7	3	14	11	22	23	17	15	19	18	1	20						
13	8	12	5	9	7	3	14	11	22	23	15	19	17	1	18	20						
14	8	12	5	9	7	3	14	11	22	23	15	19	17	1	18	20						
15	8	12	5	9	7	3	14	11	22	23	15	19	17	1	18	20						
16	8	12	5	9	7	3	14	11	22	23	15	19	17	1	18	20						
17	8	12	5	9	3	14	11	22	7	15	23	19	17	1	20	18						
18	12	5	9	8	3	14	11	7	22	15	19	17	1	23	20	18						
19	12	5	8	9	3	14	11	7	15	22	19	17	1	23	20	18						
20	12	5	8	9	3	14	11	7	15	22	17	19	23	1	20	18						
21	12	5	8	14	9	11	3	7	15	22	17	23	1	19	20	18						
22	12	8	5	14	7	11	9	3	22	15	17	23	1	19	20	18						
23	12	8	14	7	5	9	3	11	22	15	23	1	17	20	19	18						
24	12	8	7	14	5	9	3	11	22	15	23	1	17	19	18							
25	8	12	7	5	9	3	14	11	22	15	23	1	17	19	18							
26	8	12	7	5	9	3	14	11	22	15	23	1	19	17	18							
27	8	12	7	5	9	3	14	11	22	15	23	1	19	17	18							
28	8	12	7	5	9	3	14	11	22	15	1	17	19	18								
29	8	12	7	5	9	3	14	11	22	15	1	17	19	18								
30	8	12	5	7	9	3	14	11	22	15	1	17	19	18								
31	8	12	5	9	3	14	11	7	22	15	1	17	19	18								
32	8	12	5	9	3	14	11	7	22	15	1	17	19	18								
33	8	12	5	9	3	14	11	7	22	15	1	17	19	18								
34	8	12	5	9	14	11	7	15	1	17	18											
35	8	12	5	9	14	11	7	15	1	17	18											
36	8	12	5	9	14	11	7	15	1	17	18											
37	8	12	5	9	14	11	7	15	1	17	18											
38	8	12	5	9	14	11	7	15	1	17	18											
39	8	5	9	14	11	12	7	15	1	17	18											
40	8	5	9	14	11	7	12	15	1	17	18											
41	8	5	9	14	11	7	15	1	17	18												
42	8	5	9	14	11	7	15	1	17	18												
43	8	5	9	14	11	7	15	7	17	18												
44	8	5	9	14	11	7	15	1	17	18												
45	8	5	9	14	11	7	15															

Best result for a Bridgestone shod runner:

Jarno Trulli, Prost Mugen Honda, *4th*

CLASSIFICATION & RETIREMENTS

Pos	Driver	Team	Time
1.	Berger	Benetton Renault	in 1h20'59"046
2.	Schumacher	Ferrari	at 17"527
3.	Hakkinen	McLaren Mercedes	at 24"770
4.	Trulli	Prost Mugen Honda	at 27"165
5.	Schumacher	Jordan Peugeot	at 29"995
6.	Alesi	Benetton Renault	at 34"717
7.	Nakano	Prost Mugen Honda	at 1'19"722
8.	Hill	Arrows Yamaha	at 1 lap
9.	Fontana	Sauber Petronas	at 1 lap
10.	Verstappen	Tyrrell Ford	at 1 lap
11.	Fisichella	Jordan Peugeot	puncture

Lap	Driver	Team	Reason
0	Marquès	Minardi Hart	transmission
1	Irvine	Ferrari	accident
1	Frentzen	Williams Renault	accident
2	Coulthard	McLaren Mercedes	accident
9	Diniz	ArrowsYamaha	accident
9	Herbert	Sauber Petronas	accident
24	Katayama	Minardi Hart	out of fuel
28	Magnussen	Stewart Ford	engine
34	Barrichello	Steward Ford	engine
34	Salo	Tyrrell Ford	clutch
34	Villeneuve	Williams Renault	off

FASTEST LAPS

	Driver	Time	Lap
1.	Berger	1'45"747	9
2.	Alesi	1'45"917	20
3.	R. Schum.	1'46"127	24
4.	Fisichella	1'46"274	34
5.	Hill	1'46"560	10
6.	M. Schum.	1'46"603	43
7.	Trulli	1'46"733	23
8.	Hakkinen	1'46"831	9
9.	Villeneuve	1'47"044	24
10.	Barrichello	1'47"074	28
11.	Fontana	1'47"908	27
12.	Nakano	1'47"939	24
13.	Magnussen	1'48"189	14
14.	Diniz	1'48"836	5
15.	Herbert	1'49"184	3
16.	Salo	1'49"611	25
17.	Verstappen	1'50"159	4
18.	Katayama	1'50"161	22
19.	Coulthard	2'22"236	1
20.	Frentzen	3'13"699	1
21.	Irvine	3'16"256	1

TENTH ROUND

GROSSER MOBIL 1 PREIS VON DEUTSCHLAND, HOCKENHEIM

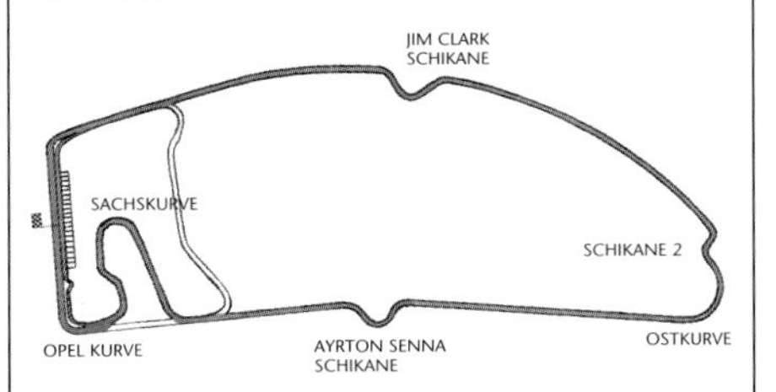

Date :	July 27, 1997
Length :	6823 meters
Distance :	45 laps, 307.035 km
Weather :	sunny, 32 degrees

CHAMPIONSHIPS

(after ten rounds)

Drivers :

1.	Michael SCHUMACHER	53
2.	Jacques VILLENEUVE	43
3.	Jean ALESI	22
4.	Gerhard BERGER	20
5.	Heinz-H. FRENTZEN	19
6.	Eddie IRVINE	18
7.	Olivier PANIS	15
8.	David COULTHARD	14
	Mika HAKKINEN	14
10.	Ralf SCHUMACHER	9
11.	Giancarlo FISICHELLA	8
12.	Johnny HERBERT	7
13.	Rubens BARRICHELLO	6
14.	Alexander WURZ	4
15.	Jarno TRULLI	3
16.	Mika SALO	2
17.	Nicola LARINI	1
	Shinji NAKANO	1
	Damon HILL	1

Constructors :

1.	Ferrari	71
2.	Williams / Renault	62
3.	Benetton / Renault	46
4.	McLaren / Mercedes	28
5.	Prost / Mugen Honda	19
6.	Jordan / Peugeot	17
7.	Sauber / Petronas	8
8.	Stewart / Ford	6
9.	Tyrrell / Ford	2
10.	Arrows / Yamaha	1

RACE SUMMARY

- Berger leads Fisichella and Michael Schumacher at the start.
- Frentzen makes a bad start and tangles with Irvine on the first lap. Both cars limp back to the pits and retire.
- Berger is pulling away fast. Running a two stop strategy his car is clearly lighter than most of his rivals who have chosen to stop only once.
- In third place, Villeneuve is having hard time fighting off Trulli in the Prost.
- After the pit stops, the placings remain the same and the Benettons are only ones in the leading bunch to stop twice.
- On lap 34, Villeneuve gets it wrong and retires.
- Fisichella, running in a solid second place, suffers a puncture.
- A problem with the refuelling rig, which did not deliver its full payload, means Michael Schumacher has to make an additional splash 'n dash stop in the F 310 B with five laps to go. He keeps his second place.

All results

WEEK-END GOSSIP

• Cheating at Ferrari?

Michael Schumacher leaves nothing to chance. At every grand prix, as he starts the final formation lap, he always spins his wheels in the spot from which he will start the race. In theory, the rubber he puts down, will give him that extra bit of grip when the lights go out.

This alone is not enough to explain the fantastic starts the German has been pulling off recently. *«I am sure everything Ferrari is doing is within the law,»* suggested Patrick Head. *«But I admit I was surprised to see the amount of traction the Ferrari had, as it came out of the last corner at Magny-Cours. In fact, there was a strange noise emanating from the car at that point.»*

Head was therefore suggesting that Ferrari might be using a form of traction control similar to the one used to limit the cars' speed in the pit-lane, which would temporarily cut the fuel supply to the engine to stop the wheels from spinning. After McLaren finally lodged a protest, the FIA clarified the situation, admitting the Ferrari system was within the law.

However, the matter did not end there. In Montreal, Williams accused Ferrari of having used 31 tyres, instead of the 28 allowed per driver, on Michael Schumacher's car, when he won the Canadian Grand Prix. Unfortunately, the race officials were unable to verify this claim as the marshals tasked with monitoring tyre activity in the Ferrari pit had got their figures mixed up!

Finally, the legality of the fuel used by Ferrari was also called into question, with McLaren accusing the Scuderia and its fuel partner Shell, of using refrigerated additives in the fuel cell, just before the start of the races.

These additives served to stabilise the fuel, producing therefore an illegal gain in power. At Shell, they maintained that the FIA was perfectly aware of the situation since the start of the season. Therefore, in Germany, every move Ferrari made was very closely monitored.

• Flotation sinks

The flotation of Formula 1 on the Stock Market looked unlikely to ever happen.

Initially scheduled for 14th July, it had been delayed until September and there were signs the whole idea might be dropped completely. *«A second hand car salesman has more morals than the higher echelons of the Stock Market,»* commented Bernie Ecclestone.

• Honda returns

The Japanese car manufacturer, Honda, which won five world championship crowns between 1987 and 1991, announced in Tokyo that it would return to Formula 1 in the year 2000. Nonetheless, this was still unofficial.

Paul Stewart, Phil Collins and Michael Schumacher. The musician, who lives in Switzerland, was paying his first ever visit to a grand prix.

The return of Super Damon

The reigning world champion had practically been forgotten all season. At the wheel of his Arrows, he had struggled with a lack of performance and reliability.
So it staggered everyone that the Englishman managed to lead almost every lap of the Hungarian Grand Prix. In Budapest, Damon Hill was once again on majestic form and the only reason he had to give second best to Jacques Villeneuve was that his gearbox had jammed in gear. Nevertheless, he was still the hero of Budapest.

MARLBORO MAGYAR NAGYDÍJ
BUDAPEST

▷ The reigning world champion qualified in third place

Jacques Villeneuve had the bit between his teeth for this race. He had to stop Michael Schumacher running away with the championship. He certainly stuck with him in qualifying as the Canadian was right alongside the German on the front row.

Damon's delight

The drivers are unanimous in their condemnation of the Budapest track. They complain about its lack of overtaking opportunities. The only straight is a measly five hundred metres long and leads into a fast corner, which requires very little braking. Passing another car in the race is pretty much impossible.
This gave the qualifying session an added sense of urgency and when the dust had settled, it was Damon Hill who provided the biggest surprise of the day. The Englishman somehow managed to stick his modest Arrows-Yamaha in third place, having never done better than ninth, so far this season.
The reigning world champion was as flabbergasted as anyone else. *«I have to admit I am very surprised, but delighted, to be this high up. It is completely unexpected. This morning, I was hoping I might be able to get in the top ten, but I never thought about the second row!»*
Pulling the Arrows up from the lower reaches of the grid was a monumental achievement, but it seemed that Hill had managed it. *«I think today shows we are making real progress,»* he stressed. *«Because I don't think this circuit suits us any better than any other, My car is quite well balanced, even if it is a long way off being one of the best.»* Hill put his progress down to two factors. *«Since he joined Arrows two months ago, John Barnard has made several detail changes to the car. I am also very surprised at the performance of our tyres here. Bridgestone has never tested on this track and the Japanese have come up with a compound that seems ideally suited to the circuit. Can I win? Yes I think so.»* Cloud cuckoo land or a real chance?

Michael Schumacher makes sure of pole ahead of Villeneuve

«So that's where the track goes!» Jan Magnussen kicks up some gravel during qualifying. It was not the best of weekends for this sort of behaviour as Jack Nasser, Ford's Number 2 was in Budapest. Ford's presence on the car was evident in a huge «Ka» logo on the engine cover. The things people do to keep the boss happy. ▷ ▽

In Budapest, Michael Schumacher recorded his third pole position of the season.
Once again, the German managed to combine skill and speed to put his new lightweight F 310 B (see page 168) ahead of the rest. *«You do not really notice the difference with the new chassis on the lap time,»* he explained. *«But it seems better balanced, which is important on a circuit like this one, where you have to run with a lot of downforce.»* As for the race, the Ferrari driver was quite optimistic. *«I am quite confident, but race strategy will be the key element. Apart from deciding how many times to stop, the other vital ingredient will be to push as hard as possible!»*
Jacques Villeneuve, who would also start from the front row, was happy to be there, thanks to modifications made to the set-up of his FW19 overnight. He was pleased to be back at the front. *«Last year, I remember I started the race behind Michael, before going on to win. It was a fun race and I hope history will repeat itself this year. The team has made a lot of progress since Hockenheim and we will be working hard tonight. We will give Michael a run for his money and I think it will be a drag race down to the first corner.»*
With Mika Hakkinen completing the second row in his McLaren, the scene was set for an interesting tussle with four different cars in the top four places.
While Ron Dennis as usual lamented the fact that the grid positions of his cars did not represent their true potential, Hakkinen himself was delighted. *«I am sure we can do something good in the race.»*

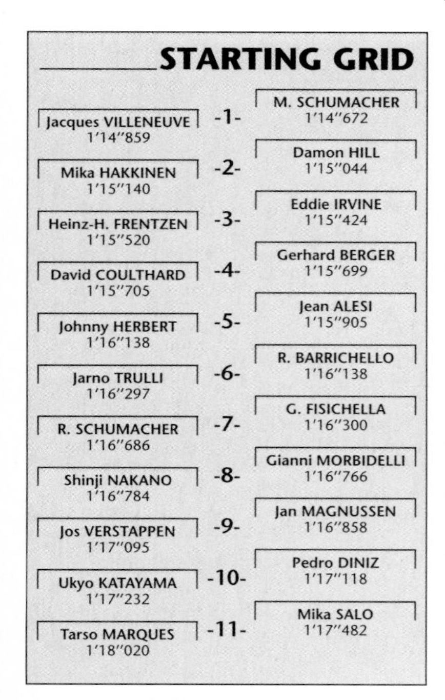

STARTING GRID

	Row	
Jacques VILLENEUVE 1'14"859	-1-	M. SCHUMACHER 1'14"672
Mika HAKKINEN 1'15"140	-2-	Damon HILL 1'15"044
Heinz-H. FRENTZEN 1'15"520	-3-	Eddie IRVINE 1'15"424
David COULTHARD 1'15"705	-4-	Gerhard BERGER 1'15"699
Johnny HERBERT 1'16"138	-5-	Jean ALESI 1'15"905
Jarno TRULLI 1'16"297	-6-	R. BARRICHELLO 1'16"138
R. SCHUMACHER 1'16"686	-7-	G. FISICHELLA 1'16"300
Shinji NAKANO 1'16"784	-8-	Gianni MORBIDELLI 1'16"766
Jos VERSTAPPEN 1'17"095	-9-	Jan MAGNUSSEN 1'16"858
Ukyo KATAYAMA 1'17"232	-10-	Pedro DINIZ 1'17"118
Tarso MARQUES 1'18"020	-11-	Mika SALO 1'17"482

It's Super Damon

With his hair in a mess and dripping with sweat, Damon Hill had rediscovered the glory days in Budapest. The Englishman put on a stunning display of brilliance and talent, to lead the race with an advantage that sometimes stretched to 30 seconds over all his rivals. Having taken the lead on lap eleven, Hill looked like a certain winner of the Hungarian Grand Prix, until three laps from the chequered flag that is. «*Everything was going fine,*» he said. «*I had slowed the pace so as not to take any risks, but coming out of the back chicane, my throttle stuck open. At first I hoped it was nothing to worry about, but then it happened again three corners later. The gearbox got stuck in second gear. I forced it and found third, but nothing else. The engine even cut out twice and I thought I would have to park it, so it's a miracle I managed to finish second.*»
Damon Hill's race was all the more remarkable, as up until now, the Arrows was more famous for its ability to suffer mechanical problems than for its race performance.
At the start of the season, the Englishman had broken down five times in six grands prix. In Budapest, the team demonstrated it was on the verge of consigning the bad times to a distant memory.
«*Of course I am disappointed not to have won,*» continued the world champion. «*However, on the other hand, I have known worse disappointments in my career. I think I will have fond memories of this weekend.*»
As in qualifying, Hill attributed much of his success to his Bridgestone tyres. «*As the chassis has not evolved that much, it is the tyres that have made the biggest difference. They were fantastic.*»
Last year, cynics in the paddock maintained that Hill owed his title to the superiority of his car. In Budapest, they had to eat their words, because, at the wheel of a car which was a long way off being a Williams or a Ferrari, the Englishman's driving display had proved he was one of the best. When the time came to negotiate his 1998 contract, this result would certainly add to his worth in the driver market.

△
Perfectly synchronised champagne spraying on the podium. Surprising really, when one considers that Hill and Herbert were out of practice as this was their first attempt of the season.

Heinz-Harald Frentzen racing to win

Heinz-Harald Frentzen richly deserves a bad luck medal. After the first pit-stops at the Hungaroring, he found himself with a comfortable lead and seemed on the way to victory.
Until lap 30, when part of the refuelling pressure relief valve on his car broke and petrol started to leak onto the exhaust system, causing a small fire.
It was a very rare occurrence which the Williams team found hard to swallow. So did the driver. «*It was a shame, because everything had been going well up until then. I was the only one to have started on hard tyres and this strategy was beginning to pay off. I could have gone quicker if I had to.*»

Villeneuve makes up for lost time

Jacques Villeneuve only led one lap of the Hungarian Grand Prix, but it was the best one and the last one. In Budapest, the Canadian lucked in when all looked lost, as, with barely three kilometres left to run, the doors to victory were opened for him by Damon Hill's misfortune.
«*Of course I was lucky,*» admitted the Canadian. «*But I'll take whatever comes my way. At Hockenheim, I came home without a single point. That's life.*» Starting from the front row of the grid, Villeneuve made a complete mess of his getaway, coming round in fifth place at the end of the first lap. Making the most of problems encountered by Michael Schumacher, Frentzen and Hakkinen, the Canadian found himself in second place behind Damon Hill, without having had to overtake another car. «*When I found myself behind Damon, I was hoping he would not finish the race, because I could not keep up with him. He was literally flying,*» he admitted.
Once his wish came true, Villeneuve won the Hungarian Grand Prix and picked up ten very important points. With Michael Schumacher finishing only fourth, he now had but a slim three point lead over the Canadian. We were in for a hot time.
The Ferrari driver's problems started in the warm-up, when he went off the track and damaged the monocoque of his lightweight F 310 B. The German thus had to start the race in the spare car, which he had hardly sat in all weekend and which had a nasty surprise in store for him. «*It was incredible! My rear tyres were destroyed after just three or four laps,*» he recounted. «*I had to change them three times. We never had this problem in practice. I don't understand it. It was a shame Damon did not win. He deserved to.*»

«Yes I am very satisfied.» In Budapest, Jacques Villeneuve resorted to his favourite cliche to sum up his feelings, after his luckiest win of the year.
▽

IN THE POINTS

1.	Jacques VILLENEUVE	Rothmans Williams Renault	1 h 45'47"149
2.	Damon HILL	Danka Arrows Yamaha	at 9"079
3.	Johnny HERBERT	Red Bull Sauber Petronas	at 20"445
4.	M. SCHUMACHER	Scuderia Ferrari Marlboro	at 30"501
5.	Ralf SCHUMACHER	B&H Total Jordan Peugeot	at 30"715
6.	Shinji NAKANO	Prost Gauloises Blondes	at 41"512

Fastest lap : H.-H. FRENTZEN, lap 25, 1'18"372, avg. 182.269 km/h

In qualifying, Damon Hill had stopped the clocks with third fastest time. Pedro Diniz tried to do the same and this is what happened: a superb prang and 19th place on the grid!

△ Johnny Herbert's third place was a real morale booster for Peter Sauber. This result should have been repeated on other occasions this season, but for the team's wretched luck.

The regulations give the nod to Ferrari

«We feel very frustrated with what is happening at the moment.» Jacques Villeneuve's Renault engineer, Denis Chevrier was not mincing his words. The French constructor had been caught out by the new interpretation the FIA had applied to the regulations appertaining to engines (see page 161.) It was now perfectly legal to replace the direct relationship between the accelerator pedal and the amount of opening of the fuel inlet, by a calculated relationship, which took engine speed into account.
This meant that sudden surges of power could be avoided, effectively cutting out wheelspin under acceleration. *«We find it regrettable that the FIA has changed the interpretation of the regulation, halfway through the season,»* continued Chevrier. *«Because, since traction control was banned, we have been working on making the engine work more progressively and to be less peaky. Therefore, we do not have much to gain from the new interpretation.»* Two months before it was due to pull out of Formula 1, Renault no doubt had no intention of making fundamental changes to its engines.
Over at Ferrari, it seemed that such a system was already waiting in the wings. *«We were opposed to this change of interpretation of the regulations,»* explained Jean Todt. *«But naturally, as what was previously forbidden is now allowed, we are working on it flat out.»*
The 046/2 Ferrari engine was known for its power, but also for the brutal way it delivered that power. An anti-wheelspin device therefore constituted a definite advantage for Michael Schumacher.
In Budapest, Ferrari also announced the arrival of a new chassis for its F 310 B. *«We have gained about ten kilos,»* explained Jean Todt. *«In any case, we were already on the minimum weight limit, but losing still more weight allows us to better distribute the ballast, in order to lower the centre of gravity. It is not a big difference, maybe one tenth of a second per lap. But at the point we have reached, every tenth counts.»* Only Schumacher had the new chassis in Hungary, as only one had been built in time.

Happy Herbert

The race has been over for half an hour. Peter Sauber, leaning on the team transporter, is on his mobile phone.
At that moment, Johnny Herbert finally returns from the post-race press conference for the top three finishers. Peter Sauber spots his driver, forgets his phone and gives the little Englishman a big hug. It seemed as though the man from Zurich had been waiting a long time for this moment, as his last podium finish was in 1996 at Monaco.
This year, after a promising start to the season, the Sauber team had suffered from a lot of bad luck, which was finally put to one side in the Hungarian GP, when Johnny Herbert made the most of the misfortunes of others. *«I was a bit lucky,»* agreed the Englishman. *«But the team has worked so hard for the last few weeks, that it really deserves this third place.»*
Herbert was only tenth on the grid, but he took off like a rocket, which allowed him to slip past the two Benettons immediately. *«Before the race, I was hoping to pass Alesi or Berger at the first corner, but I never thought I would get both of them! Then I managed to catch up to the pack, which was being held up by Michael Schumacher, which meant I could save my tyres. We knew the rubber would be a critical factor.»*
After his two pit-stops, Johnny found himself behind Villeneuve and ahead of Michael Schumacher. From then, he only had to keep an eye on the gap to the Ferrari. *«I was watching the gap throughout the race,»* he admitted. *«There was no way I could catch Villeneuve, as every time I pushed a bit harder, my tyres were giving me trouble. The most important thing was to maintain my concentration and I was very relieved to see the chequered flag.»*
As far as Herbert was concerned, this result proved what progress the team had made. *«The main problem with the car is its instability on low fuel loads. It jumps over the bumps and we always end up a long way back on the grid.»*

▷ Damon Hill was going shopping. In Budapest, the future of the reigning world champion was still unclear. McLaren? Sauber? Prost? Benetton? All options still seemed possible.

▷ The more the season went on, the more Shinji Nakano deserved his place in the Prost team. In Budapest he scored his second point, finishing sixth, over thirty seconds ahead of Jarno Trulli. In the race, he even dared attack Michael Schumacher and to push Eddie Irvine off into the scenery on the final lap.

PRACTICE TIMES

No	Driver	Make/Engine/Chassis	Practice Friday	Practice Saturday	Qualifying	Warm-up
1.	Damon Hill	Arrows/Yamaha/A18/5 (B)	1'18"161	1'16"556	1'15"044	1'17"953
2.	Pedro Diniz	Arrows/Yamaha/A18/4 (B)	1'20"002	1'17"117	1'17"118	1'17"696
3.	Jacques Villeneuve	Williams/Renault/FW19/4 (G)	1'18"805	1'15"500	1'14"859	1'17"393
4.	Heinz-Harald Frentzen	Williams/Renault/FW19/5 (G)	1'17"884	1'15"431	1'15"520	1'17"614
5.	Michael Schumacher	Ferrari/Ferrari/F310B/178 (G)	1'17"583	1'16"032	1'14"672	1'16"996
6.	Eddie Irvine	Ferrari/Ferrari/F310B/173 (G)	1'18"734	1'16"274	1'15"424	1'17"781
7.	Jean Alesi	Benetton/Renault/B197/2 (G)	1'19"358	1'16"205	1'15"905	1'19"013
8.	Gerhard Berger	Benetton/Renault/B197/4 (G)	1'18"923	1'16"373	1'15"699	1'17"875
9.	Mika Hakkinen	McLaren/Mercedes/MP4/12/5 (G)	1'20"176	1'15"839	1'15"140	1'17"579
10.	David Coulthard	McLaren/Mercedes/MP4/12/6 (G)	1'17"810	1'15"998	1'15"705	1'19"246
11.	Ralf Schumacher	Jordan/Peugeot/197/6 (G)	1'18"368	1'16"343	1'16"686	1'19"673
12.	Giancarlo Fisichella	Jordan/Peugeot/197/4 (G)	1'18"686	1'17"757	1'16"300	1'19"145
14.	Jarno Trulli	Prost/Mugen Honda/JS45/3 (B)	1'17"848	1'16"175	1'16"297	1'18"114
15.	Shinji Nakano	Prost/Mugen Honda/JS45/2 (B)	1'20"414	1'16"841	1'16"784	1'18"499
16.	Johnny Herbert	Sauber/Petronas/C16/3 (G)	1'18"796	1'16"739	1'16"138	1'18"050
17.	Gianni Morbidelli	Sauber/Petronas/C16/6 (G)	1'19"567	1'18"043	1'16"766	1'18"632
18.	Jos Verstappen	Tyrrell/Ford/025/4 (G)	1'19"346	1'18"025	1'17"095	1'19"332
19.	Mika Salo	Tyrrell/Ford/025/1 (G)	1'20"106	1'18"087	1'17"482	1'20"432
20.	Ukyo Katayama	Minardi/Hart/M197/4 (B)	1'19"521	1'17"605	1'17"232	1'17"890
21.	Tarso Marquès	Minardi/Hart/M197/2 (B)	1'20"707	1'19"912	1'18"020	1'20"778
22.	Rubens Barrichello	Stewart/Ford/SF1/2 (B)	1'18"565	1'17"129	1'16"138	1'19"122
23.	Jan Magnussen	Stewart/Ford/SF1/3 (B)	1'18"856	1'17"864	1'16"858	1'20"154

CLASSIFICATION & RETIREMENTS

Pos	Driver	Team	Time
1.	Villeneuve	Williams Renault	in 1h45'47"149
2.	Hill	Arrows Yamaha	at 9"079
3.	Herbert	Sauber Petronas	at 20"445
4.	Schumacher	Ferrari	at 30"501
5.	Schumacher	Jordan Peugeot	at 30"715
6.	Nakano	Prost Mugen Honda	at 41"512
7.	Trulli	Prost Mugen Honda	at 1'15"552
8.	Berger	Benetton Renault	at 1'16"409
9.	Irvine	Ferrari	accident
10.	Katayama	Minardi Hart	at 1 lap
11.	Alesi	Benetton Renault	at 1 lap
12.	Marquès	Minardi Hart	at 2 laps
13.	Salo	Tyrrell Ford	at 2 laps

Lap	Driver	Team	Reason
5	Magnussen	Stewart Ford	accident
7	Morbidelli	Sauber Petronas	engine
12	Hakkinen	McLaren Mercedes	hydraulics
29	Barrichello	Stewart Ford	engine
29	Frentzen	Williams Renault	refuelling valve
42	Fisichella	Jordan Peugeot	spin
53	Diniz	Arrows Yamaha	off
61	Verstappen	Tyrrell Ford	pression
65	Coulthard	McLaren Mercedes	hyraulics

FASTEST LAPS

	Driver	Time	Lap
1.	Frentzen	1'18"372	25
2.	Villeneuve	1'19"066	15
3.	Fisichella	1'19"366	37
4.	Irvine	1'19"527	44
5.	Hill	1'19"648	13
6.	R. Schum.	1'19"651	48
7.	M. Schum.	1'19"684	28
8.	Berger	1'19"923	52
9.	Nakano	1'20"003	26
10.	Hakkinen	1'20"161	4
11.	Diniz	1'20"317	46
12.	Coulthard	1'20"329	19
13.	Alesi	1'20"573	57
14.	Herbert	1'20"606	28
15.	Katayama	1'20"672	46
16.	Trulli	1'21"074	71
17.	Morbidelli	1'21"167	4
18.	Barrichello	1'21"409	23
19.	Salo	1'21"578	67
20.	Magnussen	1'21"628	3
21.	Verstappen	1'21"676	43
22.	Marquès	1'21"874	45

WEEK-END GOSSIP

- **An end in sight?**

The row between Frank Williams, Ron Dennis and Ken Tyrrell on the one hand and Bernie Ecclestone on the other, could soon be over. One year after the three team owners refused to sign the Concorde Agreement, they met with Ecclestone for over an hour on the Friday. According to Dennis, grounds for agreement should be found before the end of the season.

Gianni is back

«Look, I've got some here and look on this side as well.» In Hungary, Gianni Morbidelli was proudly showing off the scars from 34 stitches that decorated his lower left arm.

These and the metal plates holding the bones together were all that was left of the testing accident at Magny-Cours back at the end of June. *«I'm fine,»* beamed the little Italian with the big smile. *«I started training just two days after the plates were put in.»*

It was the week after Hockenheim that Morbidelli got back behind the wheel of his Sauber for the first time, at Ferrari's private Fiorano test track. *«I was a little bit worried for the first few laps,»* he said. *«I cannot bend my arm they way I used to and I was worried I would have problems in the tight corners. But in fact, everything went well and after a few laps I was back in the swing of it.»*

The return of Morbidelli was a big relief for Peter Sauber as it meant he no longer had to run the team's test driver, Norberto Fontana, who had made too many mistakes in the past three races to deserve a place on the grid. However, Sauber would have preferred to run Alexander Wurz in the second car, which is why Morbidelli was not too optimistic about his future with the team. *«I do not have a contract with Sauber,»* he pointed out. *«I am employed by Ferrari and I am on loan to Sauber. The situation could end on Sunday night.»*

- **«Fisico» goes off**

In the race, it was obvious that Michael Schumacher was holding up the cars behind him, in the hope of scoring a few points.

Ralf, right behind his brother, was making no effort to get past. Not being part of the family, Giancarlo Fisichella had no such qualms about trying to pass Michael.

Unfortunately, he ended up in the gravel trap thanks to a very determined Ferrari driver. *«That's racing! I was a lot quicker than Michael, but he shut the door on me and I found myself on a very dirty part of the track. I spun immediately. It was not his fault, but I am very disappointed.»*

LAP CHART

position:	1	2	3	4	5	6	7	8	9	10	11	12	13	14	15	16	17	18	19	20	21	22
start:	5	3	1	9	6	4	8	10	7	16	22	14	12	11	17	15	23	18	2	20	19	21
1	5	1	6	9	3	4	10	16	7	8	14	22	12	11	15	18	20	19	21	2	17	23
2	5	1	6	9	3	4	10	16	7	8	14	22	12	11	15	18	20	19	21	2	17	23
3	5	1	6	9	3	4	10	16	7	8	14	22	12	11	15	18	20	19	21	2	17	23
4	5	1	6	9	3	4	10	16	7	8	14	22	12	11	15	18	20	19	21	2	17	23
5	5	1	6	9	3	4	10	16	7	8	14	22	12	11	15	18	20	19	21	2	17	23
6	5	1	6	9	3	4	10	16	7	8	14	22	12	11	15	18	20	19	21	2	17	
7	5	1	9	3	4	10	16	7	6	8	14	22	12	11	15	18	20	19	21	2	17	
8	5	1	9	3	4	10	16	7	8	14	22	12	11	15	18	20	19	21	2	6		
9	5	1	9	3	4	10	16	7	14	22	12	11	15	8	18	20	19	21	2	6		
10	5	1	9	3	4	10	16	7	14	22	12	11	15	8	18	20	19	21	2	6		
11	1	5	9	3	4	10	16	7	14	22	12	11	15	8	18	20	19	21	2	6		
12	1	5	9	3	4	10	16	7	14	22	12	11	15	8	18	20	19	21	6	2		
13	1	5	3	4	10	16	7	14	22	12	11	15	8	18	20	19	6	21	2			
14	1	3	4	10	16	5	7	14	22	12	11	15	8	18	20	6	19	21	2			
15	1	3	4	10	16	7	14	22	12	11	15	5	8	18	6	20	19	21	2			
16	1	3	4	10	16	7	14	22	12	11	15	5	8	6	20	19	21	18	2			
17	1	3	4	10	16	7	14	22	12	11	15	5	8	6	20	19	21	18	2			
18	1	3	4	10	16	7	14	22	12	11	15	5	6	8	20	21	19	18	2			
19	1	3	4	10	16	7	14	22	12	11	15	5	6	8	20	21	18	2	19			
20	1	3	4	10	16	7	14	22	12	11	15	5	6	8	21	20	18	2	19			
21	1	3	4	10	16	7	14	22	12	11	15	5	6	8	21	18	2	19	20			
22	1	3	4	10	16	14	22	12	7	11	15	5	6	8	21	18	2	19	20			
23	1	3	4	10	16	14	22	12	11	15	5	7	6	8	18	2	19	20	21			
24	1	4	3	10	16	14	22	12	11	15	5	7	6	8	18	2	20	19	21			
25	1	4	16	3	10	14	12	15	22	5	11	6	7	8	18	2	20	19	21			
26	4	1	16	3	10	12	15	5	14	6	22	11	8	7	18	2	20	19	21			
27	4	1	3	10	12	5	15	16	6	14	22	11	7	18	2	20	19	8	21			
28	4	1	3	10	5	12	16	6	14	22	15	11	7	18	2	20	19	8	21			
29	4	1	3	10	5	16	6	12	14	22	15	11	7	18	2	20	19	8	21			
30	1	3	10	5	16	6	12	14	15	11	7	18	2	20	8	19	21					
31	1	3	10	5	16	6	12	14	15	11	7	18	2	20	8	19	21					
32	1	3	10	5	16	6	12	14	15	11	7	18	2	20	8	19	21					
33	1	3	10	5	16	6	12	15	14	11	7	18	2	20	8	19	21					
34	1	3	10	16	5	6	12	15	14	11	7	18	2	20	8	19	21					
35	1	3	10	16	5	12	6	15	14	11	7	18	2	20	8	19	21					
36	1	3	10	16	5	12	15	14	11	6	7	18	2	20	8	19	21					
37	1	3	10	16	5	12	15	14	11	6	7	2	20	18	8	19	21					
38	1	3	10	16	5	12	15	14	11	6	7	2	20	8	18	19	21					
39	1	3	10	16	5	12	15	14	11	6	7	2	20	8	18	19	21					
40	1	3	10	16	5	12	15	11	14	6	7	2	20	8	18	19	21					
41	1	3	10	16	5	12	15	11	14	6	7	2	20	8	18	19	21					
42	1	3	10	16	5	12	15	11	14	6	7	2	20	8	18	19	21					
43	1	3	10	16	5	15	11	6	14	7	2	20	8	18	21	19						
44	1	3	10	16	5	15	11	6	14	7	20	2	8	18	21	19						
45	1	3	10	16	5	15	11	6	14	7	20	8	2	18	21	19						
46	1	3	10	16	5	15	11	6	7	20	14	8	2	18	21	19						
47	1	3	10	16	5	15	11	6	7	20	14	8	2	18	21	19						
48	1	3	10	16	5	11	6	15	7	14	8	2	20	18	21	19						
49	1	3	10	16	5	11	6	15	7	14	8	2	20	18	21	19						
50	1	3	10	16	5	11	6	15	7	14	8	2	20	18	21	19						
51	1	3	10	5	11	6	16	15	14	7	2	20	8	18	21	19						
52	1	3	10	6	16	5	15	11	14	2	20	8	7	18	21	19						
53	1	3	10	6	16	5	15	11	14	2	20	8	7	18	21	19						
54	1	3	10	6	16	5	11	15	14	20	8	7	18	21	19							
55	1	3	10	6	16	5	11	15	14	8	20	7	18	21	19							
56	1	3	10	6	16	5	11	15	14	8	20	7	18	21	19							
57	1	3	10	16	5	11	15	6	14	8	20	7	18	21	19							
58	1	3	10	16	5	11	15	6	14	8	20	7	18	21	19							
59	1	3	10	16	5	11	15	6	14	8	20	7	18	21	19							
60	1	3	10	16	5	11	15	6	14	8	20	7	18	21	19							
61	1	3	10	16	5	11	15	6	14	8	20	7	21	18	19							
62	1	3	10	16	5	11	15	6	14	8	20	7	21	19								
63	1	3	10	16	5	11	15	6	14	8	20	7	21	19								
64	1	3	10	16	5	11	15	6	14	8	20	7	21	19								
65	1	3	10	16	5	11	6	15	14	8	20	7	21	19								
66	1	3	16	5	11	6	15	14	8	20	7	21	19									
67	1	3	16	5	11	6	15	14	8	20	7	21	19									
68	1	3	16	5	11	6	15	14	8	20	7	21	19									
69	1	3	16	5	11	6	15	14	8	20	7	21	19									
70	1	3	16	5	11	6	15	14	8	20	7	21	19									
71	1	3	16	5	11	6	15	14	8	20	7	21	19									
72	1	3	16	5	11	6	15	14	8	20	7	21	19									
73	1	3	16	5	11	6	15	14	8	20	7	21	19									
74	1	3	16	5	11	6	15	14	8	20	7	21	19									
75	1	3	16	5	11	6	15	14	8	20	7	21	19									
76	1	3	16	5	11	6	15	14	8	20	7											
77	3	1	16	5	11	15	14	8														

ELEVENTH ROUND

MARLBORO MAGYAR NAGYDÍJ, BUDAPEST

Date : August 10, 1997
Length : 3968 meters
Distance : 77 laps, 305.536 km
Weather : sunny, 31 degrees

◁ *«It's your brain that needs cooling, not your feet.» A traditional sight in Budapest. The chess players in the Gellert baths make the most of the splendid weather in Hungary in the summer of 1997.*

Best result for a Bridgestone shod runner:

Damon Hill, Arrows Yamaha, *2nd*

CHAMPIONSHIPS

(after eleven rounds)

Drivers:

	Driver	Points
1.	Michael SCHUMACHER	56
2.	Jacques VILLENEUVE	53
3.	Jean ALESI	22
4.	Gerhard BERGER	20
5.	Heinz-H. FRENTZEN	19
6.	Eddie IRVINE	18
7.	Olivier PANIS	15
8.	David COULTHARD	14
	Mika HAKKINEN	14
10.	Ralf SCHUMACHER	11
	Johnny HERBERT	11
12.	Giancarlo FISICHELLA	8
13.	Damon HILL	7
14.	Rubens BARRICHELLO	6
15.	Alexander WURZ	4
16.	Jarno TRULLI	3
17.	Mika SALO	2
	Shinji NAKANO	2
19.	Nicola LARINI	1

Constructors :

	Constructor	Points
1.	Ferrari	74
2.	Williams / Renault	72
3.	Benetton / Renault	46
4.	McLaren / Mercedes	28
5.	Prost / Mugen Honda	20
6.	Jordan / Peugeot	19
7.	Sauber / Petronas	12
8.	Arrows / Yamaha	7
9.	Stewart / Ford	6
10.	Tyrrell / Ford	2

RACE SUMMARY

- Michael Schumacher leads away from Hill. Villeneuve, having started from second place, has already dropped to fifth.
- Hill passes Schumacher on lap 11. In second place, Hakkinen retires two laps later.
- Schumacher is quickly losing ground and pits on lap 15. He rejoins in 12th place and finds himself stuck behind Nakano.
- After the first pit-stops, Frentzen leads. He is planning to make only one stop, but retires on lap 29 when his fuel filler falls off going down the straight.
- Hill is back in the lead and pulls away from the Villeneuve-Coulthard tandem.
- Further back, Schumacher cannot keep up with Herbert. Having made three pit stops, he is holding up his brother Ralf, Irvine and Nakano.
- In third place, Coulthard retires on lap 66 and Herbert and his Sauber inherit third place.
- Three laps to go and Hill slows dramatically and cannot stop Villeneuve driving past him to win.

Marlboro
Asprey

Schumi defies the elements

What a talent! At Spa, Michael Schumacher confirmed that he is simply on a different level to the rest of his little friends. At the start of the race, with the track still soaked, he was pulling away from the field at the rate of six seconds per lap. After the race, even Jacques Villeneuve admitted the German was the best.
His performance put every other driver in the shade, although it is worth mentioning a great drive to second place, from Giancarlo Fisichella.

BELGIAN GRAND PRIX
SPA-FRANCORCHAMPS

The Canadian gets pole

The Villeneuve counter-attack

As pole sitter in 1996, Jacques Villeneuve seemed to like the Spa circuit, or at least he did in the dry. On Friday, in the rain, he was nowhere to be seen, down in 17thspot, struggling with an ill-handling car. But on Saturday, the sun came out to play and so did the Canadian. He annihilated the opposition.
Right from the start of the qualifying session, he did a time that nobody would beat. *«In fact, once the track was dry, our settings were excellent,»* said Jacques at the end of the hour. *«We had done a lot of work on it on Friday night, based on what we learnt last year. I didn't have to touch anything on the car and I was able to concentrate on finding the best lines and the limit of my tyres.»*
After the crisis in Hungary, all the Goodyear runners apparently decided to play it safe and chose the harder tyre rather than the softer, grippier option. So there were to be no surprises in the race. *«Those who have taken a risk with their tyre choice will pay a high price in the race,»* warned Villeneuve. *«Today, the track had plenty of grip at the start of the session, but then when the sun came out, it became very slippery.»*

Great excitement in the Ferrari garage on Saturday. Michael Schumacher was paid a visit by Carl Lewis and Leroy Burrell. The two American sprinters and motor racing fans were the guests of Marlboro. ▷ ▽

Jean Alesi on the front row

Next up on in qualifying was a surprising Jean Alesi, who managed to stick his Benetton-Renault on the front row for the first time this season.
The man from Avignon was very pleased with himself. *«I am very happy, because this year, the winners have nearly always started from the top grid positions. As I have never qualified well, I have not stood a chance. This time, it will be a different story.»*
Saturday had not been a good day for Michael Schumacher. In the morning session, he had already found a problem with his race car. *«I don't want to say much about it,»* he commented tersely. *«All I will say is that it was too serious to fix for qualifying.»*
So the Ferrari driver qualified at the wheel of his spare car. It was not fitted with the Spec. 2 engine and it did not have the lightweight chassis. Under the circumstances, his third place on the grid could be seen as quite an achievement. *«I did not expect to do so well, that's for sure. But I am still worried, as we have no idea what settings to use for the race.»*

STARTING GRID

		Jacques VILLENEUVE 1'49"450
Jean ALESI 1'49"759	-1-	M. SCHUMACHER 1'50"293
G. FISICHELLA 1'50"470	-2-	Mika HAKKINEN 1'50"503
R. SCHUMACHER 1'50"520	-3-	Heinz-H. FRENTZEN 1'50"656
Pedro DINIZ 1'50"853	-4-	Damon HILL 1'50"970
David COULTHARD 1'51"410	-5-	Johnny HERBERT 1'51"725
R. BARRICHELLO 1'51"916	-6-	Gianni MORBIDELLI 1'52"094
Jarno TRULLI 1'52"274	-7-	Gerhard BERGER 1'52"391
Shinji NAKANO 1'52"749	-8-	Eddie IRVINE 1'52"793
Jan MAGNUSSEN 1'52"886	-9-	Mika SALO 1'52"897
Ukyo KATAYAMA 1'53"544	-10-	Jos VERSTAPPEN 1'53"725
Tarso MARQUES 1'54"505	-11-	

Busy session

Right at the start of the session, Pedro Diniz was the first to set a time worthy of a qualifying lap. Then he was knocked off the perch by Johnny Herbert, who was in turn dethroned by Jean Alesi, then Heinz-Harald Frentzen, Giancarlo Fisichella, Michael Schumacher and finally Jacques Villeneuve. All this in the space of 15 minutes.
Finally, it was Fisichella who slotted in behind the top trio to record fourth fastest time. It was a pleasant surprise. "I did not expect to qualify so well. But the car is finally well set up and this is the result."
Frentzen was yet again in difficulty, down in seventh place. He had to qualify in the spare car, set up for Villeneuve and got bogged down in traffic.

Schumacher, like a duck to water

△
Having disposed of Alesi and Villeneuve on the opening lap, Michael Schumacher ran away from the field at a rate of 6, 7, and even 11 seconds per lap. What a talent!

They had made the short trip from Germany in their tens of thousands to support their hero. They were not disappointed. At Spa-Francorchamps Michael Schumacher put on a virtuoso driving display, dominating the elements and the opposition with a supernatural ease.
In the morning warm-up he had only been 15th fastest, reflecting Ferrari's poor form. A form that would change when, only minutes before the start, the clouds came over and an almost tropical downpour hit the Ardennes. Jumping into his spare car, the German also chose to fit intermediate, lightly grooved tyres. *«I could see the sky was turning to blue again behind the trees,»* explained Michael the meteorologist. *«We chose the tyres accordingly and it was the right decision.»*

It had already stopped raining when the lights went out to start the Belgian Grand Prix. But the standing water all over the track persuaded the organisers to start the event behind the safety car.
This situation had not occurred since Suzuka in 1994. *«I think that starting behind the safety car was the right decision,»* said the Ferrari driver. *«A normal start would have been too dangerous.»*
After three laps politely spent behind the safety car, Schumacher did not take long to spring into action, attacking Jean Alesi at the La Source hairpin in a very risky move. *«I thought our cars would touch,»* admitted the German. *«But sliding in at that speed, I reckoned it would be very soft and would not do any damage. Luckily, Jean moved over and we never came together.»*

Half a lap later, the Ferrari closed in on Villeneuve's Williams and took the lead, before building up a gap of historical proportions: six seconds after five laps, 17 seconds the following lap, then one minute and eight seconds on lap 13. The opposition was destroyed.
From then on, all the German had to do was keep an eye on his lead and win his fourth race of the season as he pleased, while the public applauded his achievement. *«The crowd was fantastic,»* revealed Schumacher. *«It was like at Monza last year. While they played the National Anthem, my head was empty as I took in the atmosphere. I think it was my best win of the season.»*
The German now had a 12 point lead over Jacques Villeneuve, with five grands prix to go.

Hakkinen in the wars

◁
Mika Hakkinen did not have long to enjoy his third place. He was disqualified a few days after the Belgian Grand Prix. He would have done better to start from the back of the grid. At least then all his efforts would not have been in vain.

It was one problem after another for Mika Hakkinen this weekend. On Saturday morning, the Finn had a major high speed accident, when one of rear wheels flew off his car. In the afternoon, he qualified sixth, only to have his time disallowed as the scrutineers deemed that the fuel in his McLaren did not conform to previously submitted samples.
He should have started from the back of the grid, but the team lodged an appeal and he was allowed to start from his original place. He finished in third place, but a few days later, when the appeal was heard, he was finally disqualified. Which meant onn extra point for Villeneuve.

IN THE POINTS

1. M. SCHUMACHER	Scuderia Ferrari Marlboro	1 h 33'46"717
2. Giancarlo FISICHELLA	B&H Total Jordan Peugeot	at 26"753
3. Mika HAKKINEN	West McLaren Mercedes	at 30"856
4. Heinz-H. FRENTZEN	Rothmans Williams Renault	at 32"147
5. Johnny HERBERT	Red Bull Sauber Petronas	at 39"025
6. Jacques VILLENEUVE	Rothmans Williams Renault	at 42"103

Fastest lap : J. VILLENEUVE, lap 43, 1'52"692, avg. 222.596 km/h

A spectacular flying display on the kerbs at the Spa chicane. Jan Magnussen definitely wins the high jump prize in this game. All the evidence pointed to the fact that the Belgian circuit did not suit the Stewart-Fords, which would look in much better shape in Austria and at the Nurburgring.

TEXACO
Havoline
MALAYSIA
VISIT

△ Seldom seen. The right rear wheel of Heinz-Harald Frentzen's FW19 decides to make its own way in the world. An extremely rare occurrence, which luckily ended without serious consequences, apart from some extra work for the mechanics.

A fifth place finish for the Sauber of Johnny Herbert, who managed to fight off the advances of Jacques Villeneuve in the final stages of the race. ▷ ▽

Villeneuve makes the wrong tyre choice.....yet again

11h30 on Sunday morning. In the warm-up, the final dress rehearsal before the race, Jacques Villeneuve sets fastest time and confirms his position as quickest man on the Belgian track, having secured pole position the previous day. Everything seems in place for him to dominate the Belgian Grand Prix.
15h42 on Sunday afternoon. As he steps out of the cockpit of Williams-Renault Number 3, Jacques Villeneuve admits he has been beaten. Showing the strain of his efforts, he took a few moments to get over a race in which he set his best lap right at the end, when he was giving chase to Johnny Herbert in the Sauber. Only sixth, the Canadian had to give best to Michael Schumacher: which he did with a sense of fair play. *«I made the wrong choice of tyres,»* admitted Villeneuve immediately. *«For two days we have been running in temperatures of around 30 degrees and the car was badly set up for the wet. But I have to admit that Michael proved today that he is the best. In the wet and not only in the wet.»*
18h00 on Sunday evening. Having got over the emotions of the event, the Canadian has changed his tune. *«I don't understand why the safety car stayed on the track for so long at the start of the race,»* he complained. *«It was not right, because it allowed the track to dry out and favour those who chose intermediate tyres.»*
In his standing frame in a corner of his motorhome, Frank Williams shared his drivers' anger. *«I do not think it is legal to leave the safety car out for so long.»*

Blame passed onto the team

The rules state the start can be given behind the safety car in the case of "exceptional circumstances," but nowhere does it state how many laps the safety car can do in front of the field. Having obviously made the wrong tyre choice, Villeneuve tried to pass the blame onto his team.
«I think it is the team's job to go and check on the grid what tyres the other runners are using. The only thing I wanted to do today was to finish in front of Michael and if I had known he was on intermediates, I would have done the same.»

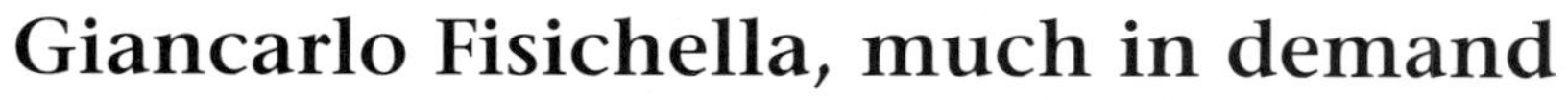

Giancarlo Fisichella, much in demand

Giancarlo Fisichella goes from strength to strength. In Spa, the Roman finished a brilliant second after driving a faultless race. *«I started on intermediate tyres, like Michael and it was the right choice,»* he revealed. *«But I could not have done anything about him and I could do nothing about it as I watched him pull away.»* From now on, Fisico's aim was a victory. *«I finished third in Canada and second here. Logic demands that I win in Monza.»*

However, in the background, storm clouds were gathering over the young Italian's future. While he had already signed a contract to drive for Benetton in 1998, his current employer Eddie Jordan, did not want to let him go. *«My contract with Giancarlo is for two years and I have every intention of having it respected,»* declared the Irishman after the race. The future of the most sought after of the crop of young talent would therefore have to be decided in the courts.

PRACTICE TIMES

No	Driver	Make/Engine/Chassis	Practice Friday	Practice Saturday	Qualifying	Warm-up
1.	Damon HIll	Arrows/Yamaha/A18/5 (B)	2'08"372	1'52"402	1'50"970	1'53"365
2.	Pedro Diniz	Arrows/Yamaha/A18/4 (B)	2'10"153	1'56"360	1'50"853	1'53"557
3.	Jacques Villeneuve	Williams/Renault/FW19/4 (G)	2'11"706	1'50"407	1'49"450	1'52"415
4.	Heinz-Harald Frentzen	Williams/Renault/FW19/5 (G)	2'10"914	1'51"179	1'50"656	1'53"777
5.	Michael Schumacher	Ferrari/Ferrari/F310B/179 (G)	2'09"272	1'52"562	1'50"293	1'54"593
6.	Eddie Irvine	Ferrari/Ferrari/F310B/173 (G)	2'10"993	2'07"786	1'52"793	1'55"993
7.	Jean Alesi	Benetton/Renault/B197/2 (G)	2'07"371	1'50"947	1'49"759	1'52"837
8.	Gerhard Berger	Benetton/Renault/B197/4 (G)	2'06"802	1'52"057	1'52"391	1'53"531
9.	Mika Hakkinen	McLaren/Mercedes/MP4/12/7 (G)	2'10"413	2'06"429	1'50"503	1'54"282
10.	David Coulthard	McLaren/Mercedes/MP4/12/6 (G)	2'09"288	1'52"604	1'51"410	1'53"846
11.	Ralf Schumacher	Jordan/Peugeot/197/6 (G)	2'12"750	1'52"682	1'50"520	1'52"619
12.	Giancarlo Fisichella	Jordan/Peugeot/197/5 (G)	2'11"093	1'51"625	1'50"470	1'53"999
14.	Jarno Trulli	Prost/Mugen Honda/JS45/3 (B)	2'09"772	1'55"895	1'52"274	1'53"760
15.	Shinji Nakano	Prost/Mugen Honda/JS45/2 (B)	2'10"272	1'54"299	1'52"749	1'55"202
16.	Johnny Herbert	Sauber/Petronas/C16/3 (G)	2'09"772	1'53"977	1'51"725	1'52"628
17.	Gianni Morbidelli	Sauber/Petronas/C16/6 (G)	2'11"262	1'54"310	1'52"094	1'54"448
18.	Jos Verstappen	Tyrrell/Ford/025/4 (G)	2'14"048	1'54"799	1'53"725	1'54"895
19.	Mika Salo	Tyrrell/Ford/025/1 (G)	2'13"256	1'53"929	1'52"897	1'55"588
20.	Ukyo Katayama	Minardi/Hart/M197/4 (B)	2'10"231	1'54"150	1'53"544	1'54"570
21.	Tarso Marquès	Minardi/Hart/M197/2 (B)	2'11"778	1'54"521	1'54"505	1'54"868
22.	Rubens Barrichello	Stewart/Ford/SF1/2 (B)	2'08"238	1'52"688	1'51"916	1'56"062
23.	Jan Magnussen	Stewart/Ford/SF1/3 (B)	2'12"545	1'54"608	1'52"886	1'55"695

LAP CHART

position :	1	2	3	4	5	6	7	8	9	10	11	12	13	14	15	16	17	18	19	20	21	22
start:	3	7	5	12	9	11	4	2	1	10	16	22	17	14	8	15	6	23	19	20	18	21
1	3	7	5	12	4	9	2	1	10	16	22	17	8	15	6	23	19	20	21	18	11	14
2	3	7	5	12	9	4	2	1	10	16	22	17	8	15	6	23	19	20	21	18	11	14
3	3	7	5	12	9	4	2	1	10	16	22	17	8	15	6	23	19	20	18	21	11	14
4	3	7	5	12	9	4	2	1	10	16	22	17	8	23	6	15	19	20	21	18	11	14
5	5	3	7	12	9	4	2	1	10	16	22	17	23	8	6	15	19	21	20	18	11	14
6	5	12	7	9	4	2	10	1	3	16	22	17	23	8	6	21	20	19	18	11	14	
7	5	12	9	7	4	10	2	1	16	22	23	17	8	21	6	20	18	3	19	11	14	
8	5	12	9	10	2	16	1	23	8	17	22	4	18	21	7	20	3	19	6	11	14	
9	5	12	9	10	2	16	1	23	17	8	18	21	7	3	20	4	19	11	6	14		
10	5	9	12	10	2	16	1	23	17	18	7	21	3	20	8	4	6	11	19	14		
11	5	9	2	16	23	10	17	18	12	7	3	21	1	8	4	20	6	19	11	14		
12	5	9	2	23	7	12	16	1	17	10	8	4	18	21	3	6	19	20	11	14		
13	5	7	12	23	9	16	10	1	8	4	18	2	3	6	17	19	21	20	11	14		
14	5	7	12	9	16	10	4	8	1	18	3	2	6	19	17	23	21	20	11	14		
15	5	7	12	9	16	10	4	8	18	3	1	2	19	6	17	23	21	20	11	14		
16	5	7	12	9	16	10	4	8	18	3	2	6	19	17	23	1	21	20	11	14		
17	5	7	12	9	16	4	10	8	18	3	2	6	19	17	23	21	11	20	1	14		
18	5	7	12	9	16	4	10	8	18	3	2	6	19	17	3	11	21	20	1	14		
19	5	7	12	9	16	4	10	8	3	18	6	2	19	17	23	11	20	1	14			
20	5	7	12	9	16	4	8	3	18	6	2	19	23	17	11	20	1	14				
21	5	7	12	9	4	16	8	3	18	6	2	19	23	17	11	20	1	14				
22	5	7	12	9	4	16	8	3	18	6	2	19	23	17	20	1	14					
23	5	7	12	9	4	16	8	3	18	6	2	19	23	17	20	1	14					
24	5	12	9	4	7	16	8	3	18	6	2	19	23	17	20	1	14					
25	5	12	9	7	16	3	4	18	6	2	8	19	23	17	20	1	14					
26	5	12	9	7	16	3	4	6	2	8	19	23	17	1	20	14						
27	5	12	9	7	16	3	4	6	2	8	19	23	17	1	20	14						
28	5	12	9	7	16	3	4	6	2	8	19	17	23	1	20	14						
29	5	12	9	7	16	3	4	6	2	8	19	17	23	1	20	14						
30	5	12	7	16	3	9	4	2	6	8	17	19	23	1	20	14						
31	5	12	7	16	3	9	4	2	8	6	17	19	23	1	20	14						
32	5	12	7	9	4	16	2	8	3	6	17	19	23	1	20	14						
33	5	12	9	4	16	7	8	3	2	6	17	19	23	1	20	14						
34	5	12	9	4	16	7	3	8	6	2	17	19	23	1	20	14						
35	5	12	9	4	16	7	3	6	8	2	19	17	23	1	20	14						
36	5	12	9	4	16	3	7	6	8	2	19	17	23	1	20	14						
37	5	12	9	4	16	3	7	6	8	2	19	17	23	1	20	14						
38	5	12	9	4	16	3	7	8	6	2	17	19	23	1	20	14						
39	5	12	9	4	16	3	8	6	2	7	17	19	23	1	20	14						
40	5	12	9	4	16	3	8	6	2	7	17	19	23	1	20	14						
41	5	12	9	4	16	3	8	6	2	7	17	19	23	1	20	14						
42	5	12	9	4	16	3	8	6	2	7	17	19	23	1	20	14						
43	5	12	9	4	16	3	8	6	2	7	17	19	23									
44	5	12	9	4	16	3	8	2	7	17												

Best result for a Bridgestone shod runner:

Pedro Diniz, Arrows Yamaha, 8th

CHAMPIONSHIPS

(after twelve rounds)

Drivers :

	Driver	Points
1.	Michael SCHUMACHER	66
2.	Jacques VILLENEUVE	54
3.	Heinz-H. FRENTZEN	22
	Jean ALESI	22
5.	Gerhard BERGER	20
6.	Eddie IRVINE	18
	Mika HAKKINEN	18
8.	Olivier PANIS	15
9.	David COULTHARD	14
	Giancarlo FISICHELLA	14
11.	Johnny HERBERT	13
12.	Ralf SCHUMACHER	11
13.	Damon HILL	7
14.	Rubens BARRICHELLO	6
15.	Alexander WURZ	4
16.	Jarno TRULLI	3
17.	Mika SALO	2
	Shinji NAKANO	2
19.	Nicola LARINI	1

Constructors :

	Constructor	Points
1.	Ferrari	84
2.	Williams / Renault	76
3.	Benetton / Renault	46
4.	McLaren / Mercedes	32
5.	Jordan / Peugeot	25
6.	Prost / Mugen Honda	20
7.	Sauber / Petronas	14
8.	Arrows / Yamaha	7
9.	Stewart / Ford	6
10.	Tyrrell / Ford	2

CLASSIFICATION & RETIREMENTS

Pos	Driver	Team	Time
1.	Schumacher	Ferrari	in 1h33'46"717
2.	Fisichella	Jordan Peugeot	at 26"753
3.	Hakkinen	McLaren Mercedes	at 30"856
4.	Frentzen	Williams Renault	at 32"147
5.	Herbert	Sauber Petronas	at 39"025
6.	Villeneuve	Williams Renault	at 42"103
7.	Berger	Benetton Renault	at 1'03"741
8.	Diniz	Arrows Yamaha	at 1'25"931
9.	Alesi	Benetton Renault	at 1'42"008
10.	Morbidelli	Sauber Petronas	at 1'42"582
11.	Irvine	Ferrari	accident
12.	Salo	Tyrrell Ford	at 1 lap
13.	Magnussen	Stewart Ford	at 1 lap
14.	Hill	Arrows Yamaha	tyre
15.	Katayama	Minardi Hart	engine
16.	Trulli	Prost Mugen Honda	at 2 laps

Lap	Driver	Team	Reason
5	Nakano	Prost Mugen Honda	electronics
8	Barrichello	Stewart Ford	suspension
18	Marquès	Minardi Hart	off
19	Coulthard	McLarenMercedes	spin
21	Schumacher	Jordan Peugeot	spin
25	Verstappen	Tyrrell Ford	spin

FASTEST LAPS

	Driver	Time	Lap
1.	Villeneuve	1'52"692	43
2.	Herbert	1'53"615	44
3.	Berger	1'53"649	43
4.	Diniz	1'53"652	42
5.	Frentzen	1'53"874	43
6.	Hill	1'54"074	41
7.	Hakkinen	1'54"175	43
8.	Fisichella	1'54"688	39
9.	Morbidelli	1'54"818	39
10.	Trulli	1'55"152	37
11.	Irvine	1'55"290	29
12.	M. Schum.	1'55"340	41
13.	Alesi	1'55"348	30
14.	Katayama	1'55"413	41
15.	Magnussen	1'55"726	41
16.	Salo	1'56"919	43
17.	R. Schum.	1'57"784	16
18.	Coulthard	1'59"169	16
19.	Verstappen	1'59"409	16
20.	Marquès	2'02"753	16
21.	Barrichello	2'16"804	5
22.	Nakano	2'19"161	5

TWELTH ROUND

BELGIAN GRAND PRIX, SPA-FRANCORCHAMPS

LES COMBES · MALMÉDY · RAIDILLON · KEMMEL · L'EAU ROUGE · POUHON · RIVACE · LA SOURCE · BUS STOP · BLANCHIMONT · FAGNES · STAVELOT

Date : August 24, 1997
Length : 6967 meters
Distance : 44 laps, 306.577 km
Weather : rainy then sunny, 16 degrees

WEEK-END GOSSIP

• **A disaster at Benetton**

It should have been Jean Alesi's day. He qualified in second place at Spa, proving his Benetton was on form. However, when the time came to add up the scores, Alesi finished down in ninth place, two positions behind Gerhard Berger, who in seventh spot, also failed to score any points. A disaster.

The Frenchman, who started on full rain tyres, complained of a mechanical problem. *«The car began to lose grip at around half-distance. At first I thought it was the tyres. I stopped to change them, but it was even worse. In fact, it turns out that some part of the rear suspension had broken. We will have to wait until the car has been checked to find out exactly what the problem was.»*

• **McLaren confirms its driver line-up**

The driver transfer market was beginning to take shape. On Friday afternoon, Damon Hill, who had been having talks with McLaren, put out a press statement saying his dealings with the Anglo-German team had broken down. *«I was negotiating with McLaren-Mercedes, but they made me an offer that I had no option but to refuse. It was in no way in line with the talks we had and it proved that the team was not serious about having me as one of its drivers.»* A nice smack in the mouth!

One hour later, McLaren put out its own release, stating that both its current drivers, David Coulthard and Mika Hakkinen had been retained for 1998.

• **Olivier Panis is back**

Of course, he had a pair of crutches with him, but they were more of a mental support than a physical one. Olivier Panis was back in Spa. *«I am being careful,»* he explained. *«My doctors have asked me not to put any pressure on my legs. That is why I cannot do any running. Most of my rehabilitation involves cycling and swimming.»*

The Frenchman had made the trip to Belgium to announce he had renewed his contract with the Prost team. *«I spoke to Alain about it a long time ago. He knew my two broken legs would only be a temporary interruption, without any effect on the long term. He wanted to keep me and I wanted to stay. We quickly reached an agreement.»*

For Panis, the visit to Spa marked the end of the worst part of his career. The countdown to his racing comeback had started.

• **Renewed support**

The 21st August was an important day for the Prost team. Apart from signing the contract with Olivier Panis, the team also announced it had renewed its deal with the team's title sponsor SEITA. The cigarette manufacturer had signed on for three more years until the year 2000.

RACE SUMMARY

- A storm floods the track twenty minutes before the start, which is given behind the safety car. It stays out on the track for three laps. The rain has stopped on most parts of the circuit.
- From third on the grid, Michael Schumacher passes Alesi on lap 5. A short distance later he also takes Villeneuve to go into the lead.
- On lap 6 Fisichella gets past Alesi and attacks Villeneuve, who pits for intermediate tyres. He rejoins in 18th place.
- On lap 8 Frentzen, who was 5th is overtaken by Diniz and Herbert.
- Berger is the first to change to slicks on lap 9. Fisichella does the same, while Hill fits intermediates again.
- Diniz and Herbert pass Coulthard and the Brazilian is provisionally third.
- Villeneuve stops a second time, this time for slicks and rejoins in 13th place.
- In second place, Hakkinen straightlines the chicane at Combes, but keeps going. He then pits for slick tyres.
- On lap 13 Michael Schumacher stops for slicks and takes the opportunity to refuel at the same time. By this stage he already has a lead of one minute and seven seconds.
- Villeneuve is on a charge through the field and passes Hill on lap 16.
- The run of refuelling stops leaves the order unchanged.
- On the last lap, Diniz tries to pass Irvine, crashing into him at the Combes chicane. They both retire.

▽ *Spectacular Spa. Even in the rain, the Ardennes circuit is a gem.*

A team win

David Coulthard took his second win of the season at Monza, thanks to McLaren's clever strategy. He started with a heavy fuel load and therefore took less time to refuel than the other drivers.
This allowed the Scotsman to pass Alesi and Frentzen, to take control of a very boring Italian Grand Prix.
There was virtually no overtaking on an afternoon when the cars appeared to be taking part in a concours d'elegance rather than a motor race.

68° GRAN PREMIO CAMPARI D'ITALIA
MONZA

Jean Alesi and Giancarlo Fisichella - the people's choice

At the instigation of Damon Hill, there was a one minute silence in the pit-lane at Monza on Saturday, in memory of Princess Diana, who died the previous weekend. ▽

«Forza Jean. Monza e ancora con te.» (Go on Jean, Monza is still with you.) This giant banner, unfurled in the main grandstand, directly opposite the Benetton pit, proved that Jean Alesi was still loved by the tifosi, even though he no longer drives for Ferrari.
On Saturday, the man from Avignon thanked them for their support with a fine pole position - his first for three years - his only other pole dating back to the very same Italian Grand Prix in 1994.
«Of course I have a French passport and I speak French better than Italian. But my family comes from Sicily and my heart is Italian.» At the end of the session, Jean Alesi could not put his happiness into words. *«I have had a lot of bad luck on this track in recent years, but I have always loved it. I feel comfortable here. The support from the fans was incredible and I felt as though they were pushing me down the straights.»*
They had given him just enough help and no more, as he was only 52 thousandths of a second up on Heinz-Harald Frentzen and had a 76 thousandth advantage over Giancarlo Fisichella.
All told, the lead in the classification changed eight times in the most hotly contested qualifying session of the season.
Having secured his second pole, Alesi was hoping his favourite circuit would also allow him to score his second win.
«I think I've got a good chance of winning this grand prix,» he concluded. *«The car is competitive on full tanks and I think it should go well. But I think it will be a very close race and the pit-stops will play a key role.»* He was to be proved right on that score.

«Fisico» third

Giancarlo Fisichella topped the time sheets for a long time, before being knocked off his perch at the end of the session, when he was also summoned to meet the Italian Stewards, after ignoring yellow flags being waved at the site of Jarno Trulli's accident.
The time Gianvarlo Fisichella set on that lap was disallowed, but luckily for the Italian, it was not his best lap of the session. *«Of course I am very excited at the idea of starting from third place. I think I will have a good race, because my car is excellent with a heavy fuel load. I just hope it does not get any hotter as we would have to change the settings. At the very least, I hope to get on the podium.»*

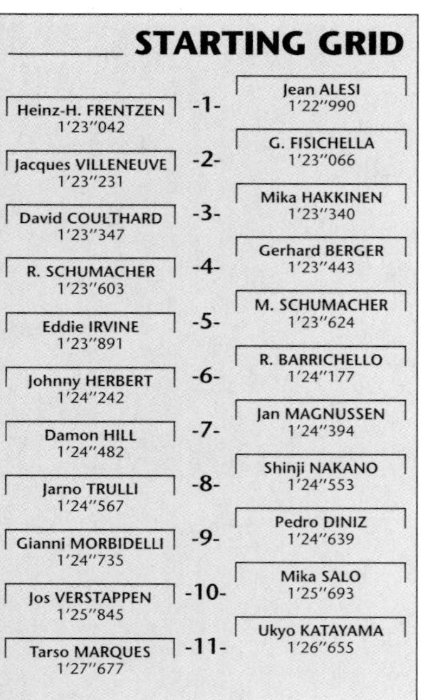

STARTING GRID

	Row	
		Jean ALESI 1'22"990
Heinz-H. FRENTZEN 1'23"042	-1-	G. FISICHELLA 1'23"066
Jacques VILLENEUVE 1'23"231	-2-	Mika HAKKINEN 1'23"340
David COULTHARD 1'23"347	-3-	Gerhard BERGER 1'23"443
R. SCHUMACHER 1'23"603	-4-	M. SCHUMACHER 1'23"624
Eddie IRVINE 1'23"891	-5-	R. BARRICHELLO 1'24"177
Johnny HERBERT 1'24"242	-6-	Jan MAGNUSSEN 1'24"394
Damon HILL 1'24"482	-7-	Shinji NAKANO 1'24"553
Jarno TRULLI 1'24"567	-8-	Pedro DINIZ 1'24"639
Gianni MORBIDELLI 1'24"735	-9-	Mika SALO 1'25"693
Jos VERSTAPPEN 1'25"845	-10-	Ukyo KATAYAMA 1'26"655
Tarso MARQUES 1'27"677	-11-	

▷ *«I don't believe it. The paparazzi even follow me on the track now!» On Saturday morning, Michael Schumacher and his F 310 B are towed back to the pits. In the afternoon he qualified in ninth spot, his worst performance of the season.*

David Coulthard wins it, thanks to his strategy

Jean Alesi had got pole position. His car was running well on full tanks and he made a good start. Leading from the grid, he was holding off Heinz-Harald Frentzen and David Coulthard, who were close behind. The Frenchman had every right to expect his second grand prix victory.
However, as the chequered flag fell, he was only second, but nobody could hold him responsible. On lap 32, the Frenchman made his pit-stop at the same time as David Coulthard. Everything depended on the skill of the mechanics. The seconds ticked by and Alesi would later admit he was as tense as at the start of a race. It was Coulthard who was the first to get back on the track.
The game was over. The Scotsman, with a clear track ahead of him, only had to stay on the road to take his second win of the season. *«After the pit-stop, I was much more relaxed,»* said Coulthard. *«I was in cruise mode and just had to make sure I made no mistakes.»*
He admitted the race had been won in the pits. *«It was a team victory and the mechanics were really part of it. I expected to get out ahead of Jean. We had decided to brim the tank before the start, which meant we needed to take less fuel on board during the pit-stop. That saved us one second over a normal stop.»*
The McLaren tactic had worked so well that Coulthard also managed to get ahead of Frentzen. The German had stopped three laps earlier and had the nasty surprise of finding himself in third place after Coulthard and Alesi had stopped, as these two had really put the hammer down for a couple of laps before coming into pit lane.
Coulthard had laid the groundwork for his win at the start. From sixth on the grid, he came round the first corner in third place. *«I made a very good start as I have been working on them for a while now. At the start, you can overtake someone in a matter of seconds, whereas once the race is underway, it can take as much as 20 laps to get by.»*
While Jean Alesi could only finish second, he was keen to point out his mechanics were not to blame. *«The guys did a great job,»* he insisted. *«But the fuel filler on our car prevents us from refuelling as quickly as some of the others. We could not have done better. Of course I am disappointed. I did my best, but I knew it would be impossible to pass David, unless he made a mistake.»*

Problem solved

There is no such thing as a discrete celebration at McLaren.
One hour after the finish, Mercedes motor sport boss Norbert Haug has turned the volume up full blast on the motorhome sound system, as the champagne flowed in celebration of victory, in the presence of Daimler-Benz director, Jurgen Hubbert, who had made the trip to Monza.
Watching the scene from a distance, Ron Dennis was savouring the moment, stating that McLaren had solved its problems. *«We have had a few reliability problems recently,»* he admitted. *«But we have traced the probable cause and changed our manufacturing process for some components. I think from now on we will be challenging to win on a more regular basis.»* Sadly subsequent events, in Austria and the Nurburgring, would prove him wrong.
In Monza, Mika Hakkinen could have made the team's joy complete, but for a puncture on his second set of tyres, which forced him to make an extra stop. He finished ninth.

△ *Chequered flag.*
On the pit wall, the McLaren mechanics had every reason to celebrate David Coulthard's success, as they had been instrumental in achieving it.

Herbert has a lucky escape

It is lap 39 and the battle between Johnny Herbert and Ralf Schumacher has been going on since the first corner, although it looks as though the Sauber driver is going to conserve his advantage ahead of the Jordan to the flag. Then suddenly, Ralf Schumacher overtakes him after slipstreaming down the pit straight. The two cars are neck and neck as they brake for the first chicane and the German moves over to the right, literally pushing the Englishman off onto the grass. At over 330 km/h at this point, Herbert's accident is frightening and comes to an end in a pile of tyres. *«He suddenly swerved to the right and I had nowhere to go,»* said Herbert, trembling with rage when he got back to the pits.
The Englishman had escaped unhurt from the crash, but this did not lessen the anger he felt towards Ralf Schumacher:
«I like racing another driver. I like to have a good fight for a place, but not like this. This guy does not realise he must give others some room. What he did was pointless and unacceptable. It shows he is just a novice with no experience of racing at high speed.»

Ralf *«thought»* Johnny had enough room

In his defence, *«Schumi 2»* said he *«thought»* Johnny Herbert had enough room to get by. As it went off the track, the Sauber had clipped the Jordan's rear wheel and the German was also eliminated in the accident.

◁ *"I tell you, I was this close to disaster." Johnny Herbert gets over his fright and explains to the marshals what happened. Ralf Schumacher's thoughtlessness could have had serious consequences.*

IN THE POINTS

	Driver	Team	Time
1.	David COULTHARD	West McLaren Mercedes	1 h 17'04"609
2.	Jean ALESI	Mild Seven Benetton Renault	at 1"937
3.	Heinz-H. FRENTZEN	Rothmans Williams Renault	at 4"343
4.	Giancarlo FISICHELLA	B&H Total Jordan Peugeot	at 5"871
5.	Jacques VILLENEUVE	Rothmans Williams Renault	at 6"416
6.	M. SCHUMACHER	Scuderia Ferrari Marlboro	at 11"481

Fastest lap : M. HAKKINEN, lap 49, 1'24"808, avg. 244.929 km/h

TRULLI
E
PlayStation
MUGEN
LOISES
BiC

Jarno Trulli spent this weekend in the gravel traps, going off in both Saturday sessions. Alain Prost was not best pleased with Jarno.
The Frenchman accepted that one could crash in qualifying, chasing a quick time, but not in free practice when it is time to find a good set-up for the car.

△
Yet another second place for Jean Alesi - the 15th of his career. Very frustrating.

The duellists are left behind

The tifosi had no chance to show their appreciation for Michael Schumacher. At Monza, the German had a quiet race to finish sixth, one place behind his rival, Jacques Villeneuve. *«Considering the problems we had in practice, I am quite happy with this result,»* he said. *«I have only lost one point to Jacques, so it could have been worse.»*
According to the German, the worst was now over. *«The championship is very open of course, but I think the next few tracks will suit our car better. Here, with very little downforce, nothing worked properly.»*
At Williams, Jacques Villeneuve made the best of a bad job. After failing to slow down when yellow flags were waved in the morning, he had received a one race ban, suspended for a staggering nine races. His afternoon was not much better, as he finished fifth and only clawed back one point of his deficit to Schumacher. *«We knew this track would not suit our chassis. I have caught up a little bit, but not enough.»*
In the closing stages of the race, the Canadian was right behind Fisichella's Jordan, which in turn, was glued to Frentzen's Williams. *«I could not pass Giancarlo, because I lost downforce if I got too close,»* complained Villeneuve. *«I was hoping that Heinz, who was in front, would slow him down enough for me to get by, but he did not do it. It's a shame.»*
The Monza topography had relegated the Ferraris and Williams to the lower orders. It was a bad experience which could be seen as a blip in the usual progress of these two teams.

«HH» ready to help Jacques

Stepping down from the third place on the podium, Heinz-Harald Frentzen did not have much to say about his race.
His race had also been a case of sitting in a queue, without any chance of overtaking. *«At the start, I felt I was quicker than Jean* (Alesi) *but I couldn't do anything about it. I had a little bit of understeer and I did not want to push too hard, in case I damaged my tyres. Towards the end, I tried to push harder, in the hope Jean would make a mistake, but it is very difficult here to find a gap and get through.»*
Having led for several laps, «HH» actually lost the race in the pits. *«Maybe I stopped too soon,»* he confessed. *«I must say that when you decide on a strategy before the the race, it is difficult to be 100% certain what to do and what not to do. Once the race is over, it is easy to see what the right choice would have been.»*
Questioned as to his intentions regarding Villeneuve, the German replied that he could have helped him. *«Would I let Jacques through if he was behind me? Why not?»* was his short reply.

▷
Sylvester Stallone paid a high-profile visit to Monza. He announced the signing of a contract with Bernie Ecclestone to make a film about Formula 1. No doubt he would play the role of the "star driver who has an accident but gets over it and just manages to win the world championship." The part of Bernie Ecclestone would have to go to Al Pacino, famous for his role in "The Godfather," naturally.

Hill is looking for a seat

Time was running out for Damon Hill as summer came to an end. Having failed in his negotiations with McLaren, Sauber and Jordan, none of them feeling disposed to meet the Englishman's salary demands, he was still without a seat for 1998.
The week before Monza, he had talks with Alain Prost, who had been a long time admirer of the reigning world champion. The only sticking point was Hill's demand for a 5.6 million pound salary, which Alain Prost was not ready to pay. Bernie Ecclestone, the prime mover in this sport, seemed to be on Hill's case as Damon was the sole focus of interest in grand prix racing in England. Ecclestone therefore felt it was essential to find him a competitive drive, to increase the value of the contract he was planning to sign with British Sky Broadcasting for digital grand prix coverage in the UK.

PRACTICE TIMES

No	Driver	Make/Engine/Chassis	Practice Friday	Practice Saturday	Qualifying	Warm-up
1.	Damon HIll	Arrows/Yamaha/A18/5 (B)	1'26"502	1'24"892	1'24"482	1'26"364
2.	Pedro Diniz	Arrows/Yamaha/A18/4 (B)	1'26"246	1'25"243	1'24"639	1'26"511
3.	Jacques Villeneuve	Williams/Renault/FW19/4 (G)	1'24"837	1'23"194	1'23"231	1'25"683
4.	Heinz-Harald Frentzen	Williams/Renault/FW19/5 (G)	1'23"991	1'23"658	1'23"042	1'25"962
5.	Michael Schumacher	Ferrari/Ferrari/F310B/180 (G)	1'26"224	1'23"815	1'23"624	1'26"228
6.	Eddie Irvine	Ferrari/Ferrari/F310B/179 (G)	1'25"340	1'24"236	1'23"891	1'26"907
7.	Jean Alesi	Benetton/Renault/B197/2 (G)	1'24"847	1'23"262	1'22"990	1'25"836
8.	Gerhard Berger	Benetton/Renault/B197/4 (G)	1'25"559	1'23"898	1'23"443	1'26"028
9.	Mika Hakkinen	McLaren/Mercedes/MP4/12/7 (G)	1'25"096	1'23"346	1'23"340	1'24"234
10.	David Coulthard	McLaren/Mercedes/MP4/12/4 (G)	1'25"050	1'23"434	1'23"347	1'25"093
11.	Ralf Schumacher	Jordan/Peugeot/197/6 (G)	1'25"422	1'23"387	1'23"603	1'24"937
12.	Giancarlo Fisichella	Jordan/Peugeot/197/5 (G)	1'25"050	1'23"329	1'23"066	1'25"118
14.	Jarno Trulli	Prost/Mugen Honda/JS45/3 (B)	1'25"317	1'24"749	1'24"567	1'25"493
15.	Shinji Nakano	Prost/Mugen Honda/JS45/2 (B)	1'26"727	1'25"034	1'24"553	1'25"608
16.	Johnny Herbert	Sauber/Petronas/C16/3 (G)	1'25"845	1'24"316	1'24"242	1'26"115
17.	Gianni Morbidelli	Sauber/Petronas/C16/6 (G)	1'26"696	1'25"391	1'24"735	1'27"012
18.	Jos Verstappen	Tyrrell/Ford/025/4 (G)	1'26"755	1'25"925	1'25"845	1'27"496
19.	Mika Salo	Tyrrell/Ford/025/3 (G)	1'26"608	1'25"561	1'25"693	1'26"037
20.	Ukyo Katayama	Minardi/Hart/M197/4 (B)	1'26"891	1'26"709	1'26"655	1'28"279
21.	Tarso Marquès	Minardi/Hart/M197/2 (B)	1'28"388	1'27"929	1'27"677	1'38"060
22.	Rubens Barrichello	Stewart/Ford/SF1/2 (B)	1'26"421	1'24"379	1'24"177	1'25"860
23.	Jan Magnussen	Stewart/Ford/SF1/3 (B)	1'25"488	1'24"436	1'24"394	1'27"343

LAP CHART

position :	1	2	3	4	5	6	7	8	9	10	11	12	13	14	15	16	17	18	19	20	21	22
start:	7	4	12	3	9	10	8	11	5	6	22	16	23	1	15	14	2	17	19	18	20	21
1	7	4	10	12	3	9	5	8	6	16	11	14	23	1	22	19	15	17	2	18	21	20
2	7	4	10	12	3	9	5	8	6	16	11	14	23	1	22	19	15	17	2	18	20	21
3	7	4	10	12	3	9	5	8	6	16	11	14	23	1	22	19	15	17	2	18	20	21
4	7	4	10	12	3	9	5	8	6	16	11	14	23	1	22	19	15	17	18	2	20	21
5	7	4	10	12	3	9	5	8	6	16	11	14	23	1	22	19	15	17	18	21	20	
6	7	4	10	12	3	9	5	8	6	16	11	14	23	1	22	19	15	17	18	21	20	
7	7	4	10	12	3	9	5	8	6	16	11	14	23	1	22	19	15	17	18	21	20	
8	7	4	10	12	3	9	5	8	6	16	11	14	23	1	22	19	15	17	18	21	20	
9	7	4	10	12	3	9	5	8	6	16	11	14	23	1	22	19	15	17	18	21		
10	7	4	10	12	3	9	5	8	6	16	11	14	23	1	22	19	15	17	18	21		
11	7	4	10	12	3	9	5	8	6	16	11	14	23	1	22	19	15	17	18	21		
12	7	4	10	12	3	9	5	8	6	16	11	14	23	1	22	19	15	17	18	21		
13	7	4	10	12	3	9	5	8	6	16	11	14	23	1	22	19	15	17	21			
14	7	4	10	12	3	9	5	8	6	16	11	14	23	1	22	19	15	17	21			
15	7	4	10	12	3	9	5	8	6	16	11	14	23	1	22	19	15	17	21			
16	7	4	10	12	3	9	5	8	6	16	11	14	23	1	22	15	17	19	21			
17	7	4	10	12	3	9	5	8	6	16	11	14	23	1	15	17	22	19	21			
18	7	4	10	12	3	9	5	8	6	16	11	14	1	15	17	23	22	19	21			
19	7	4	10	12	3	9	5	8	6	16	11	14	1	15	17	23	22	19	21			
20	7	4	10	12	3	9	5	8	6	16	11	14	1	15	17	23	22	19	21			
21	7	4	10	12	3	9	5	8	6	16	11	14	1	15	17	23	22	19	21			
22	7	4	10	12	3	9	5	8	6	16	11	14	1	15	17	23	22	19	21			
23	7	4	10	12	3	9	5	8	6	16	11	14	1	15	17	23	22	19	21			
24	7	4	10	12	3	9	5	8	6	16	11	14	1	15	17	23	22	19	21			
25	7	4	10	12	3	9	5	8	6	16	11	14	1	15	17	23	22	19	21			
26	7	4	10	12	3	9	5	8	6	16	11	14	1	15	17	23	22	19	21			
27	7	4	10	12	3	9	5	8	6	16	11	14	1	15	17	23	22	19	21			
28	7	4	10	12	9	5	8	6	16	11	3	14	1	15	17	23	22	19	21			
29	7	10	12	9	5	8	4	6	16	11	3	1	15	17	14	23	22	19	21			
30	7	10	12	9	5	8	6	4	11	3	1	16	15	17	14	23	19	22	21			
31	7	10	9	5	8	6	12	4	11	3	1	15	16	17	14	23	19	22	21			
32	9	5	8	10	7	6	4	12	3	16	11	1	14	15	17	19	22	21				
33	9	5	8	10	7	4	12	3	6	16	11	1	14	15	19	17	22	21				
34	5	10	9	7	4	12	3	8	6	16	11	1	14	15	17	22	21					
35	10	7	4	9	12	3	5	8	6	16	11	1	14	15	17	22	21					
36	10	7	4	9	12	3	5	9	6	16	11	1	14	15	17	22	21					
37	10	7	4	12	3	5	8	6	16	11	1	14	15	9	17	22	21					
38	10	7	4	12	3	5	8	6	16	11	1	14	15	9	17	22	21					
39	10	7	4	12	3	5	8	6	1	14	15	9	17	22	11	21						
40	10	7	4	12	3	5	8	6	1	14	15	9	17	22	21							
41	10	7	4	12	3	5	8	6	1	14	15	9	17	22	21							
42	10	7	4	12	3	5	8	6	1	14	15	9	17	22	21							
43	10	7	4	12	3	5	8	6	1	14	15	9	17	22	21							
44	10	7	4	12	3	5	8	6	1	14	9	15	17	22	21							
45	10	7	4	12	3	5	8	6	1	14	9	15	17	22	21							
46	10	7	4	12	3	5	8	6	1	14	9	15	17	22	21							
47	10	7	4	12	3	5	8	6	9	14	15	17	22	21								
48	10	7	4	12	3	5	8	6	9	14	15	17	22	21								
49	10	7	4	12	3	5	8	6	9	14	15	17	22	21								
50	10	7	4	12	3	5	8	6	9	14	15	17	22	21								
51	10	7	4	12	3	5	8	6	9	14	15	17	22									
52	10	7	4	12	3	5	8	6	9	14	15	17	22									
53	10	7	4	12	3	5	8	6	9	14	15											

BRIDGESTONE

Best result for a Bridgestone shod runner:

Jarno Trulli, Prost Mugen Honda, ***10th***

CLASSIFICATION & RETIREMENTS

Pos	Driver	Team	Time
1.	Coulthard	McLaren Mercedes	in 1h17'04"609
2.	Alesi	Benetton Renault	at 1"937
3.	Frentzen	Williams Renault	at 4"343
4.	Fisichella	Jordan Peugeot	at 5"871
5.	Villeneuve	Williams Renault	at 6"416
6.	Schumacher	Ferrari	at 11"481
7.	Berger	Benetton Renault	at 12"471
8.	Irvine	Ferrari	at 17"639
9.	Hakkinen	McLaren Mercedes	at 49"373
10.	Trulli	Prost Mugen Honda	at 1'02"706
11.	Nakano	Prost Mugen Honda	at 1'03"327
12.	Morbidelli	Sauber Petronas	at 1 tour
13.	Barrichello	Stewart Ford	at 1 tour
14.	Marquès	Minardi Hart	at 3 tours

Lap	Driver	Team	Reason
4	Diniz	Arrows Yamaha	suspension
8	Katayama	Minardi Hart	tyre
12	Verstappen	Tyrrell Ford	gearbox
31	Magnussen	Stewart Ford	gearbox
33	Salo	Tyrrell Ford	engine
38	Herbert	Sauber Petronas	off
39	Schumacher	Jordan Peugeot	accident
46	Hill	Arrows Yamaha	engine

FASTEST LAPS

	Driver	Time	Lap
1.	Hakkinen	1'24"808	49
2.	Frentzen	1'25"600	47
3.	Berger	1'25"653	47
4.	Irvine	1'25"655	53
5.	Villeneuve	1'25"715	20
6.	M. Schum.	1'25"863	47
7.	R. Schum.	1'25"909	31
8.	Fisichella	1'25"960	28
9.	Coulthard	1'25"975	31
10.	Alesi	1'26"067	52
11.	Nakano	1'26"383	53
12.	Herbert	1'26"572	27
13.	Trulli	1'26"718	44
14.	Hill	1'27"081	27
15.	Morbidelli	1'27"257	26
16.	Magnussen	1'27"447	21
17.	Barrichello	1'27"571	20
18.	Salo	1'28"004	12
19.	Verstappen	1'28"227	9
20.	Diniz	1'28"569	3
21.	Marquès	1'29"116	7
22.	Katayama	1'29"133	3

THIRTEENTH ROUND

68° GRAN PREMIO CAMPARI D'ITALIA, MONZA

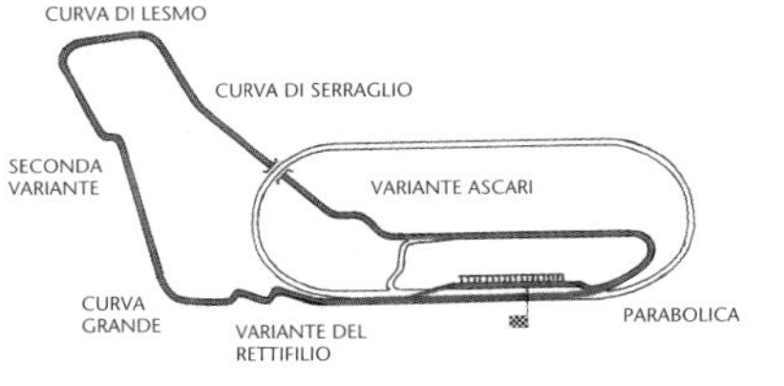

Date : September 7, 1997
Length: 5769.5 meters
Distance : 53 laps, 305.785 km
Weather : sunny, 26 degrees

CHAMPIONSHIPS

(after thirteen rounds)

Drivers :

1. Michael SCHUMACHER 67
2. Jacques VILLENEUVE 57
3. Jean ALESI......................................28
4. Heinz-H. FRENTZEN.......................27
5. David COULTHARD 24
6. Gerhard BERGER............................21
7. Eddie IRVINE...................................18
8. Giancarlo FISICHELLA 17
9. Olivier PANIS 15
10. Mika HAKKINEN 14
11. Johnny HERBERT............................14
12. Ralf SCHUMACHER........................11
13. Damon HILL 7
14. Rubens BARRICHELLO.....................6
15. Alexander WURZ 4
16. Jarno TRULLI 3
17. Mika SALO..2
    Shinji NAKANO 2
19. Nicola LARINI 1

Constructors :

1. Ferrari..85
2. Williams / Renault..........................84
3. Benetton / Renault.........................53
4. McLaren / Mercedes.......................38
5. Jordan / Peugeot 28
6. Prost / Mugen Honda 20
7. Sauber / Petronas 15
8. Arrows / Yamaha 7
9. Stewart / Ford 6
10. Tyrrell / Ford...................................2

WEEK-END GOSSIP

• BMW with Williams

The deal is done! The rumours had been doing the rounds for several months. BMW had decided to return to Formula 1 in the year 2000, as Williams' engine partner.
The official announcement was made on the Monday after Monza at the Frankfurt Motor Show, by Karl-Heinz Kalbfell, marketing director for the Munich car maker. BMW had already taken part in 91 grands prix between 1982 and 1987, supplying several teams, most notably Brabham. In 1983, with Nelson Piquet at the wheel, the German company had been the first to win a world championship with a turbocharged engine. Today, it could no longer stand by and watch Mercedes make the most of Formula 1's popularity in Germany.
For the Williams team, this announcement secured its long term future. For 1988 and 1989, the team already had a contract with Mecachrome, partly financed by BMW no less.

• No Malaysia

There would be no Malaysian Grand Prix in 1998. Bernie Ecclestone declared that, as yet, no Far Eastern country was ready to let the circus come to town.
The devaluation of their local currency had not helped the Korean promoters, who had assumed their deal was in place.

• The USA takes up the running

Millionaire Don Panoz, who recently bought the Road Atlanta circuit, was planning to modernise all its facilities in order to host a grand prix in 1999. Bernie Ecclestone, who has always been a fan of the Road Atlanta circuit and apparently tried to buy the track in the early 90s, would apparently support the project. Also in the USA, Chris Pook, organiser of the old Long Beach Grand Prix, was rumoured to be working on a new project.

• South Africa as well

The South Africans would also like to see another grand prix in their country in 1998. Since Nelson Mandela came to power, the political situation has definitely improved, with several large companies investing in the country.

• Farewell to Concorde

The famous Concorde Agreement could soon be a thing of the past. It seemed that Max Mosley was planning to abolish it, pure and simple, adding a few financial clauses to the F1 sporting regulations.

• Modernised Monza

Monza had replaced the flat kerbs in use the previous year, with raised ones which were harder to ride over. The general opinion among the drivers was that this was an improvement.

RACE SUMMARY

- Alesi leads from Frentzen and Coulthard after the start. The Scotsman made a great getaway, as he had been sixth on the grid.
- While Alesi pulls out a small lead, Coulthard closes on Frentzen. Behind them comes a trio of cars- Fisichella, Villeneuve and Hakkinen.
- Michael Schumacher gets away well. He is seventh, but losing ground to Hakkinen.
- There are no overtaking moves until the pit-stops. Of the leading group, the Williams are the first to stop. It was a tactical error.
- Thanks to the speed of his mechanics, Coulthard gets ahead of Frentzen and Alesi during the pit-stops.
- The positions do not change from now until the flag. Except in the fight for ninth place, where Ralf Schumacher pushes Herbert off the track. Both cars are eliminated.
- Coulthard wins the most tedious race of the season, from Alesi and Frentzen. The German got close to the Benetton, but was unable to pass it.

It was just like the good old days in Monza. A huge crowd was present as Michael Schumacher and his Ferrari was in with a chance of winning the team's first world title since 1979. No tifosi dared miss the show. On Sunday, an all-time record 150,000 strong crowd poured into the Autodromo.

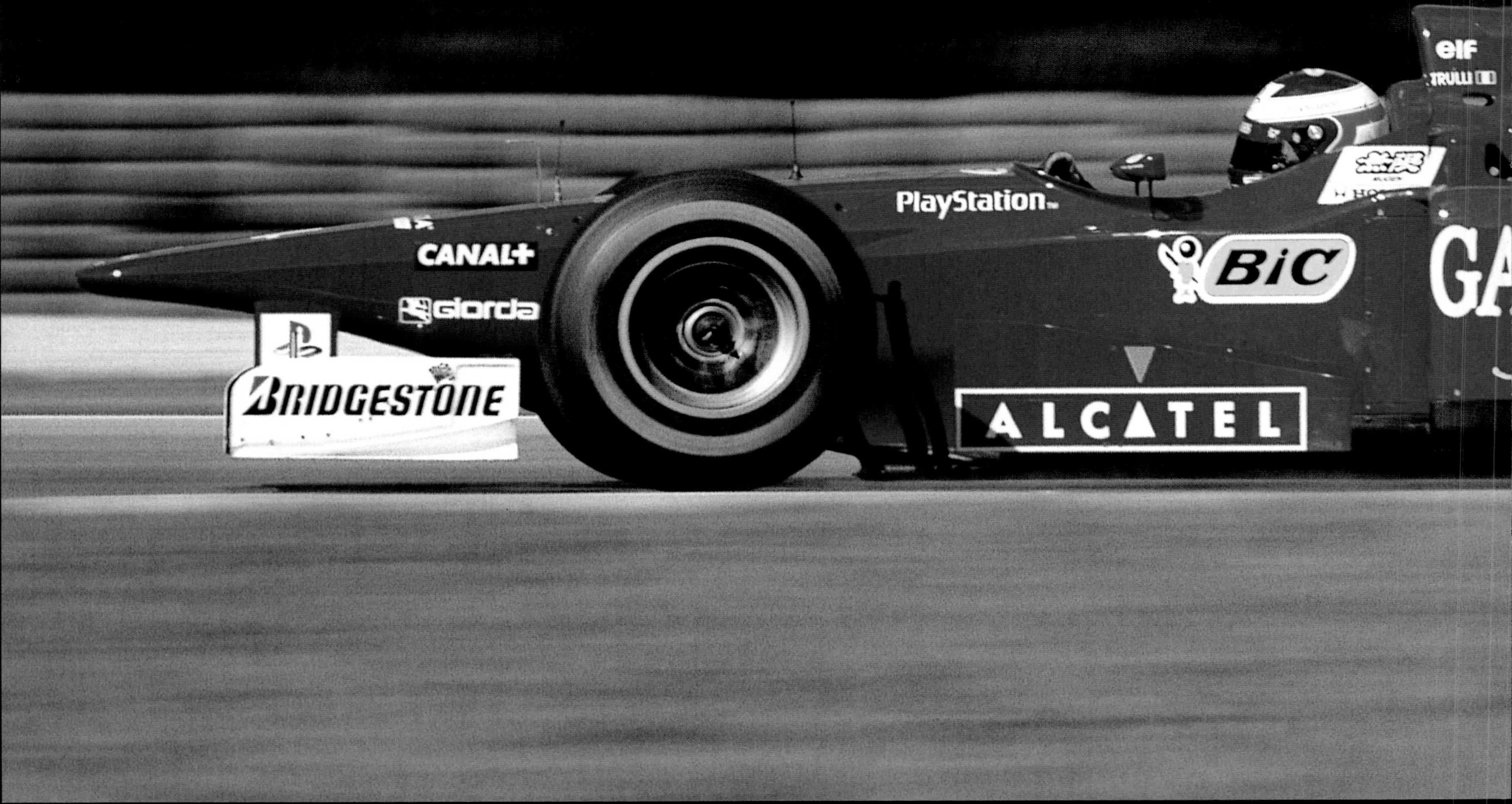
elf
TRULLI
PlayStation
CANAL+
BiC
BRIDGESTONE
ALCATEL

Farewell Jarno

Against a backdrop of the Styria mountains, Jarno Trulli demonstrated that the Prost Mugen-Honda had rediscovered the fine form it had shown earlier in the summer. The Italian led for almost half the race, before his engine failed. He was not too upset. Olivier Panis would be back to claim his seat at the Nurburgring, but he had made his mark.

Jacques Villeneuve also had a day to remember in Spielberg. Winning the race, he closed the gap to the championship leader down to a single point.

However, Michael Schumacher will not want to remember the Austrian Grand Prix. Penalised for overtaking under a yellow flag, he had to fight tooth and nail to claim sixth place.

GROSSER PREIS VON ÖSTERREICH
SPIELBERG

△ *Jean Alesi qualified down in 15th place, having started from pole two weeks earlier in Monza! In Spielberg, the Frenchman suffered from the closeness of the lap times, with 14 cars lapping in the same second. This was an outright record in the history of Formula 1.*

With the circuit situated at over 30,000 feet, it was certainly chilly for practice in the mornings. ▽▷

Jacques Villeneuve in attack mode

Jacques Villeneuve seems immune to pressure, or at least any time the season reaches a critical point, he manages to extract the maximum from his car.

In Austria, when the time came and it was vital for him to close the gap in the championship, he managed to snatch himself an important pole position at the end of the most hotly contested qualifying session of the season.

The gaps were so small on Saturday afternoon, that the slightest error was penalised with a free fall down the order. In these circumstances, Jacques Villeneuve put together a perfect lap. *«I must say the session was pretty exciting,»* puffed Jacques as he stepped from his car. *«When I went out for my final run, I knew I had to make up a gap of two tenths of a second on Mika* (Hakkinen). *I was absolutely flat-out and it worked. I must say I am very happy to be back on pole, because after yesterday and this morning's practice, I did not think I could do better than fifth or sixth. We just made a small change in the lunch break and then everything went a lot better.»* The Canadian did not expect the race to be child's play however. *«The weather needs to be very good tomorrow,»* he continued. *«Because we cannot get our tyres up to temperature when it is cool. I am worried about Mika but even more about Jarno* (Trulli.) *He will have nothing to lose in the race and his tyres might make all the difference.»*

For Mika Hakkinen, second on the grid, the Austrian Grand Prix provided the chance to make up for all his bad luck this season. *«The car is really great,»* rejoiced the Finn. *«It is very important to be on the front row here. It was my goal and I am pleased to have done it.»*

Trulli on the second row

As Olivier Panis had announced he would be back for the Nurburgring, the Italian Jarno Trulli was driving his last race here for the Prost team. He had every intention of bowing out in style as he managed to qualify in third place on the grid on Saturday. His session had started badly though, when his engine blew up before he had completed one flying lap. *«At that moment, I thought it was all over,»* he recounted after the session, sporting a smile from ear to ear. *«There were only forty minutes to go to the end of the session and the spare car was not ready. But the mechanics did a great job.»*

His third place owed something to the tyres Bridgestone had brought here. Alain Prost was quick to praise Trulli's performance. *«What Jarno has done today is really remarkable,»* he stressed.

STARTING GRID

	Row	
		Jacques VILLENEUVE 1'10"304
Mika HAKKINEN 1'10"398	-1-	
		Jarno TRULLI 1'10"511
Heinz-H. FRENTZEN 1'10"670	-2-	
		R. BARRICHELLO 1'10"700
Jan MAGNUSSEN 1'10"893	-3-	
		Damon HILL 1'11"025
Eddie IRVINE 1'11"051	-4-	
		M. SCHUMACHER 1'11"056
David COULTHARD 1'11"076	-5-	
		R. SCHUMACHER 1'11"186
Johnny HERBERT 1'11"210	-6-	
		Gianni MORBIDELLI 1'11"261
G. FISICHELLA 1'11"299	-7-	
		Jean ALESI 1'11"382
Shinji NAKANO 1'11"596	-8-	
		Pedro DINIZ 1'11"615
Gerhard BERGER 1'11"620	-9-	
		Ukyo KATAYAMA 1'12"036
Jos VERSTAPPEN 1'12"230	-10-	
		Tarso MARQUES 1'12"304
Mika SALO 1'14"246	-11-	

A big crowd turned out right from the start of practice. The Austrians certainly seemed pleased to rediscover their national grand prix on the calendar once more. From the biggest to the smallest. ▽

The Canadian's big day

Over dinner on Saturday night, on the eve of the Austrian Grand Prix, Jacques Villeneuve risked a prediction as to his result in the race. *«You wait and see. I will do the triple,»* he confided to his friend and manager Craig Pollock. *«I've got pole position and tomorrow I will win the race and set the fastest lap.»*
He was uncannily clairvoyant and in Spielberg, once the race was over, Pollock was proud to recount the tale.
«Jacques is not in the habit of making predictions like this,» he confided. *«He had a special feeling about this win.»*
While Villeneuve did indeed win the race and set the fastest lap, his afternoon's work was no picnic, mainly as the result of a very poor start. *«I came off the clutch too quickly, that's for sure,»*admitted the Canadian. *«I got wheelspin and I was even passed by Mika* (Hakkinen) *and Jarno* (Trulli). *Shortly after that, Barrichello also got by. I knew I had a problem with my tyre temperatures and that I would need at least five or six laps to get maximum grip out of them. I just bided my time.»*
Once this had happened, Villeneuve stepped up the pace and re-passed Rubens Barrichello's Stewart, which had been second behind Trulli in the Prost, who was leading the dance. *«I was not too worried about Rubens,»* he continued. *«But I did not want to take any risks in passing him, which is why I took my time. However, I was worried about not being able to catch Jarno* (Trulli).*»*
The Prost was indeed ten seconds ahead. Lap by lap, his Bridgestone tyres began to go off, which allowed Jacques to take the lead during the pit stops. From that moment on, all he had to do was keep his lead under control.
For the Canadian, this win in Austria pretty much re-set the trip meter on the championship. *«It is a bit of a special win because of my duel with Michael. I could not have done any better than win the race, so I am even happier to see he only scored one point today. It's a great day.»*

Thanks to Olivier Panis

Jarno Trulli was one of the heroes of the Austrian Grand Prix. For the first 37 laps of the race, the Italian had the honour of allowing Alain Prost to see one of his cars lead a grand prix for the first time in his capacity as a team owner. Sadly, the party came to a sudden end when the Mugen-Honda engines in both cars broke just seconds apart.
Alain Prost was not nicknamed «The Professor» for nothing. The race was barely over, before the Frenchman was analysing it in his usual scrupulous fashion. *«Sometimes we have scored points when we did not deserve to. Today, it was the other way around. We deserved a good result and we go home with nothing to show for it. But I am not too disappointed, as we have proved we are really competitive.»*
The return of Olivier Panis was scheduled for the following weekend in the Luxembourg Grand Prix. The Prost situation could only improve, especially as the returning driver had already had an effect on the team since he stepped back in the cockpit two weeks earlier. *«In Magny-Cours, Olivier did a time that would have put him in pole position for the French Grand Prix,»* was the news from the Prost team. *«But more importantly he has re-drawn the engine mapping on the Mugen-Honda as he did not like its brutal power delivery. This certainly helped Jarno to qualify so well here.»*

IN THE POINTS

	Driver	Team	Time
1.	Jacques VILLENEUVE	Rothmans Williams Renault	1 h 27'35"999
2.	David COULTHARD	West McLaren Mercedes	at 2"909
3.	Heinz-H. FRENTZEN	Rothmans Williams Renault	at 3"962
4.	Giancarlo FISICHELLA	B&H Total Jordan Peugeot	at 12"127
5.	Ralf SCHUMACHER	B&H Total Jordan Peugeot	at 31"859
6.	M. SCHUMACHER	Scuderia Ferrari Marlboro	at 33"410

Fastest lap : J. VILLENEUVE, lap 36, 1'11"814, avg. 216.709 km/h

▽ *Jarno Trulli led 37 laps of the Austrian Grand Prix, confirming the progress shown by the Prost team in qualifying.*

"Look out below!" Jean Alesi gives flying lessons as a result of crashing with Eddie Irvine (the damage caused by the Benetton can be seen on the right side of the Ferrari.) Once back on terra firma, Alesi took off again, this time in a rage against the Irishman. "If it were not for the fact I knew it would cost me a 10,000 dollar fine, I would have punched him in the face!"

MILD SEVEN
MILD SEVEN
BENETTON
POWER BY RENAULT
Gillette
FedEx
GOODYEAR
TELECOM

▷
Michael Schumacher left Austria with his lead over Jacques Villeneuve reduced to almost nothing thanks to his 10 seconds penalty Ironically this came about as a result of an incident involving his very own team-mate Eddie Irvine.

Schumacher pleads not guilty

«I did not see anything. I assure you I did not see anything.» After the race, Michael Schumacher could do nothing but repeat this phrase over and over again. As far as he was concerned, the ten second penalty, which dropped him from third to ninth was totally baffling.
The Austrian stewards reckoned he overtook Heinz-Harald Frentzen under braking for the Remus corner, at the precise moment when yellow flags were hung out, because of an accident involving Jean Alesi and Eddie Irvine. Overtaking «under a yellow» is strictly forbidden.
«I was right behind Heinz-Harald and Gerhard. I was trying to attack them and was concentrating on the inside of the corner,» said Schumacher in justifying his actions. *«When I saw a replay of the incident with footage taken from my on-board camera, I realised there was no way I could have seen the yellow flags, because when they were shown, I was already on the right of Heinz-Harald and Gerhard was right in front of me, so I could not see the flags as our wheels were very close together. You can be sure that if I had seen anything I would not have overtaken.»*
Told over the radio about the penalty, the German started to get very hot under the helmet. *«As far as I was concerned, I had done nothing wrong. I had every reason to be angry. But I calmed down and tried to make the best of a bad situation.»*
Having sat through his ten second penalty, the German went out onto the track in ninth place. There were still twenty laps to go and Schumacher put the hammer down. With two laps remaining he was seventh behind Damon Hill and literally pushed the Englishman out of the way at the Remus corner to snatch one point for sixth place. It was slim consolation. *«I leave this race with mixed feelings,»* he said. *«On the one hand I threw away five points, but on the other, I could see in the race that I could have caught up with Villeneuve. The car handled better than I had expected, which is a good sign for the end of the season.»*

Hill chooses Jordan

The Friday afternoon of the Italian Grand Prix, Eddie Jordan and Damon Hill find themselves by chance sitting next to one another in a press conference.
Damon Hill takes the opportunity to let Jordan know he is available. *«Unfortunately, you are out of my price range,»* quips the Irishman, whose reputation for being careful with money seems like an impossible barrier to the two men getting together.
However, two days later, unexpected circumstances change the situation. On Sunday evening after the Italian Grand Prix, Hill is due to fly back to England in Arrows boss Tom Walkinshaw's private plane.
But when he gets to Milan airport, Hill discovers that Walkinshaw has left without him. At a loss as to what to do, he bumps into Eddie Jordan who offers him a lift in his own aircraft. It is during this flight that the two men find some common ground.
So on Friday morning, the Jordan team is proud to announce that the reigning world champion would be joining them for the 1998 and 1999 seasons.
For Hill, whose other options had all evaporated, this was pretty much his last chance, although he denied he was clinging to this offer like a drowning man to a lifebelt.

Jean Alesi signs a two year deal with Sauber

The day after finishing second at Monza, Jean Alesi had paid a secret visit to the Sauber factory at Hinwil, near Zurich.
For the moment, it was only a first meeting. But rumours were spreading like wild fire that the Benetton driver would be moving to the Swiss team.
These rumours were confirmed on the Monday before the Austrian Grand Prix: Jean Alesi would drive for Sauber in 1998 and 1999. Financially, the Frenchman had done a good deal. Thanks to a generous budget courtesy of sponsors Red Bull and Petronas, Peter Sauber had managed to meet Alesi's demands, estimated at six million dollars per year for two years.
The driver himself naturally refused to comment on the figure, preferring to explain why he had been drawn to the Swiss team. *«The Sauber team really surprised me this season,»* he explained. *«I think it has all the necessary attributes in place to join the select band of top teams in the future.»*
After five years with Ferrari and two with Benetton, it was clear that Jean Alesi, with 131 grands prix under his belt, was going to bring invaluable experience to the Hinwil engineers to help them develop next year's C17.
«Jean Alesi has been one of the top drivers for years,» said Peter Sauber. *«Over the past few years we have improved our team from a technical point of view and we have significantly increased the number of staff. It was about time that we employed drivers who matched the targets we have set ourselves.»*
In other words, to win races soon.

Eddie Jordan and Flavio Briatore share the woes of team management. Jordan: «OK, I'll give you Fisichella. But if you knew how much Hill has cost me...» Briatore: «Tell me about it. That's just why I'm taking two youngsters as they are dirt cheap.»
▷ ▽

Plenty of action on the Spielberg track. Here, Pedro Diniz, starting from 17th place is holding up the traffic, including Morbidelli, Irvine, Nakano and... Gerhard Berger. In front of his home crowd, the Austrian could do no better than tenth. «It is not quite what I had expected from my home race. But when you really want things to go well, they always go badly.»
▽

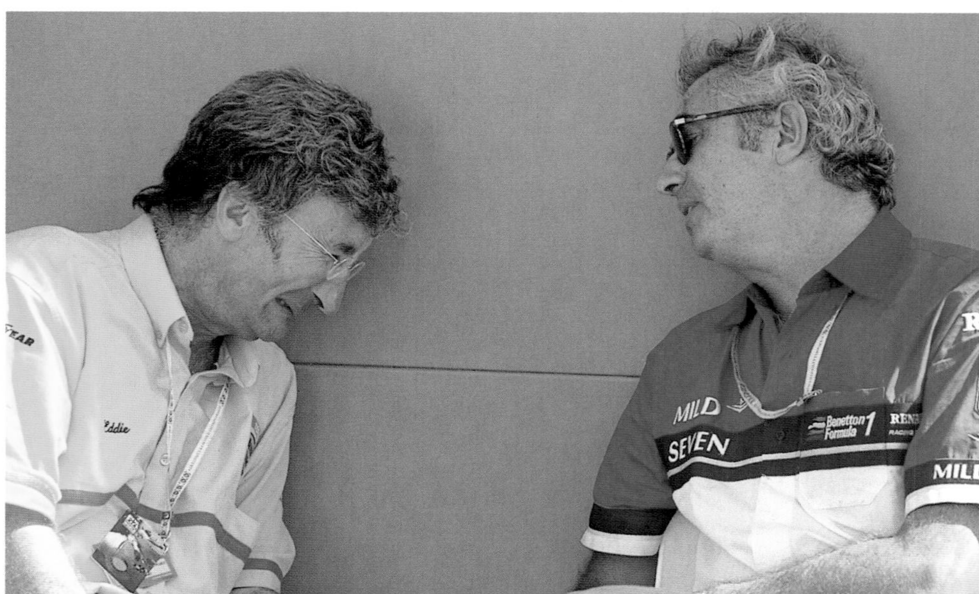

PRACTICE TIMES

No	Driver	Make/Engine/Chassis	Practice Friday	Practice Saturday	Qualifying	Warm-up
1.	Damon Hill	Arrows/Yamaha/A18/5 (B)	1'12"614	1'11"471	1'11"025	1'13"929
2.	Pedro Diniz	Arrows/Yamaha/A18/4 (B)	1'12"519	1'10"782	1'11"615	1'13"625
3.	Jacques Villeneuve	Williams/Renault/FW19/4 (G)	1'11"638	1'10"798	1'10"304	1'13"695
4.	Heinz-Harald Frentzen	Williams/Renault/FW19/5 (G)	1'11"527	1'11"300	1'10"670	1'13"755
5.	Michael Schumacher	Ferrari/Ferrari/F310B/180 (G)	1'12"265	1'11"018	1'11"056	1'13"173
6.	Eddie Irvine	Ferrari/Ferrari/F310B/179 (G)	1'12"548	1'10"824	1'11"051	1'13"621
7.	Jean Alesi	Benetton/Renault/B197/2 (G)	1'12"820	1'11"346	1'11"382	1'15"266
8.	Gerhard Berger	Benetton/Renault/B197/4 (G)	1'12"283	1'12"109	1'11"620	1'14"276
9.	Mika Hakkinen	McLaren/Mercedes/MP4/12/7 (G)	1'11"902	1'10"872	1'10"398	1'12"803
10.	David Coulthard	McLaren/Mercedes/MP4/12/4 (G)	1'11"967	1'11"752	1'11"076	1'13"227
11.	Ralf Schumacher	Jordan/Peugeot/197/6 (G)	1'13"041	1'11"933	1'11"186	1'13"510
12.	Giancarlo Fisichella	Jordan/Peugeot/197/4 (G)	1'11"899	1'11"927	1'11"299	1'13"224
14.	Jarno Trulli	Prost/Mugen Honda/JS45/3 (B)	1'12"935	1'10"815	1'10"511	1'12"868
15.	Shinji Nakano	Prost/Mugen Honda/JS45/2 (B)	1'13"280	1'11"698	1'11"596	1'14"466
16.	Johnny Herbert	Sauber/Petronas/C16/7 (G)	1'12"751	1'11"513	1'11"210	1'13"692
17.	Gianni Morbidelli	Sauber/Petronas/C16/6 (G)	1'12"966	1'12"561	1'11"261	1'13"603
18.	Jos Verstappen	Tyrrell/Ford/025/4 (G)	1'14"188	1'13"187	1'12"230	1'14"766
19.	Mika Salo	Tyrrell/Ford/025/5 (G)	1'14"079	1'13"574	1'14"246	1'15"340
20.	Ukyo Katayama	Minardi/Hart/M197/4 (B)	1'13"348	1'12"285	1'12"036	1'17"435
21.	Tarso Marquès	Minardi/Hart/M197/2 (B)	1'14"739	1'13"038	1'12"304	disqualifié
22.	Rubens Barrichello	Stewart/Ford/SF1/2 (B)	1'11"798	1'11"387	1'10"700	1'13"509
23.	Jan Magnussen	Stewart/Ford/SF1/3 (B)	1'13"286	1'11"785	1'10"893	1'15"894

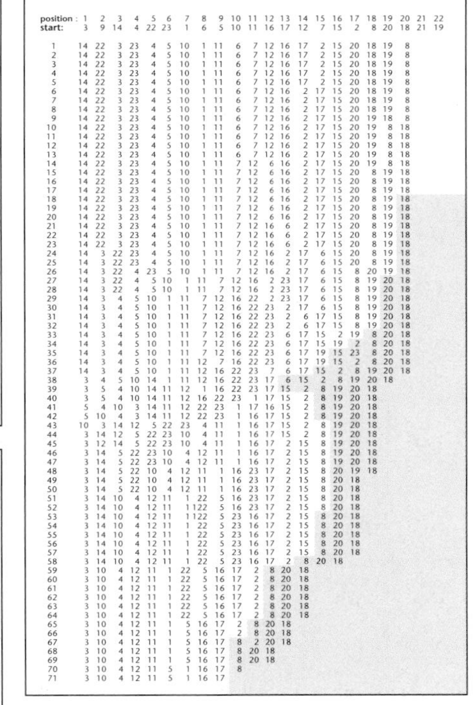

LAP CHART

position:	1	2	3	4	5	6	7	8	9	10	11	12	13	14	15	16	17	18	19	20	21	22
start:	3	9	14	4	22	23	1	6	5	10	11	16	17	12	7	15	2	8	20	18	21	19
1	14	22	3	23	4	5	10	1	11	6	7	12	16	17	2	15	20	18	19	8		
2	14	22	3	23	4	5	10	1	11	6	7	12	16	17	2	15	20	18	19	8		
3	14	22	3	23	4	5	10	1	11	6	7	12	16	17	2	15	20	18	19	8		
4	14	22	3	23	4	5	10	1	11	6	7	12	16	17	2	15	20	18	19	8		
5	14	22	3	23	4	5	10	1	11	6	7	12	16	17	2	15	20	18	19	8		
6	14	22	3	23	4	5	10	1	11	6	7	12	16	2	17	15	20	18	19	8		
7	14	22	3	23	4	5	10	1	11	6	7	12	16	2	17	15	20	18	19	8		
8	14	22	3	23	4	5	10	1	11	6	7	12	16	2	17	15	20	18	19	8		
9	14	22	3	23	4	5	10	1	11	6	7	12	16	2	17	15	20	19	18	8		
10	14	22	3	23	4	5	10	1	11	6	7	12	16	2	17	15	20	19	8	18		
11	14	22	3	23	4	5	10	1	11	6	7	12	16	2	17	15	20	19	8	18		
12	14	22	3	23	4	5	10	1	11	6	7	12	16	2	17	15	20	19	8	18		
13	14	22	3	23	4	5	10	1	11	6	7	12	16	2	17	15	20	19	8	18		
14	14	22	3	23	4	5	10	1	11	7	12	6	16	2	17	15	20	19	8	18		
15	14	22	3	23	4	5	10	1	11	7	12	6	16	2	17	15	20	8	19	18		
16	14	22	3	23	4	5	10	1	11	7	12	6	16	2	17	15	20	8	19	18		
17	14	22	3	23	4	5	10	1	11	7	12	6	16	2	17	15	20	8	19	18		
18	14	22	3	23	4	5	10	1	11	7	12	6	16	2	17	15	20	8	19	18		
19	14	22	3	23	4	5	10	1	11	7	12	6	16	2	17	15	20	8	19	18		
20	14	22	3	23	4	5	10	1	11	7	12	6	16	2	17	15	20	8	19	18		
21	14	22	3	23	4	5	10	1	11	7	12	16	6	2	17	15	20	8	19	18		
22	14	22	3	23	4	5	10	1	11	7	12	16	6	2	17	15	20	8	19	18		
23	14	22	3	23	4	5	10	1	11	7	12	16	6	2	17	15	20	8	19	18		
24	14	3	22	23	4	5	10	1	11	7	12	16	2	17	6	15	20	8	19	18		
25	14	3	22	23	4	5	10	1	11	7	12	16	2	17	6	15	20	8	19	18		
26	14	3	22	4	23	5	10	1	11	7	12	16	2	17	6	15	8	20	19	18		
27	14	3	22	4	5	10	1	11	7	12	16	2	23	17	6	15	8	19	20	18		
28	14	3	22	4	5	10	1	11	7	12	16	2	23	17	6	15	8	19	20	18		
29	14	3	4	5	10	1	11	7	12	16	22	2	23	17	6	15	8	19	20	18		
30	14	3	4	5	10	1	11	7	12	16	22	23	2	17	6	15	8	19	20	18		
31	14	3	4	5	10	1	11	7	12	16	22	23	2	6	17	15	8	19	20	18		
32	14	3	4	5	10	1	11	7	12	16	22	23	2	6	17	15	8	19	20	18		
33	14	3	4	5	10	1	11	7	12	16	22	23	6	17	15	2	19	8	20	18		
34	14	3	4	5	10	1	11	7	12	16	22	23	6	17	15	19	2	8	20	18		
35	14	3	4	5	10	1	11	7	12	16	22	23	6	17	19	15	23	8	20	18		
36	14	3	4	5	10	1	11	12	7	16	22	23	6	17	19	15	2	8	20	18		
37	14	3	4	5	10	1	11	12	16	22	23	7	6	17	15	2	8	19	20	18		
38	3	4	5	10	14	1	11	12	16	22	23	17	6	15	2	8	19	20	18			
39	3	5	4	10	14	11	12	1	16	22	23	17	15	2	8	19	20	18				
40	3	5	4	10	14	11	12	16	22	23	1	17	15	2	8	19	20	18				
41	5	4	10	3	14	11	12	22	23	1	17	16	15	2	8	19	20	18				
42	5	10	4	3	14	11	12	22	23	1	16	17	15	2	8	19	20	18				
43	10	3	14	12	5	22	23	4	11	1	16	17	15	2	8	19	20	18				
44	3	14	12	5	22	23	10	4	11	1	16	17	15	2	8	19	20	18				
45	3	12	14	5	22	23	10	4	11	1	16	17	2	15	8	19	20	18				
46	3	14	5	22	23	10	4	12	11	1	16	17	2	15	8	19	20	18				
47	3	14	5	22	23	10	4	12	11	1	16	17	2	15	8	19	20	18				
48	3	14	5	22	10	4	12	11	1	16	23	17	2	15	8	20	19	18				
49	3	14	5	22	10	4	12	11	1	16	23	17	2	15	8	20	18					
50	3	14	5	22	10	4	12	11	1	16	23	17	2	15	8	20	18					
51	3	14	10	4	12	11	1	22	5	16	23	17	2	15	8	20	18					
52	3	14	10	4	12	11	1122	5	16	23	17	2	15	8	20	18						
53	3	14	10	4	12	11	1122	5	23	16	17	2	15	8	20	18						
54	3	14	10	4	12	11	1	22	5	23	16	17	2	15	8	20	18					
55	3	14	10	4	12	11	1	22	5	23	16	17	2	15	8	20	18					
56	3	14	10	4	12	11	1	22	5	23	16	17	2	15	8	20	18					
57	3	14	10	4	12	11	1	22	5	23	16	17	2	15	8	20	18					
58	3	14	10	4	12	11	1	22	5	23	16	17	2	8	20	18						
59	3	10	4	12	11	1	22	5	16	17	2	8	20	18								
60	3	10	4	12	11	1	22	5	16	17	2	8	20	18								
61	3	10	4	12	11	1	22	5	16	17	2	8	20	18								
62	3	10	4	12	11	1	22	5	16	17	2	8	20	18								
63	3	10	4	12	11	1	22	5	16	17	2	8	20	18								
64	3	10	4	12	11	1	22	5	16	17	2	8	20	18								
65	3	10	4	12	11	1	5	16	17	2	8	20	18									
66	3	10	4	12	11	1	5	16	17	2	8	20	18									
67	3	10	4	12	11	1	5	16	17	8	2	20	18									
68	3	10	4	12	11	1	5	16	17	8	20	18										
69	3	10	4	12	11	1	5	16	17	8	20	18										
70	3	10	4	12	11	5	1	16	17	8												
71	3	10	4	12	11	5	1	16	17													

BRIDGESTONE

Best result for a Bridgestone shod runner:

Damon Hill, Arrows Yamaha, *7th*

CLASSIFICATION & RETIREMENTS

Pos	Driver	Team	Time
1.	Villeneuve	Williams Renault	in 1h27'35"999
2.	Coulthard	McLaren Mercedes	at 2"909
3.	Frentzen	Williams Renault	at 3"962
4.	Fisichella	Jordan Peugeot	at 12"127
5.	Schumacher	Jordan Peugeot	at 31"859
6.	Schumacher	Ferrari	at 33"410
7.	Hill	Arrows Yamaha	at 37"207
8.	Herbert	Sauber Petronas	at 49"057
9.	Morbidelli	Sauber Petronas	at 1'06"455
10.	Berger	Benetton Renault	at 1 lap
11.	Katayama	Minardi Hart	at 2 laps
12.	Verstappen	Tyrrell Ford	at 2 laps
13.	Diniz	Arrows Yamaha	engine
14.	Barrichello	Stewart Ford	off

Lap	Driver	Team	Reason
1	Hakkinen	McLaren Mercedes	engine
38	Alesi	Benetton Renault	accident
39	Irvine	Ferrari	accident
49	Salo	Tyrrell Ford	gearbox
58	Nakano	Prost Mugen Honda	engine
59	Magnussen	Stewart Ford	engine
59	Trulli	Prost Mugen Honda	engine

FASTEST LAPS

	Driver	Time	Lap
1.	Villeneuve	1'11"814	36
2.	M. Schum.	1'12"169	71
3.	Coulthard	1'12"207	65
4.	Frentzen	1'12"223	55
5.	Fisichella	1'12"375	64
6.	Barrichello	1'12"535	55
7.	Herbert	1'12"574	34
8.	Trulli	1'12"598	30
9.	Magnussen	1'12"605	38
10.	Berger	1'12"624	66
11.	Irvine	1'12"704	35
12.	Morbidelli	1'12"826	71
13.	R. Schum.	1'12"862	65
14.	Hill	1'12"903	53
15.	Alesi	1'12"953	29
16.	Nakano	1'13"010	57
17.	Diniz	1'13"074	63
18.	Verstappen	1'13"708	69
19.	Salo	1'13"862	34
20.	Katayama	1'14"394	63
21.	Hakkinen	1'31"574	1

FOURTEENTH ROUND

GROSSER PREIS VON ÖSTERREICH, SPIELBERG

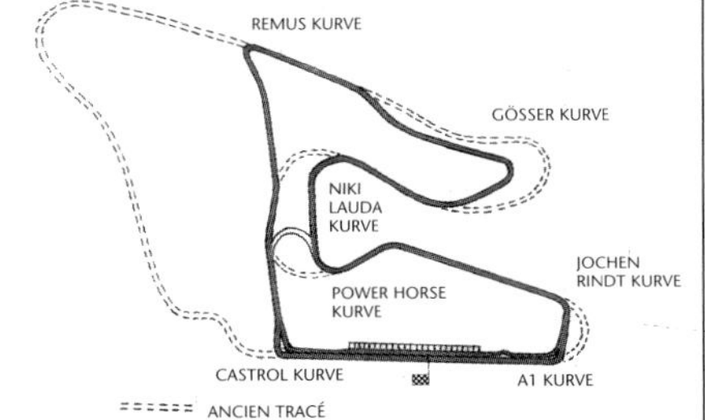

Date : September 21, 1997
Length : 4323 meters
Distance : 71 laps, 306.933 km
Weather : sunny,19 degrees

CHAMPIONSHIPS

(after fourteen rounds)

Drivers :

1. Michael SCHUMACHER 68
2. Jacques VILLENEUVE 67
3. Heinz-Harald FRENTZEN 31
4. David COULTHARD 30
5. Jean ALESI.....................................28
6. Gerhard BERGER...........................21
7. Giancarlo FISICHELLA 20
8. Eddie IRVINE................................18
9. Olivier PANIS 15
10. Mika HAKKINEN 14
    Johnny HERBERT...........................14
12. Ralf SCHUMACHER.......................13
13. Damon HILL 7
14. Rubens BARRICHELLO.....................6
15. Alexander WURZ 4
16. Jarno TRULLI 3
17. Mika SALO......................................2
    Shinji NAKANO 2
19. Nicola LARINI 1

Constructors :

1. Williams / Renault.........................98
2. Ferrari...86
3. Benetton / Renault.........................53
4. McLaren / Mercedes.......................44
5. Jordan / Peugeot 33
6. Prost / Mugen Honda.....................20
7. Sauber / Petronas 15
8. Arrows / Yamaha 7
9. Stewart / Ford 6
10. Tyrrell / Ford...................................2

RACE SUMMARY

- Hakkinen leads at the start from Trulli and Villeneuve. Barrichello also passes the Canadian on the first lap.
- Hakkinen retires at the end of the first lap with a blown engine and Trulli leads.
- The Prost pulls away from Barrichello and Villeneuve. Behind them, Magnussen is slowing a pack of cars, including, Frentzen, Michael Schumacher, Coulthard and Hill.
- On lap 24 Villeneuve re-takes Barrichello and closes on Trulli.
- On lap 38, Trulli is the first to refuel. When Villeneuve does the same two laps later, he emerges in the lead.
- On lap 39, Irvine collides with Alesi, launching the Benetton into the air. The yellow flags come out. Michael Schumacher overtakes Frentzen at this point.
- Schumacher finds himself in the lead for two laps before pitting. He exits the pits in third place and sets off in pursuit of Trulli.
- On lap 49, Michael Schumacher comes in for a ten second stop-go penalty for having passed Frentzen under the yellow flags. He is now ninth.
- On lap 58, both Prosts retire a few seconds apart, with engine failure.
- Michael Schumacher manages to pass Damon Hill on the last lap to finish sixth. Villeneuve wins and makes up nine points on Schumacher in the championship.

WEEK-END GOSSIP

- **Wurz with Fisico**

Alexander Wurz and Giancarlo Fisichella will be team-mates at Benetton next season. A few days before the Austrian Grand Prix, a London court ruled in the custody battle over little Giancarlo, between Benetton and Jordan. It would be Mummy Benetton who would look after him in 1998.

- **The Bergers are coming**

Local hero Gerhard Berger had thousands of supporters at his home race. On Thursday, the Austrian radio station, ORF announced it was offering free travel from Vienna to Spielberg, as well as admission to the track to first listeners called Berger who rang in. The places were all filled in a matter of minutes and on Sunday, three coach loads of Bergers arrived to support their famous namesake.

- **Marques has lost too much weight**

On Saturday, several hours after the qualifying session, Tarso Marques was disqualified by the Austrian stewards. Scrutineering checks revealed his car was three kilos under the regulation minimum weight. It turned out it was the driver who had lost these three kilos.

Weighed at the beginning of the season, Tarso Marques had lost weight since then. This was enough to put the Minardi under the minimum weight. It is forbidden to go on a diet in F1.

Set out in the hills of Styria, in the heart of Austria, the Spielberg track had none of the charms of the old Osterreichring, which had hosted the grand prix up until 1987. At least the setting was as splendid as ever.

Canadian Kismet

On Michael Schumacher's home turf at the Nurburgring, Jacques Villeneuve only had to sit back and wait for things to go his way, before winning the grand prix as he pleased.
The road was left clear for the Canadian after both McLarens, which had seemed unbeatable on this track, retired.
With Michael Schumacher knocked out of the race by his brother at the first corner, Villeneuve found himself with a nine point lead with two rounds remaining...

GROSSER PREIS VON LUXEMBOURG
NÜRBURGRING

First pole position for the Finn. And a first pole position for Mercedes since the 1955 Italian Grand Prix

△
Olivier Panis was making his big comeback at the Nurburgring. On Saturday, he ended up in eleventh place on the grid. «The car was not too bad,» he explained. «I made some adjustments during the session to get more grip in the last chicane, but I was blocked by a Stewart on my last lap.»

Mika's first

One week earlier in Spielberg, Mika Hakkinen had lost out to Jacques Villeneuve in the fight for pole position by just 94 thousandths of a second. On the Nurburgring track, the Finnish driver got his revenge, as he beat the Canadian by 89 thousandths. This give him his first ever pole position at the 93rd attempt.
It was enough to make Mika Hakkinen more than happy. Not the most expansive of drivers, the Finn nevertheless managed a few smiles after pulling off this notable achievement. *«I have been fighting for this for ten years, trying to get to the number one position on the starting grid,»* he said. *«I hope this pole position will mark a new beginning to my career.»*
It was also the first pole position for the Mercedes engine, since the team had retired from Formula 1 in 1955, before coming back to the sport with the Sauber team in 1994.
On Saturday, the event was celebrated with an impromptu party under the Mercedes motorhome awning.
Glass of champagne in hand, Mario Ilien, the father of the Mercedes engine, was more than proud of his achievement, as was Norbert Haug, the three pointed star's motor sport boss of the German company.
«I think we deserve this pole position,» he said. *«After all, Mika has missed out on it three times already this season, by less than two tenths of a second.»*
The following day, Mika Hakkinen would celebrate his 29th birthday. He promised he would be trying to offer himself a race win as a present.

Olivier Panis back behind the wheel

Olivier Panis was still limping a tiny bit, but that apart, everything was going very well thank you. On Friday, 103 days after his accident in the Canadian Grand Prix, he was back in action in F1 again.
Calm, relaxed and in great shape, the Frenchman seemed as happy as a little boy with his first electric train set. *«Everything is fine,»* he reassured everyone. *«I am 100% recovered. The private testing I did last week proved that I have not lost my touch.»* At Magny-Cours, Olivier Panis had indeed run off 175 laps over four days, including a lap of 1m 13.9s., six tenths under Michael Schumacher's pole position time at the French Grand Prix! *«The first two weeks after the accident were not easy. But once the doctors told me I would make a full recovery, I knew this was only a hiccough in my career and I concentrated completely on my comeback.»*

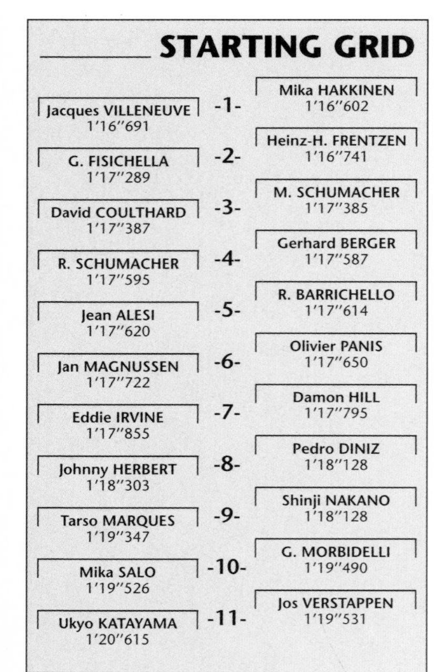

STARTING GRID

Jacques VILLENEUVE 1'16"691	-1-	Mika HAKKINEN 1'16"602
G. FISICHELLA 1'17"289	-2-	Heinz-H. FRENTZEN 1'16"741
David COULTHARD 1'17"387	-3-	M. SCHUMACHER 1'17"385
R. SCHUMACHER 1'17"595	-4-	Gerhard BERGER 1'17"587
Jean ALESI 1'17"620	-5-	R. BARRICHELLO 1'17"614
Jan MAGNUSSEN 1'17"722	-6-	Olivier PANIS 1'17"650
Eddie IRVINE 1'17"855	-7-	Damon HILL 1'17"795
Johnny HERBERT 1'18"303	-8-	Pedro DINIZ 1'18"128
Tarso MARQUES 1'19"347	-9-	Shinji NAKANO 1'18"128
Mika SALO 1'19"526	-10-	G. MORBIDELLI 1'19"490
Ukyo KATAYAMA 1'20"615	-11-	Jos VERSTAPPEN 1'19"531

▷
«Taste that Bernie!» On Saturday, Ferrari had made a little(?) cake to celebrate Michael Schumacher's 100th grand prix. As cocky as ever, the German took the opportunity to give Bernie Ecclestone the custard pie treatment, much to Jean Todt's amusement (right.) What a nerve!

◁
«Sorry Michael. I did not see you there.» Ralf Schumacher flies over the pack at the first corner and apart from putting himself out of the race, he also accounts for his elder brother, Giancarlo Fisichella and Ukyo Katayama. It was his biggest mistake of the season, to add to all his others.

Seventh win of the season for Jacques Villeneuve

Is God a French-Canadian?

It was Jacques Villeneuve's lucky day. He made a mess of his start and tangled with team-mate, Heinz-Harald Frentzen at the first corner. By some miracle, the Canadian's car was undamaged, while a second later, his championship rival, Michael Schumacher, was eliminated in a separate incident.
One could be forgiven for thinking that this was to be Villeneuve's last brush with Lady Luck for the day. Wrong.
As the race settled down, Villeneuve was in third place, powerless to challenge the two McLaren-Mercedes, when suddenly, he saw the track clear itself in front of his Williams when David Coulthard and Mika Hakkinen retired within moments of one another, on laps 42 and 43. If there was a motor racing God, He was French- Canadian that day. *«I could not have beaten the McLarens if they had kept going,»* admitted Villeneuve after the race. *«Both Mika and David made excellent starts. I don't know how they do that. We will have to look into it, so that we do not get caught out in future.»*
Thrust into the lead, Villeneuve found himself with a comfortable 40 seconds cushion over his pursuers, which in itself gave him a few headaches. *«Actually, this was the most difficult part of the race,»* he continued. *«At first I eased up, to look after the car. But when you do that there is a danger of going to sleep. The team told me I was starting to lose ground, so I decided to speed up again to maintain my concentration. I think the team might have preferred me to think more about the car.»*
Jacques Villeneuve was obviously delighted with his day, as from this point on, the championship was almost his. *«I always thought I could win this season, even when I was a long way back. But now, I am almost sure of it,»* he said with a big beaming smile.
The Canadian added that, in Japan in two weeks time, he felt he could maintain the upper hand over his rival. *«I love Suzuka circuit and I think the long corners will suit our car perfectly. What is more, all the psychological pressure is now on Michael's shoulders. I know I am going to be very calm.»*
With Jean Alesi second, Heinz-Harald Frentzen third and Gerhard Berger fourth, it had been a clean sweep for Renault. With only three grands prix remaining before it pulled out of the sport, the French constructor had proved it had not given up yet.
Jean Alesi blames his team
Tenth on the grid, Jean Alesi was not exactly hopeful before the off, but he somehow managed to finish second. *«I could not believe it. Before my second pit-stop I was eighth and when I got back on the track I was second. I do not understand how it happened!»* In fact, it was his bad start that saved him. *«Yes I made a very average start, but it meant I was able to avoid the first corner accident!*
This result has come at just the right time to shake the team up a bit. People tend to think the championship is already over and they are going to sleep.»

Heinz-Harald gets his wires crossed

At the Nurburgring, Heinz-Harald Frentzen finished on the third step of the podium, for the fourth time in a row.
Throughout the final stages of the race, the German tried to pass Jean Alesi's Benetton, but to no avail.
No doubt he could have finished ahead, if not for a mistake at the first corner. *«Jacques and I touched at the end of the straight,»* he recounted. *«It was nothing serious. But in the heat of the moment, I hit the cut-out switch and the engine died. It took me a few seconds to work out why. I switched it on again and it fired up, but I lost a lot of places.»*
Indeed he did, as he came round in 13th place at the end of the first lap. *«I was disheartened but I knuckled down to it and set off in pursuit.»*

Just as in Austria, both Williams drivers made it to the podium.
◁▽

«I don't think I am going to get very far.» «Fisico's» front suspension is well modified after the first corner accident.
▽

Schumacher versus Schumacher

It took barely 400 metres for the race to turn into a disaster for the Schumacher family. Having made what he described as the best start of his career, Ralf found himself sandwiched between his team-mate and his brother Michael. As three into two does not go, the ensuing accident was inevitable. Ralf's Jordan flew over Michael's Ferrari, breaking its front right suspension. *«I suppose we should be happy no one was hurt,»* commented Ralf, *«But I am very unhappy for myself and for my brother.»*
The accident saw all three drivers retire. *«My suspension was bent and there was nothing I could do. It was nobody's fault. It was a racing accident,»* said a philosophical Michael Schumacher. However, one wonders what the atmosphere was like during Sunday night's family dinner.
Michael stayed at the track to the end, to see Villeneuve take victory. "I think there is not much chance for the championship now," he concluded.

IN THE POINTS

1.	Jacques VILLENEUVE	Rothmans Williams Renault	1 h 31'27"843
2.	Jean ALESI	Mild Seven Benetton Renault	at 11"770
3.	Heinz-H. FRENTZEN	Rothmans Williams Renault	at 13"480
4.	Gerhard BERGER	Mild Seven Benetton Renault	at 16"416
5.	Pedro DINIZ	Danka Arrows Yamaha	at 43"147
6.	Olivier PANIS	Prost Gauloises Blondes	at 43"750

Fastest lap : H.-H. FRENTZEN., lap 32, 1'18"805, avg. 208.128 km/h

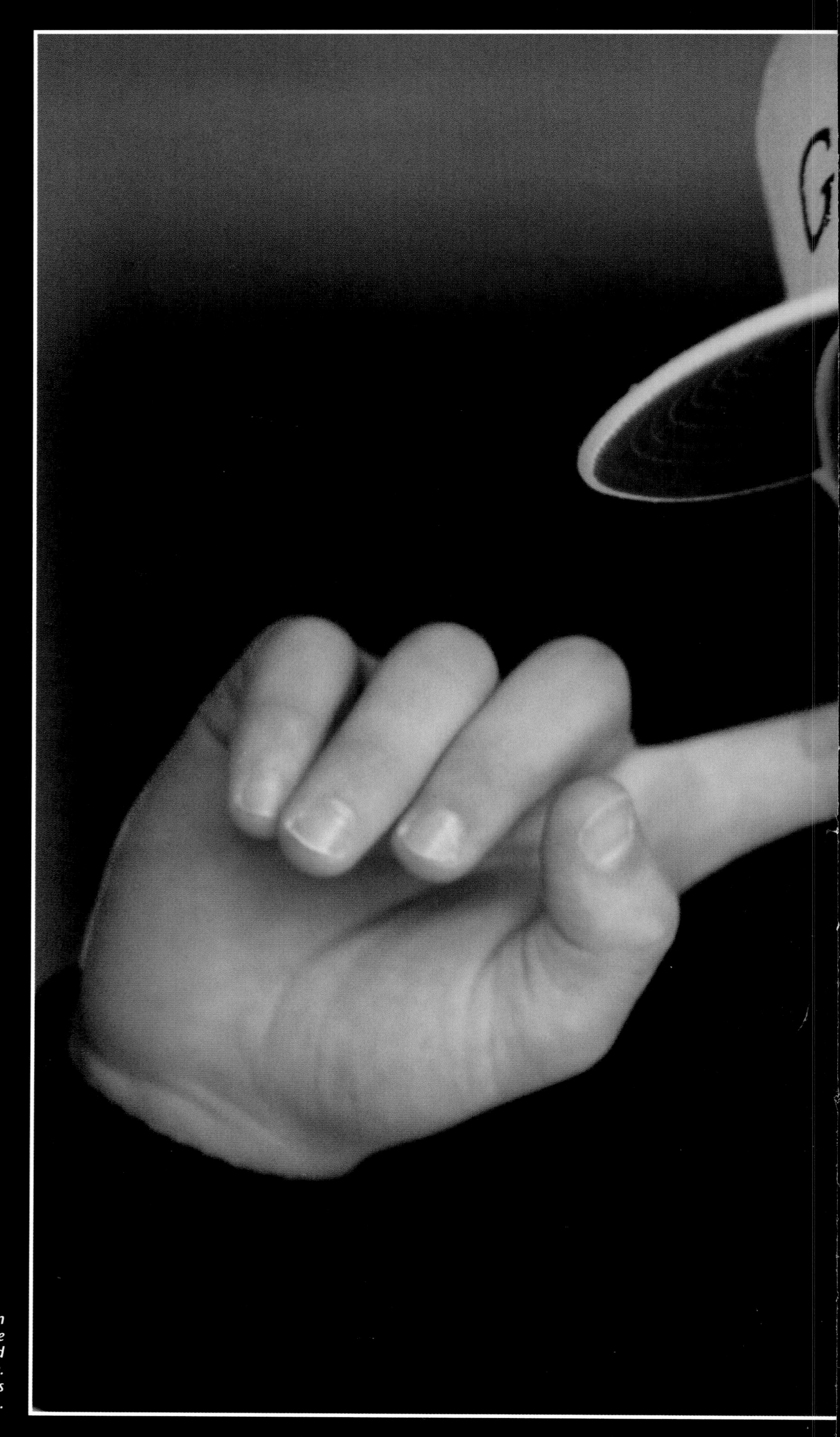

Ralf Schumacher ended his Nurburgring race with his tail between his legs. His carelessness had caused his brother's retirement on the very first corner of the Luxembourg Grand Prix. At the time, he did not know it had also cost him the world title.
In order not to listen to further criticism, all he could do was block his ears up.

NTHER

Mika Hakkinen and David Coulthard led the race comfortably, until forced to retire when their Mercedes engines broke.

Mystery surrounds McLaren

With the Luxembourg Grand Prix taking place on German soil, Mercedes were hoping to put on a good show.
Everything went well for the three pointed star in practice with Mika Hakkinen managing to get pole position. Then, in the race, both Anglo-German cars looked as though they were heading for an easy win, until they were both forced to retire with blown engines.
Had they decided to play to the crowd, pushing their engines beyond the limit? It was impossible to find out. Once the chequered flag had fallen, the Mercedes motorhome was deserted. The company bigwigs had fled the nest. Mercedes boss Norbert Haug had apologised to his drivers via the team's press release, adding that: *«The problem will be solved very soon.»*
Jacques Villeneuve, who had run third behind them for a long time, was still confused. *«We had guessed correctly that McLaren would get away in front and would only make one pit-stop. We therefore decided to stop twice, so that we would not get stuck behind them. What surprises me is that, with this strategy, they should have taken on more fuel and their pit-stops should have been longer than ours. I cannot understand why it turned out the other way round.»*
While Williams took 8.8 seconds to send the Canadian on his way, Coulthard's pit stop took less than five seconds and Hakkinen's was completed in under seven. What Villeneuve was hinting at was, that in order to refuel so quickly, there must have been some «slight» modification to the refuelling system and therefore some «slight» bending of the rules.
This would be surprising from a team as serious and irreproachable as McLaren. Unless the team was convinced its cars would not make it to the finish and they therefore did not put in sufficient fuel.

Williams has solved its problems

At the start of the season, the Williams-Renault was so dominant that its designers seemed to have gone to sleep. Convinced of the superiority of the FW19, they concentrated on the FW20 from March onwards.
It was a big mistake, as by July, the Ferraris had caught up with the Williams in terms of performance. Patrick Head confirmed this at the Nurburgring. *«Heinz- Harald* (Frentzen) *had told us there was a structural problem right from the start of the season,»* he explained. *«But as Jacques had no complaints and Heinz was a new boy, we put these remarks down to his difficulty in adapting to the team. And we did nothing about it. It was only at Hockenheim that our telemetry data confirmed there was indeed a problem with the chassis.»*
This discovery had the effect of a good kick up the backside.
Putting its 1998 challenger to one side for the moment, the Williams task force set about correcting the fault. As Jacques Villeneuve's wins in the last two grands prix proved, the mission had been successful. *«We have not really solved our problem,»* claimed Patrick Head nevertheless. *«But let us say that we have done a lot of work and managed to identify and limit the damage.»*
The task was made that much harder by the fact their chief aerodynamicist, Adrian Newey, had left for McLaren before the start of the season. *«We have some new staff,»* admitted Head. *«It has taken them some time to get in the swing of things. But everything is sorted now. We still have a few new developments in the pipeline and then we will concentrate on our 1998 programme again, as we have slipped behind with it.»*

Dave Richard's dream becomes reality

For the past few years, the Benetton team has been one of the brightest stars in the paddock. Between 1994 and 1995, with a little help from Michael Schumacher, the team won 19 races and took three world titles. Team boss Flavio Briatore was the king of the paddock.
Since then, the situation has changed drastically. The team's two technical directors - Rory Byrne and Ross Brawn - left for Ferrari and the atmosphere at the heart of the team has deteriorated. One victory is all the team has to show for two years of effort. Discouraged by all of this, Briatore decided to throw in the towel, according to rumour, with a little prompting from the Benetton family.
The effect of this decision was not long in coming, when David Richards was crowned as his successor at the Luxembourg Grand Prix. *«When I got up this morning and put my Benetton team kit on for the first time, I felt like a little boy on his first day at a new school,»* declared the Englishman at an impromptu press conference at the team motorhome. *«Alessandro Benetton has given me full powers, but I do not plan to come in and change everything immediately,»* he continued. *«In any case, I do not have any short term objectives and I am delighted to be working with two young drivers next season (Alexander Wurz and Giancarlo Fisichella) but my objectives are fixed more on the year 2000 and beyond.»*
Trained as an accountant, David Richards has been involved in the world of rallying for 20 years. He will continue to run his company, Prodrive, while running the Benetton team. *«This dual role will not pose a problem,»* he assured everyone. *«I will just have to delegate. I have always wanted to be involved in Formula 1. It is the dream of everyone who works in motor sport. At one time, I thought about setting up my own team, or of buying an existing one. But it would have been impossible to contemplate winning for at least two or three years. So, when Alessandro Benetton offered me this job, I accepted immediately. Now I have come in with a top team and today is the realisation of a dream.»*

David Richards started his new job on Sunday night at the Luxembourg Grand Prix. At the Nurburgring, he had simply been an observer.

The Stewarts performed brilliantly at the Nurburgring in the early part of the race. Just as at Spielberg, one week earlier, they suffered from a lack of reliability.

«My dear Ralf, all Germany is behind you. But mind you do not get in the way of your brother Michael.» Chancellor Helmut Kohl gives Ralf Schumacher some advice on the grid.

PRACTICE TIMES

No	Driver	Make/Engine/Chassis	Practice Friday	Practice Saturday	Qualifying	Warm-up
1.	Damon Hill	Arrows/Yamaha/A18/5 (B)	1'19"091	1'18"180	1'17"795	1'20"051
2.	Pedro Diniz	Arrows/Yamaha/A18/4 (B)	1'19"750	1'18"788	1'18"128	1'20"558
3.	Jacques Villeneuve	Williams/Renault/FW19/4 (G)	1'19"640	1'17"395	1'16"691	1'19"548
4.	Heinz-Harald Frentzen	Williams/Renault/FW19/5 (G)	1'18"926	1'17"158	1'16"741	1'19"493
5.	Michael Schumacher	Ferrari/Ferrari/F310B/178 (G)	1'18"954	1'17"567	1'17"385	1'19"512
6.	Eddie Irvine	Ferrari/Ferrari/F310B/180 (G)	1'19"708	1'19"139	1'17"855	1'20"011
7.	Jean Alesi	Benetton/Renault/B197/2 (G)	1'18"794	1'18"233	1'17"620	1'19"918
8.	Gerhard Berger	Benetton/Renault/B197/4 (G)	1'18"434	1'17"778	1'17"587	1'20"121
9.	Mika Hakkinen	McLaren/Mercedes/MP4/12/3 (G)	1'17"998	1'17"220	1'16"602	1'17"959
10.	David Coulthard	McLaren/Mercedes/MP4/12/6 (G)	1'18"912	1'17"884	1'17"387	1'19"088
11.	Ralf Schumacher	Jordan/Peugeot/197/6 (G)	1'18"713	1'17"948	1'17"595	1'19"569
12.	Giancarlo Fisichella	Jordan/Peugeot/197/4 (G)	1'19"034	1'17"390	1'17"289	1'19"490
14.	Olivier Panis	Prost/Mugen Honda/JS45/3 (B)	1'19"412	1'18"106	1'17"650	1'19"970
15.	Shinji Nakano	Prost/Mugen Honda/JS45/2 (B)	1'20"073	1'19"031	1'18"699	1'28"017
16.	Johnny Herbert	Sauber/Petronas/C16/7 (G)	1'20"373	1'17"953	1'18"303	1'19"754
17.	Giancarlo Morbidelli	Sauber/Petronas/C16/6 (G)	1'21"387	1'20"256	1'19"490	1'20"291
18.	Jos Verstappen	Tyrrell/Ford/025/4 (G)	1'20"947	1'20"064	1'19"531	1'21"695
19.	Mika Salo	Tyrrell/Ford/025/5 (G)	1'21"118	1'19"490	1'19"526	1'21"391
20.	Ukyo Katayama	Minardi/Hart/M197/4 (B)	1'38"344	1'19"883	1'20"615	1'21"251
21.	Tarso Marquès	Minardi/Hart/M197/2 (B)	1'21"424	1'19"609	1'19"347	1'21"477
22.	Rubens Barrichello	Stewart/Ford/SF1/2 (B)	1'18"339	1'17"778	1'17"614	1'20"377
23.	Jan Magnussen	Stewart/Ford/SF1/3 (B)	1'20"592	1'18"167	1'17"722	1'20"463

LAP CHART

position :	1	2	3	4	5	6	7	8	9	10	11	12	13	14	15	16	17	18	19	20	21	22
départ :	9	3	4	12	5	10	8	11	22	7	14	23	1	6	2	16	15	21	17	19	18	20
1	9	10	3	22	7	23	1	2	16	5	14	6	4	21	8	15	19	18	17	20		
2	9	10	3	22	7	23	1	2	16	14	6	4	8	15	5	19	17	18				
3	9	10	3	22	7	23	1	2	16	14	6	4	8	15	19	17	18					
4	9	10	3	22	7	23	1	2	16	14	6	4	8	15	19	17	18					
5	9	10	3	22	7	23	1	2	16	14	6	4	8	15	19	17	18					
6	9	10	3	22	7	23	1	2	16	14	6	4	8	15	19	17	18					
7	9	10	3	22	7	23	1	2	16	14	6	4	8	15	19	17	18					
8	9	10	3	22	7	23	1	2	16	14	8	4	6	15	19	17	18					
9	9	10	3	22	7	23	1	2	16	14	8	4	6	15	19	17	18					
10	9	10	3	22	7	23	1	2	16	8	4	14	6	15	19	17	18					
11	9	10	3	22	7	23	1	2	16	8	4	14	6	15	19	17	18					
12	9	10	3	22	7	23	1	2	16	8	4	14	6	15	17	19	18					
13	9	10	3	22	7	23	1	2	16	8	4	14	6	15	17	19	18					
14	9	10	3	22	7	23	1	2	16	8	4	14	6	15	17	19	18					
15	9	10	3	22	7	23	1	2	16	8	4	14	6	15	17	19	18					
16	9	10	3	22	7	23	1	2	8	4	16	14	6	15	17	19	18					
17	9	10	3	22	7	23	1	8	2	4	14	6	17	19	18	16						
18	9	10	3	22	7	23	1	8	2	4	14	6	17	19	18	16						
19	9	10	3	22	7	23	1	8	2	4	14	6	17	19	18	16						
20	9	10	3	22	7	23	1	8	2	4	14	6	17	19	18	16						
21	9	10	3	22	23	1	8	4	2	14	6	7	17	19	18	16						
22	9	10	3	22	23	1	4	2	14	6	7	17	8	19	18	16						
23	9	10	3	22	23	1	4	2	14	7	17	8	18	16	19							
24	9	10	3	22	23	1	4	2	14	7	8	18	16	17	19							
25	9	10	3	22	23	1	4	2	7	14	8	16	17	19	18							
26	9	10	3	22	23	1	4	2	7	14	8	16	17	19	18							
27	9	10	3	22	23	1	4	2	7	14	8	16	17	19	18							
28	9	10	3	22	23	1	4	2	7	14	8	16	17	19	18							
29	10	9	3	22	23	1	4	2	7	14	8	16	17	19	18							
30	10	9	3	22	23	1	4	2	7	14	8	16	17	19	18							
31	10	9	3	22	23	1	2	7	14	8	4	16	17	19	18							
32	9	10	3	22	23	1	2	7	14	8	4	16	17	19	18							
33	9	10	3	22	23	1	2	7	14	8	4	16	17	19	18							
34	9	10	3	22	23	1	2	7	14	8	4	16	17	19	18							
35	9	10	3	22	23	1	2	7	14	8	4	16	17	19	18							
36	9	10	3	22	23	1	2	7	14	8	4	16	17	19	18							
37	9	10	3	22	23	2	7	14	8	4	16	17	1	19	18							
38	9	10	3	23	22	2	7	14	8	4	16	17	1	19	18							
39	9	10	3	22	23	7	14	2	8	4	16	17	1	19	18							
40	9	10	3	22	7	8	4	14	16	2	17	1	19	23	18							
41	9	10	3	22	7	8	4	16	2	14	1	19	17	18								
42	9	10	3	22	7	8	4	16	2	14	1	19	17	18								
43	9	3	22	7	8	4	2	14	16	1	17	19	18									
44	3	7	8	4	2	14	16	1	17	19	18											
45	3	4	8	7	2	14	16	1	17	19	18											
46	3	4	7	8	2	14	16	1	17	19	18											
47	3	4	7	8	2	14	16	1	17	19	18											
48	3	7	4	8	2	14	16	1	17	19	18											
49	3	7	4	8	2	14	16	1	17	19	18											
50	3	7	4	8	2	14	16	1	17	19	18											
51	3	7	4	8	2	14	16	1	17	19												
52	3	7	4	8	2	14	16	1	17	19												
53	3	7	4	8	2	14	16	1	17	19												
54	3	7	4	8	2	14	16	1	17	19												
55	3	7	4	8	2	14	16	1	17	19												
56	3	7	4	8	2	14	16	1	17	19												
57	3	7	4	8	2	14	16	1	17	19												
58	3	7	4	8	2	14	16	1	17	19												
59	3	7	4	8	2	14	16	1	17	19												
60	3	7	4	8	2	14	16	1	17	19												
61	3	7	4	8	2	14	16	1	17	19												
62	3	7	4	8	2	14	16	1	17	19												
63	3	7	4	8	2	14	16	1	17	19												
64	3	7	4	8	2	14	16	1	17	19												
65	3	7	4	8	2	14	16	1	17	19												
66	3	7	4	8	2	14	16	1	17	19												
67	3	7	4	8	2	14	16	1														

Best result for a Bridgestone shod runner:

Pedro Diniz, Arrows-Yamaha, *5th*

CLASSIFICATION & RETIREMENTS

Pos	Driver	Team	Time
1.	Villeneuve	Williams Renault	in 1h31'27"843
2.	Alesi	Benetton Renault	at 11"770
3.	Frentzen	Williams Renault	at 13"480
4.	Berger	Benetton Renault	at 16"416
5.	Diniz	Arrows Yamaha	at 43"147
6.	Panis	Prost Mugen Honda	at 43"593
7.	Herbert	Sauber Petronas	at 44"354
8.	Hill	Arrows Yamaha	at 44"777
9.	Morbidelli	Sauber Petronas	at 1 tour
10	Salo	Tyrrell Ford	at 1 tour

Lap	Driver	Team	Reason
1	Fisichella	Jordan Peugeot	accident
1	Schumacher	Jordan Peugeot	accident
2	Katayama	Minardi Hart	accident
2	Marquès	Minardi Hart	electric failure
3	Schumacher	Ferrari	accident
17	Nakano	Prost Mugen Honda	engine
23	Irvine	Ferrari	electric failure
41	Magnussen	Stewart Ford	transmission
43	Coulthard	McLaren Mercedes	engine
44	Barrichello	Stewart Ford	hydraul. pressure
44	Hakkinen	McLaren Mercedes	engine
51	Verstappen	Tyrrell Ford	transmission

FASTEST LAPS

	Driver	Time	Lap
1.	Frentzen	1'18"805	32
2.	Hakkinen	1'19"576	27
3.	Alesi	1'19"716	65
4.	Villeneuve	1'19"838	31
5.	Coulthard	1'19"920	23
6.	Berger	1'19"996	61
7.	Hill	1'20"407	64
8.	Herbert	1'20"518	33
9.	Barrichello	1'20"737	25
10.	Morbidelli	1'20"865	31
11.	Panis	1'21"086	29
12.	Diniz	1'21"262	25
13.	Magnussen	1'21"448	32
14.	Irvine	1'21"793	13
15.	Nakano	1'21"969	14
16.	Salo	1'21"996	26
17.	Verstappen	1'22"455	30

FIFTEENTH ROUND

GRAND PRIX DU LUXEMBOURG, NÜRBURGRING

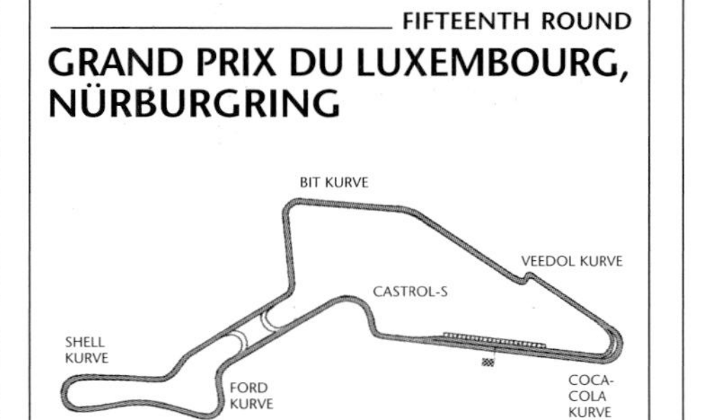

Date : September 28, 1997
Length: 4555 meters
Distance : 67 laps, 305.235 km
Weather : sunny, 20 degrees

CHAMPIONSHIPS

(after fifteen rounds)

Drivers :

1. Jacques VILLENEUVE 77
2. Michael SCHUMACHER 68
3. Heinz-Harald FRENTZEN 35
4. Jean ALESI 34
5. David COULTHARD 30
6. Gerhard BERGER 24
7. Giancarlo FISICHELLA 20
8. Eddie IRVINE 18
9. Olivier PANIS 16
10. Mika HAKKINEN 14
    Johnny HERBERT 14
12. Ralf SCHUMACHER 13
13. Damon HILL 7
14. Rubens BARRICHELLO 6
15. Alexander WURZ 4
16. Jarno TRULLI 3
17. Mika SALO 2
    Pedro DINIZ 2
    Shinji NAKANO 2
20. Nicola LARINI 1

Constructors :

1. Williams / Renault 112
2. Ferrari 86
3. Benetton / Renault 62
4. McLaren / Mercedes 44
5. Jordan / Peugeot 33
6. Prost / Mugen Honda 21
7. Sauber / Petronas 15
8. Arrows / Yamaha 9
9. Stewart / Ford 6
10. Tyrrell / Ford 2

RACE SUMMARY

- At the start, Hakkinen maintains his pole position advantage, while Coulthard makes an excellent start to move into second place.
- Villeneuve and Frentzen touch at the first corner, without any damage being done. Behind them, a serious crash eliminates both Jordans and Michael Schumacher.
- Frentzen comes round in 13th place at the end of the first lap and starts to climb through the field.
- Hakkinen quickly pulls out a big lead at the front, ahead of the Coulthard-Villeneuve tandem.
- Behind these three, Barrichello is fourth and Alesi fifth. The Frenchman started from tenth on the grid and had made the most of the confusion at the first corner.
- The Williams have decided on a two stop strategy, while McLaren would stop only once.
- Coulthard and Hakkinen retire one after the other on the pit straight, just two minutes apart.
- Villeneuve thus inherits the lead and simply has to cruise to the flag.
- Alesi finishes second, just ahead of Frentzen and Berger. Panis is still stuck behind Diniz and finishes sixth.

WEEK-END GOSSIP

• Villeneuve and Frentzen confirmed

On the Monday after the Luxembourg Grand Prix, Williams confirmed that both its drivers, Jacques Villeneuve and Heinz-Harald Frentzen, would be staying with the team in 1998.
However, it was not impossible for the Canadian to leave the team at the end of the season, as there was a clause in his contract stating he was entitled to leave Williams if he won the world championship.

• Cosmetic modifications

On Saturday afternoon, Bernie Ecclestone, FIA President Max Mosley and all the team owners met to discuss the 1998 sporting regulations, the technical ones having been established a long time ago.
While there had been much talk of major changes, including a possible return to Friday qualifying, all that came out of the meeting were a few minor cosmetic details. Most notably, the fact that Friday practice would start at 10h30 instead of 11h00. It took over three hours for F1's finest to reach this decision!

• Dudot to Prost

On Tuesday, the Prost team announced that Bernard Dudot would be joining them as technical director as from 1st November.
Before concentrating exclusively on engines, the Frenchman had been a chassis engineer for Renault and thus brought the benefits of a global overview to the team.

▽ *The old Nurburg castle still majestically dominates the area. The Eifel region has a lot of charm, but for its cold weather.*

Villeneuve in the eye of the hurricane

At Suzuka, it was Michael who was laughing and Jacques who was crying. Excluded from the race for ignoring the yellow flags when he was already running under a suspended ban, the Canadian tried his best to prevent a Michael Schumacher victory. However, ably seconded by his team-mate Eddie Irvine, the German took ten points off his championship rival. Ferrari had bet everything on this race and had won the lot. The final round of the season was shaping up to be very exciting.

FUJI TELEVISION JAPANESE GRAND PRIX SUZUKA

A pig of a day

High drama in Suzuka: after qualifying in pole position, Jacques Villeneuve was excluded from the Japanese Grand Prix, before being reinstated under appeal.
The day had actually started well for Jacques Villeneuve. At the end of the session, the Canadian had claimed his ninth pole position of the season, just ahead of Michael Schumacher. It looked like being a thrilling race between the two world championship contenders.
However, a few hours later, the prospect of this confrontation evaporated when the Stewards at Suzuka decided to disqualify Villeneuve. Timetable of a disastrous day for the Canadian:
9h30: In the morning's free practice session, Jos Verstappen parked his Tyrrell in the grass with a fuel pick-up problem. Although the Dutchman had left his car a long way off the track, the Japanese marshals were waving yellow flags. Of the nine cars who went past these, only three slowed down, but Villeneuve set his best time of the session. Knowing that he is under a one race ban for a similar offence, this mistake was about to cost him dear. The rule regarding yellow flags is abundantly clear. «Waved yellow flag: slow down.»
14h15: After qualifying, the Canadian mentioned the incident. *«I clearly saw the yellow flags. If they had been waved in a corner, I would have slowed down. But on a straight it was not necessary.»*
15h00: Villeneuve is summoned to the Stewards for not slowing down, along with Michael Schumacher, Johnny Herbert, Ukyo Katayama, Rubens Barrichello and Heinz-Harald Frentzen.
17h50: After long deliberation, the decision is announced. Jacques Villeneuve is excluded from the Japanese Grand Prix. The Williams team has one hour to appeal against the decision. The other five drivers are all hit with a suspended one race ban.
18h30: The Williams team announces it wishes to appeal.
19h10: The Stewards announce that Villeneuve will be able to race under appeal.
19h15: Surrounded by dozens of journalists Villeneuve appears from the hut that serves as the Williams office. *«What has happened to me today is very difficult to accept,»* he says simply. *«I would state that six of the nine cars on the track at that time, committed the same offence, which leads us to think that there are good reasons to appeal. I will fight to the end, but this championship is by far the hardest one I have ever competed in.»*
The curtain falls. The final act should have taken place at the FIA Appeal Tribunal, which was due to meet the following week.
A few days later, Max Mosley was in Munich. During a conference he gave there, he advised the Williams team to withdraw its appeal so as not to risk seeing the race ban doubled. Williams took the advice...

◁ *Confronted by the media, Villeneuve does a good job of hiding his true feelings after his disqualification.*

▽ *Ukyo Katayama announced in Suzuka that he was going to retire. It was a hard blow for all his fans.*

STARTING GRID

	Pos.	
		Jacques VILLENEUVE 1'36"071
M. SCHUMACHER 1'36"133	-1-	
		Eddie IRVINE 1'36"466
Mika HAKKINEN 1'36"469	-2-	
		Gerhard BERGER 1'36"561
Heinz-H. FRENTZEN 1'36"628	-3-	
		Jean ALESI 1'36"682
Johnny HERBERT 1'36"906	-4-	
		Giancarlo FISICHELLA 1'36"917
Olivier PANIS 1'37"073	-5-	
		David COULTHARD 1'37"095
R. BARRICHELLO 1'37"343	-6-	
		R. SCHUMACHER 1'37"443
Jan MAGNUSSEN 1'37"480	-7-	
		Shinji NAKANO 1'37"588
Pedro DINIZ 1'37"853	-8-	
		Damon HILL 1'38"022
Gianni MORBIDELLI 1'38"556	-9-	
		Ukyo KATAYAMA 1'38"983
Tarso MARQUES 1'39"678	-10-	
		Jos VERSTAPPEN 1'40"259
Mika SALO 1'40"529	-11-	

Ferrari plays its final card

Before Suzuka, nine points down on Villeneuve with two rounds to go, at the wheel of a Ferrari that seemed inferior to the Williams, Michael Schumacher's situation seemed delicate, not to say desperate. All Villeneuve had to do to win the title in Japan was score one more point than his rival.
In these circumstances, the Scuderia decided to play its Joker. It arrived with its F 310 B sporting a revolutionary new electronic throttle - claimed to be an «anti- wheelspin» device, along with a lightweight front wing which flexed nearer the ground under aerodynamic forces, which had only just been tested at Fiorano, the week before.
Now they had to sit back and hope these changes made the difference. *«As long as I have a chance of winning the title, I will cling to it,»* said Schumacher. *«There is nothing to lose now. If it works, all well and good. If it breaks, that's just bad luck. I rate my chances at about 30%.»*

A tactical victory

Michael Schumacher takes his helmet off and falls into the arms of Jean Todt. The victory which had just fallen to the German could not have come at a better time. *«I have to say, it has been a very long time since I can remember having such a fantastic day,»* said the Ferrari driver, congratulating himself. *«Because it is not only a grand prix I have won, but also a ticket to the championship.»* It's fantastic.

The victory came after what was certainly not an easy day at the office. In the early stages, Michael Schumacher was held up by Jacques Villeneuve. The start was particularly heart stopping with the Canadian zig-zagging in front of the German. *«I don't think Jacques tried anything dangerous. I hoped he would be professional enough not to try anything stupid. But as he knew he would not be allowed to keep any points today, his only tactic was to hold me up and hope that others would take the opportunity to pass me. So it was not a surprise and it did not work. Jacques did brake a bit early sometimes going into the corners and we touched two or three times.»*

Not wanting to take the slightest risk, Schumacher preferred to wait for the pit-stops to mount his attack and indeed he took the lead when his rival pitted, re-joining just behind him. *«Jacques tried a very dangerous move there, »* added Schumacher. *«There is a sort of agreement between the drivers that anyone coming out of the pits must stay on their line. But Jacques cut right across in front of me and we could have had a very serious accident, given the difference in speeds at that point. It was not really necessary from someone who is fighting for the world championship.»*

Ferrari then called on Eddie Irvine to help his team leader and the Irishman duly slowed down the Canadian, who lost even more time at his second pit-stop with a fuel problem.

Out in front, Schumacher did not have a moment's rest. After the second series of pit-stops, Heinz-Harald Frentzen began to give chase and finished just one second behind the Ferrari. But it was all in vain and the craziest race of the season ended in total triumph for the Scuderia.

Irvine was waiting for the «phone call from the boss»

Eddie Irvine was third and explained he had to modify his strategy during the grand prix. *«When we saw that Villeneuve was holding us up, we changed tactics and I decided to overtake everyone. Jacques tried to close the door on me, but I managed to get past on the outside. From then on, I only had to sit and wait for the instructions from the team. We had discussed it before the race and I agreed to do all I could to help Michael. When I took the lead, I just had to wait for the phone call from the team. When it came, I did as I was told, that's all.»* A model team player, when one considers he thus sacrificed his first grand prix win.

Frentzen is powerless to help

When the time came that Villeneuve would have liked to count on his support, in the same way that Schumacher was able to count on Irvine, Heinz-Harald Frentzen did not succeed in his mission, which was to take a few precious points away from his fellow countryman. *«Of course I would have liked to take these four points off Michael, but it did not work. I had a very solitary race.»*

Champagne! In winning at Suzuka, Ferrari had chosen just the right moment to come out on top.

The lights go out. Jacques Villeneuve finishes his swerving manoeuvre and pulls across Michael Schumacher.

▽

IN THE POINTS

	Driver	Team	Time
1.	M. SCHUMACHER	Scuderia Ferrari Marlboro	1 h 29'48"446
2.	Heinz-H. FRENTZEN	Rothmans Williams Renault	at 1"378
3.	Eddie IRVINE	Scuderia Ferrari Marlboro	at 26"384
4.	Mika HAKKINEN	West McLaren Mercedes	at 27"129
5.	Jacques VILLENEUVE	Rothmans Williams Renault	at 39"776
6.	Jean ALESI	Mild Seven Benetton Renault	at 40"403

Fastest lap : H.-H. FRENTZEN, lap 48, 1'38"942, avg. 213.361 km/h

Jacques Villeneuve in the eye of the hurricane. Suzuka was a black weekend for the Canadian, who had turned a nine point advantage into a one point deficit behind Michael Schumacher.

▷ Frank Williams follows Michael Schumacher's race on his TV monitors.

Frank Williams makes history

Frank Williams did not have a completely wasted Japanese weekend. Jacques Villeneuve had lost his lead over Michael Schumacher in the Drivers' Championship, but the team had still won the Constructors' World Championship. It might be something of an honorary title, which does not really interest the fans, but it does give team owners more bargaining power when it comes to negotiating bigger budgets with sponsors. This could be why the canny Mr. Williams rates it above the drivers' title.
The Williams team now had 120 points to Ferrari's 100 and with one race to go, the gap could not be made up.
The British team thus picked up its ninth title, an outright record in the history of Formula 1. This performance is all the more remarkable as Williams did not win its first championship until 1980. Nine titles in 18 years is an extraordinary feat.

Suzuka atmosphere - The Japanese circuit is considered to be the most beautiful on the calendar, after Spa. ▽

Ferrari now seems to have the upper hand

Second place for Heinz-Harald Frentzen, 1.3 seconds down on Michael Schumacher. This result handed Williams the Constructors' title, but did not really help Villeneuve much in his fight for the crown. ▷ ▽

David Richards and Mika Hakkinen. Apparently the newest boss in the pit-lane seems to be enjoying Formula 1, although it certainly is not the performance of his cars which makes him so happy. ▽

When he arrived in the Suzuka paddock on Thursday, Michael Schumacher only gave himself a 30% chance of winning the championship. His car could not match the pace of the Williams and making up the nine points on Villeneuve seemed like a tall order.
Then came the Canadian's black Saturday. Disqualified from the grand prix, he had broken the thread of victory which should have led him inexorably to the world title. Out of sorts in Suzuka, he then tried to trip up the triumphal march of the Ferraris. It was in pure vain.
With a one point lead over Villeneuve, Michael Schumacher now seemed perfectly placed to walk off with his third world title.
While the Canadian would arrive in Jerez under an angry cloud after his Japanese disqualification, Michael Schumacher would turn up in his usual relaxed mood. In Suzuka, the German had proved his Ferrari was a match for the Williams and this new found competitiveness had come at exactly the right moment to cause the Canadian still further worry.
In Japan, the good fortune that had abandoned him in the previous two races had returned to offer Schumacher its support.
The spiral of success was now turning in his favour. On Sunday night, he reckoned his chances of taking the title had gone up to 50%, which was something of a conservative estimate.

«Villeneuve held us up a lot today»

Jean Todt is not what you could call one of the fun people of Formula 1. The serious expression Ferrari's sporting director maintains at all times only makes way for a smile when something wonderful occurs.
The race in Suzuka was one of those moments. All smiles, he was more than willing to give his comments on what was one of his greatest triumphs. *«Naturally I am very happy. We have proved today that we are on the right road.»*
However, when asked if he would not have preferred a less political win, in other words, without the exclusion of Jacques Villeneuve, Jean Todt's demeanour changed back to its more usual self.
«Villeneuve held us up a lot today. But I have little to say about him. All I know is that we have one more grand prix in two weeks time. I hope it will be a good race and that it will produce a worthy champion.»

PRACTICE TIMES

No	Driver	Make/Engine/Chassis	Practice Friday	Practice Saturday	Qualifying	Warm-up
1.	Damon Hill	Arrows/Yamaha/A18/5 (B)	1'39"898	1'38"514	1'38"022	1'40"227
2.	Pedro Diniz	Arrows/Yamaha/A18/4 (B)	1'42"893	1'39"702	1'37"853	1'40"576
3.	Jacques Villeneuve	Williams/Renault/FW19/4 (G)	1'40"616	1'37"758	1'36"071	1'40"061
4.	Heinz-Harald Frentzen	Williams/Renault/FW19/5 (G)	1'39"398	1'37"755	1'36"628	1'39"084
5.	Michael Schumacher	Ferrari/Ferrari/F310B/178 (G)	1'40"460	1'38"403	1'36"133	1'39"163
6.	Eddie Irvine	Ferrari/Ferrari/F310B/180 (G)	1'38"903	1'38"910	1'36"466	1'39"233
7.	Jean Alesi	Benetton/Renault/B197/2 (G)	1'39"454	1'37"905	1'36"682	1'44"098
8.	Gerhard Berger	Benetton/Renault/B197/4 (G)	1'40"422	1'38"147	1'36"561	1'40"685
9.	Mika Hakkinen	McLaren/Mercedes/MP4/12/4 (G)	1'40"724	1'37"481	1'36"469	1'38"113
10.	David Coulthard	McLaren/Mercedes/MP4/12/6 (G)	1'39"945	1'39"537	1'37"095	1'39"784
11.	Ralf Schumacher	Jordan/Peugeot/197/6 (G)	1'38"911	1'37"372	1'37"443	1'38"547
12.	Giancarlo Fisichella	Jordan/Peugeot/197/5 (G)	1'40"720	1'37"649	1'36"917	1'40"312
14.	Olivier Panis	Prost/Mugen Honda/JS45/3 (B)	1'38"941	1'38"816	1'37"073	1'39"370
15.	Shinji Nakano	Prost/Mugen Honda/JS45/2 (B)	1'40"653	1'38"343	1'37"588	1'39"553
16.	Johnny Herbert	Sauber/Petronas/C16/7 (G)	1'39"840	1'37"929	1'36"906	1'39"418
17.	Gianni Morbidelli	Sauber/Petronas/C16/6 (G)	1'44"736	1'39"546	1'38"556	
18.	Jos Verstappen	Tyrrell/Ford/025/3 (G)	1'42"290	1'41"370	1'40"259	1'42"835
19.	Mika Salo	Tyrrell/Ford/025/5 (G)	1'42"587	1'40"905	1'40"529	1'42"021
20.	Ukyo Katayama	Minardi/Hart/M197/4 (B)	1'41"158	1'39"995	1'38"983	1'41"685
21.	Tarso Marquès	Minardi/Hart/M197/2 (B)	1'46"282	1'41"348	1'39"678	1'41"480
22.	Rubens Barrichello	Stewart/Ford/SF1/4 (B)	1'40"937	1'38"723	1'37"343	1'41"983
23.	Jan Magnussen	Stewart/Ford/SF1/3 (B)	1'42"000	1'38"947	1'37"480	1'40"345

CLASSIFICATION & RETIREMENTS

Pos	Driver	Team	Time
1.	Schumacher	Ferrari	in 1h29'48"446
2.	Frentzen	Williams Renault	at 1"378
3.	Irvine	Ferrari	at 26"384
4.	Hakkinen	McLaren Mercedes	at 27"129
5.	Villeneuve	Williams Renault	at 39"776
6.	Alesi	Benetton Renault	at 40"403
7.	Herbert	Sauber Petronas	at 41"630
8.*	Fisichella	Jordan Peugeot	at 56"825
9.	Berger	Benetton Renault	at 1'00"429
10.	Schumacher	Jordan Peugeot	at 1'22"036
11.	Coulthard	McLaren Mercedes	engine
12.	Hill	Arrows Yamaha	at 1 lap
13.	Diniz	Arrows Yamaha	at 1 lap
14.	Verstappen	Tyrrell Ford	at 1 lap

Lap	Driver	Team	Reason
4	Magnussen	Stewart Ford	off
7	Barrichello	Stewart Ford	off
9	Katayama	Minardi Hart	engine
23	Nakano	Prost Mugen Honda	ball bearings
37	Panis	Prost Mugen Honda	engine
47	Salo	Tyrrell Ford	engine
47	Marquès	Minardi Hart	transmission

FASTEST LAPS

	Driver	Time	Lap
1.	Frentzen	1'38"942	48
2.	M. Schum.	1'39"268	48
3.	Alesi	1'39"381	29
4.	R. Schum.	1'39"737	46
5.	Coulthard	1'39"771	52
6.	Irvine	1'39"935	15
7.	Berger	1'39"998	48
8.	Hakkinen	1'40"151	24
9.	Villeneuve	1'40"163	22
10.	Fisichella	1'40"217	45
11.	Herbert	1'40"266	49
12.	Panis	1'40"430	34
13.	Hill	1'41"419	35
14.	Nakano	1'41"608	15
15.	Diniz	1'41"611	33
16.	Marquès	1'42"699	34
17.	Salo	1'42"996	20
18.	Verstappen	1'43"051	49
19.	Barrichello	1'43"883	3
20.	Magnussen	1'44"089	3
21.	Katayama	1'44"403	5

LAP CHART

position :	1	2	3	4	5	6	7	8	9	10	11	12	13	14	15	16	17	18	19	20	21	22
start :	3	5	6	9	8	4	7	16	12	14	10	22	11	23	15	2	1	17	20	21	18	19
1	3	5	9	6	4	8	7	16	10	12	23	22	1	11	14	21	2	15	18	19	20	
2	3	6	5	9	4	8	7	16	10	12	23	22	1	11	14	21	2	15	18	19	20	
3	6	3	5	9	4	8	7	16	10	12	23	22	1	11	14	21	2	15	18	19	20	
4	6	3	5	9	4	7	8	16	10	12	22	1	11	14	21	2	15	18	19	20		
5	6	3	5	9	4	7	8	16	10	12	22	1	11	14	21	2	15	18	19	20		
6	6	3	5	9	4	7	8	16	10	12	22	1	11	14	21	15	2	18	19	20		
7	6	3	5	9	4	7	8	16	10	12	1	14	11	21	15	2	18	19	20			
8	6	3	5	9	4	7	8	16	10	12	1	14	11	21	15	2	18	19	20			
9	6	3	5	9	4	7	8	16	10	12	1	14	11	21	15	2	18	19				
10	6	3	5	9	4	7	8	16	10	12	1	14	11	21	15	2	18	19				
11	6	3	5	9	4	7	8	16	10	12	1	14	11	21	15	2	18	19				
12	6	3	5	9	4	7	8	16	10	12	1	14	11	21	15	2	18	19				
13	6	3	5	9	4	7	8	16	10	12	1	14	11	21	15	2	18	19				
14	6	3	5	4	7	16	10	12	1	9	14	11	8	15	21	2	18	19				
15	6	3	5	4	16	12	1	9	14	11	7	8	15	10	21	2	18	19				
16	6	3	5	4	16	12	1	9	7	11	8	15	10	21	2	14	18	19				
17	3	5	4	6	16	12	9	1	7	11	8	10	15	21	2	14	19	18				
18	3	5	4	6	16	12	9	7	11	8	10	21	2	14	1	15	19	18				
19	3	4	6	16	5	12	9	7	11	8	10	14	1	2	15	21	18	19				
20	3	4	6	16	5	12	9	7	11	8	10	14	1	15	2	21	18	19				
21	4	6	5	3	9	12	7	11	8	16	10	14	1	15	2	21	18	19				
22	6	5	3	4	9	7	8	16	11	10	12	14	1	2	21	18	19	15				
23	6	5	3	4	9	7	8	16	10	12	14	1	11	2	21	18	19					
24	6	5	3	4	9	7	8	16	10	12	14	1	11	2	21	18	19					
25	5	6	3	4	9	7	8	16	10	12	14	1	11	2	21	18	19					
26	5	6	3	4	9	7	8	16	10	12	14	1	11	2	21	18	19					
27	5	6	3	4	9	7	16	10	12	14	8	1	11	2	21	18	19					
28	5	6	3	4	9	16	7	10	12	14	8	1	11	2	21	18	19					
29	5	6	3	4	9	16	7	10	12	14	8	1	11	2	21	18	19					
30	5	6	3	4	9	16	7	10	12	14	8	1	11	2	21	18	19					
31	5	6	4	16	7	9	3	10	12	14	8	1	11	2	21	18	19					
32	5	6	4	16	7	9	3	10	12	14	8	1	11	2	21	18	19					
33	5	4	6	16	7	9	3	10	12	8	1	11	14	2	21	18	19					
34	4	5	6	16	7	9	3	10	12	8	1	11	14	2	21	19	18					
35	4	5	6	16	7	9	3	10	12	8	1	11	14	21	2	19	18					
36	4	5	6	16	7	9	3	12	8	10	1	11	14	21	2	19	18					
37	4	5	6	16	7	9	3	12	8	10	11	1	2	21	19	18						
38	5	4	6	7	9	3	8	16	10	12	11	1	2	21	19	18						
39	5	4	6	7	9	3	16	8	10	12	1	11	2	21	19	18						
40	5	4	6	7	9	3	16	10	12	8	1	11	2	21	19	18						
41	5	4	6	9	3	7	16	10	12	8	11	1	2	21	19	18						
42	5	4	6	9	3	7	16	10	12	8	11	1	2	21	19	18						
43	5	4	6	9	3	7	16	10	12	8	11	1	2	21	19	18						
44	5	4	6	9	3	7	16	10	12	8	11	1	2	21	19	18						
45	5	4	6	9	3	7	16	10	12	8	11	1	2	21	19	18						
46	5	4	6	9	3	7	16	10	12	8	11	1	2	21	19	18						
47	5	4	6	9	3	7	16	10	12	8	11	1	2	18								
48	5	4	6	9	3	7	16	10	12	8	11	1	2	18								
49	5	4	6	9	3	7	16	10	12	8	11	1	2	18								
50	5	4	6	9	3	7	16	10	12	8	11	1	2	18								
51	5	4	6	9	3	7	16	10	12	8	11	1	2	18								
52	5	4	6	9	3	7	16	10	12	8	11	1	2	18								
53	5	4	6	9	3	7	16	12	8	11												

SIXTEENTH ROUND

FUJI TELEVISION JAPANESE GRAND PRIX, SUZUKA

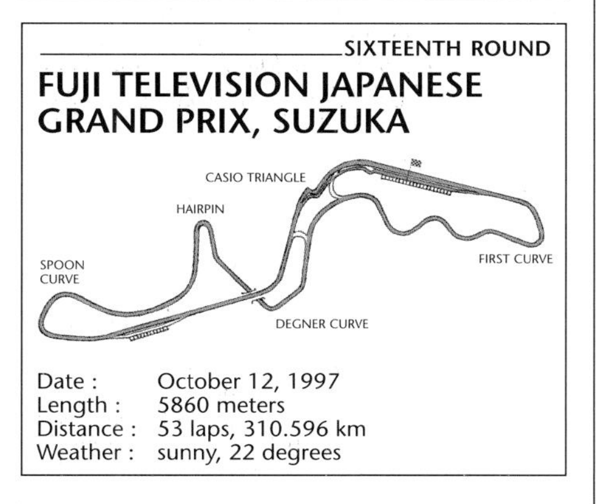

Date : October 12, 1997
Length : 5860 meters
Distance : 53 laps, 310.596 km
Weather : sunny, 22 degrees

Best result for a Bridgestone shod runner:

Damon Hill, Arrows Yamaha, *12th*

CHAMPIONSHIPS

(after sixteen rounds)

Drivers :

1. Michael SCHUMACHER 78
2. Jacques VILLENEUVE 77
3. Heinz-H. FRENTZEN......................41
4. Jean ALESI.....................................35
5. David COULTHARD 30
6. Gerhard BERGER...........................24
7. Eddie IRVINE.................................22
8. Giancarlo FISICHELLA 20
9. Mika HAKKINEN 17
10. Olivier PANIS 16
11. Johnny HERBERT...........................14
12. Ralf SCHUMACHER.......................13
13. Damon HILL 7
14. Rubens BARRICHELLO....................6
15. Alexander WURZ 4
16. Jarno TRULLI 3
17. Mika SALO.......................................2
    Pedro DINIZ 2
    Shinji NAKANO 2
20. Nicola LARINI 1

Constructors :

1. Williams / Renault.......................120
2. Ferrari..100
3. Benetton / Renault........................63
4. McLaren / Mercedes.....................41
5. Jordan / Peugeot 28
6. Prost / Mugen Honda...................21
7. Sauber / Petronas 15
8. Arrows / Yamaha 9
9. Stewart / Ford 6
10. Tyrrell / Ford...................................2

RACE SUMMARY

- At the start, Villeneuve gets the jump on Schumacher and leads.
- Behind the two rivals, Hakkinen leads Irvine, but the Irishman passes the Finn on lap 2.
- Villeneuve is holding up the field and Irvine makes the most of it to take the lead, by passing Villeneuve round the outside of the chicane under braking!
- Irvine rapidly builds up a big lead. After a few laps, Villeneuve ups his pace, but Schumacher is still less than a second behind.
- Schumacher refuels on lap 18. Villeneuve copies him and re-joins in third place, closing rapidly on the Ferrari.
- Irvine, 11 seconds ahead of his team-mate, slows down and lets him pass. He then slows down to block Villeneuve.
- During the second set of pit-stops, Villeneuve loses time refuelling and re-joins in 7thplace.
- Frentzen pulls out of the pits just ahead of Irvine and begins to give chase to Schumacher.
- Schumacher loses three seconds trying to lap Hill and manages to finish just ahead of Frentzen.

WEEK-END GOSSIP

• Stewart confirms Magnussen

Nothing changes at Stewart for next season. While Rubens Barrichello had his seat booked a long time ago, the young Dane, Jan Magnussen had a longer wait to have his future confirmed.

• Concorde goes to court

With no solution to the Concorde Agreement in sight, the three teams who had refused to sign it decided to take the matter to court, citing a violation of Articles 86 and 87 of the Treaty of Rome, which forbid cartels and abuse of power.

• Driver meeting

The drivers' association, the GPDA, met on the Thursday before the grand prix, for two and half hours. Jackie Stewart, as the original founder of the GPDA back in the Sixties, was invited to become an honorary member. Apart from that, the only decision it put forward to the FIA was a list of corners it considered dangerous, as well as a request to have the current high nose configuration sported by most cars altered, as it was considered dangerous in the case of side impacts.

• Jean Alesi speaks Japanese

Jean Alesi is a big star in Japan. Tokyo was plastered with advertising hoardings showing the Benetton driver playing with the new Sony Playstation '97, which had been launched on the Thursday before the race. A TV commercial even showed the Frenchman giving a commentary on the game in Japanese. A truly historic event!

Suzuka means 130,000 spectators and a sell-out every year. But it also means «Motopia,» a theme park based around the car.

▽

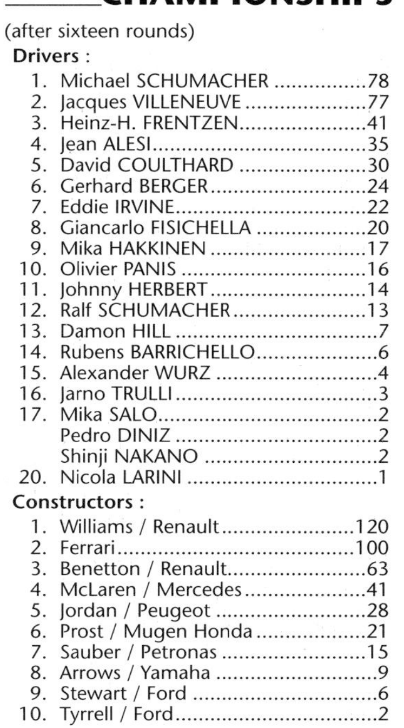

Jacq
Villene
FIA
Form
Wo
Cham
SONAX
Rothmans

It all came down to one corner

It was a titanic struggle: having qualified alongside one another on the grid, with identical times, Jacques Villeneuve and Michael Schumacher engaged in a frantic battle at the European Grand Prix. The championship awaited which ever one finished ahead of the other.
It was all over in a second on lap 48, when Villeneuve mounted his attack and the two rivals collided. Michael was eliminated and Jacques was world champion.
The season had ended with a simple case of road rage.

GRAND PRIX OF EUROPE
JEREZ

△ The first three set identical lap times, to the nearest thousandth of a second. You had to be there to believe it.

Dead heat between the first three

A final folly

Unbelievable, mind-blowing, historic, fantastic: words cannot describe the grid for the European Grand Prix. Jacques Villeneuve, Michael Schumacher and Heinz- Harald Frentzen all set an identical time, to the nearest thousandth of a second!
Given that setting times to the same tenth is very unlikely, the probability of such an event must be around one in a million! Such a situation had never been seen before in Formula 1. What made it all the more unlikely, was that two of the drivers involved were the men who were fighting for the title, Jacques Villeneuve and Michael Schumacher. As the Canadian himself said: *«If I had not been there myself, I would have thought it was fixed!»* Indeed, many voices raised doubts about the veracity of the times, so incredible was the event.
The Canadian was the first to set the time and would therefore start from pole, something he seemed very happy to do. *«I am not too surprised to find myself in front,»* he declared. *«Everything has gone well since we got here. The car is working so well, we have hardly had to touch the settings. I am very, very confident for the race.»*
For his part, Michael Schumacher did not sound too disappointed at having missed out on pole position, despite having set the same time. *«When I finished my lap, I knew I was in the 1m 21s. But I did not know if I was ahead of Jacques or behind him. Anyway, it's not important. I am on the front row and that is what counts. To be honest, being on pole or second makes little difference. Everything will depend on who makes the best start.»*
Apparently quite relaxed, the Ferrari driver claimed he felt under no undue pressure. Jacques Villeneuve meanwhile, seemed a bit more tense.
«I felt under more pressure in Suzuka than here,» he said all the same. *«Here, I must make sure I finish at all costs. Apart from that, the situation is simple. There is no race tactic or complicated pit-stop strategy. All I have to do is finish ahead of Michael!»*
Heinz-Harald Frentzen, taciturn as ever, had little to say about the qualifying session. *«I knew my third lap was really good and I thought I could qualify in front. But the track was a little bit slower at the end and there was nothing I could do.»*
All the ingredients for a cliff hanger of a race were now in place.

High Society at the Renault party. Alain Prost, Damon Hill, Nigel Mansell and the four 1997 drivers. Also present, the main directors of the French firm as well as Alessandro and Luciano Benetton. ▷ ▽

Renault says its farewells to Formula 1

The setting was sumptuous: a huge private hacienda set in the Cadiz hinterland about 50 kilometres from Jerez. It was there, among palm trees and flamenco dancers that Renault had organised a giant party to celebrate its retirement from Formula 1.
It was Saturday night and the atmosphere was electric. Jacques Villeneuve was still chasing the championship and the Renault directors desperately wanted to bow out with one more title. *«We aim for total quality,»* explained Christian Contzen, Renault- Sport's Managing Director. *«We will not be satisfied unless we get both the drivers' and constructors' titles. And to finish a grand prix with all four of our cars in the top four places. Looking at it closely, until now, that is something we have only achieved on two occasions. Technology certainly teaches you humility,»* he added in his usual mystifying style.
For this special occasion, Renault had invited all the drivers whom they had powered to a world championship: Nigel Mansell, Alain Prost and Damon Hill. Only Michael Schumacher failed to show up, claiming he was too busy at the track. During the evening, all the major players in Renault's F1 history took the opportunity to underline just how brightly the company had shined in this discipline. Its president, Louis Schweitzer made the point that it was because of all the success it had enjoyed that Renault was pulling out. While Bernard Dudot made the point that a Renault win was taken for granted these days. *«People did not bother coming to see us when we won, but only when we had problems. We realised that in Monaco in 1996, when Damon Hill's engine broke. It had not happened to us since 1993 and we had never received so much press coverage as we did that day. It was our failure that had become newsworthy.»*
Today, Renault has pulled out of F1 with a remarkable record (see page 13.) Next season, the engines will be taken over and developed by Mecachrome, who will supply them, at a price, to Williams and Benetton. But the same heart will not be beating inside the cylinders.

STARTING GRID

M. SCHUMACHER 1'21"072	-1-	Jacques VILLENEUVE 1'21"072
Damon HILL 1'21"130	-2-	Heinz-H. FRENTZEN 1'21"072
David COULTHARD 1'21"476	-3-	Mika HAKKINEN 1'21"369
Gerhard BERGER 1'21"656	-4-	Eddie IRVINE 1'21"610
Jean ALESI 1'22"011	-5-	Olivier PANIS 1'21"735
R. BARRICHELLO 1'22"222	-6-	Jan MAGNUSSEN 1'22"167
Johnny HERBERT 1'22"263	-7-	Pedro DINIZ 1'22"234
R. SCHUMACHER 1'22"740	-8-	Shinji NAKANO 1'22"351
Norberto FONTANA 1'23"281	-9-	Giancarlo FISICHELLA 1'22"804
Tarso MARQUES 1'23"854	-10-	Ukyo KATAYAMA 1'23"409
Jos VERSTAPPEN 1'24"301	-11-	Mika SALO 1'24"222

IT'S JACQUES!

Jacques Villeneuve took the chequered flag and became the Formula 1 World Champion. On the pit wall, the entire Williams team exploded with joy. A long hard season was finally over. Swarming around the podium, the mechanics all donned yellow wigs to take the mickey out of their «Blondie». Up above them, on the third step of the podium, the Canadian was all smiles. He seemed to be far away in another world.
A few moments later, in the press conference, he took his seat next to the winner on the day, Mika Hakkinen.
Overjoyed at the first win of his career, the Finn burst into tears. A furtive glance across at Villeneuve revealed that he too had tears rolling down his cheeks.
Later however, the Canadian would deny having cried with joy, simply because by the end of the afternoon, he still could not come to terms with what had happened to him. *«I think it will take some time for this world championship to sink in. I find it very hard to explain how I feel right now. The season has been so long and hard. But it is a feeling of intense happiness. I've finally done it!»*
After the press conference, Villeneuve surrendered himself to countless television interviews before returning to his team, who immediately carried him shoulder high. *«I have to thank all the team,»* he added later. *«A world title is won as much in the factory as on the track. We brought in several changes to the car this season and each one of them represents a lot of hard work. Just last week, the Renault engineers worked on the engine rather than spend time with their families. A world title represents an enormous amount of work.»*
In Jerez, Villeneuve withstood the strongest pressure a driver can know in his career and he did not let up for one second of the 69 laps of the European Grand Prix.

It's in the bag! Jacques Villeneuve crosses the finish line in third place, but it was enough to take the world championship title.

For the Canadian, this title came at the end of a season which had been far from rosy. *«It was the toughest championship of my career,»* he confirmed. *«I had to fight non-stop to get back the lead from Michael. After Nurburgring, I thought everything was in place and then the situation was overturned in Japan. It was really hard right down to the final lap. I lost a lot of hair this season.»*
Jacques Villeneuve left the circuit with his manager. *«We are going to have one hell of a party tonight,»* he said. He richly deserved it.

69 qualifying laps

Jacques Villeneuve ran an almost perfect race. Attacking all the way, the Canadian was more aggressive than ever as he matched Schumacher's fiendish pace. The only thing he messed up was his start. *«I was very surprised to see how quickly Michael took off,»* he explained. *«I think I made a perfectly good start, it you look at the cars behind me. But I don't how he did it. He seemed to be stuck to the track. Of course I was frustrated to find myself behind him, but I soon realised that I was actually quicker than him, especially as my first set of tyres was not very good. I had started on old rubber and I knew I would have to wait for the pit-stops to fit the new sets.»*
After his first stop, Villeneuve took up the chase once more, but without success. *«It was very tiring physically. I was always flat out without a moment's rest,»* he continued. *«It was like doing a long series of qualifying laps!»*

The chase is on. The European Grand Prix turned into an amazing pursuit race between the two championship rivals.

Michael Schumacher comes back to the pits by scooter. A race that had started so well ended in disaster on lap 48.

IN THE POINTS

	Driver	Team	Time
1.	Mika HAKKINEN	West McLaren Mercedes	1 h 38'57"771
2.	David COULTHARD	West McLaren Mercedes	at 1"654
3.	Jacques VILLENEUVE	Rothmans Williams Renault	at 1"803
4.	Gerhard BERGER	Mild Seven Benetton Renault	at 1"919
5.	Eddie IRVINE	Scuderia Ferrari Marlboro	at 3"789
6.	Heinz-H. FRENTZEN	Rothmans Williams Renault	at 4"537

Fastest lap : H.-H. FRENTZEN, lap 30, 1'23"135, avg. 191.745 km/h

The McLarens had come full circle: after winning the first grand prix in Australia, the silver arrows were successful once again, doing the double in the final race at Jerez.

A sad race incident

It was after his second pit-stop that Jacques Villeneuve mounted the attack that would decide the outcome of the championship. Diving down the inside at Dry Sack Corner, the Canadian braked extremely late to draw level with Michael Schumacher.

Totally taken by surprise - if he had not been, he would have kept the inside line - the German could not bear to see his rival overtake him and jerked the steering wheel to drive into the Williams side pod. If he had made contact with one of the two wheels it could have been fatal. Luckily for the Canadian, the Ferrari only hit his left radiator. *«It was a hard knock,»* recounted Villeneuve. *«I thought it was all over. I carried on, but the car was handling strangely down the straights. I did two slow laps and when I saw the suspension was still okay, I pushed on again. I think the mechanics were more worried than I was, but I am very surprised to have finished the race.»*

The Canadian knew he had taken a big risk with this move. *«I was aware that Michael could take me out,»* he continued. *«In fact, I think the move only had a 50% chance of success. But I had noticed that my car was definitely better after I fitted new tyres and I could not wait to attack. It would have been pointless to finish second and I preferred taking the risk of finishing in the gravel than to stay behind until the end.»* The move paid off, as it was the Ferrari which was stuck in the gravel. *«It serves him right,»* added Villeneuve.

A few hours before the race, during the drivers' briefing, Bernie Ecclestone himself intervened to ask the championship contenders to race in the spirit of fair play. *«If one or other of the drivers takes the other out, then the punishment will be draconian,»* he had warned. Evidently his words were not heeded.

At the time, rumours doing the rounds of the paddock suggested that Schumacher could be excluded from the first grand prix of the 1998 season, but the Stewards finally decided it was a «racing incident». However, the following day, the FIA announced it had summoned the German to appear before them on 11th November to explain his actions. After the race, a grim looking Schumacher refused to admit he was at fault. *«With Bernie, we talked about my forthcoming holidays,»* he insisted on repeating. *«My car was perfect and I think I could have kept ahead of Jacques to the finish. I do not think I made a mistake. I have known better days, but that is racing.»* Although he claimed his Ferrari was fine, rumours quickly spread that in fact it was leaking water from a radiator and it would not have made it to the finish. The team had seen this on the telemetry and informed their driver, which could certainly explain his attempt at knocking Villeneuve out of the race.

Hakkinen could not believe it

96 starts for one win! In Jerez, Mika Hakkinen took the first Grand Prix victory of his long career in Formula 1. It went virtually unnoticed amidst all the celebrations for Jacques Villeneuve's first world championship title.

It was all the more unnoticed as the new champion did not put up a fight against the two McLarens, handing them victory on a plate on the final lap. *«I had no need to defend my position against the McLarens,»* he explained. *«Mika had been kind enough to stay behind me at the beginning of the race, even though he was quicker than me. So I let him win. It was not a sacrifice, it was just an exchange of favours.»* For the Finn, who was still third three laps from the flag, this first win was completely unexpected. *«It's fantastic, it's incredible,»* he babbled after the finish. *«It was an exciting race from start to finish for me. It is true I was quicker than Jacques in the early part of the race. But as he was fighting for the championship I did not want to take any risks and so I chose to stay behind him. But I never thought for one moment I would win the race. I was able to pass David* (Coulthard) *at a point where you cannot really overtake and then Jacques did not put up a fight. Fantastic.»*

The manner of victory owed something to a pre-planned agreement between Williams and McLaren. Ron Dennis had discussions with Frank Williams prior to the race and was seen in conversation with Patrick Head on the grid. It would seem that in exchange for helping Villeneuve, Williams had agreed to gift McLaren the race if possible.

PRACTICE TIMES

No	Driver	Make/Engine/Chassis	Practice Friday	Practice Saturday	Qualifying	Warm-up
1.	Damon Hill	Arrows/Yamaha/A18/5 (B)	1'22"898	1'21"780	1'21"130	1'24"231
2.	Pedro Diniz	Arrows/Yamaha/A18/4 (B)	1'24"797	1'22"750	1'22"234	1'25"103
3.	Jacques Villeneuve	Williams/Renault/FW19/4 (G)	1'22"922	1'21"593	1'21"072	1'23"849
4.	Heinz-Harald Frentzen	Williams/Renault/FW19/5 (G)	1'23"124	1'21"263	1'21"072	1'24"089
5.	Michael Schumacher	Ferrari/Ferrari/F310B/178 (G)	1'23"532	1'22"120	1'21"072	1'24"063
6.	Eddie Irvine	Ferrari/Ferrari/F310B/180 (G)	1'23"695	1'22"820	1'21"610	1'24"560
7.	Jean Alesi	Benetton/Renault/B197/3 (G)	1'23"174	1'21"814	1'22"011	1'24"540
8.	Gerhard Berger	Benetton/Renault/B197/5 (G)	1'23"923	1'21"525	1'21"656	1'23"160
9.	Mika Hakkinen	McLaren/Mercedes/MP4/12/5 (G)	1'23"024	1'20"856	1'21"369	1'23"016
10.	David Coulthard	McLaren/Mercedes/MP4/12/6 (G)	1'23"440	1'20"738	1'21"476	1'23"359
11.	Ralf Schumacher	Jordan/Peugeot/197/6 (G)	1'23"678	1'21"881	1'22"740	1'24"386
12.	Giancarlo Fisichella	Jordan/Peugeot/197/5 (G)	1'24"263	1'22"438	1'22"804	1'25"377
14.	Olivier Panis	Prost/Mugen Honda/JS45/3 (B)	1'22"735	1'21"364	1'21"735	1'23"166
15.	Shinji Nakano	Prost/Mugen Honda/JS45/2 (B)	1'24"735	1'21"671	1'22"351	1'24"125
16.	Johnny Herbert	Sauber/Petronas/C16/7 (G)	1'24"507	1'22"065	1'22"263	1'24"012
17.	Norberto Fontana	Sauber/Petronas/C16/2 (G)	1'25"134	1'22"404	1'23"281	1'24"795
18.	Jos Verstappen	Tyrrell/Ford/025/3 (G)	1'25"327	1'23"742	1'24"301	1'26"307
19.	Mika Salo	Tyrrell/Ford/025/5 (G)	1'25"025	1'24"429	1'24"222	1'25"419
20.	Ukyo Katayama	Minardi/Hart/M197/4 (B)	1'24"329	1'22"512	1'23"409	1'25"159
21.	Tarso Marquès	Minardi/Hart/M197/2 (B)	1'26"816	1'23"369	1'23"854	1'25"707
22.	Rubens Barrichello	Stewart/Ford/SF1/2 (B)	1'22"964	1'22"117	1'22"222	1'25"275
23.	Jan Magnussen	Stewart/Ford/SF1/3 (B)	1'23"685	1'21"605	1'22"167	1'24"309

LAP CHART

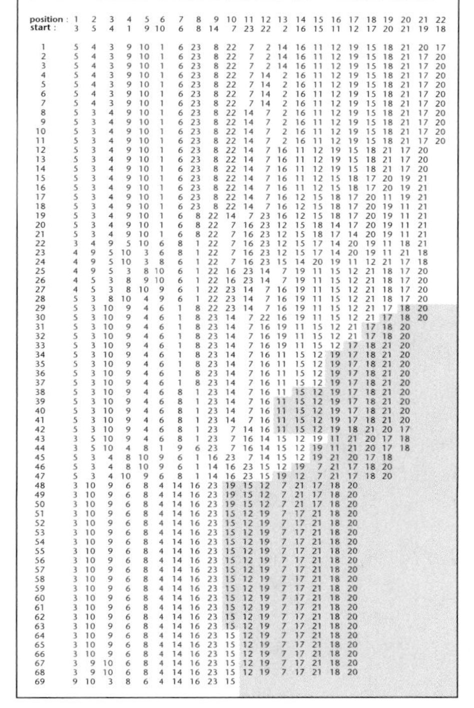

position :	1	2	3	4	5	6	7	8	9	10	11	12	13	14	15	16	17	18	19	20	21	22
start :	3	5	4	1	9	10	6	8	14	7	23	22	2	16	15	11	12	17	20	21	19	18
1	5	4	3	9	10	1	6	23	8	22	7	2	14	16	11	12	19	15	18	21	20	17
2	5	4	3	9	10	1	6	23	8	22	7	2	14	16	11	12	19	15	18	21	17	20
3	5	4	3	9	10	1	6	23	8	22	7	2	14	16	11	12	19	15	18	21	17	20
4	5	4	3	9	10	1	6	23	8	22	7	14	2	16	11	12	19	15	18	21	17	20
5	5	4	3	9	10	1	6	23	8	22	7	14	2	16	11	12	19	15	18	21	17	20
6	5	4	3	9	10	1	6	23	8	22	7	14	2	16	11	12	19	15	18	21	17	20
7	5	4	3	9	10	1	6	23	8	22	7	14	2	16	11	12	19	15	18	21	17	20
8	5	3	4	9	10	1	6	23	8	22	14	7	2	16	11	12	19	15	18	21	17	20
9	5	3	4	9	10	1	6	23	8	22	14	7	2	16	11	12	19	15	18	21	17	20
10	5	3	4	9	10	1	6	23	8	22	14	7	2	16	11	12	19	15	18	21	17	20
11	5	3	4	9	10	1	6	23	8	22	14	7	2	16	11	12	19	15	18	21	17	20
12	5	3	4	9	10	1	6	23	8	22	14	7	16	11	12	19	15	18	21	17	20	
13	5	3	4	9	10	1	6	23	8	22	14	7	16	11	12	19	15	18	21	17	20	
14	5	3	4	9	10	1	6	23	8	22	14	7	16	11	12	19	15	18	21	17	20	
15	5	3	4	9	10	1	6	23	8	22	14	7	16	11	12	15	18	17	20	19	21	
16	5	3	4	9	10	1	6	23	8	22	14	7	16	11	12	15	18	17	20	19	21	
17	5	3	4	9	10	1	6	23	8	22	14	7	16	12	15	18	17	20	11	19	21	
18	5	3	4	9	10	1	6	23	8	22	14	7	16	12	15	18	17	20	19	11	21	
19	5	3	4	9	10	1	6	8	22	14	7	23	16	12	15	18	17	20	19	11	21	
20	5	3	4	9	10	1	6	8	22	7	16	23	12	15	18	14	17	20	19	11	21	
21	5	3	4	9	10	1	6	8	22	7	16	23	12	15	18	17	14	20	19	11	21	
22	3	4	9	5	10	6	8	1	22	7	16	23	12	15	17	14	20	19	11	18	21	
23	4	9	5	10	3	6	8	1	22	7	16	23	12	15	17	14	20	19	11	21	18	
24	4	9	5	10	3	8	6	1	22	7	16	23	15	14	20	19	11	12	21	17	18	
25	4	9	5	3	8	10	6	1	22	16	23	14	7	19	11	15	12	21	18	17	20	
26	4	5	3	8	9	10	6	1	22	16	23	14	7	19	11	15	12	21	18	17	20	
27	4	5	3	8	10	9	6	1	22	23	14	7	16	19	11	15	12	21	18	17	20	
28	5	3	8	10	4	9	6	1	22	23	14	7	16	19	11	15	12	21	18	17	20	
29	5	3	10	9	4	6	1	8	22	23	14	7	16	19	11	15	12	21	17	18	20	
30	5	3	10	9	4	6	1	8	23	14	7	22	16	19	11	15	12	21	17	18	20	
31	5	3	10	9	4	6	1	8	23	14	7	16	19	11	15	12	21	17	18	20		
32	5	3	10	9	4	6	1	8	23	14	7	16	19	11	15	12	21	17	18	20		
33	5	3	10	9	4	6	1	8	23	14	7	16	19	11	15	12	17	18	21	20		
34	5	3	10	9	4	6	1	8	23	14	7	16	11	15	12	19	17	18	21	20		
35	5	3	10	9	4	6	1	8	23	14	7	16	11	15	12	19	17	18	21	20		
36	5	3	10	9	4	6	1	8	23	14	7	16	11	15	12	19	17	18	21	20		
37	5	3	10	9	4	6	1	8	23	14	7	16	11	15	12	19	17	18	21	20		
38	5	3	10	9	4	6	8	1	23	14	7	16	11	15	12	19	17	18	21	20		
39	5	3	10	9	4	6	8	1	23	14	7	16	11	15	12	19	17	18	21	20		
40	5	3	10	9	4	6	8	1	23	14	7	16	11	15	12	19	17	18	21	20		
41	5	3	10	9	4	6	8	1	23	14	7	16	11	15	12	19	17	18	21	20		
42	5	3	10	9	4	6	8	1	23	7	14	16	11	15	12	19	18	21	20	17		
43	3	5	10	9	4	6	8	1	23	7	16	14	15	12	19	11	21	20	17	18		
44	3	5	10	4	8	1	9	6	23	7	16	14	15	12	19	11	21	20	17	18		
45	5	3	4	8	10	9	6	1	16	23	7	14	15	12	19	21	20	17	18			
46	5	3	4	8	10	9	6	1	14	16	23	15	12	19	7	21	17	18	20			
47	5	3	4	10	9	6	8	1	14	16	23	15	19	12	7	21	17	18	20			
48	3	10	9	6	8	4	14	16	23	19	15	12	7	21	17	18	20					
49	3	10	9	6	8	4	14	16	23	19	15	12	7	21	17	18	20					
50	3	10	9	6	8	4	14	16	23	19	15	12	7	21	17	18	20					
51	3	10	9	6	8	4	14	16	23	15	12	19	7	17	21	18	20					
52	3	10	9	6	8	4	14	16	23	15	12	19	7	17	21	18	20					
53	3	10	9	6	8	4	14	16	23	15	12	19	7	17	21	18	20					
54	3	10	9	6	8	4	14	16	23	15	12	19	7	17	21	18	20					
55	3	10	9	6	8	4	14	16	23	15	12	19	7	17	21	18	20					
56	3	10	9	6	8	4	14	16	23	15	12	19	7	17	21	18	20					
57	3	10	9	6	8	4	14	16	23	15	12	19	7	17	21	18	20					
58	3	10	9	6	8	4	14	16	23	15	12	19	7	17	21	18	20					
59	3	10	9	6	8	4	14	16	23	15	12	19	7	17	21	18	20					
60	3	10	9	6	8	4	14	16	23	15	12	19	7	17	21	18	20					
61	3	10	9	6	8	4	14	16	23	15	12	19	7	17	21	18	20					
62	3	10	9	6	8	4	14	16	23	15	12	19	7	17	21	18	20					
63	3	10	9	6	8	4	14	16	23	15	12	19	7	17	21	18	20					
64	3	10	9	6	8	4	14	16	23	15	12	19	7	17	21	18	20					
65	3	10	9	6	8	4	14	16	23	15	12	19	7	17	21	18	20					
66	3	10	9	6	8	4	14	16	23	15	12	19	7	17	21	18	20					
67	3	9	10	6	8	4	14	16	23	15	12	19	7	17	21	18	20					
68	3	9	10	6	8	4	14	16	23	15	12	19	7	17	21	18	20					
69	9	10	3	8	6	4	14	16	23	15												

CLASSIFICATION & RETIREMENTS

Pos	Driver	Team	Time
1.	Hakkinen	McLaren Mercedes	in 1h38'57"771
2.	Coulthard	McLaren Mercedes	at 1"654
3.	Villeneuve	Williams Renault	at 1"803
4.	Berger	Benetton Renault	at 1"919
5.	Irvine	Ferrari	at 3"789
6.	Frentzen	Williams Renault	at 4"537
7.	Panis	Prost Mugen Honda	at 1'07"145
8.	Herbert	Sauber Petronas	at 1'12"961
9.	Magnussen	Stewart Ford	at 1'17"487
10.	Nakano	Prost Mugen Honda	at 1'18"215
11.	Fisichella	Jordan Peugeot	at 1 lap
12.	Salo	Tyrrell Ford	at 1 lap
13.	Alesi	Benetton Renault	at 1 lap
14.	Fontana	Sauber Petronas	at 1 lap
15.	Marquès	Minardi Hart	at 1 lap
16.	Verstappen	Tyrrell Ford	at 1 lap
17.	Katayama	Minardi Hart	at 1 lap

Lap	Driver	Team	Reason
12	Diniz	Arrows Yamaha	spin
31	Barrichello	Stewart Ford	gearbox
45	Schumacher	Jordan Peugeot	water leak
48	Hill	Arrows Yamaha	gearbox
48	Schumacher	Ferrari	off

FASTEST LAPS

	Driver	Time	Lap
1.	Frentzen	1'23"135	30
2.	Berger	1'23"361	31
3.	M. Schum.	1'23"692	42
4.	Villeneuve	1'23"906	42
5.	Panis	1'23"941	45
6.	Alesi	1'23"975	27
7.	Coulthard	1'24"006	27
8.	Hakkinen	1'24"072	28
9.	Irvine	1'24"266	37
10.	Hill	1'24"274	40
11.	Nakano	1'24"679	45
12.	Fontana	1'25"154	32
13.	Herbert	1'25"159	30
14.	Salo	1'25"237	37
15.	Magnussen	1'25"370	31
16.	Fisichella	1'25"434	45
17.	R. Schum.	1'25"895	34
18.	Marquès	1'25"947	55
19.	Barrichello	1'26"169	13
20.	Katayama	1'26"215	27
21.	Verstappen	1'26"369	40
22.	Diniz	1'26"434	3

SEVENTEENTH ROUND

GRAND PRIX OF EUROPE JEREZ

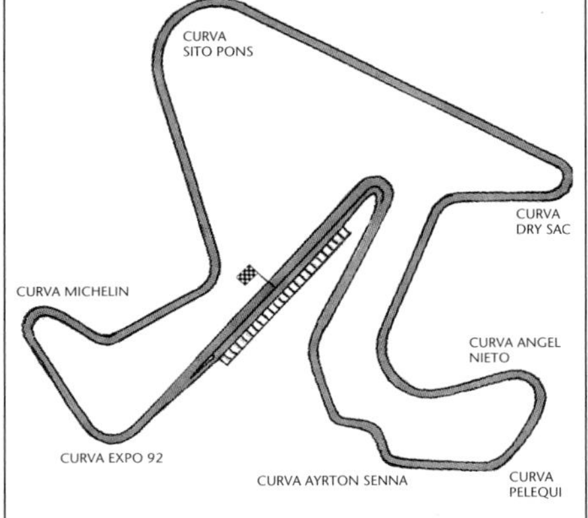

Date : October 6, 1997
Length : 4428 meters
Distance : 69 laps, 305.532 km
Weather : sunny, 27 degrees

CHAMPIONSHIPS

(after seventeen rounds)

Drivers:

1. Jacques VILLENEUVE 81
2. Michael SCHUMACHER 78
3. Heinz-H. FRENTZEN 42
4. David COULTHARD 36
5. Jean ALESI 36
6. Gerhard BERGER 27
7. Mika HAKKINEN 27
8. Eddie IRVINE 24
9. Giancarlo FISICHELLA 20
10. Olivier PANIS 16
11. Johnny HERBERT 15
12. Ralf SCHUMACHER 13
13. Damon HILL 7
14. Rubens BARRICHELLO 6
15. Alexander WURZ 4
16. Jarno TRULLI 3
17. Mika SALO 2
    Pedro DINIZ 2
    Shinji NAKANO 2
20. Nicola LARINI 1

Constructors :

1. Williams / Renault 123
2. Ferrari 102
3. Benetton / Renault 67
4. McLaren / Mercedes 63
5. Jordan / Peugeot 33
6. Prost / Mugen Honda 21
7. Sauber / Petronas 16
8. Arrows / Yamaha 9
9. Stewart / Ford 6
10. Tyrrell / Ford 2

RACE SUMMARY

- Villeneuve is slow off the line and is passed by Michael Schumacher and Frentzen.
- Schumacher pulls out a lead in the early stages. Frentzen cannot keep up and lets Villeneuve by on lap 8.
- Villeneuve and Schumacher are locked in a fascinating duel, both men trading fastest laps.
- Gradually, Schumacher pulls out a small gap which has reached 5.2 seconds when the pit-stops begin.
- After his first stop, Schumacher is held up by Frentzen and Coulthard, allowing Villeneuve to close up.
- When Frentzen and Coulthard pit, Schumacher is once again in the lead, with Villeneuve right behind him. On lap 30, the Canadian is badly held up by Fontana's Sauber before lapping him. He is now 3.2 seconds behind Schumacher.
- After his second stop, Schumacher slows the pace. Villeneuve takes just two laps to catch him and attacks at Dry Sack Corner. Schumacher deliberately drives into him and is forced to retire.
- Although damaged, Villeneuve's car keeps going. The Canadian slows right down, allowing both McLarens to pass him on the final lap.

WEEK-END GOSSIP

• Party pooper

In Germany and Italy, it was time for the Schumacher party. In Kerpen, the little town where Michael grew up, 800 people had gathered in the little «Michael Museum» created there. At Maranello, 18,000 tifosi jostled one another in the town square to watch the grand prix on a giant screen. So many people, so much disappointment.

• Yellow flags

Michael Schumacher passed by some yellow flags in qualifying. But they were stationary, not waved as was the case in Suzuka. *«I clearly saw these flags,»* affirmed Michael. *«But as they were stationary, I did not have to slow down as it simply means you must drive within your limits.»* All the same, he did set his fastest time at that moment.

Blue skies and whitewashed buildings - the charm of Andalusia.
▽

△
«Mirror, mirror on the wall, tell me what the future of Formula 1 will hold.» Reflections in the windows of the Barcelona circuit press office.

Bernard Dudot's life with Renault was coming to an end as he prepared for a new adventure: from the 1st November he took up the position of technical director with Prost Grand Prix.
▽

All change for 1998

Formula 1 is on the eve of a cultural revolution. When the time came to draw up a new set of technical regulations to come into effect at the start of the 1998 season, the engineers from all the teams opted for "Mini-Formula 1 cars." Narrower by 20 centimetres, fitted with grooved tyres, the 1998 F1 cars will be very different to the ones we have seen in 1997. It could well upset the balance of power in the sport.
The reduced width of the cars, means a smaller wing surface. Combined with tyres that also have less grip, the result will be lower cornering speeds. Experts reckon that lap times will increase by two or three seconds, a deficit which will no doubt be made up over the next two years.
In a straight line, the narrower cars will be able to hit higher top speeds. This combined with a slower cornering speed means that braking distances should be considerably increased. From this conclusion springs the hope we will witness more overtaking.
In 1997, it was noticeable that the performance level of most of the cars was very similar and overtaking manoeuvres were becoming an endangered species.
The first tests with cars modified to the 1998 specification did not leave the drivers with a favourable impression. The general comment was that they had insufficient grip. Life could be very exciting come the 8th March 1998.

No smoke without fire in Formula 1

FIA President Max Mosley dropped something of a bombshell at Jerez on the Saturday of the European Grand Prix.
Speaking at a press conference, he gave the sporting authority's views on the implications of the new anti-tobacco legislation which the European Community is planning to adopt. Hold on tight, you are in for a shock! *«If these anti-tobacco laws are applied in Europe, our plans are quite straightforward,»* explained Mosley. *«We will reduce the number of races in Europe to the same number which currently run without tobacco advertising - that is to say, three: Great Britain, Germany and normally France. At the moment we have nine races in Europe, which would be reduced to three, each race being run once every three years.*
Therefore, the British Grand Prix at Silverstone would only count towards the World Championship once every three years. In the intervening years, the organisers would be free to hold other races as they pleased, but they would not count towards the championship. As for races held in Europe, but not affected by European legislation - Monaco and Hungary - these would naturally be maintained as they are now. Of course, we would need to replace the six missing races. On this point, I can already say where four of them would be held, because we are under considerable pressure from Asian countries who want to organise grands prix. These pressures come from various sources, but principally because 70% of the grand prix TV audience comes from this part of the world. In any case, the plans to ban tobacco advertising are unlikely to come into effect for the next three to five years, which allows us ample time to sort out our championship. Even though the teams will not tell us the exact amounts, tobacco sponsorship represents between 200 and 300 million dollars per year for them and we cannot afford to lose that.»
«This position does not signify that the FIA encourages cigarette smoking. We have carried out numerous independent surveys, which show that banning advertising actually increases young people's cigarette consumption, rather than reduce it. I think governments should study the question of why young people start smoking.»
Mosley went on to explain that the FIA was in contact with government and was willing to negotiate over the permitted size of "tobacco" logos.
Whatever the outcome, it seems clear that the face of Formula 1 is bound to change in the near future.

Little change behind the wheel

As every year, those drivers unhappy with their lot have decided to switch teams for 1998. Most conspicuously fitting into that category were Damon Hill, Jean Alesi and Gerhard Berger. All three are veterans in the sport and all three endured a less than brilliant 1997 season.

Damon Hill and his lawyer Michael Breen spent the summer cruising the paddock in search of a team which might be interested in the services of the 1996 World Champion. After talks with Sauber failed, he got quite far down the road with McLaren-Mercedes, before it became apparent the silver team was going to stick with its two current drivers.

Hill then turned to Prost Grand Prix. The Englishman proved somewhat naive in believing the French team was about to offer him a crock of gold, just when Alain Prost was using all his business acumen to limit unnecessary expenditure and save his money for essentials. Finally and against all expectation, Hill found a berth with Eddie Jordan. The Irishman's careful approach to money seemed an impossible barrier to this marriage. In 1997, Jordan had lined up two "free" drivers and it seemed very unlikely that he would countenance a world champion as greedy as Damon Hill.

Finally, the team's title sponsor picked up the bill and everything slotted into place.

For his part, Jean Alesi was also looking to flee the Benetton nest. After two years of bitter failure, the Frenchman no longer wanted to stay with a team that appeared to be crumbling. From the start of the summer it was apparent that Flavio Briatore would no longer be at the helm in 1998 and there were strong doubts about the Benetton family's commitment to maintaining its F1 team.

In his search for a new home, Jean Alesi reached the same conclusion as Damon Hill; that there were in fact very few seats available. He also knocked on Sauber's door and reached an agreement. A marriage between the calm Swiss team owner and the effervescent French driver seemed unlikely. The sparks are likely to fly between them.

As for Gerhard Berger, with 13 seasons in the sport, he reached the only logical conclusion and announced before the final race of 1997, that he was hanging up his helmet. Although he refused to rule out the possibility of a comeback at a later date.

In 1998, apart from Benetton, which is putting its faith in two young drivers, Wurz and Fisichella, the majority of teams have opted for status quo on the driver front. Prost is likely to choose Trulli to second Panis, while McLaren, Williams, Ferrari and Stewart will line up with the same drivers as in 1997.

At the back of the grid, Tyrrell had not made a decision by the end of the season, nor had Giancarlo Minardi. For them the choice of driver will invariably come down to the size of the wallets on offer.

△ *Jean Alesi will start a new life in 1998. After five years with Ferrari and two at Benetton, the Frenchman will drive for the Sauber team.*

◁ *A glance at the wings in Formula 1 is enough to realise just how much the sport relies on the tobacco industry.*

Mecachrome on a par with Renault?

With Renault pulling out, a chapter in Formula 1 history comes to an end. In Jerez, after the race, the atmosphere was a mixture of joy, at Villeneuve's championship and sadness for the people from Viry-Chatillon.

However, for most of the race team, their racing days are not yet over, as Mecachrome, which had taken over the Renault engines under license, would be employing the majority of them.

Nothing guarantees that the RS9B "Mecachrome" will be developed with the same energy and the same talent as the Renault engines. For the new French engine builder, this will be a purely commercial operation, with engines being sold to both the contracted teams, Williams and Benetton. For the first of these two, cost will not be a concern, as the Mecachrome invoices will be paid by BMW, who will supply the Grove team as from the year 2000.

The splendid setting of Melbourne will once again provide the backdrop for the season opener in 1998. ▽

Recap of the 1997 season

Position in championship	Driver	Make	Australian Grand Prix	Brazilian Grand Prix	Argentinian Grand Prix	San Marino Grand Prix	Monaco Grand Prix	Spanish Grand Prix	Canadian Grand Prix	French Grand Prix	British Grand Prix	German Grand Prix	Hungarian Grand Prix	Belgian Grand Prix	Italian Grand Prix	Austrian Grand Prix	Luxemburg Grand Prix	Japanese Grand Prix	European Grand Prix	Number of pole-positions	Number of victories	Number of fastest laps	Number of laps in the lead	Number of km in the lead	Final classif. in Championship
1	Jacques VILLENEUVE	Williams Renault	A	1	1	A	A	1	A	4	1	A	1	5	5	1	1	5	3	10	7	3	349	1'602	81
2	Michael SCHUMACHER	Ferrari	2	5	A	2	1	4	1	1	A	2	4	1	6	6	A	1	A	3	5	3	300	1'393	78
3	Heinz-H. FRENTZEN	Williams Renault	8	9	A	1	A	8	4	2	A	A	A	3	3	3	3	2	6	1	1	6	76	379	42
4	David COULTHARD	McLaren Mercedes	1	10	A	A		6	7	7	4	A	A	A	1	2	A	11	2	–	2	1	77	396	36
5	Jean ALESI	Benetton Renault	A	6	7	5	A	3	2	5	2	6	11	8	2	A	2	6	13	1	–	–	32	184	36
6	Gerhard BERGER	Benetton Renault	4	2	6	A	9	10	–	–	–	1	8	6	7	10	4	9	4	1	1	2	41	272	27
7	Mika HAKKINEN	McLaren Mercedes	3	4	5	6	A	7	A	A	A	3	A	D	9	A	A	4	1	1	1	1	50	234	27
8	Eddie IRVINE	Ferrari	A	16	2	3	3	12	A	3	A	A	9	10	8	A	A	3	5	–	–	–	23	125	24
9	Giancarlo FISICHELLA	Jordan Peugeot	A	8	A	4	6	9	3	9	7	11	A	2	4	4	A	8	11	–	–	1	7	48	20
10	Olivier PANIS	Prost Mugen Honda	5	3	A	8	4	2	11	–	–	–	–	–	–	–	6	A	7	–	–	–	–	–	16
11	Johnny HERBERT	Sauber Petronas	A	7	4	A	A	5	5	8	A	A	3	4	A	8	7	7	8	–	–	–	–	–	15
12	Ralf SCHUMACHER	Jordan Peugeot	A	A	3	A	A	A	A	6	5	5	5	A	A	A5	A	10	A	–	–	–	–	–	13
13	Damon HILL	Arrows Yamaha	A	17	A	A	A	A	9	12	6	8	2	13	A	7	8	12	A	–	–	–	62	246	7
14	Rubens BARRICHELLO	Stewart Ford	A	A	A	A	2	A	A	A	A	A	A	A	13	4	A	A	A	–	–	–	–	–	6
15	Alexander WURZ	Benetton Renault	–	–	–	–	–	–	A	A	3	–	–	–	–	–	–	–	–	–	–	–	–	–	4
16	Jarno TRULLI	Minardi Hart	9	12	9	A	A	15	A	–	–	–	–	–	–	–	–	–	–	–	–	–	–	–	–
		Prost Mugen Honda	–	–	–	–	–	–	–	10	8	4	7	16	10	A	–	–	–	–	–	–	37	160	3
17	Mika SALO	Tyrrell Ford	A	13	8	9	5	A	A	A	A	A	13	11	A	A	10	A	12	–	–	–	–	–	2
18	Pedro DINIZ	Arrows Yamaha	10	A	A	A	A	A	8	A	A	A	A	7	A	13	5	13	A	–	–	–	–	–	2
19	Shinji NAKANO	Prost Mugen Honda	7	14	A	A	A	A	6	A	11	7	6	A	11	A	A	A	10	–	–	–	–	–	2
20	Nicola LARINI	Sauber Petronas	6	11	A	7	A	–	–	–	–	–	–	–	–	–	–	–	–	–	–	–	–	–	1
	Then, by alphabetical order :																								
	Norberto FONTANA	Sauber Petronas	–	–	–	–	–	–	–	A	9	9	–	–	–	–	–	–	14	–	–	–	–	–	–
	Ukyo KATAYAMA	Minardi Hart	A	18	A	11	10	A	A	11	A	A	10	14	A	11	A	A	17	–	–	–	–	–	–
	Jan MAGNUSSEN	Stewart Ford	A		10	A	7	13	A	A	A	A	A	12	A	A	A	A	9	–	–	–	–	–	–
	Tarso MARQUES	Minardi Hart	–	–	–	–	–	–	–	A	10	A	12	A	14	D	A	A	15	–	–	–	–	–	–
	Gianni MORBIDELLI	Sauber Petronas	–	–	–	–	–	14	10	–	–	–	A	9	12	9	9	F	–	–	–	–	–	–	–
	Riccardo ROSSET	Lola Ford	NQ	–	–	–	–	–	–	–	–	–	–	–	–	–	–	–	–	–	–	–	–	–	–
	Vincenzo SOSPIRI	Lola Ford	NQ	–	–	–	–	–	–	–	–	–	–	–	–	–	–	–	–	–	–	–	–	–	–
	Jos VERSTAPPEN	Tyrrell Ford	A	15	A	10	8	11	A	A	A	10	A	A	A	12	A	14	16	–	–	–	–	–	–

Nber of Grand Prix contested

Patrese	256
Berger	210
DeCesaris	208
Piquet	204
Prost	199
Alboreto	194
Mansell	187
G. Hill	176
Laffite	176
Lauda	171
Boutsen	163
Senna	161
Brundle	158
Watson	152
Arnoux	149
Warwick	147
Reutemann	146
E. Fittipaldi	144
Jarier	135
Alesi	135
Cheever	132
Regazzoni	132
Ma. Andretti	128
Brabham	126
Peterson	123
Ickx	116
Jones	116
Rosberg	114
Tambay	114
Hulme	112
Scheckter	112
Surtees	111
Martini	119
Herbert	113
De Angelis	108
Alliot	107
Mass	105
Bonnier	102
M. Schumacher	102
McLaren	101
Stewart	99
Siffert	97
Amon	96
Hakkinen	96
Depailler	95
Katayama	95
Capelli	94
Hunt	92
Beltoise	86
Gurney	86
Palmer	84
D. Hill	84
Surer	82
Trintignant	82
Barrichello	81
Johansson	79
Nannini	77
Ghinzani	76
Nakajima	74
Brambilla	74
Gugelmin	74
Stuck	74
Clark	72
Pace	72
Modena	70
Pironi	70
Then :	
Morbidelli	68
Frentzen	65
Irvine	65
Panis	59
Coulthard	58
Salo	52
Diniz	50
Larini	49
Verstappen	48
J. Villeneuve	33
Fisichella	25
Magnussen	17
Nakano	17
R. Schumacher	17
Rosset	16
Trulli	14
Marquès	12
Fontana	4
Wurz	3

Nber of poles

Senna	65
Prost	33
Clark	33
Mansell	32
Fangio	28
Lauda	24
Piquet	24
D. Hill	20
Andretti	18
Arnoux	18
Stewart	17
M. Schumacher	17
Moss	16
Ascari	14
Hunt	14
Peterson	14
Brabham	13
G. Hill	13
Ickx	13
J. Villeneuve	13
Berger	12
Rindt	10
Surtees	8
Patrese	8
Laffite	7
Fittipaldi	6
P. Hill	6
Jabouille	6
Jones	6
Reutemann	6
Amon	5
Coulthard	5
Farina	5
Regazzoni	5
Rosberg	5
Tambay	5
Hawthorn	4
Pironi	4
De Angelis	3
Brooks	3
T. Fabi	3
Gonzales	3
Gurney	3
Jarier	3
Scheckter	3
Then :	
Alesi	2
Frentzen	1
Barrichello	1
Hakkinen	1

Nber of victories

Prost	51
Senna	41
Mansell	31
Stewart	27
M. Schumacher	27
Clark	25
Lauda	25
Fangio	24
Piquet	23
D. Hill	21
Moss	16
Brabham	14
Fittipaldi	14
G. Hill	14
Ascari	13
Andretti	12
Jones	12
Reutemann	12
J. Villeneuve	11
Hunt	10
Peterson	10
Scheckter	10
Berger	10
Hulme	8
Ickx	8
Arnoux	7
Brooks	6
Laffite	6
Rindt	6
Surtees	6
G. Villeneuve	6
Patrese	6
Alboreto	5
Farina	5
Regazzoni	5
Rosberg	5
Watson	5
Gurney	4
McLaren	4
Boutsen	3
P. Hill	3
Hawthorn	3
Pironi	3
Coulthard	3
Then :	
Herbert	2
Panis	1
Panis	1
Alesi	1
Frentzen	1
Hakkinen	1

Number of fastest laps

Prost	41
Mansell	30
Clark	28
M. Schumacher	28
Lauda	25
Fangio	23
Piquet	23
Berger	21
Moss	20
D. Hill	19
Senna	19
Regazzoni	15
Stewart	15
Ickx	14
Jones	13
Patrese	13
Arnoux	12
Ascari	11
Surtees	11
Andretti	10
Brabham	10
G. Hill	10
Hulme	9
Peterson	9
J. Villeneuve	9
Hunt	8
Laffite	7
G. Villeneuve	7
Farina	6
Fittipaldi	6
Gonzalez	6
Gurney	6
Hawthorn	6
P. Hill	6
Pironi	6
Scheckter	6
Frentzen	6
Pace	5
Watson	5
Coulthard	5
Alesi	4
Alboreto	4
Beltoise	4
Depailler	4
Reutemann	4
Siffert	4
Then :	
Fisichella	1
Hakkinen	1

Total number of points scored

Prost	798.5
Senna	614
Piquet	485.5
Mansell	482
M. Schumacher	440
Lauda	420.5
Berger	385
Stewart	360
D. Hill	333
Reutemann	310
G. Hill	289
E. Fittipaldi	281
Patrese	281
Fangio	277.5
Clark	274
Brabham	261
Scheckter	255
Hulme	248
Laffite	228
Alesi	225
Regazzoni	212
Jones	206
Peterson	206
McLaren	196.5
Alboreto	186.5
Moss	186.5
Arnoux	181
Ickx	181
Ma. Andretti	180
Surtees	180
Hunt	179
Watson	169
Then :	
J. Villeneuve	159
Hakkinen	118
Coulthard	117
Herbert	82
Frentzen	71
Panis	54
Irvine	52
Barrichello	51
Fisichella	20
R. Schumacher	13
Salo	12
Verstappen	11
Katayama	5
Wurz	4
Trulli	3
Diniz	2
Nakano	2
Larini	

Number of laps in the lead

Senna	2'999
Prost	2'705
Mansell	2'099
Clark	2'039
Stewart	1'893
Lauda	1'620
Piquet	1'572
M. Schumacher	1'568
D. Hill	1'325
G. Hill	1'073
Brabham	827
Andretti	799
Peterson	706
Berger	695
Scheckter	671
Reutemann	648
Hunt	634
J. Villeneuve	634
Jones	594
Patrese	568
G. Villeneuve	533
Ickx	529
Arnoux	506
Rosberg	506
Fittipaldi	459
Hulme	436
Rindt	387
Regazzoni	361
Surtees	310
Coulthard	310
Pironi	295
Watson	287
Laffite	279
Alesi	271
Alboreto	218
Tambay	197
Gurney	191
P. Hill	189
Jabouille	184
Amon	183
Brooks	173
Depailler	165
Then :	
Frentzen	76
Hakkinen	66
Trulli	37
Herbert	27
Irvine	23
Panis	16
Fisichella	7
Barrichello	4

Nber of km in the lead

Senna	13'613
Prost	12'575
Clark	10'189
Mansell	9'642
Stewart	9'077
Piquet	7'465
M. Schumacher	7'211
Lauda	7'188
D. Hill	6'062
G. Hill	4'618
Brabham	4'541
Andretti	3'577
Berger	3'456
Reutemann	3'309
Peterson	3'304
Hunt	3'229
Ickx	3'067
J. Villeneuve	2'972
Jones	2'877
Scheckter	2'837
Patrese	2'571
Arnoux	2'561
G. Villeneuve	2'244
Rosberg	2'137
Surtees	2'131
Fittipaldi	2'122
Rindt	1'905
Hulme	1'900
Regazzoni	1'855
P. Hill	1'715
Brooks	1'525
Gurney	1'518
Laffite	1'476
Coulthard	1'455
Alesi	1'297
Watson	1'245
Pironi	1'238
Jabouille	978
Tambay	975
Alboreto	927
Von Trips	787
Amon	784
Then :	
Frentzen	379
Hakkinen	319
Trulli	160
Herbert	149
Irvine	125
Panis	53
Fisichella	48
Barrichello	18

Abbreviations : A = retired; NQ = not qualified; NPQ = not prequalified; F = forfeit; D = disqualified, NC = finished but not classified (insufficient distance covered). ARG = Argentina; AUS = Australia; AUT = Austria; BEL = Belgium; BRE = Brazil; CAN = Canada; DAL = Dallas; ESP = Spain; EUR = Europe; FIN = Finland; FRA = France; GB = England; GER =Germany; HOL = The Netherlands; ITA = Italy; JAP = Japan; MEX = Mexico; MON = Monaco; NZ = New-Zealand; PAC = Pacific; POR = Portugal; RSM = San Marino; SA = South Africa; SUE = Sweden; SUI = Switzerland; USA = Etats-Unis; USAE = East USA; USAW = West USA; VEG = Las Vegas. NB : Laps in the lead only since 1957.

The 48 World Champions

Year	Driver	Nationality	Make	Nber of races	Nber of poles	Nber of victories	Nber fastest laps
1950	Giuseppe Farina	ITA	Alfa Roméo	7	2	3	3
1951	Juan Manuel Fangio	ARG	Alfa Roméo	8	4	3	5
1952	Alberto Ascari	ITA	Ferrari	8	5	6	5
1953	Alberto Ascari	ITA	Ferrari	9	6	5	4
1954	Juan Manuel Fangio	ARG	Mercedes/Maserati	9	5	6	3
1955	Juan Manuel Fangio	ARG	Mercedes	7	3	4	3
1956	Juan Manuel Fangio	ARG	Lancia/Ferrari	8	5	3	3
1957	Juan Manuel Fangio	ARG	Maserati	8	4	4	2
1958	Mike Hawthorn	GB	Ferrari	11	4	1	5
1959	Jack Brabham	AUS	Cooper Climax	9	1	2	1
1960	Jack Brabham	AUS	Cooper Climax	10	3	5	3
1961	Phil Hill	USA	Ferrari	8	5	2	2
1962	Graham Hill	GB	BRM	9	1	4	3
1963	Jim Clark	GB	Lotus Climax	10	7	7	6
1964	John Surtees	GB	Ferrari	10	2	2	2
1965	Jim Clark	GB	Lotus Climax	10	6	6	6
1966	Jack Brabham	AUS	Brabham Repco	9	3	4	1
1967	Dennis Hulme	NZ	Brabham Repco	11	0	2	2
1968	Graham Hill	GB	Lotus Ford	12	2	3	0
1969	Jackie Stewart	GB	Matra Ford	11	2	6	5
1970	Jochen Rindt	AUT	Lotus Ford	13	3	5	1
1971	Jackie Stewart	GB	Matra Ford	11	6	6	3
1972	Emerson Fittipaldi	BRE	Lotus Ford	12	3	5	0
1973	Jackie Stewart	GB	Tyrrell Ford	15	3	5	1
1974	Emerson Fittipaldi	BRE	McLaren Ford	15	2	3	0
1975	Niki Lauda	AUT	Ferrari	14	9	5	2
1976	James Hunt	GB	McLaren Ford	16	8	6	2
1977	Niki Lauda	AUT	Ferrari	17	2	3	3
1978	Mario Andretti	USA	Lotus Ford	16	8	6	3
1979	Jody Scheckter	SA	Ferrari	15	1	3	1
1980	Alan Jones	AUS	Williams Ford	14	3	5	5
1981	Nelson Piquet	BRE	Brabham Ford	15	4	3	1
1982	Keke Rosberg	FIN	Williams Ford	16	1	1	0
1983	Nelson Piquet	BRE	Brabham BMW Turbo	15	1	3	4
1984	Niki Lauda	AUT	McLaren TAG Porsche Turbo	16	0	5	5
1985	Alain Prost	FRA	McLaren TAG Porsche Turbo	16	2	5	5
1986	Alain Prost	FRA	McLaren TAG Porsche Turbo	16	1	4	2
1987	Nelson Piquet	BRE	Williams Honda Turbo	16	4	3	4
1988	Ayrton Senna	BRE	McLaren Honda Turbo	16	13	8	3
1989	Alain Prost	FRA	McLaren Honda	16	2	4	5
1990	Ayrton Senna	BRE	McLaren Honda	16	10	6	2
1991	Ayrton Senna	BRE	McLaren Honda	16	8	7	2
1992	Nigel Mansell	GB	Williams Renault	16	14	9	8
1993	Alain Prost	FRA	Williams Renault	16	13	7	6
1994	Michael Schumacher	GER	Benetton Ford	14	6	8	9
1995	Michael Schumacher	GER	Benetton Renault	17	4	9	7
1996	Damon Hill	GB	Williams Renault	16	9	8	5
1997	Jacques Villeneuve	CAN	Williams Renault	17	10	7	3

Constructors' Championship 1997

Position	Make	Nber of points	Nber of poles	Nber of victories	Nb. fastest laps	Nb. laps in lead	Nb. km in lead
1.	Williams Renault	123	11	8	9	425	1981
2.	Ferrari	102	3	5	3	323	1518
3.	Benetton Renault	67	2	1	2	73	456
4.	McLaren Mercedes	63	1	3	2	127	630
5.	Jordan Peugeot	33	0	0	1	7	48
6.	Prost Mugen Honda	21	0	0	0	37	160
7.	Sauber Petronas	16	0	0	0	0	0
8.	Arrows Yamaha	9	0	0	0	62	246
9.	Stewart Ford	6	0	0	0	0	0
10.	Tyrrell Ford	2	0	0	0	0	0

Nb. of constructors' championship titles

(exists since 1958)

9 : Williams 1980 - 81 - 86 - 87-92 - 93-94-96-97

8 : Ferrari 1961 - 64 - 75 - 76 77 - 79 - 82 - 83

7: Lotus 1963 - 65 - 68 - 70-72 - 73 - 78

McLaren 1974 - 84 - 85 - 88-89 - 90 - 91

2 : Cooper 1959 - 60
Brabham 1966 - 67

1 : Vanwall 1958
BRM 1962
Matra 1969
Tyrrell 1971
Benetton 1995

Number of poles per make

Make	Poles
Ferrari	121
Lotus	107
Williams	107
McLaren	80
Brabham	39
Renault	31
Benetton	15
Tyrrell	14
Alfa Roméo	12
BRM	11
Cooper	11
Maserati	10
Ligier	9
Mercedes	8
Vanwall	7
March	5
Matra	4
Shadow	3
Lancia	2
Arrows	1
Honda	1
Jordan	1
Lola	1
Porsche	1
Wolf	1

Nber of victories per make

Make	Victories
Ferrari	113
McLaren	107
Williams	103
Lotus	79
Brabham	35
Benetton	26
Tyrrell	23
BRM	17
Cooper	16
Renault	1
Alfa Roméo	10
Maserati	9
Matra	9
Mercedes	9
Vanwall	9
Ligier	9
March	3
Wolf	3
Honda	2
Hesketh	1
Penske	1
Porsche	1
Shadow	1

Nber of fastest laps per make

Ferrari	126
Williams	109
McLaren	71
Lotus	70
Brabham	41
Benetton	36
Tyrrell	20
Renault	18
BRM	15
Maserati	15
Alfa Roméo	14
Cooper	13
Matra	12
Ligier	11
Mercedes	9
March	7
Vanwall	6
Surtees	4
Eagle	2
Honda	2
Shadow	2
Wolf	2
Ensign	1
Gordini	1
Hesketh	1
Lancia	1
Parnelli	1
Jordan	1

Family picture of the 1997 Championship, in Melbourne. Standing, from left to right : Eddie Irvine, Rubens Barrichello, Jan Magnussen, David Coulthard, Mika Hakkinen, Ralf Schumacher, Giancarlo Fisichella, Ricardo Rosset, Vincenzo Sospiri. Middle : Michael Schumacher, Jarno Trulli (at the time with Minardi), Ukyo Katayama, Jacques Villeneuve, Heinz-Harald Frentzen, Shinji Nakano and Olivier Panis. Sitting : Jos Verstappen, Mika Salo, Pedro Diniz, Damon Hill, Nicola Larini, Johnny Herbert, Gerhard Berger and Jean Alesi.

Sporting regulations

The FIA will organise the FIA Formula One World Championship (the Championship) which is the property of the FIA and comprises two titles of World Champion, one for drivers and for for constructors. It consists of the Formula One Grand Prix races which are included in the Formula One calendar and in respect of which the ASNs and organisers have signed the organisation agreement provided for in the 1997 Concorde Agreement (Events). All the participating parties (FIA, ASNs, organisers, competitors and circuits) undertake to apply as well as observe the rules governing the Championship and must hold FIA Super Licences which are issued to drivers, competitors, officials, organisers and circuits.

LICENCES

10. All drivers, compet.itors and officials participating in the Championship must hold a FIA Super licence. Applications for Super Licences must be made to the FIA through the applicant's ASN. The driver's name will remain on the super license for one year.

CHAMPIONSHIP EVENTS

12. Events are reserved for Formula One cars as defined in the Technical Regulations.

13. Each Event will have the status of an international restricted competition.

14. The distance of all races (from start signal to chequered flag, excluding the formation lap referred to in Art. 142) shall be equal to the least number of complete laps which exceed a distance of 305 km, save only that should two hours elapse before the scheduled race distance is completed, the leader will be shown the chequered flag when he crosses the start/finish line (the Line) at the end of the lap during which such period of two hours shall end. The Line is a single line which crosses both the track and the pit lane.

15. The maximum number of events in the Championship is 17, the minimum is 8.

17. An Event which is cancelled with less than three months written notice to the FIA will not be considered for inclusion in the following year's Championship unless the FIA judges the cancellation to have been due to force majeure.

18. An Event may be cancelled if fewer than 12 cars are available for it.

WORLD CHAMPIONSHIP

19. The Formula One World Champion Driver's Title will be awarded to the driver who has scored the highest number of points, taking into consideration all the results obtained during the events which have actually taken place.

20. Points will not be awarded for the Championship unless the driver has driven the same car throughout the race in the Event in question.

21. The title of Formula One World Champion for Constructors will be awarded to the make which has scored the highest number of points, taking into account all the results obtained by a maximum of 2 cars per make.

22. The constructor of an engine or rolling chassis is the person (including any corporate or unincorporated body) which owns the intellectual property rights to such engine or chassis. The make of an engine or chassis is the name attributed to it by its constructor. If the make of the chassis is not of the same as that of the engine, the title will be awarded to the former which shall always precede the latter in the name of the car.

23. Points for both titles will be awarded at each Event according to the following scale :

1st : 10 points;

2nd : 6 points;

3rd : 4 points;

4th : 3 points;

5th : 2 points;

6th : 1 point.

24. If a race is stopped under Arts. 158 and 159, and cannot be restarted, no points will be awarded in case A, half points will be awarded in case B and full points will be awarded in case C.

25. Drivers finishing first, second and third in the Championship must be present at the annual FIA Prize Giving ceremony. Any such driver who is absent will be liable to a maximum fine of US $ 50,000.00. All competitors shall use their best endeavours to ensure that their drivers attend as aforesaid.

DEAD HEAT

26. Prizes and points awarded for all the positions of competitors who tie, will be added together and shared equally.

27. If two or more constructors or drivers finish the season with the same number of points, the higher place in the Championship (in either case) shall be awarded to :

a) the holder of the greatest number of 1st places,

b) if the number of first places is the same, the holder of the greatest number of second places,

c) if the number of second places is the same, the holder of the greatest number of third places and so on until a winner emerges,

d) if this procedure fails to produce a result, the FISA will nominate the winner according to such criteria as it thinks fit.

COMPETITORS APPLICATIONS

43. Applications to compete in the Championship may be submitted to the FIA at any time between 1 November and 15 November each year (...). Successful applicants are automatically entered in all events of the Championship and will be the only competitors at Events.

45. A competitor may change the make and type of engine at any time during the Championship. All points scored with an engine different (in make and type) to that which was first entered in the Championship will count (and will be aggregated) for the assessment of Benefits and for determining team positions for pre-qualifying purposes, however such points will not count towards (nor be aggregated for) the FIA Formula One Constructors Championship.

46. (...) All applicants who did not take part in the entire Championship for the previous year must also deposit US$500,000.00 with the FIA when submitting their application. (...)

47. All applications will be studied by the FIA which will publish the list of cars and drivers accepted together with their race numbers on 1 December (or the following Monday if 1 December falls on a week-end), having first notified unsuccessful applicants as set out in article 43.

48. No more than two entries will be accepted from any one competitor.

INCIDENTS

54. Incident means any occurrence or series of occurrences involving one or more drivers, or any action by any driver, which is reported to the stewards by the race director (or noted by the stewards and referred to the race director for investigation) which :

- necessitated the stopping of a race under Article 158;

- constituted a breach of these Sporting Regulations or the Code;

- caused a false start by one or more cars;

- caused an avoidable collision;

- forced a diver off the track;

- illegitimately prevented a legitimate overtaking manoeuvre by a driver;

- illegitimately impeded another driver during overtaking.

55. It shall be at the discretion of the stewards to decide, upon a report or a request by the race director, if a driver or drivers involved in an incident shall be penalised. If a driver is involved in a collision or incident (see Art. 54) he must not leave the circuit without the consent of the stewards.

56. The stewards may impose a time penalty on any driver involved in an incident.

57. Should the Stewards decide to impose a time penalty, the following procedure shall apply :

a) The stewards shall, no later than twenty-five minutes after the moment at which the Incident occurred, give written notification of the time penalty which has been imposed to an official of the team concerned on the pitwall; this penalty will also be transmistted on the video monitors as rapidly as possible.

b) Subject to e) below, after notification has been given to the team pursuant to a) above, the relevant driver may cover no more than three complete laps before entering the pits and proceeding to his pit where he shall remain for the period of time penalty. During the time the car is stationary it may not be worked on unless the engine stops, in which case it may be started after the time penalty period has elapsed.

c) When the time penalty period has elapsed the driver may rejoin the race.

d) Any breach or failure to comply with Articles 57 b) or 57 c) may result in the car being excluded.

e) If an incident for which a time penalty is imposed occurs with 12 or less complete laps remaining to the finish of the race, the stewards shall have the right to add the time penalty to the elapsed time of the driver concerned.

58. Any determination made or any penalty imposed pursuant to Article 56 shall be without prejudice to the operation of Articles 160 or 161 of the Code.

CHANGES OF DRIVER

61. During a season, each team will be permitted one driver change for their first car and will be permitted to have three drivers for their second car who may be changed at any time provided that any driver change is made in accordance with the Code and before the start of qualifying practice. After 18:00 on the day of scrutineering, a driver change may only take place with the consent of the stewards. In all other circumstances, competitors will be obliged to use the drivers they nominated at the time of entering the Championship except in case of force majeure which will be considered seperately. Any new driver may score points in the Championship.

NUMBER OF CARS PARTICIPATING

63. The number of cars allowed to start the race is limited to 26. For practice the number is limited to 30, except for the free practice on race day which is open only to those cars which have qualified for the race.

64. Should the number of cars entered in the Championship exceed 30 the following procedure will be used :

- 26 places in qualifying practice will be reserved for constructors' cars according to the classification in the World Championship for Constructors of the two previous half seasons (...)

- 4 places will be made available to other cars according to pre-qualifying practice.

- Those cars not included in the 26 automatically admitted to qualifying practice will take part in a timed practice session two days before the race (see Art. 118) and the 4 fastest of them will then be allowed to take part in free and qualifying practice sessions (see Arts. 119 and 120) together with the aforementioned 26.

RACE NUMBERS AND NAME OF CAR

65. Each car will carry the race number of its driver (or his replacement) as published by the FIA at the beginning of the season. When a car is shown on a 25 cm television monitor in such a way as to substantially fill the screen in at least one dimension, its race number must be clearly visible from the front and from either side of the car respectively.

66. The name or the emblem of the make of the car must appear on the front of the nose of the car and in either case be at least 25 mm in its largest dimension. The name of the driver will also appear on the bodywork, on the outside of the cockpit, or on the driver's helmet and be clearly legible.

PIT LANE

69. a) For the avoidance of doubt and for description purposes, the pit lane shall be divided into two lanes. The lane closest to the pit wall is designated the «fast lane» and the lane closest to the garages is designated the «inner lane», and is the only area where any work can be carried out on a car.

b) Competitors must not paint lines on any part of the pit lane.

c) No equipment may be left in the fast lane. A car may enter the fast lane only with the driver sitting in the car behind the steering wheel in his normal position even when the car is being pushed.

d) Team personnel are only allowed in the pit lane immediately before they are required to work on a car and must withdraw as soon as the work is complete.

SPORTING CHECKS

71. At the first Event of each Championship, the FIA will check all licences.

SCRUTINEERING

73. Initial scrutineering of the car will take place between 10h00 and 18h00 on the day before first practice in the garage assigned to each team.

74. Unless a waiver is granted by the stewards, competitors who do not keep to these time limits will not be allowed to take part in the Event.

75. No car may take part in the Event until it has been passed by the scrutineers.

76. The scrutineers may :

a) check the eligibility of a car or of a competitor at any time during an Event.

b) require a car to be dismantled by the competitor to make sure that the conditions of eligibility or conformity are fully satisfied.

c) require a competitor to pay the reasonable expenses which exercise of the powers mentioned in this Article may entail.

d) require a competitor to supply them with such parts or samples as they may deem necessary.

78. The race director or the clerk of the course may require that any car involved in an accident be stopped and checked.

80. The stewards will publish the findings of the scrutineers each time cars are checked during the Event. These results will not include any specific figure except in respect of fuel analysis or where a car is found to be in breach of the Technical Regulations.

SUPPLY OF TYRES IN THE CHAMPIONSHIP AND TYRE LIMITATION DURING THE EVENT

81. Supply of tyres : No tyre may be used in the Championship unless the company supplying such tyre accepts and adheres to the following conditions :

- one tyre supplier present in the Championship: this company must equip 100% of the entered teams on ordinary commercial terms.

- two tyre suppliers present : each of them must, if called upon to do so, be prepared to equip up to 60% of the entered teams on ordinary commercial terms.

- three or more tyre suppliers present : each of them must, if called upon to do so, be prepared to equip up to 40% of the entered teams on ordinary commercial terms.

- each tyre supplier must undertake to provide only two specifications of dry-weather tyre at each Event, each of which must be of one homogenous compound only;

- if, in the interests of maintaining current levels of circuit safety, the FIA deems it necessary to reduce tyre grip, it shall introduce such rules as the tyre suppliers may advise or, in the absence of advice which achieves the FIA's objectives, specify the maximum permissible contact areas for front and rear tyres.

82. Quantity and type of tyres :

a) The same driver may not use more than a total of thirty-six dry-weather tyres and twenty-eight wet-weather tyres throughout the entire duration of the Event.

Prior to the qualifying practice each driver may use two specifications of dry-weather tyres but must, before qualifying practice begins, nominate which specification of tyre he will use for the remainder of the Event.

For qualifying practice, warm up and the race each driver may use no more than twenty-eight tyres (fourteen front and fourteen rear).

b) A wet-weather tyre is a tyre which is designed for use on a wet track and has a contact area which is less than 75% of that of an equivalent size dry-weather tyre. Wet-weather tyres may only be used after the track has been declared wet by the race director.

83. The control procedure will be as follows :

a) All tyres which are to be used at an Event will be marked with a unique identification.

b) At any time during an Event, and at his absolute discretion, the FIA technical delegate may select the dry-weather tyres to be used by any Team from among the total stock of tyres which such Team's designated supplier has present at the Event.

c) During initial scrutineering, each competitor may have up to thirty-six dry-weather tyres and twenty-eight wet-weather tyres for each of his drivers ready for marking in his garage. Tyres not marked during initial scrutineering can be marked at other times by arrangement with the FIA technical delegate.

d) From among the twenty-eight dry-weather tyres chosen for each car for qualifying practice, warm up and the race, the FIA technical delegate will choose at random sixteen tyres (eight front and eight rear) which are the only dry-weather tyres which such car may use in qualifying practice.

e) A competitor wishing to replace an already marked unused tyre by another unused one must present both tyres to the FIA technical delegate.

84. The use of tyres without appropriate markings is strictly forbidden.

WEIGHING

85. The weight of any car may be checked during the Event as follows :

a) All drivers entered in the Championship will be weighed, wearing their complete racing apparel, at the first Event of the season. If a driver is entered later in the season he will be weighed at his first Event.

b) During qualifying practice

1) the FIA will install weighing equipment in an area as close to the first pit as possible, this area will be used for the weighing procedure;

2) cars will be selected at random to undergo the weighing procedure. The FIA technical delegate will inform the driver by means of a red light at the pit entrance that his car has been selected for weighing;

3) having been signalled (by means of a red light), that his car has been selected for weighing, the driver will proceed directly to the weighing area and stop his engine;

4) the car will then be weighed and the result given to the driver in writing;

5) if the car is unable to reach the weighing area under its own power it will be placed under the exclusive control of the marshals who will take the car to be weighed;

6) a car or driver may not leave the weighing area without the consent of the FIA technical delegate.

c) After the race : Each car crossing the line will be weighed. If a car is weighed without the driver the weight determined under 2 above will be added to give the total weight required under Article 4. of the Technical Regulations.

d) Should the weight of the car be less than that specified in Article 4.1 of the Technical Regulations when weighed under b) or c) above, the car and the driver will be excluded from the Event save where the deficiency in weight results from the accidental loss of a component of the car due to force majeure.

e) No solid, liquid, gas or other substance or matter of whatsoever nature may be added to, placed on, or removed from a car after it has been selected for weighing or has finished the race or during the weighing procedure. (...)

f) Only scrutineers and officials may enter the weighing area. No intervention of any kind is allowed there unless authorised by such officials.

86. Any breach of these provisions for the weighing of cars may result in the exclusion of the relevant car.

SPARE CAR

89. A competitor may use several cars for practice and the race provided that :

a) he uses no more than two cars (one car for a one car Team) for free practice on each of the two practice days;

b) he uses no more than three cars (two cars for a one car Team) during qualifying practice;

c) they are all of the same make and were entered in the Championship by the same competitor;

d) they have been scrutineered in accordance with these Sporting Regulations;

e) each car carries its driver's race number.

90. Changes of car may only take place in the pits under supervision of the marshals.

91. No change of car will be allowed after the green light (see Article 142) provided always that if a race has to be restarted under Article 160 Case A, the moment after which no car change will be allowed shall be when the green light for the subsequent start is shown.

GENERAL SAFETY

93. Drivers are strictly forbidden to drive their car in the opposite direction to the race unless this is absolutely necessary in order to move the car from a dangerous position. A car may be pushed to remove it from a dangerous position as directed by the marshals.

94. Any driver intending to leave the track or to go to his pits or the paddock area must signal his intention to do so in good time making sure that he can do this without danger.

96. A driver who abandons a car must leave it in neutral or with the clutch disengaged and with the steering wheel in place.

97. Repairs to a car may be carried out only in the paddock, pits and on the grid.

99. Save as provided in Articl 141, refuelling is allowed only in the pits.

102. Save as specifically authorised by the Code or these Sporting Regulations, no one except the driver may touch a stopped car unless it is in the pits or on the starting grid.

104. During the periods commencing 15 minutes prior to and ending 5 minutes after every practice session and the period between the green lights being illuminated (Article 142) and the time when the last car enters the parc fermé, no one is allowed on the track with the exception of :

a) marshals or other authorised personnel in the execution of their duty;

b) drivers when driving or under the direction of the marshals;

c) and mechanics under Article 143 only.

105. During a race, the engine may only be started with the starter, except :

a) in the pit lane where the use of an external starting device is allowed (...).

107. A speed limit of 80 km/h in practice and 120 km/h in the race, or such other speed limits as the Permanent Bureau of the Formula One Commission may decide, will be enforced in the pit lane. During practice and reconnaissance laps (see Article 139), any driver who exceeds the limit will be fined a maximum of US$10,000 (US$20,000 in case of a second offence in the same Championship season). During the race, the stewards may impose a time penalty on any driver who exceeds the limit.

108. If a driver has serious mechanical difficulties during practice or the race, he must leave the track as soon as it is safe to do so.

109. The car's rear light must be illuminated at all times when it is running on wet-weather tyres. The technical delegate may check the light at any time until 15 minutes before the green light. No penalty will be imposed if the light fails during a race, nor need the car be stopped.

110. Only six team members per participating car (all of whom shall have been issued with and wearing special identification) are allowed in the signalling area during practice and the race. (...)

112. The race director, the clerk of the course or the FIA medical delegate can require a driver to have a medical examination at any time during an Event.

113. A breach of the provisions of the Code or these Sporting Regulations relating to general safety discipline may result in the exclusion of the car and driver concerned from the Event.

PRE-QUALIFYING PRACTICE, FREE PRACTICE, QUALIFYING PRACTICE AND WARM UP

115. No driver may start in the race without taking part in qualifying practice.

116. During practice there will be a green/red light at the pit exit. Cars may only leave the pit lane when the green light is on.

117. During the Event, the circuit shall not be used for any purpose other than the Event except after all practice has finished on each day and during the period beginning after the free practice on race day and ending 60 minutes before the pit lane is opened or at other times with the written consent of the FIA.

118. Should it be necessary for certain cars to pre-qualify in accordance with Article 64, the practice session will take place two days (Monaco, three days) before the race from 08h00 to 09h00.

119. Free practice sessions will take place :

a) two days (Monaco : three days) before the race from 11.00 to 12.00 and from 13.00 to 14.00.

b) the day before the race from 09.00 to 9.45 and from 10.15 to 11.00.

c) Each driver is allowed a maximum of 30 laps free practice on each day. Any extra lap(s) completed will be deducted from such driver's qualifying practice.

120. Qualifying practice will take place :

a) The day before the race from 13.00 - 14.00.

b) Subject to Article 119(c), each driver is allowed a maximum of 12 laps qualifying practice. Should a driver complete more than 12 laps, all times recorded by the driver will be cancelled.

121. Warm up : a free practice session will take place on race day; it will last 30 minutes and start 4 hours and 30 minutes before the starting time of the race.

122. The interval between the free and qualifying

practice session may never be less than 1 hour and 30 minutes.

Only in the most exceptional circumstances can a delay in free practice or other difficulty on race morning result in a delay to the starting time of the race.

123. If a car stops during practice it must be removed from the track as quickly as possible so that its presence does not constitute a danger or hinder other competitors. If the driver is unable to drive the car from a dangerous position, it shall be the duty of the marshals to assist him. If any such assistance results in the car being driven or pushed back to the pits, the car may not be used again in that session. Additionally, if the assistance is given during pre-qualifying practice or qualifying practice, all the driver's lap times for that session will be cancelled.

124. The clerk of the course may interrupt practice as often and for as long as he thinks necessary to clear the track or to allow the recovery of a car. In the case of free practice only, the clerk of the course with the agreement of the stewards of the meeting may decline to prolong the practice period after an interruption of this kind.

Furthermore if, in the opinions of the stewards, a stoppage is caused deliberately, the driver concerned may have his times from that session cancelled and may not be permitted to take part in any other practice session that day.

126. Should one or more sessions be thus interrupted, no protest can be accepted as to the possible effects of the interruption on the qualification of drivers admitted to start.

127. All laps covered during qualifying practice will be timed to determine the driver's position at the start in accordance with the prescriptions of Article 132. With the exception of a lap on which a red flag is shown (see Article 158) each time a car crosses the Line it will be deemed to have completed one lap. On a circuit where the Line is situated before the first pit, any car which stops on the circuit having already completed its total allocation of laps, will be deemed to have covered an extra lap.

STOPPING THE PRACTICE

128. Should it become necessary to stop the practice because the circuit is blocked by an accident or because weather or other conditions make it impossible to continue, the Clerk of the Course shall order a red flag and the abort lights to be shown at the start Line. Simultaneously, red flags will be shown at all marshal posts. When the signal is given to stop all cars shall immediately reduce speed and proceed slowly back to their respective pits and all cars abandoned on the track will be removed to a safe place. Any lap during which the red flag is shown will not be counted towards a car's total lap allocation for that session.

PRESS CONFERENCES

129. The FIA press delegate will choose a maximum of five drivers who must attend a press conference in the media centre for a period of one hour at 15:00 on the Thursday of the Event (on Wednesday in Monaco). These driver's Teams will be notified no less than 48 hours before the conference. In addition, a maximum of two Team personalities may be chosen by the FIA press delegate to attend this press conference.

On the Friday of the Event (on Thursday in Monaco), a minimum of three and a maximum of six drivers and/or team personalities, (other than those who attended the press conference on the previous day and subject to the consent of the team principal), will be chosen by ballot or rota by the FIA press delegate during the Event and must make themselves available to the media for a press conference in the media centre for a period of one hour at 15:30.

130. Immediately after qualifying practice the first three drivers in qualifying will be required to make themselves available for television interviews in the unilateral room and then attend a press conference in the media centre for a maximum period of 30 minutes.

THE GRID

131. At the end of qualifying practice, the fastest time achieved by each driver will be officially published (see Article 63).

132. The grid will be drawn up in the order of the fastest time achieved by each driver. Should two or more drivers have set identical times, priority will be given to the one who set it first.

133. The fastest driver will start the race from the position on the grid which was the pole position in the previous year or, on a new circuit, has been designated as such by the FIA safety delegate.

134. Any driver whose best qualifying lap exceeds 107% of the pole position time will not be allowed to take part in the race, save for exceptional circumstances accepted as such by the stewards of the Event. Should there be more than one driver accepted in this manner, their order will be determined by the stewards.

135. The final starting grid will be publihed after the warm up on race day. Any competitor whose car(s) is (are) unable to start for any reason whatsoever (or who has good reason to believe that their car(s) will not be ready to start) must inform the clerk of the course accordingly at the earliest opportunity and, in any event, not later than 45 minutes before the start of the race. If one or more cars are withdrawn the grid will be closed up accordingly.

137. Any car which has not taken up its position on the grid by the time the ten minute signal is shown will not be permitted to do so and must start from the pits in accordance with Article 140.

BRIEFING

138. A briefing by the race director will take place one hour after the end of warm up on race day in the location allocated for this purpose. All competitors (or their appointed representatives) and drivers of those cars which are eligible to take part in the race must be present throughout the briefing, under penalty of exclusion from the race.

STARTING PROCEDURE

139. 30 minutes before the time for the start of the race, the cars will leave the pits to cover one reconnaissance lap. At the end of this lap they will stop on the grid in starting order with their engines stopped. Should they wish to cover more than one reconnaissance lap, this must be done by driving down the pit lane at a greatly reduced speed between each of the laps.

140. 17 minutes before the starting time, a warning signal announcing the closing of the pit exit in 2 minutes will be given.

15 minutes before the starting time, the pit exit will be closed and a second warning signal will be given. Any car which is still in the pits can start from the pits, but only under the direction of the marshals. It may be moved to the pit exit only with the driver in position. Where the pit exit is immediately after the Line, cars will join the race when the whole field has passed the pit exit on its first racing lap. Where the pit exit is immediately before the Line, cars will join the race as soon as the whole field has crossed the Line after the start.

141. During the starting procedure, refuelling and wheel changes will be allowed on the starting grid until the 5 minute signal is shown. Refuelling on the starting grid may only be carried out using one unpressurised container with a maximum capacity of 12 litres. This container may not be refilled during the starting procedure and must be fitted with one or more dry break couplings connecting it to the car.

142. The approach of the start will be announced by signals shown ten minutes, five minutes, three minutes, one minute and thirty seconds before the start of the formation lap, each of which will be accompanied by an audible warning.

When the ten minute signal is shown, everybody except drivers, officials and team technical staff must leave the grid.

When the one minute signal is shown, engines will be started and all team technical staff must leave the grid.

When the green lights are illuminated, the cars will begin the formation lap with the pole position driver leading. During this lap practice starts are forbidden and the formation must be kept as tight as possible.

Overtaking during the formation lap is only permitted if a car is delayed when leaving its grid position and cars behind cannot avoid passing it without unduly delaying the remainder of the field. In this case, drivers may only overtake to re-establish the original starting order.

Any driver who is delayed leaving the grid may not overtake another moving car if he was stationary after the remainder of the cars had crossed the Line, and must start the race from the back of the grid. If more than one driver is affected, they must form up at the back of the grid in the order they left to complete the formation lap.

A time penalty will be imposed on any driver who, in the opinion of the Stewards, unnecessarily overtook another car during the formation lap.

143. Any driver who is unable to start the formation lap must raise his arm and, after the remainder of the cars have crossed the Line, his mechanics may attempt to rectify the problem under the supervision of the marshals. If the car is still unable to start the formation lap it will be pushed into the pit lane by the shortest route and the mechanics may work on the car again.

144. When the cars come back to the grid at the end of the formation lap, they will stop on their respective grid positions, keeping their engines running. Once all the cars have come to a halt the five-second signal will appear followed by the four, three, two and one second signals. At any time after the one second signal appears, the race will be started by extinguishing all red lights.

146. Any car which is unable to maintain starting order during the entire formation lap or is moving when the one second light comes on must enter the pit lane and start from the pits as specified in Article 140.

147. If, after returning to the starting grid at the end of the formation lap, a driver's engine stops and he is unable to restart the car, he must immediately raise his hands above his head and the marshal responsible for that row must immediately wave a yellow flag.

If the start is delayed, (see Article 148) a marshal with a yellow flag will stand in front of the car concerned to prevent it from moving until the whole field has left the grid. The driver may then follow the procedure set out in Articles 143 and 146. As in Article 144, other cars will maintain their grid positions and the vacant position(s) will not be filled. Should there be more than one driver in this situation, their new positions at the back of the grid will be determined in accordance with their relative positions on the grid at the start of the formation lap.

148. If a problem arises when the cars reach the starting grid at the end of the formation lap the following procedure shall apply :

a) If the race has not been started, the abort lights will be switched on, all engines will be stopped and the new formation lap will start 5 minutes later with the race distance reduced by one lap. The next signal will be the three minute signal.

b) If the race has been started, the marshals alongside the grid will wave their yellow flags to inform the drivers that a car is stationary on the grid.

c) If, after the start, a car is immobilised on the starting grid, it shall be the duty of the marshals to push it into the pit lane by the fastest route. If the driver is able to re-start the car whilst it is being pushed he may rejoin the race.

d) If the driver is unable to start the car whilst it is being pushed his mechanics may attempt to start it in the pit lane. If the car then starts it may rejoin the race. The driver and mechanics must follow the instructions of the track marshals at all times during such a procedure.

149. Should Article 148 apply, the race will neverthelesss count for the Championship no matter how often the procedure is repeated, or how much the race is shortened as a result.

150. No refuelling will be allowed on the grid if more than one start procedure proves necessary under Article 148.

151. A time penalty will be imposed for a false start judged using an FIA supplied transponder which must be fitted to the car as specified.

152. Only in the following cases will any variation in the start procedure be allowed :

a) If the track is dry throughout all practice sessions but becomes wet (or vice-versa) after the end of the warm up and at least 60 minutes before the starting time, a 15 minute free practice may be allowed.

b) If it starts to rain after the five-minute signal but before the race is started, the abort lights will be shown on the Line and the starting procedure will begin again at the 15 minute point. If necessary the procedure set out in Article 148 will be followed.

c) If the start of the race is imminent and in the opinion of the race director, the volume of water on the track is such that it cannot be negotiated safely even on wet-weather tyres, the avort lights will be shown on the Line simultaneously with a «10» board with a red background.

This «10» board with a red background will mean that there is to be a delay of ten minutes before the starting procedure can be resumed. If weather conditions have improved at the end of that ten minute period, a «10» board with a green background will be shown. The «10» board with a green background will mean that the green light will be shown in ten minutes.

Five minutes after the «10» board with the green background is shown, the starting procedure will begin and the normal starting procedure signals (i.e. 5, 3, 1 min., 30 second) will be shown.

If however, the weather conditions have not improved within ten minutes after the «10» board with the red background was shown, the abort lights will be shown on the Line and the «10» board with the red background will be shown again which will mean a further delay of ten minutes before the starting procedure can be resumed.

This procedure may be repeated several times.

At any time when a «10» board (with either a red or green background) is shown, it will be accompanied by an audible warning.

d) If the race is started behind the safety car, Article 157 m) will apply.

THE RACE

154. A race will not be stopped in the event of rain unless the circuit is blocked or it is dangerous to continue (see Article 158).

155. If a car during the race (except under Article 148 c and d), it must be removed from the track as quickly as possible so that its presence does not constitute a danger or hinder other competitors. If the driver is unable to drive the car from a dangerous position, it shall be the duty of the marshals to assist him. If any such assistance results in the engine starting and the driver rejoining the race, the car will be excluded from the results of the race.

156. During the race, drivers leaving the pit lane will do so on their own responsibility. However, a flashing yellow light will be shown at the pit exit and a marshal with a blue flag will warn of cars approaching.

SAFETY CAR

157. (...) b) 30 minutes before the race start time the safety car will take up position at the front of the grid and remain there until the five-minute signal is given. At this point (except under m) below) it will cover a whole lap of the circuit and enter the pit lane. If Article 152 a) applies, the safety car will take up its position at the front of the grid as soon as the 15 minute practice session has finished.

c) The safety car may be brought into operation to neutralise a race upon the decision of the clerk of the course. It will be used only if competitors or officials are in immediate physical danger but the circumstances are not such as to necessitate stopping the race.

d) When the order is given to deploy the safety car during the race, all observer's posts (including the Line) will display immobile yellow flags and a board «SC» which shall be maintained until the intervention is over.

e) During the race, the safety car with its revolving lights on, will start from the pit lane and will join the track regardless of where the race leader is.

f) All the competing cars will form up in line behind the safety car no more than 5 car lengths apart. All overtaking is forbidden (except under m) below), unless a car is signalled to do so from the safety car.

g) When ordered to do so by the clerk of the course the observer in the car will use a green light to signal to any cars between it and the race leader that they should pass. These cars will continue at reduced speed and without overtaking until they reach the line of cars behind the safety car.

h) The safety car shall be used at least until the leader is behind it and all remaining cars are lined up behind him.

Once behind the safety car, the race leader must keep within 5 car lengths of it and all remaining cars must keep the formation as tight as possible.

i) While the safety car is in operation, competing cars may stop at their pit, but may only rejoin the track when the green light at the pit exit is on. It will be on at all times except when the safety car and the line of cars following it are about to pass or are passing the pit exit. A car rejoining the track will proceed at reduced speed until it reaches the end of the line of cars behind the safety car.

j) When the clerk of the course calls in the safety car, it must extinguish all the revolving lights and enter the pits at the end of that lap. As the safety car is entering the pits the flags and boards at the observer's posts will be withdrawn.

k) When the safety car has pulled off the circuit and the cars are approaching the Line, green lights will be shown. All observer's posts will then show a green flag. Overtaking remains strictly forbidden until the cars pass the green light at the Line. The green flags will be withdrawn after one lap.

l) Each lap completed while the safety car is in service will be counted as a race lap.

m) In exceptional circumstances, the race may be started behind the safety car. In this case, at the five-minute signal its revolving yellow lights will be turned on. This is the signal to the drivers that the race will be started behind the safety car. When the green lights are shown, the safety car will leave the grid with all cars following in grid order no more than 5 car lengths apart. There will be no formation lap and race will start when the leading car crosses the line for the first time.

Overtaking, during the first lap only, is permitted if a car is delayed when leaving its grid position and cars behind cannot avoid passing it without unduly delaying the remainder of the field. In this case, drivers may only overtake to re-establish the original starting order.

Any driver who is delayed leaving the grid may not overtake another moving car if he was stationary after the remainder of the cars had crossed the Line, and must form up at the back of the line of cars behind the safety car. If more than one driver is affected, they must form up at the back of the field in the order they left the grid.

A time penalty will be imposed on any driver who, in the opinion of the Stewards, unnecessarily overtook another car during the first lap.

STOPPING A RACE

158. Should it become necessary to stop the race because the circuit is blocked by an accident or because weather or other conditions make it dangerous to continue, the clerk of the course shall order a red flag and the abort lights to be shown at the Line.

Simultaneously, red flags will be shown at all marshal posts.

When the signal is given to stop all cars shall immediately reduce speed in the knowledge that :

- the race classification will be that at the end of the penultimate lap before the lap in which the signal to stop the race was given,

- race and service vehicles may be on the track,

- the circuit may be totally blocked because of an accident,

- weather conditions may have made the circuit undriveable at racing speed,

- the pit lane will be open.

159. The procedure to be followed varies according to the number of laps completed by the race leader before the signal to stop the race was given :

Case A. Less than two full laps. If the race can't be restarted, Article 160 will apply.

Case B. Two or more full laps but less than 75% of the race distance (rounded up to the nearest whole number of laps). If the race can be restarted, Article 161 will apply.

Case C. 75 % or more of the race distance (rounded up to the nearest whole number of laps). The cars will be sent directly to the Parc Fermé and the race will be deemed to have finished when the leading car crossed the line for the penultimate time before the race was stopped.

RESTARTING A RACE

160. Case A.

a) The original start shall be deemed null and void.

b) The length of the restarted race will be the full original race distance.

c) The drivers who are eligible to take part in the race shall be eligible for the restart either in their original car or in a spare car.

d) After the signal to stop the race has been given, all cars able to do so will proceed directly but slowly to either :

- the pit lane or,

- if the grid is clear, to their original grid position or,

- if the grid is not clear, to a position behind the last grid position as directed by the marshals.

e) All cars may be worked on.

f) Refuelling will be allowed until the five minute signal is shown.

161. Case B.

a) The race shall be deemed to be in two parts, the first of which finished when the leading car crossed the Line for the penultimate time before the race was stopped.

b) The length of the second part will be three laps less than the length of the original race less the first part.

c) The grid for the second part will be a standard grid with the cars arranged in the order in which they finished the first part.

d) Only cars which took part in the original start will be eligible and then only if they returned to the grid under their own power by an authorized route to either the pit lane or to a position behind the last grid position as directed by the marshals.

e) No spare car will be eligible.

f) Cars may be worked on in the pits or on the grid. If work is carried out on the grid, this must be done in the car's correct grid position and must in no way impede the re-start.

g) If a car returns to the pits if may be refuelled. If a car is refuelled it must take the re-start from the back of the grid and, if more than one car is involved, their positions will be determined by their order on the penultimate lap before the race was stopped. In this case their original grid positions will be left vacant.

162. In both Case A and Case B :

a) 10 minutes after the stop signal, the pit exit will close.

b) 15 minutes after the stop signal, the five minute signal will be shown, the grid will close and the normal start procedure will recommence.

c) Any car which is unable to take up its position on the grid before the five minute signal will be directed to the pits. It may then start from the pits as specified in Article 140. The organiser must have sufficient personnel and equipment available to enable the foregoing timetable to be adhered to even in the most difficult circumstances.

FINISH

163. The end-of-race signal will be given at the Line as soon as the leading car has covered the full race distance in accordance with Article 14. Should two hours elapse before the full distance has been covered, the end-of-race signal will be given to the leading car the first time it crosses the Line after such time has elapsed.

164. Should for any reason (other than under Article 158) the end-of-race signal be given before the leading car completes the scheduled number of laps, or the prescribed time has been completed, the race will be deemed to have finished when the leading car last crossed the Line before the signal was given. Should the end-of-race signal be delayed for any reason, the race will be deemed to have finished when it should have finished.

165. After receiving the end-of-race signal all cars must proceed on the circuit directly to the parc fermé without stopping and without receiving any object whatsoever and without any assistance (except that of the marshals if necessary).

Any classified car which cannot reach the parc fermé under its own power will be placed under the exclusive control of the marshals who will take the car to the parc fermé.

PARC FERME

166. Only those officials charged with supervision may enter the parc fermé. No intervention of any kind is allowed there unless authorised by such officials.

167. When the parc fermé is in use, parc fermé regulations will apply in the area between the Line and the parc fermé entrance.

168. The parc fermé shall be sufficiently large and secure that no unauthorised persons can gain access to it.

CLASSIFICATION

169. The car placed first will be the one having covered the scheduled distance in the shortest time, or, where appropriate, passed the Line in the lead at the end of two hours, All cars will be classified taking into account the number of complete laps they have covered, and for those which have completed the same number of laps, the order in which they crossed the Line.

170. If a car takes more than twice the time of the winner's fastest lap to cover its last lap this last lap will not be taken into account when calculating the total distance covered by such car.

171. Cars having covered less than 90 % of the number of laps covered by the winner (rounded down to the nearest whole number of laps), will not be classified.

172. The official classification will be published after the race. It will be the only valid result subject to any amendments which may be made under the Code and these Sporting Regulations.

PODIUM CEREMONY

173. The drivers finishing the race in 1st, 2nd and 3rd positions and a representative of the winning constructor must attend the prize-giving ceremony on the podium and abide by the podium procedure (...), and immediately thereafter make themselves available for a period of 90 minutes for the purpose of television unilateral interviews and the press conference in the media centre.

Meaning of the flags

White flag : service vehicle on track
Blue flag : (immobile) : a car is close behind you
(waving) : a car is about to overtake you
Yellow flag : (immobile) : overtaking is prohibited, danger
(waving) immediate danger, slow down
Red flag : (by marshals and the Clerk of the race) : stopping of the race on the Line
Green flag : end of danger, free track
Yellow with red stripes flag : danger, slippery surface
Black flag : (with car number) : stop on the next lap
Black with yellow circle flag : your car is in danger
Black and white flag : non-sporting behaviour, warning
Chequered flag : end of the race or of the practice